★ ARTHUR LEE ★

SOUTHERN BIOGRAPHY SERIES
William J. Cooper, Jr., Editor

Arthur Lee by Charles Willson Peale.

ARTHUR LEE

★ A VIRTUOUS REVOLUTIONARY ★

Louis W. Potts

Louisiana State University Press
BATON ROUGE AND LONDON

DESIGNER: Joanna Hill
TYPEFACE: Garamond
TYPESETTER: G & S Typesetters, Inc.
PRINTER AND BINDER: Thomson-Shore, Inc.

Portions of this book originally appeared, in somewhat different form, in the *Journal of Psychohistory* and in W. Robert Higgins (ed.), *The Revolutionary War in the South* (1979), copyright © 1979 by Duke University Press.

LIBRARY OF CONGRESS CATALOGING IN PUBLICATION DATA

Potts, Louis W 1944–
Arthur Lee, a virtuous revolutionary.

(Southern biography series)
Bibliography: p.
Includes index.
1. Lee, Arthur, 1740–1792. 2. United States—
Foreign relations—Revolution, 1775–1783. 3. Dip-
lomats—United States—Biography. I. Title.
II. Series.
E302.6.L38P67   973.3'2'0924 [B]   80-21831
ISBN 0-8071-0785-9

Arthur Lee, a man of whom I cannot think without emotion; a man too early in the service of his country to avoid making a multiplicity of enemies; too honest, upright, faithful, and intrepid to be popular; too often obliged by his principles and feelings to oppose Machiavelian intrigues, to avoid the destiny he suffered. This man never had justice done him by his country in his lifetime, and I fear he never will have by posterity. His reward cannot be in this world.

JOHN ADAMS TO RICHARD BLAND LEE, AUGUST 11, 1819

Contents

Illustrations

Acknowledgments

My contacts over the years with colleagues, fellow scholars, and institutions have been of great benefit to me in the production of this work. To paraphrase a toast once made by Abraham Lincoln: to all my friends—they are too numerous to be now named individually, while there is not one of them who is not too dear to be forgotten or neglected.

Curators of manuscripts have been most resourceful in satisfying my inquiries. The collections of the Perkins Library at Duke University, the American Philosophical Society, the Benjamin Franklin Papers at Yale University, Colonial Williamsburg, and especially the Alderman Library at the University of Virginia, were made accessible and proved nourishing through the efforts of their fine staffs. I am grateful for permission to quote materials from the Arthur Lee Papers and Lee Family Papers at the University of Virginia and from the Duane, Benjamin Franklin, and Sol Feinstone Collections at the American Philosophical Society.

I owe a special debt of gratitude to Jessie M. Fraser of Sweet Briar College. It was the late Professor Fraser who painstakingly collected transcripts of Arthur Lee's correspondence from various depositories to augment the holdings of the Alderman Library. Her labors, which continued from the 1930s to the 1950s, were of immeasurable benefit to my research. I am deeply grateful.

Friendly criticism enhanced my craftsmanship. John R. Alden provided orientation and boosted my enthusiasm at critical junctures. John J. Fitzpatrick and Cecil Currey challenged my interpretations appropriately. Richard Forry and Richard McKinzie helped recast my articulations. Judy Bailey's role as editor was that of scholarly midwifery. She performed it with care. Joanna Zauchenberger aided in translations. I only wish I could have learned more from their insights.

Responsive typing and further refinements in presentation were performed by Claire Hildebrand, Debbie Scheel, and Elizabeth Bailey McIntyre.

Financial assistance and accompanying intangible sustenance came from Duke University Fellowships, a research stipend from Colonial Williamsburg, Inc., and twice from Dean Herwig G. Zauchenberger and the Research Council at the University of Missouri-Kansas City.

Brian, Jennifer, and Bridget, as children should, kept their father in tune with life so that he would be refreshed for further sorties into history.

Annetta has been my ultimate benefactress.

★ ARTHUR LEE ★

★ PROLOGUE ★

That Restless Genius

The frigate *Alliance*, pride of the Continental Navy, symbolized the harmony of the French and American nations. Yet, in the summer of 1780, the twenty-six-gun square-rigger was the stage for dispute between commanders, discord among crew and officers, and ultimately, two mutinies.[1] Embroiled in these controversies was the embattled American envoy, Arthur Lee. Whether aboard the *Alliance* or on diplomatic assignment in Europe, dissension and disruption swirled around Arthur Lee. Wherever he traveled, storm clouds gathered.

Lee's role in the *Alliance* affair was typical of his entire career: his brand of public spirit cast him as the antagonist of such patriots as John Paul Jones and Benjamin Franklin. Jones dubbed Lee "the Wasp" and considered the Virginian and his cohorts "to be *English* at the bottom of their hearts."[2] Franklin, vexed by Lee's behavior, responded, "That Genius must either find or make a quarrel wherever he is. The only excuse for him that his conduct will admit of, is his being at times out of his Senses. . . . if some of the many Enemies he provokes do not kill him sooner he will die in a madhouse."[3] Jones and Franklin feared that Lee would wreck the Franco-American entente and thus threaten the prospects of a successful war for independence in America. Lee suspected the personal ambitions of Franklin and Jones and believed the diplomatic aims of France jeopardized the hopes of American revolutionaries like himself.[4]

1. Richard B. Morris, "The Revolution's Caine Mutiny," *American Heritage*, XI (April, 1960), 10–13, 88–91; Samuel E. Morison, *John Paul Jones: A Sailor's Biography* (Boston, 1959), 299.
2. Morison, *John Paul Jones*, 177; John Paul Jones to Benjamin Franklin, June 21, 1780, in Benjamin Franklin Papers, American Philosophical Society, Philadelphia, XVIII, 2.
3. Franklin to Samuel Wharton, June 17, 1780, in Albert H. Smyth (ed.), *The Writings of Benjamin Franklin Collected and Edited with a Life and Introduction* (10 vols.; New York, 1905), VIII, 96.
4. Arthur Lee to the Committee of Correspondence, July 16, 1778, in Arthur

The *Alliance* affair of 1780 entangled congressmen in Philadelphia, radicals in Boston, American representatives throughout Europe, as well as the ministry of Louis XVI. Uproar prevailed. The year before, Congress had recalled Lee from his post in Paris. It was rumored he was *persona non grata* at the French court as well as inimical toward his American colleagues. Yet it was not easy for Franklin and the Comte de Vergennes, the French foreign minister, to rid themselves of the pest. Lee was sent packing first to Brest and then to L'Orient to seek passage to America in late February. Finally Franklin, as director of American naval affairs in European waters, arranged for Lee to sail on the *Alliance*, then being outfitted at L'Orient under the eyes of John Paul Jones. Franklin's judgment was uncharacteristically faulty; he had cast the factious Lee into a hornets' nest.

The fact was that since 1778 Lee had suspected Jones of politicking with French and American war profiteers. Further, Jones was then having trouble locating a shipment of arms as cargo and negotiating with a balky crew. The commander's troubles with the *Alliance* could be traced to the epic duel the previous September between the *Bonhomme Richard* and the *Serapis*. Jones claimed that during that struggle the *Alliance*, under the command of Pierre Landais, had fired on fellow Americans. When Franklin acceded to Jones and removed Landais, the crew of the *Alliance* grew hostile and demanded that their former commander be restored to his post. They hoped that such a move would lead to a restoration of their prize money.[5] Franklin's conciliatory efforts were for naught.

At L'Orient, Lee and Landais leagued against Jones. Landais, veteran of the French navy but currently possessor of a captain's commission from Congress, rivaled Lee as a single-minded and captious personality. His naval record documented his inability either to command a crew or to obey orders. John Adams, after a voyage aboard the *Alliance* with Landais in command, characterized him as "jealous of everything, . . . he knows not how to treat his officers, nor his passengers, nor anybody else. . . . he is bewildered—an absent-minded bewildered man, an embarrassed mind."[6]

Lee Papers (Accession No. 8709), Manuscripts Department, University of Virginia Library, Charlottesville, Box 5.

5. Charles O. Paullin, "Admiral Pierre Landais," *Catholic Historical Review*, XVII (October, 1931), 296–307.

6. Quoted in Lincoln Lorenz, *John Paul Jones: Fighter for Freedom and Glory* (Annapolis, 1943), 257.

While outfitting the ship dragged on through the spring of 1780, Franklin proposed that Landais submit his grievances to a board of inquiry in America. Overburdened by controversy, the American plenipotentiary warned Landais, "I waive, therefore, any dispute with you. But I charge you not to meddle with the command of the *Alliance*, or to create any disturbance on board her, as you will answer the contrary at your peril." The Frenchman, however, had taken his case to cronies Arthur Lee and Alexander Gillon. Taking it upon himself to act as supreme arbiter, Lee weighed the arguments of Landais and Jones (*in absentia*) for the command of the *Alliance* and declared the congressional commission of the Frenchman superior to the Jones authorization signed by Franklin. The *Alliance* affair offered Lee an opportunity to embarrass and undermine Franklin. He urged Landais to defy Franklin's power in France by usurping Jones's command.[7]

While Jones dallied, Landais boarded ship on June 13 and took command. Within an hour he set sail and moved into the channel off L'Orient to await developments. Jones sped to Paris to enlist the aid of Franklin and the French authorities in order to regain command. Reacting promptly, the elderly American diplomat ordered Landais to quit the *Alliance*, enjoined the crew to obey Jones, and instructed Jones to leave Lee off the passenger list. Jones was mystified by Lee's conduct. He would have expected the Virginian to oppose Landais, originally an adventurer recruited by Silas Deane, another of Lee's antagonists. Jones suspected Lee was acting against him because he "would not become the enemy of the venerable, the wise, and good Franklin." Such was the interpretation Jones penned for his congressional sponsor Robert Morris, another American leader who would later feel the ire of Lee.[8]

Between June 20 and July 7, the drama at L'Orient heightened. De-

7. Franklin to Pierre Landais, June 7, 1780, in Francis Wharton (ed.), *The Revolutionary Diplomatic Correspondence of the United States* (6 vols.; Washington, D.C., 1882–89), III, 572–73; Arthur Lee to John Paul Jones, June 13, 1780, in Paul R. Hoffman and John L. Molyneaux (eds.), *The Lee Family Papers* (8 reels microfilm; Charlottesville, 1966), VI, 683; Arthur Lee to Captain Pierre Landais, June 17, 1780, in Lorenz, *John Paul Jones*, 415; Arthur Lee to Landais, June 25, 1780, in Hoffman and Molyneaux (eds.), *Lee Family Papers*, VI, 686–87.

8. Franklin to Landais, June 16, 1780, Franklin to the crew of the *Alliance*, June 16, 1780, Franklin to Jones, June 17, 1780, all in Wharton (ed.), *Correspondence*, III, 786–801; Jones to Robert Morris, June 27, 1780, in Wharton (ed.), *Correspondence*, III, 820–22.

parture of the *Alliance* was thwarted by the guns of the French, both ashore and afloat, as well as a boom across the channel. While Jones enlisted French military support for possible assault on the frigate, Landais and Lee counseled aboard ship. Ultimately, and inexplicably, Jones gave up and permitted the frigate to put to sea. Before sailing, Lee's baggage and two nephews were brought aboard but the intended cargo of armaments was not; neither was a large carriage the Virginia republican sought to bring to America.[9]

The alliance between Landais and Lee lasted only until their ship reached open water. Lee, finding the Frenchman unfit for command, connived with officers, crew, and passengers. The relationship grew testy. At dinner one evening, the Virginia gentleman, once trained as a physician, complained of unsanitary drinking water. His pride pricked, the distraught captain countered with a lecture on shipboard protocol, then brandished a carving knife, and challenged Lee to a duel once they made landfall.

Smoldering discontent among the crew ignited as the *Alliance* neared Newfoundland. Although the winds were fair, Landais obdurately refused to unfurl the sails—inexplicable behavior. On August 5, Lee and the other passengers appealed to the captain to stop loitering and proceed to America "as the whole crew are dissatisfied with not making sail." When the sailors aligned with Lee, Landais retired to sulk in his cabin. Five days later the officers, unable to control the crew, produced a written report of the dangerous anarchy aboard the *Alliance*. Landais ignored it. This act was interpreted by the junior officers as an abdication of command. Lieutenant James Degge, an outspoken critic of Landais, was chosen to take control of the ship for the duration of the voyage. When at last the ship reached Boston on August 15, Landais had to be pulled from his cabin. Lee scurried ashore to converse with James Warren and other patriot leaders of Massachusetts.[10]

It was rumored then and since that Arthur Lee was the architect of the

---

9. Lorenz, *John Paul Jones*, 418–30; Morison, *John Paul Jones*, 273, 296–98.

10. Copy of a petition to sail to Captain Landais, August 5, 1780, in Hoffman and Molyneaux (eds.), *Lee Family Papers*, VI, 717. Among the signatures are those of Arthur Lee and his two nephews, Thomas and Ludwell Lee, sons of Richard Henry Lee; Morris, "Revolution's Caine Mutiny," 88–89; copy of a petition from the officers of the *Alliance* to Captain Landais, August 10, 1780, in Hoffman and Molyneaux (eds.), *Lee Family Papers*, VI, 722.

"great confusion . . . extraordinary conduct . . . dark business" aboard the *Alliance*. At his court-martial in Boston and in later publications, Landais asserted that the Virginian exhorted him to defy Franklin and then, in mid-Atlantic, cunningly fomented mutiny.[11] As had Franklin, Landais portrayed Lee as an artful and malicious conspirator. Lee's connection with Warren, head of the navy board in Boston, together with his own lengthy testimony, resulted in a verdict that left Lee relatively unscathed by the inquiry. In the end, only the bulk of Lee's personal goods, shipped at public expense, caused much comment.

The denouement of the *Alliance* affair was neither swift nor even-handed. Landais was broken in rank and barred from further service in the Continental Navy. Returning to his homeland, he joined the French fleet (during the French Revolution) but spent his last twenty-one years in America, petitioning unsuccessfully for reimbursement from Congress. He died in poverty in 1818. Lieutenant Degge was also dismissed from the service, a mild fate in contrast to the death penalty that usually faced mutineers. The destiny of the frigate was more fortunate; under the command of John Barry, the *Alliance* later achieved fame that outweighed the ignominy gained under Landais.[12]

The episode was neither critical nor prominent in Lee's career; extensive service in the Virginia House of Delegates and the Continental Congress lay before him. The incident, nonetheless, symbolized his entire life. The themes present in the *Alliance* episode recurred throughout his career. His existence, which he later termed "this odd chapter of accidents," was perpetually filled with controversies that yielded him notoriety, frustration, alienation, and often ridicule. The Arthur Lee known to his contemporaries was a zealot: hot-tempered, quarrelsome, and unbending. He

11. Marine Committee to Commissioners of the Navy Board of Boston, September 5, 1780, "Marine Committee Letterbook. 1776–1780," Miscellaneous Papers of the Continental Congress, 1774–1789, in Record Group 11, Microcopy 322, Roll 6, National Archives; Pierre de Landais, *Memorial to Justify Peter Landais' Conduct During the Late War* (Boston, 1784), 4–17, 52; Navy Board of the Eastern Department (Captain John Barry presiding), "Courtmartial of Captain Peter Landais, November 20, 1780–January 7, 1781 and Lieutenant James Degge, January 11–25, 1781," Papers of the Continental Congress, 1774–1789, Record Group 360, Microcopy 257, Roll 200, National Archives.

12. *Dictionary of American Biography*, X, 567–68; Gardner W. Allen, *A Naval History of the American Revolution*, (2 vols.; New York, 1972) 527–29; Morris, "Revolution's Caine Mutiny," 90–91.

was intelligent yet passionate, aristocratic in demeanor yet unrestrained in spirit, and he readily plunged into the fervor and clamor of the times. Throughout it all he lived by the credo that "The good of the public must be above all things most dear to me—that is the essence of true republicanism."[13] He tirelessly aspired to be *the* virtuous patriot of the American Revolution. Half his lifetime was devoted to a myriad of roles and responsibilities in public service. But, although blessed with considerable talents, he could not transcend temperamental frailties and excesses. For Arthur Lee there were many elements of tragedy in the American Revolution. The American republic that arose owed more to the handiwork of Franklin than to the visions of Lee. The exploits of Jones rather than the exertions of Lee formed the basis of our national myth.

13. Arthur Lee, "Indian Journal," December 24, 1784, in Richard Henry Lee, *The Life of Arthur Lee, LL.D., Joint Commissioner to the Court of France, and Sole Commissioner to the Courts of Spain and Prussia, During the Revolutionary War* (2 vols.; Boston, 1829) II, 389–93; Arthur Lee to Thomas Lee Shippen, March 26, 1792 in Arthur Lee Papers, Box 5.

CHAPTER I

Foes Are Not Wanting
to the Best on Earth

Stratford Hall, the mansion near the bluffs of the upper Potomac River in the area known as the Northern Neck, is both a shrine and a symbol of the Lee family of Virginia. At the time of Arthur Lee's birth, on December 21, 1740, the newly built home was the center of a regional drive to manipulate politics in the colony and to control a domain in the American interior. Stratford Hall suggested key elements of Arthur's inner struggles over social prestige, political power, and financial success. Its size, which rivaled that of the capitol at Williamsburg, marked the eminence to which Lees were to aim. Its style, which emulated homes of English gentry, denoted Arthur's perplexing destiny, his bifurcated identity as an Anglo-American.[1]

For a century before Arthur's birth the Lees had accumulated land and status in the colony of Virginia. They had become members of a "small homogeneous elite—English by descent, Anglican in religion, and linked to one another by ties of kinship and bonds of economic interest—which monopolized the political life" of eighteenth century Virginia. Although there were more wealthy and more powerful clans along the banks of the Potomac, Rappahannock, and James rivers, few exceeded the Lees in the arts of political management. The pattern of behavior had been established by the family progenitor, Richard Lee, who had appeared in Virginia in 1638. A man of ambition and action, "the Emigrant" took advantage of the beneficent friendship of Governor William Berkeley to amass thirteen thousand acres. Similarly, he gained stature in local political circles, first in the House of Burgesses, then in the Council, and ultimately as Berkeley's secretary of state.[2]

---

1. Ethel Armes, *Stratford Hall: The Great House of the Lees* (Richmond, 1936), 50; Jack P. Greene, "Search for Identity: An Interpretation of the Meaning of Selected Patterns of Social Response in Eighteenth Century America," *Journal of Social History*, III (Spring, 1970), 189–200.

2. James A. Henretta, *The Evolution of American Society, 1700–1815: An*

Richard Lee II, second son of the Emigrant and grandfather of Arthur Lee, had dissimilar ambitions. A serious-minded scholar and business-man, Richard II was pious, headstrong, and politically conservative: he opposed the rebellion incited by Nathaniel Bacon in 1676 and only grudgingly acknowledged the ascension of William and Mary to the English throne in the Glorious Revolution in 1688. The Lee family myth, a blend of values and beliefs about the family's past and destiny, esteemed Richard II for his thought rather than for his actions. His personal library, numbering more than three hundred volumes, reflected the classical bent that he might have developed from training at Oxford.[3] That the Stratford Lees chose to send their sons to England for schooling might be traced to the scholarly inclinations of Richard II.

The builder of Stratford was Thomas Lee (1690–1750), fourth son of Richard II. Despite meager formal education and a relatively slim inheritance of twelve hundred acres, Thomas proved himself equal to the Emigrant in enterprising spirit and acquisitive zeal. He began his career in public service as a customs receiver on the Potomac and justice of the peace for Westmoreland County. At the time of his death he had served as president of the Council, commander-in-chief, and acting governor of Virginia, posts which testified to his ascendancy as head of the planter class. Like the Emigrant, Thomas Lee discovered that power was within the reach of large landholders in baronial Virginia and that such power would expand the elite's dominion. He had taken advantage of connections to assemble an estate of thirty thousand acres in the Northern Neck and on the western frontier of Virginia. At the time his last son, Arthur, was born, Thomas Lee sat as a member of the Council and was involved in land schemes along the Ohio River in territory claimed by the French, the Indians, and divers British colonies.[4]

As in other fields of endeavor, so in that of matrimony, Thomas Lee

---

Interdisciplinary Analysis (Lexington, 1973), 92; Ludwell Lee Montague, "Richard Lee, the Emigrant 1613–1664," *Virginia Magazine of History and Biography,* LXII (January, 1954), 3–49; Burton J. Hendrick, *The Lees of Virginia: Biography of a Family* (Boston, 1935), 3–26.

3. David F. Musto, "The Youth of John Quincy Adams," *Proceedings of the American Philosophical Society,* CXIII (1969), 269; Hendrick, *The Lees,* 30–47; George K. Smart, "Private Libraries in Colonial Virginia," *American Literature,* X (March, 1938), 24–52.

4. Hendrick, *The Lees,* 47–81; Cazenove G. Lee, Jr., *Lee Chronicle: Studies of*

recorded a success. In 1772 he took to wife Hannah Harrison Ludwell (1701–1750), whose family at least equaled the Lees in all respects. Thomas, despite time-consuming affairs in the colony, was not unaffectionate. In his will, written a month after Hannah died, Thomas stipulated, "I desire that I may be buried between my Late Dear Wife and my honored Mother, and that the bricks on the side next to my wife may be moved, and my Coffin placed as near hers as possible, without moving it or disturbing the remains of my mother." [5]

John Adams, in the midst of the War for American Independence, would assert that, "The family of Lee . . . has more men of merit in it than any other family." His reference was to the sons of Thomas and Hannah, whom Adams later eulogized as "that band of brothers, intrepid and unchangeable, who like the Greeks at Thermopylae, stood in the gap, in defence of their country, from the first glimmering of the Revolution in the horizon, through all its rising light, to its perfect day." [6] Despite the partisanship of such comments, it was evident to Adams and his contemporaries, that the fourth generation of Lees possessed a distinguishable set of attitudes, codes of behavior, manners, and morals. Such laudable attributes had been cultivated by a combination of experiences at Stratford and in British schools. The Lee family prepared itself for society by uncommon investment in formal training. Thomas Lee had had to teach himself Greek and Latin as an adult. He saw to it that his male offspring had no such shortcoming. Private tutoring at home and extensive schooling abroad were prescribed for his sons.

The family also nurtured within itself a distinctive view of the world, perpetuated a system of values, and devised a sense of family mission: Lees were groomed to lead. Thomas' sons perceived that their roles in society were at the upper levels of provincial politics and that they were guardians of such diverse traditions as the Whig obsession with moral decay and championing of rights, the Enlightenment's concept that events

the Early Generations of the Lees of Virginia, ed. Dorothy Mills Parker (New York, 1957), 24–52.

5. Armes, *Stratford Hall,* 535.

6. John Adams to Samuel Cooper, February 28, 1779, Adams to Richard Bland Lee, August 11, 1819 in Charles Francis Adams (ed.), *The Works of John Adams, Second President of the United States, with a Life of the Author* (10 vols; Boston, 1851), IX, 478–80, X, 382.

are managed by men, and the colonial millennial quest to achieve a perfect society. In sum, they were an elite, advocating republicanism but not democracy.[7] The fourth generation of the family, *the* Stratford Lees, all took prominent roles in Anglo-American affairs 1760–1790. Ultimately at the climax of the movement for American autonomy, the two eldest males withdrew while the four youngest defiantly enlisted in the vanguard of rebellion.

To be born a Stratford Lee in the middle of the eighteenth century was good luck. Arthur might look forward to a life of security, comfort, and prominence. Yet the combination of genetic and material inheritance did not predestine his entire future. Through his own efforts, he could transcend or dip below the family standards. In retrospect it is evident that Arthur—like numerous other colonials—departed from the inherited pattern.[8] Often the opportunities that confronted him were in conflict with his personal needs and motives or unsuited to his specific skills and competencies. The course of his life was littered with altered career goals and alienated relationships. While he tenaciously upheld the ideals of his family, he was often ill at ease in the specific roles history allotted him, perhaps a fate founded on birth order.

Arthur was the last child born to Thomas and Hannah Lee. In the thirteen years between 1727 and 1740 Hannah bore ten children, eight of whom survived infancy.[9] Arthur's sisters, Hannah and Alice, married into respectable families: the former wed Gawin Corbin of Virginia; the latter was wooed in England by Dr. William Shippen, Jr., who brought her home to Philadelphia as his wife. Arthur's two oldest brothers, raised with the expectation that they would manage their father's domain, were Philip Ludwell and Thomas Ludwell. The former was his mother's favorite and exhibited her haughty, aristocratic demeanor. The latter was passive yet popular. Arthur was close to neither. His immediate group

7. Bernard Bailyn *et al.* (eds.), *The Great Republic: A History of the American People* (Lexington, 1977), 265–68.

8. Edmund S. Morgan, *Virginians at Home: Family Life in the Eighteenth Century* (Williamsburg, 1952), 6; Bernard Bailyn, *Education in the Forming of American Society: Needs and Opportunities* (New York: 1972), 36.

9. Edmund Jennings Lee, *Lee of Virginia, 1642–1892: Biographical and Genealogical Sketches of the Descendents of Colonel Richard Lee* (Philadelphia, 1895), 125–26.

within the family was composed of Francis Lightfoot, six years his elder; Alice, born in 1736; and William, slightly more than a year his senior. The childhood experiences shared by this group went unrecorded. Arthur's adult relationships indicate that a trusting bond had developed, for he frequently practiced confession in his letters to Frank, he was embraced by Alice's family in later years, and he shared with William the most trying times of his European career. The greatest impact on Arthur's character, as well as career, was made by Richard Henry, a brother who drifted between Arthur's closest siblings and the more distant elders.

Arthur's youthful experiences, as he learned to adjust to authority and to form social relationships, contributed to his developing character. Although his surname categorized him in Virginia's political elite, his rank within the family prescribed that his career be chosen by his parents and older siblings rather than by himself. On one hand he came to resent, distrust, and detest his eldest brother, who became his authority figure. On the other hand, he had such great affection for his two brothers Richard Henry and William that he was willing to engage in duels to protect their honor. His was a world populated by powerful males, and early in his life Arthur established atypical relationships with women. Although no misogynist, the only females he felt comfortable around were kin. He tended either to ridicule women for their intellectual aspirations or to idealize them for knowing their place in the home. Only belatedly and unsuccessfully would he go suitoring for a wife.

Arthur's way of adjusting to situations and the impression he gave his contemporaries are traceable to childhood experiences. Only in his will is there any record of his disposition towards his parents. Here he mentions his "dear parents." Perhaps a premonition of his own death reminded him of them. It is not too much to argue that a sense of denial as well as abandonment were associated with memories of his parents. It is recorded that he spent his infancy in the care of a black nanny and his youth amidst the games of the plantation's slaves.[10] As an infant Arthur was refused love by

10. Arthur Lee's Will, July 27, 1792, in Arthur Lee Papers, Box 20; Richard Henry Lee, *Memoir of the Life of Richard Henry Lee and His Correspondence* (2 vols.; Philadelphia, 1825), I, 244; John F. Walzer, "A Period of Ambivalence: Eighteenth Century American Childhood," in Lloyd de Mause (ed.), *The History of Childhood* (New York, 1974), 374.

his parents; as a youngster his father's political interests and mother's disinterest led to disownment; ultimately, their deaths when he was nine robbed him of further nurture. From the basic child-parent relationship grew Arthur Lee's heightened sense of mistrust. From the infantile experiences, from the quantity and quality of parental love shown him, Arthur developed peculiar modes of looking at and acting on the world. As he learned to differentiate himself from the parental orbit, he retained an inflated sense of his own goodness—what later associates saw as self-righteousness and overconfidence. Simultaneously, he came to believe that evil was not an attribute of his own character, but that it emanated from others. Here was the source of the fears of persecution so prevalent in his mature years. Through adolescence and early adulthood Arthur Lee searched for loving replacements for his parents. He continually sought out prominent characters of his era but never trusted them completely. As his parents had done to him, so he did to others—he kept his distance.

Hannah and Thomas Lee's child rearing encouraged some offspring to fend for themselves. It is known that Arthur's mother contented herself with raising her daughters and eldest son but "gave up her younger sons, when boys, to be fed, in a great measure, by their own enterprise and exertions." [11] This practice may have been a reaction to the death of her firstborn son. As he ventured out of the nursery and learned to play on the plantation, Arthur developed a ready sense of autonomy. As he matured, however, this confidence was displaced by doubt. He cherished self-control as a child and as an adolescent, but as an adult he encountered repeated frustrations and failures that severely challenged his self-esteem, although shame never overwhelmed him.

Two early critical experiences at Stratford gave Arthur a measure of self-esteem and showed him the arbitrariness of power. They provided him a set of attitudes and modes of adaptation and contributed to his orientation toward life. [12] In a brick outbuilding at Stratford, Arthur, like his older brothers, was tutored by a Mr. Craig, a Scottish clergyman. The

11. Richard Henry Lee, *Life of Arthur Lee*, I, 11–13; Marguerite duPont Lee, *Arthur Lee, M.D., LL.D., F.R.S.* (Richmond, 1936), 3–4.

12. The model used here is influenced by James D. Barber, *The Presidential Character: Predicting Performance in the White House* (Englewood Cliffs, N.J., 1972), 3–14, Alexander L. George, "Assessing Presidential Character," *World Politics*, XXVI (1974), 234–82, and Erik H. Erikson, *Childhood and Society* (2nd ed., New York, 1963), 247–74.

Stratford Lees gave credence to the generalization of one historian that tutoring "formed the gentry of Revolutionary Virginia and nurtured in them the fierce independence and haughty provincialism that were to constitute at the same time their greatest strength and their consummate weakness in the years ahead." [13] Such education emphasized autonomy and initiative for the Lee boys.

Mr. Craig was with the boys day and night, hearing their recitations in Greek and Latin, explaining their responsibilities and privileges as budding gentlemen, and curbing their inattention. Arthur responded positively to the pedagogue's exhortations; in a family where schooling was uncommonly pursued, he was deemed the brightest. While his brothers stood out from their colonial peers because of their superior training in English schools, Arthur stood above even them; his education included attendance at Eton, an M.D. from the University of Edinburgh, and a law degree from the Middle Temple in London. Whereas he could not equal his older brothers in physical and social prowess, Arthur found a rewarding channel for his vitality in study and writing. He won early applause for his initiative and industry, and he invested energy in formal training past the midpoint of his life, concluding his law studies at the age of thrty-four. As he accomplished assignments for Craig as a youngster and as he recited lessons for the dames and tutors at Eton, so he would endlessly dispatch essays to the press on both sides of the Atlantic between 1764 and 1775. As he reaped the praises of his siblings and mentors during childhood, Lee as an adult sought recognition and reinforcement from fellow Anglo-Americans. He craved attention, respect, and praise. Never would he gain the deference he believed he had earned. Neglect and criticism brought to the surface doubts of himself and raised his ire. Formal education, which provided him values and goals, garnered from the classics and the Real Whigs, also indicated a way to realize his goals, to become a polemicist.

Arthur's profound distrust of others was reinforced by the intrafamilial strife that arose when both of his parents died. Thomas Lee had hoped that his will was so lucid that "a Lawyer will not find room to make constructions prejudicial to my Family," but for thirteen years suits and countersuits split the family and scarred the developing personalities of

13. Lawrence A. Cremin, *American Education: The Colonial Experience, 1607– 1783* (New York, 1970), 491.

the youngsters, William and Arthur.[14] Philip Ludwell, a malefic figure in Arthur's eyes, stood at the center of the controversy.

Despite the practice of partible inheritance, the oldest son, Philip Ludwell, gained the bulk of his father's estate. The will appointed him and the docile Thomas Ludwell as guardians of William and Arthur. The older brothers were commanded to educate the young two "in such a manner as they think fit, Religiously and virtuously and if necessary to bind them to a profession or Trade, so they may learn to get their living honestly." Upon his maturity Arthur was to be allotted one thousand pounds, two hundred pounds toward a home, and other potential sources of income. The younger Lees were not to enjoy the leisure and grace of plantation life. They were expected to follow the authority, discipline, and hierarchy of the family. While Arthur became the professional Lee, first as a physician and then as a lawyer, William was groomed as the family's commercial agent.

Because Philip Ludwell, Thomas Ludwell, and the third son, Richard Henry, were all in England studying at the time of their father's death, the will was not probated until July 30, 1751, following their return. Philip's autocratic handling of the estate was challenged by his siblings. It took eight years for appraisals and inventories to be completed, a delay that irritated and enraged the younger boys, who needed money to finance their education. Arthur, feeling he had been treated unfairly by his brother, joined the others in 1754 in a successful petition to secure cousin Henry Lee as a new guardian. Henry, in turn, sought a settlement from Philip, but none was forthcoming. The effort was ultimately dismissed by the courts in 1764. This experience taught Arthur alienation and deprivation. He subsequently approached others he encountered in life with the utmost suspicion, for if he could not trust a brother, whom could he trust? If the legal system never gave him his due, would life? As late as 1774 Arthur was extremely distressed by Philip's refusal to remit him educational expenses. Lack of money threatened Arthur's quests for a profession and for personal autonomy.[15] Arthur would come to view the world as populated by avaricious and cunning men like Philip, who put their own well-being ahead of all other considerations. Later Arthur fanatically

14. Armes, *Stratford Hall*, 83–100, 534–38.
15. Arthur Lee to Richard Henry Lee, December 13, 1774, in Richard Henry Lee, *Life of Arthur Lee*, I, 208–211.

battled Benjamin Franklin, Silas Deane, and Robert Morris, charging that they were seeking private fortune at the expense of the public. The charges were correct, but the true basis of his fury was that these men, in their pursuit of pelf, frustrated his own desires for political prestige and power.

In accordance with the provisions of his father's will, Philip Ludwell, probably with the advice of Thomas Ludwell and Richard Henry, decided the fate of his younger brothers. William was to learn plantation management firsthand at Stratford, while Arthur, perhaps precociously manifesting restless energy that engrossed his adulthood, was destined for English preparatory school. Perhaps this was a choice to his own taste, for he later developed an avidity for British education. Sometime after midsummer, 1751, Arthur bade farewell to Stratford to embark on a trans-Atlantic passage. To a boy not yet eleven, this doubtlessly was a fearful experience, which severely tested his self-reliance and redoubled his alienation. The anxiety of separation was reinforced by the recent loss of his parents. Yet dispatching Arthur to England was a prudent decision from the point of view of the family. Arthur's education in the mother country would uphold family tradition, while broadening the family's thrust by extending its influence to the professions.

Thus a solitary colonial child was sent from his home. During this adolescent period his character and world view further developed. He oriented himself toward life by adopting a set of perceptions and maxims about the nature of man and society. Thrown back upon himself during British schooling, he came to rely on two strategies to see him through this stress: the adoption of Richard Henry Lee as his mentor and the investment of his energy in reading the histories of Greece and Rome.

Though the evidence is not complete, it appears Arthur Lee spent the bulk of the 1750s at Eton College. Later in life he became embroiled in a controversy with John Russell, a London merchant who apparently handled bills accrued from Arthur's education, specifically "dames accounts" such as those presented by women who operated boarding houses for boys unable to find lodging in the dormitories. Arthur left no contemporary record of this stage of life.[16]

16. Richard A. Austen-Leigh (ed.), *The Eton College Register, 1753–1790* (Eton, 1921), 327; Arthur Lee to Richard Henry Lee, October 14, 1761, in Arthur Lee Papers, Box 1.

The flow of students from Virginia to British schools ebbed in Arthur's era, perhaps because of increasing indebtedness of colonial planters, perhaps because of provincial questioning of the merit of such training. Nonetheless, between 1750 and 1760, at least nineteen Virginians appear on the rolls of institutions of higher learning in Great Britain and by 1776, thirty Americans had gone through Eton. Lee, numbered among the oppidans, received training from both dames and tutors. Family legend portrays the colleger as a diligent and eager student who so impressed one instructor that he offered the lad free tutoring, which was hastily and earnestly accepted since Arthur's funds were far from reliable.[17]

Even if not harassed by bullies, the Virginian youth developed a sense of being somehow different while at Eton. It was evident that he was not equal to the nobs, the sons of British aristocrats. It is possible that the proddings of his schoolmates and others forced him to defend himself against charges that Americans were an inferior species of the genus of Briton. The fierce stance he later took in pamphlets defending Virginia and America during the 1760s and 1770s might have originated in the halls and fields of Eton. It was the British boys who added to his widening sense of identity as an American. Later he would defiantly style himself, "Junius Americanus."

The education offered by Eton largely consisted of endless hours of recitation and composition in Greek and Latin. Classical study was thought to be a valuable source of moral lessons to inspire manliness, patriotism, and love of liberty. No less an oracle than John Locke had decreed that Latin was "absolutely necessary to be a gentleman" and Greek as necessary to a scholar. Because Arthur aimed at both goals, he doggedly grappled with both tongues. The recitations Arthur endured at Eton engraved upon his memory countless quotations and numerous maxims from the history of Greece and Rome. This training gave a moralistic and pedantic cast to many of his later publications. The past for him was a storehouse not of mere illustrations but of authoritative precedents.[18]

17. Christopher Hollis, *Eton: A History* (London, 1960), 143; James Heneage Jesse, *Memoirs of Celebrated Etonians* (London, 1875), *passim*; Austen-Leigh (ed.), *Eton College Register, passim*; Douglas S. Freeman, *George Washington: A Biography* (7 vols.; New York, 1949–57), I, 132–33; William L. Sachse, *The Colonial American in Britain* (Madison, 1956), 47; Hollis, *Eton*, 145–51; Richard Henry Lee, *Life of Arthur Lee*, I, 12.

18. M. L. Clarke, *Greek Studies in England, 1700–1830* (Cambridge, 1945),

The heritage of classical antiquity from which Lee and other Americans drew was predominantly the political history of republican Rome from the first century B.C. to the end of the second century A.D. The shared focus was on the moral and political decline of the Roman republic. Writers such as Plutarch, Livy, Cicero, Tacitus, and Sallust were most favored. From these tracts the colonists envisioned a heroic age, filled with virtue, simplicity, patriotism, integrity, justice, and liberty, that had fallen victim to venal, cynical, and oppressive rulers. To erudite colonials there was no more graphic analogy to explain Augustan Britain. Republican Rome had grown rich, luxurious, corrupt, and licentious only to fall prey to the Goths who had retained their primitive virtues. Such an interpretation did not bode well for the British empire under the Hanoverians.[19]

Particularly pertinent to Arthur Lee were the histories of Sallust. These moralistic compositions repeated the theme that power, ambition, and avarice had caused the erosion of Roman character and collapse of the Roman Republic. Such observations seemed validated by Arthur's own experience. To Sallust, as to the student from Virginia, an individual's virtue was the keystone to republican society. Throughout his life Lee maintained a stance of stern integrity modeled on Sallust's portraits of the selfless aristocrats of republican Rome. Virtue was Lee's primary moral precept and the ultimate goal of his aspirations. Thus to a large extent, reading the classics, rather than parental guidance, determined his code of behavior. The lessons Arthur learned as a schoolboy from Sallust were those he later broadcast in his pamphlets and letters:

> In most countries, they who blind and enslave people, are popular and reverenced; they who would enlighten and free them, are hated and persecuted. . . . A country divided against itself, cannot stand, nor a country well united, fall. . . . It is natural, indeed too natural, for men to grasp at enormous power. . . . To save and serve their country, is the

10–15; Richard M. Gummere, *The Colonial Mind and the Classical Tradition: Essays in Comparative Culture* (Cambridge, 1963), *passim*; Bernard Bailyn, *The Ideological Origins of the American Revolution* (Cambridge, 1967), 25–26; H. Trevor Colbourn, *The Lamp of Experience: Whig History and the Intellectual Origins of the American Revolution* (Chapel Hill, 1965), 9.

19. Bailyn, *Ideological Origins*, 25; Gordon S. Wood, *The Creation of the American Republic, 1776–1787* (Chapel Hill, 1969), 48–51; Colbourn, *Lamp of Experience*, 25.

Duty of all Men. . . . Virtue and a good name is the best wealth. . . .
Corruption in a state is a deviation from our Duty to the public, upon
private motives. . . . People are generally more constant in evil habits
than in good; perservering in Grossness and Stupidity than in the Exercise of Reason, and in useful Pursuits.[20]

Sallust saw the world as a Manichean struggle in which individuals triumphed or perished as a consequence of their personal qualities. In
Sallust's world there was little shading; men were either completely good
or totally evil. Arthur Lee adopted this polar perspective.

The heroic world of Sallust came alive in the person of brother Richard Henry Lee, nearly nine years Arthur's senior. Arthur was devoted to
him and trusted him completely. There was an intimacy and a reverence
in his relationship with Richard Henry that Arthur felt for no one else.
The two brothers found themselves frequently separated by the Atlantic
Ocean—when one returned from schooling in England, the other was
dispatched there—and this remoteness led Arthur to idealize Richard
Henry. The older served as an example to emulate, a voice of authority,
and a mentor for the younger brother, and throughout his lifetime Arthur
was dependent upon him. Richard Henry financed Arthur's schooling in
Britain. Richard Henry, himself a disciple of Hampden and Sydney, led
Arthur to the writings of Locke, Montesquieu, and Pufendorf for ex-
planation of contemporary politics. Most importantly, Richard Henry's
opposition first to the Tidewater establishment in colonial Virginia and
then to parliamentary taxation reassured Arthur as he ventured into anti-
authoritarian roles.

At the age of twenty-three, Arthur observed, "Indeed my whole life
has been so much indebted to [Richard Henry's] goodness and affection,
that it is vain to think of repaying them, more than by the sincerest gratitude and esteem."[21] His subsequent life was largely an effort to follow his
mentor in ideology as well as action. Arthur relied heavily on Richard
Henry for advice in planning his career, sought praise and encouragement

20. M. L. W. Laistner, *The Great Historians* (Berkeley, 1947), 52–55; D. C.
Earl, *The Political Thought of Sallust* (Amsterdam, 1966), 7–36; Thomas Gordon (trans.), *The Works of Sallust, Translated into English with Political Discourses upon that Author, to Which Is Added a Translation of Cicero's Four Orations Against Cataline* (London, 1744), 8, 18, 32, 34, 88, 93, 183.
21. Arthur Lee to [Richard Henry Lee], December 22, 1763, in Hoffman and
Molyneaux (eds.), *Lee Family Papers*, I, 305–306.

from him, gloried in his rapid rise in Virginia political circles, and shared with him the Real Whig or "country" perspective on British government. Richard Henry inculcated a litany of virtues: to serve selflessly in public life, to contend against ubiquitous corruption in politics, and to cherish republicanism. Arthur particularly applauded his brother's "patriot spirit and love of liberty which have hitherto influenced your resolves uninjured by public corruption or party zeal."[22] Richard Henry, who became known as the Cicero of the House of Burgesses, was an early and eternal hero for Arthur, but the saintly aspirations of both men were hampered by flaws in their characters.

There is no record when Arthur Lee completed his studies at Eton and returned to America. In the customary pattern, he would have been at Eton for six years, but it was possible for an intellectually gifted student to cover more than one form per year. It appears Arthur was in Virginia in 1759 when Richard Henry joined the ranks of the republican and western forces in the Virginia Burgesses opposed to the aristocratic Tidewater faction. Yet Richard Henry did not want Arthur to become too entranced with local affairs; he preferred that Arthur return to England and Cambridge University to complete his schooling. Arthur's profession was to be medicine, perhaps because this had been Thomas Lee's wish or perhaps because Arthur wanted to learn how to minister to gout-ridden Richard Henry. A career as a doctor would have been an apt repayment by Arthur for Richard Henry's generosity. Thus in the final months of 1760 Arthur once again departed Stratford for Britain.

For the next six years, what is known of Arthur Lee comes largely from his correspondence to Richard Henry, which served several functions. Arthur recognized that he could serve as a source of information on British politics for the family in Virginia. Thus, his first letter home announced the death of George II in October, 1760: "the large Artery in his Heart burst, and in an instant He was no more." The information he could provide would grow more critical as antagonisms mounted within the British empire; as Arthur widened his correspondence to include men like John Dickinson, the Pennsylvania moderate, and Samuel Adams, Massachusetts malcontent; and as Arthur sought the position of colonial agent. In a more personal light, the correspondence provided a confessional. Arthur repeatedly recorded how he measured up to Lee family standards and as-

22. Arthur Lee to Richard Henry Lee, August 19, 1761, *Ibid.*, I, 267–69.

pirations. He sought to define himself by relating his experiences, feelings, and decisions. Some of the letters, often defensive in tone and filled with rationalization, entreated Richard Henry for his blessing and sustenance. Arthur, both as an adolescent and as an adult, emphasized the drama in his life. Career decisions, personal quests, and acquaintance with noted personages litter his correspondence. His dramaturgical bent was susceptible to exaggeration and hyperbole that, in turn, could verge on paranoia.[23]

He found some comfort at the home of his cousin Lucy Ludwell and her husband John Paradise. There Arthur discovered the renowned lexicographer, Dr. Samuel Johnson. One of the most notable celebrities of Georgian society, Johnson was then the pope of London taverns and coffeehouses. Duly impressed, Arthur recorded that "his outward appearance is very droll and uncouth, the too assiduous cultivation of his mind seems to have caused a very great neglect of his body; but for this his friends are very amply rewarded in the enjoyment of a mind most elegantly polished, enlightened and refined. . . . an intelligent mind cannot fail of receiving the most agreeable information and entertainment in his conversation." Arthur emphasized the Briton's acumen for good reason. He needed to justify the fact that Johnson had persuaded him to change his plans. Rebelling against the wishes of his father and the specific directions of Richard Henry, Arthur found refuge under Johnson's wing.

When the youthful colonial told Johnson of his intention to go to Cambridge for a career in medicine, the sage argued against such a course. For those who possessed neither abundant time nor money, Johnson recommended study at Leyden or Edinburgh. There "at a small expense and in a short time," decent medical training could be had. The Briton chortled that "the [Scottish or] foreign Education is like [a house] built to last a man's lifetime only. The English is like a Palace or Fortress intended to [last for] many ages." Johnson's advice was endorsed by Arthur's relatives in London, who agreed that Edinburgh was a superior training ground. After all, Dr. John Fothergill of London, the foremost doctor of his era and the friend of Americans, was an alumnus of Edinburgh.

23. Arthur Lee to [Richard Henry Lee], December 24, 25, 28, 1760, *Ibid.*, I, 247–49; Gordon W. Allport (ed.), *Letters From Jenny* (New York, 1965), 173.
24. Arthur Lee to [Richard Henry Lee], December 24, 25, 28, 1760, in Hoffman and Molyneaux (eds.), *Lee Family Papers*, I, 305–306.

American students, it also seemed, were more easily accepted by the Scottish faculty than by English instructors. Enlightened by such information Arthur determined to journey to Scotland for his medical training.[25] This decision was a benchmark of his independence—Arthur was defying family authority.

Edinburgh was thriving when Arthur Lee arrived. Depicted by poet Thomas Gray as the "most picturesque (at a distance) and nastiest (when near) of all capital cities," the Scottish municipality had grown upward in the form of twelve-story tenements. An observer claimed that only in Edinburgh could one walk a few blocks and meet fifty men of genius. A student, remembering the lively mood of the city, proclaimed "that it is not easy to conceive a university where industry was more general, where reading was more fashionable, where indolence and ignorance were more disreputable. Every mind was in a state of fermentation."[26] Lee would be attracted to such ferment.

The medical faculty, established in 1726, was a main source of the university's reputation. Alexander Munro, William Cullen, Joseph Black, and John Hope were luminaries who instructed Arthur Lee and his contemporaries in the 1760s. Munro, who held the chair in anatomy and was succeeded by his son of the same name, discovered the functions of lymph vessels. Many of the American students were attracted to the university by William Cullen, who stood at the head of the British medical profession. He was elevated to the chair of theory of physic in 1766. Black, Cullen's former student, was professor of chemistry and a pioneer in quantitative analysis and thermal reactions. Botanist John Hope was intensely interested in all areas of natural history. The approach of the university was to teach medicine as "a systematic science related to the great laws of material philosophy," rather than to provide practical training.[27]

Although Arthur Lee arrived at Edinburgh after classes had begun in 1761, he decided to attend Cullen's lectures on *materia medica*. The co-

25. Arthur Lee to Richard Henry Lee, March 14, 1761, *Ibid.*, I, 252–54.
26. A. J. Youngson, *The Making of Classical Edinburgh, 1750–1840* (Edinburgh, 1966), 6–21; Sachse, *Colonial American in Britain*, 56–59; D. B. Horn, *A Short History of the University of Edinburgh, 1556–1889* (Edinburgh, 1967), 94; Whitfield J. Bell, Jr., *John Morgan: Continental Doctor* (Philadelphia, 1965), 54–57.
27. Horn, *Short History*, 52–56, 76.

lonial was overwhelmed and quickly concluded that Cullen outshone all the faculty.[28] Each letter from Edinburgh to Virginia dutifully reviewed what Arthur had learned, such as Cullen's theory of disease. Arthur would ask his lecturers about remedies for Richard Henry's ills in an attempt to alleviate his brother's suffering from gout and from minor accidents. Later, during the War for Independence, Arthur loyally sent his beloved brother medicinal herbs from Spain.

Despite his zeal for medical knowledge, Arthur was far from happy at Edinburgh. Though there were an agreeable number of fellow Americans at the school, Lee felt out of place with the North Britons. His distaste might be traced to rabid anti-Scot feeling then pervading London. It was the Whig fashion to malign Scots such as the first minister, Lord Bute, who had attained places of political power. From 1761 up to the opening flashes of the War for American Independence, Lee believed Bute to be a malignant power behind George III. The persistency of such a mistaken belief was a gauge of Arthur's whiggism, if not ethnic prejudice. In Virginia such antagonism was traced to the fact that many merchants were Scots and their sharp practices irritated the planters. Whatever the source, Arthur incorporated his antipathy toward Scotsmen into the political musings he shared with Richard Henry. Soon after his arrival in Edinburgh, Arthur explained, "Nothing can be more disagreeable to me than this town and the manners of the people in it." He was particularly put off by the girls of the town, especially those who read much, "which serves to make them disagreeably opinionated without much improving their natural understanding."[29]

By the summer of 1761, Arthur had completed Cullen's lectures and had prepared for natural philosophy by self-instruction in mathematics and geometry. Concerned at news of a serious fall suffered by Richard Henry, Arthur consulted the good Dr. Cullen, "in the opinion of the world as great a physician who ever lived." A diagnosis and proposed medication were soon on their way to Virginia, together with urgent pleas

28. Arthur Lee to Richard Henry Lee, March 14, 1761, April 2-4-6, 1761, in Hoffman and Molyneaux (eds.), *Lee Family Papers*, I, 252-54, 255-260.

29. Arthur Lee to Richard Henry Lee, March 14, 1761, in Arthur Lee Papers, Box 1. Lee's contemporary, Benjamin Rush, did not share this hostility. George W. Corner (ed.), *The Autobiography of Benjamin Rush: His Travels Through Life Together with His Commonplace Book for 1789-1793* (Princeton, 1948), 38-68; Richard Pares, *George the Third and the Politicians* (Oxford, 1953), 104-109.

for funds. In May, Arthur had moved into an apothecary shop to gain instruction in the mysteries of medication and also to curtail his expenses. Neither brother Philip Ludwell nor cousin Richard Lee of Lee Hall had paid debts owed Arthur. Local sources of loans were unyielding. Arthur determined to continue his studies—midwifery, botany, chemistry, anatomy and natural philosophy were scheduled for the next year—if he could afford it. He begged Richard Henry to pressure his relatives to meet their obligations so that he might purchase dissection samples and a cadaver.[30]

It is likely that soaring aspirations and disquieting doubts pulsed in Arthur's mind as he entered the portals of the medical profession. He pursued the career with the altruistic goal "to live happily with my much loved friends and be useful to them," a goal that smoothed the rugged course of study he proposed and rendered "tolerable the painful thought of so long a Separation from all that's dear to me." His fortitude, however, was severely tested by attendance at his first surgical operation, an ordeal which gave him "so severe a shock" that he had no appetite for further observations.[31]

Still, he managed to endure, and student life was not all drudgery. Numbered among Arthur's acquaintances were Lord Cardross, a fussy and bombastic Scot, and John Berkenhout, a sometime medical student, linguist and wit. Arthur's path also crossed that of law student James Boswell. It appears both were participants in the Soaping Club, an informal convivial fraternity at Thom's Tavern. Perhaps because he feared his brother's reactions to such waywardness, Arthur never reported his weekly activities with this group. Evidently Lee did not lead as dissolute a student life as Boswell, who suffered from recurrent bouts of venereal disease. Nonetheless, Arthur corresponded with him and renewed the friendship when both were in London in the 1770s.[32]

30. Arthur Lee to Richard Henry Lee, May 31, 1761, June 28–July 4, 1761, in Hoffman and Molyneaux (eds.), *Lee Family Papers*, I, 261–63, 264–66. Arthur's instruction at Edinburgh is listed in Whitfield J. Bell, Jr., "Some American Students of 'That Shining Oracle of Physic,' Dr. William Cullen of Edinburgh, 1755–1766," *Proceedings of the American Philosophical Society*, XCIV (June, 1950), 280–281.

31. Arthur Lee to Richard Henry Lee, June 28–July 4, 1761, in Hoffman and Molyneaux (eds.), *Lee Family Papers*, I, 267–69.

32. Richard Henry Lee, *Life of Arthur Lee*, I, 13–14; Lord Cardross to Arthur Lee, October 31, 1767, in Hoffman and Molyneaux (eds.), *Lee Family Papers*, I,

In early adulthood Arthur's personality coalesced, and he crossed the threshold into intense political activity. Three episodes, only tangentially connected to his emerging role as physician, reveal Arthur's style in interpersonal relationships and in political movements. The confrontations illustrate the tactics of adaptation Lee practiced and the conclusions he drew that resulted in a distinct set of perceptions and a characteristic behavior pattern.[33] This was the identity of Arthur Lee.

Arthur's personal sense of autonomy was threatened in the first of these confrontations—the recurrent battle with his family over money. He was still subject to constant anxiety over finances and chagrined to be dependent on commercial affairs, which he regarded as beneath the notice of a truly virtuous man. At Edinburgh, as at Eton, Arthur's schooling was financed by cargoes shipped from Virginia by Richard Henry and sold through a British merchant, John Russell. Because he believed his lifestyle rather frugal for a gentleman (£419 for three years), Arthur regarded the continual harassment by the malfunctioning system as unjust and undeserved. His letters sprayed venom at those who caused his plight. He wrote of "the artful, disingenuous cunning" of cousin Richard Lee of Lee Hall who had delayed payment of debts, and he traced his predicament to Russell who appeared to be broadcasting a "malicious falsehood" that Arthur was a gambler and a bankrupt and thus a poor credit risk. Arthur hotly disputed the charges. Perhaps a sense of guilt, traceable to the Soaping Club, made him edgy, but self-righteousness won out, and he cried to Richard Henry,

> Foes are not wanting to the best on earth. God forbid that I ever should be deaf to the complaints of the oppressed and injured; but scandalous whisperings of Malice, the weak Insinuations, and malevolent Operations of Untruth I shall always dispise [sic]; Nor shall I have regarded the present Defamation so much as to answer it, had you not desired it, it can only operate to the conviction of the weak and unjust

---

495; Frederick A. Pottle, *James Boswell: the Earlier Years, 1740–1769* (New York, 1966), 47, 58; Claude C. Abbott, *A Catalogue of Papers Relating to Boswell, Johnson, and Sir William Forbes Found at Fettercairn House* (Oxford, 1936), 76.

33. James D. Barber, "Adult Identity and Presidential Style: The Rhetorical Emphasis," *Daedalus*, XCVII (Summer, 1968), 950–51; Barber, *Presidential Character*, 10.

and of such I neither desire the Favor nor regard the ill opinion, so long as I shall be conscious to myself of its being unmerited.[34]

In later disputes Arthur would rely on the same stance. He always perceived the causes of his distress as external and usually traced the discomfort to self-seeking opponents. It was the connivance of others that obstructed Arthur's will or challenged his self-esteem. The most frequent objects of his suspicions were men of commerce, whose value system was the opposite of his own posture of the selfless patriot. He believed himself blameless and denied that he sought revenge on those who thwarted him. Yet, without ever submitting his own motives to close scrutiny, he would unleash his hostility in letters to a small group of confidants and await just retribution. This recurrent behavior led historians to characterize him as "a marplot" and "cursed with a persecution complex."[35]

A second episode at Edinburgh taught Arthur lessons in opposition politics and heightened his sense of American identity. Self-conscious of their birthplace, the American students formed a virtual fraternity, often living, dining, or meeting together. In 1761 Virginians on the rolls of the medical school included Lee, Theodorick Bland, Jr., Richard Field, George Gilmer the younger, and James Blair. Under a constitution drafted by Bland, they formed the Virginia Club, which rivaled the prestigious Medical Society. The affiliation was founded on a strong sense of professionalism that affirmed the university's standards and expectations for its students. Each member was, accordingly, required by the club's constitution to promise "for the honor of his profession, not to degrade it by hereafter mingling the trade of an apothecary or a surgeon with it."[36]

In 1764 Arthur, using his position as spokesman for the Virginia Club, composed a memorial to the Virginia Council and House of Burgesses.

34. Arthur Lee to Richard Henry Lee, October 14, 1761, December 22, 1763, in Hoffman and Molyneaux (eds.), *Lee Family Papers*, I, 270–72, 305–307.

35. Mark M. Boatner III (ed.), *Encyclopedia of the American Revolution* (New York, 1966), 603–605; John R. Alden, *A History of the American Revolution* (New York, 1969), 378.

36. Bell, *John Morgan*, 70–73; Theodorick Bland, Jr., to Theodorick Bland, Sr., March 8, 1761, in Charles Campbell (ed.), *The Bland Papers* (2 vols.; Petersburg, Va., 1840), I, 18–20; Lyon G. Tyler, "The Medical Men of Virginia," *William and Mary Quarterly*, 1st ser., XIX (January, 1911), 155–56; Courtlandt Canby, "The Commonplace Book of Doctor George Gilmer," *Virginia Magazine of History and Biography*, LVI (October, 1948), 379–407; Bell, "Some American Students," 279–81.

His first engagement in public writing, it is a prolix petition. The students, in Arthur's rendition, cited their own rigorous training, their aspirations in the "salutary art of healing," and their "inexpressible concern [for] the present unguarded state of physic in our country." Virginia, he said, lay open "to the intrusion of every pretender to the medical art, who may there practice not less to the dishonor of medicine itself, than to the destruction of mankind." Medical practice should be restricted to qualified men like themselves, "properly licensed and honored with a doctor's degree." Arthur's initial venture into policy shaping proved fruitless. The petition was unanswered, and a medical license tax was not legislated in the Old Dominion until 1786.[37]

The more extensive his training, the more concern Arthur showed for his profession. It became his first cause; he threw himself wholeheartedly into it, dreaming of establishing a medical school in Philadelphia with his brother-in-law, William Shippen, Jr., and his colleague, John Morgan.[38] Their plans were never realized, for Lee did not persist in the medical profession and the other two became rivals rather than partners in Pennsylvania, but Lee's intense professionalism embroiled him in a student protest, "an accident, as rare as unexpected." The faculty of the medical school, in what became known as the Pulteney case, desired to grant degrees to two Englishmen, an apothecary of some renown and a gentleman of "plentiful fortune." Twenty-nine students, believing such action cheapened their own degrees and violated university regulations, remonstrated. The students cited the rules for conferring degrees and defended their position on moral grounds as well. Arthur believed the case affected student "honor and interest." When the faculty issued an "evasive and unsatisfactory" rejoinder, the students threatened to resign. Eventually a compromise was mediated. The first gentleman, a Fellow of the Royal Society, was to get his degree as he was of high merit and had only violated procedures. The other candidate would only be acceptable if he provided valid testimony of previous study at Oxford, a requirement evidently not easily met.

37. Wyndham B. Blanton, *Medicine in Virginia in the Eighteenth Century* (Richmond, 1931), 5–6, 90–91, 226, 399–402.
38. Bell, *John Morgan*, 72–73, 112; Arthur Lee to [Richard Henry Lee], [before September 1, 1764], in Hoffman and Molyneaux (eds.), *Lee Family Papers*, I, 310–312.

As a leader of the Virginia Club Arthur had organized this student uprising, and his advocacy became notorious among the faculty. He feared reprisals: "For however their consciences may convince them of the justice of our opposition; yet, as men, they cannot avoid feeling it as coercive of their power and . . . of their conduct." He believed his degree was in jeopardy when acceptance of his dissertation was delayed. Eventually the protest proved a success, for in 1767 Benjamin Rush informed a colleague, "Our professors have lately enacted some new laws to regulate the graduation of students. The examinations are more strict and more numerous than formerly. This will tend to keep up the reputation of the College. 'Tis now in the zenith of its glory." The 1767 *Statuta Solemnia* of the university required all course work, preliminary exams, theses, and final written exams to be rendered in Latin.[39]

Arthur's impressions of the confrontation were characteristic. He was thrilled by the excitement and the prominent role he had played. As a leader he had tasted power in manipulating his followers and negotiating with the faculty. He was certain his position "as one, who would not willingly suffer the honor of a Physician to be prostituted" was morally upright. He had participated in a worthy cause, made a name for himself, and gained a sense of achievement. Yet, his exhilaration was tempered by uneasiness over the reaction of his faculty opponents. He was "uncertain whether in any event I can venture to apply for a degree in this University." This would be the pattern of his adult life. He would throw himself fanatically into confrontations, some as sweeping as the American Revolution, others quite petty. No outcome would ever be completely satisfactory judged against Lee's perfectionist ideals. Arthur Lee, the eternal moralizer, viewed any compromise of his integrity as abject surrender.

In a third episode, Arthur involved himself in a much larger confrontation, which illustrated his attachment to his homeland and the development of his rhetorical style. He published a disparaging pamphlet wherein he took exception to Adam Smith's comments about slavery in America. On an intellectual level, this particular episode shows Lee's intellectual obstinacy and his muddled thinking; on a personal level, Lee's attraction

---

39. Benjamin Rush to Jonathan Bayard Smith, April 30, 1767, in Lyman Butterfield *et al.* (eds.), *Letters of Benjamin Rush* (2 vols.; Princeton, 1951), I, 41, Sir Alexander Grant, *The Story of the University of Edinburgh During Its First Three Hundred Years* (London, 1884), 330–32.

to Smith was typical of his propensity to seek out acquaintances of high esteem. Perhaps he hoped their renown would grace his own reputation.

In October, 1761, Lee journeyed to Glasgow to converse with Adam Smith on husbandry. At first, he found Smith "a very agreeable companion," the Scottish agricultural innovations promising, and Glasgow preferable to Edinburgh, but his optimism soon vanished. Lee was disappointed at being unable to observe highly productive drill plowing. The Virginian also found further fault with the Scots: "an uncivil, unsociable people, and utterly strangers to politeness." Conversations with Smith and travels in the British Isles prompted Lee to enter a larger political arena. In 1764 his pen produced *An Essay in Vindication of the Continental Colonies of America, from a Censure of Mr. Adam Smith, in His Theory of Moral Sentiments, with Some Reflections on Slavery in General.* The essay exhibited Arthur's distaste for slavery, an aversion he shared with Richard Henry, as well as his pride in native Virginia.[40]

The piece was as much an appraisal of slaves as it was a counterattack on British critics of slaveholding. According to Lee's reading of *Theory of Moral Sentiments,* Smith had castigated American slaveholders as vicious and inhuman in contrast to virtuous enslaved Africans. Arthur, therefore, set out first to catalogue the depravity and barbarism of Negroes in Africa, then to prove that Negro slaves in America shared the same characteristics. It was neither the environment nor the nurture offered by American slaveholders, but the nature of the victims themselves that made the practice detestable. The Americans, on whom Smith had cast "as bitter an invective as ever fell from the tongue of man," were blameless. Whether the Negroes' depravity "proceeds from a native baseness that fits their minds for all villainy; or that they never receive the benefit of education" was a question Lee left begging.[41]

Lee's style of writing is to be found already full-blown in this pamphlet, and his political opinions are taking shape. He strews throughout the work a mélange of authorities, ranging from Homer to Montesquieu.

40. Arthur Lee to Richard Henry Lee, October 21, 1761, August 28, December 22, 1763, in Hoffman and Molyneaux (eds.), *Lee Family Papers,* I, 273–75, 295–99, 305–307; Winthrop D. Jordan, *White over Black: American Attitudes Toward the Negro, 1550–1812* (Chapel Hill, 1968), 308–311.

41. [Arthur Lee], *An Essay in Vindication of the Continental Colonies of America, from a Censure of Mr. Adam Smith, in His Theory of Moral Sentiments, with Some Reflections on Slavery in General* (London, 1764), 10, 38.

Lee preferred overwhelming his readers to reasoning with them. His budding political views are apparent in the pamphlet when, in illustrating the history of Virginia, Maryland, and the Carolinas, Lee digresses to attack restraints on colonial trade. In Arthur's view the mercantile policy of Great Britain thwarted American autonomy. The colonies were "subjected to the arbitrary impositions of British merchants," who fixed "like cankers" on colonial estates and "utterly consume them." British mercantile interests dictated what American planters grew and were thus responsible for the institution of slavery. Arthur judged mercantilism a "confined and puny policy" and found it alarming that the colonists were "treated, not as fellow-subjects, but as the servants of Britain."[42] Arthur would later passionately embrace the notion that the British sought to secure the chains of bondage on the colonists rather than grant them a degree of independence. He ultimately perceived the choice as either slavery or liberty.

Arthur also used the pamphlet to challenge the British belief that slaves were ill treated in America. He attributed this generally held notion to false reports spread abroad "to catch the ears of vulgar credulity, or to gratify that strange propensity in some minds to calumny and misrepresentation." In truth, though he could not suppress thoughts of "inexpressible misery" over slavery, Lee countered that the condition of American slaves was "far happier than that of the Scotch or Irish vulgar."[43] When he later became involved in the imperial dilemma, especialy as it focused on affairs between Massachusetts citizens and British policy makers, Lee was certain that the antagonism was traceable to unreliable information from both sides of the Atlantic.

Summing up his observations on "the bondage we have imposed on the Africans," Arthur determined slavery to be "absolutely repugnant to justice" and "highly inconsistent with civil policy." The fact that barbarous, savage, and lawless Africa affirmed slavery was ample reason for civilized Christian nations to abolish it. As long as the peculiar institution persisted, it thwarted "all improvements in arts and sciences." Enslavement of blacks prejudiced the minds of the freemen by "steeling their hearts against the laudable feelings of virtue and humanity." Over the community hung the destructive threats of slave uprisings. The only solution to

42. *Ibid., passim*, 20.
43. *Ibid.*, 25.

the American dilemma was to people the colonies with Europeans. Lee believed free white labor more efficient than blacks in bondage.[44]

The repugnance Arthur displayed toward slavery and blacks was not merely rhetorical. In private correspondence he spoke of the "dastardly temper of the Negroes." What rankled the Virginian was that black slavery in the colonies symbolized "the lamentable state of dependence in which I perceive America must for many years be held by Britain." The linchpin of this subordinance was cultivation of tobacco—"a very precarious commodity"—dictated by the English. If the Americans could diversify their agricultural production, by growing more hemp and flax for instance, they would gain a measure of commercial freedom and perhaps cut into the practice of slavery. Later in his career he labored in the antislavery movement: in Williamsburg he circulated petitions to halt the slave trade and in London he communed with Granville Sharpe, the British abolitionist. Reportedly, he expected more from servants in his employ than from slaves he owned.[45]

Despite his protests against British commercial policy and university authorities, Arthur's graduation from Edinburgh was not long delayed. John Hope accepted his dissertation and awarded him a gold medal for work on the botanical and medical qualities of quinine (Peruvian bark). On September 1, 1764, the Virginian was one of seven students granted an M.D. He had become, in his own words, "a legitimate Son of Aesculapius," a reference to the mythological illegitimate son of Apollo worshiped by all those who sought cures of their pains. Although he considered his study arduous and intricate, he felt uncertain of his capabilities. His ambivalence over his professional capabilities was characteristic of Virginians within the empire. He proposed further class work at Edin-

44. *Ibid.*, 39–45. Lee persistently claimed white labor to be more efficient than black. In Congressional debate in 1783 he "gave it as his opinion that 2 slaves were not equal to 1 Freeman." William T. Hutchinson *et al.* (eds.), *The Papers of James Madison* (12 vols.; Chicago, 1962–), VI, 408.

45. Arthur Lee to Richard Henry Lee, August 15, 1769, Arthur Lee to [Richard Henry Lee], March 20, 1765, Arthur Lee to [Francis Lightfoot Lee], November 3, 1763, in Hoffman and Molyneaux (eds.), *Lee Family Papers*, I, 621–24, 326–28, 303–304; Richard K. MacMaster, "Arthur Lee's 'Address on Slavery': An Aspect of Virginia's Struggle to End the Slave Trade, 1765–1774," *Virginia Magazine of History and Biography*, LXXX (April, 1972), 141–47; Jordan, *White over Black*, 309; Richard Henry Lee, *Life of Arthur Lee*, I, 183.

burgh through the winter and a tour through Leyden, Paris, and the German universities the following spring. The capstone was to be a year in London, possibly in the clinics, before returning to America in 1766. He assured Richard Henry, "You may be satisfied, my dear Brother, that there is not the least probability of my settling any where in Britain; indeed, I think I shall require all the assistance my friends can give to support me with you; for I have not the least talent for what is called pushing one's fortune." Nonetheless his aspirations had been buoyed by Philip Lee's promise to pay both William and Arthur.[46]

Arthur was not so much attracted to home in Virginia as he was repelled by British men and institutions. At the core of this distrust was the fashionable loathing of the Scots, a mannerism that infected all his letters. He numbered himself among those who condemned "the unprincipled ambition and partiality" of the Earl of Bute, who commanded the ear of George III and who epitomized the aggressive migration of Scots to positions of power. Though Bute resigned his position as head of the administration in 1763, Lee retained the notion for more than a decade that the Scot was the real power behind the throne: it was broadcast in his later assessments of British policy. According to the young analyst of the 1760s, Scotsmen were encroaching on English independence, and their encroachment was sure to have dramatic consequences, for as Arthur remembered his Montesquieu, if the English lost "their Liberty, they could be the most abject slaves on earth."[47] Typically, Lee perceived the situation as without possible compromise: the British would be either utterly free or abjectly enslaved. Later, as the storm of the American Revolution gathered, Lee would find the same dichotomy, freedom or slavery, confronting the Americans.

Arthur's evaluations of British imperial policy abound in fears that the

46. Richard Henry Lee, *Life of Arthur Lee*, I, 13; Louis B. Wright, *The Atlantic Frontier: Colonial American Civilization, 1607–1763* (Ithaca, 1965), 64; Arthur Lee to Richard Henry Lee, September 1–2, 1764, in Hoffman and Molyneaux (eds.), *Lee Family Papers*, I, 313; Edith Hamilton, *Mythology* (Boston, 1946), 413–15.

47. Jack P. Greene, "Society, Ideology, and Politics: An Analysis of the Political Culture of Mid-Eighteenth Century Virginia," in Richard M. Jellison (ed.), *Society, Freedom, and Conscience* (New York, 1973), 75–76; Robert K. Weir, "Who Shall Rule at Home: The American Revolution as a Crisis of Legitimacy for the Colonial Elite," *Journal of Interdisciplinary History*, VI (Spring, 1976),

American colonies would be victimized. Parliamentary taxation for revenue was categorized as a mark of impending oppression.[48] Arthur exhorted the colonists to "counteract" such legislation as the Sugar Act of
1764. Americans should turn inward, establish their own manufacturing
centers, foreswear the use of British "luxuries or even conveniences,
which the parliament has been pleased to render so expensive." His suggestions anticipated the tactics espoused by the Continental Association in
1774 in a drive for economic self-sufficiency. Lee's visions were most often
antimodern. The advent of industry and urban machine-tenders was re-
pulsive to neowhig chanters, who idealized the bucolic societies of the
past.

It has often been alleged that the poem entitled "Oppression," which
appeared in London in 1765, was written by Arthur Lee. The poem,
which was later reprinted in Boston, New York and Philadelphia, was a
satirical attack on the British ministry in general and the Scots in particular:

> When tyrants skulk behind a gracious T[HRONE],
> And practice what,—their courage dare not own;
> When M[INISTE]RS like screening G[RENVIL]L rule,
> A Pedant talker, and a B[UT]EAN tool:
>
> .   .   .   .
>
> When sons of famine (a) swarm throughout our coast,
> UnKnown to fame, yet rise to ev'ry post:
> When countries groan beneath Oppression's hand,
> And pension'd blockheads riot through the land:
> When COLONIES a savage Ex[CI]SE pay,
> To feed the creatures of a motly day:
>
> .   .   .   .
>
> When dunce on dunce successive rules our S[tate],
> Who can't love P[I]TT, and who a G[RENVIL]L hate?

Although it cannot be proven that Lee was its author, it is certain that the
poem exhibits Arthur's central concerns: the threat to the British constitution, the designs of Bute and the Scots, the corruption and hypocrisy of

685; Arthur Lee to [Francis Lightfoot Lee], November 5, 1763, in Hoffman and
Molyneaux (eds.), *Lee Family Papers*, I, 303.

48. Arthur Lee to Richard Henry Lee, January 13, 1765, in Hoffman and Molyneaux (eds.), *Lee Family Papers*, I, 322–25.

the ministry, and the plight of the Americans.[49] The poem's tone, shrill and hyperbolic, is also characteristic of Arthur's writing.

Arthur was not completely put off by Britain, though. Early in 1765 he was vacillating in his choice of locale for his medical practice. He was drawn to America "by the strongest ties of family affection and patriotic love" but distraught with the prevalence of slavery. With Whiggish flourish he described England as "the Eden of the world and the land of liberty and independence, to me the most valuable of all blessings since I know not a more bitter ingredient than dependence that can enter the cup of life." The dread manifested in this letter shows the impact of Lee's analogical thoughts: he perceived the slave-master relationship to be like the connection between colony and mother country, perhaps even like that between himself and members of his family. Dependence was a badge of subordination and inferiority, while independence indicated autonomy.[50]

While Patrick Henry and other colonists angrily arose to challenge the Stamp Act in the spring of 1765, Arthur Lee toured Holland and France. A short respite at Leyden to attend lectures netted him another M.D. degree. This journey, like those of later life, was faithfully recorded in a journal. With a keen eye for architecture and the lay of the land, Arthur related history to scenery and reinforced his conceptions of political science. Of the inhabitants of the Low Countries he reported, "The liberty of the people is imaginary, and consists only in the wise and temperate legislation of their aristocracy; for such are the states, the members of which are chosen by themselves, without the participation of the people." He was then, and later, partial to such a system of government.[51]

Perhaps the young physician stayed on the European continent until the end of the year. By early 1766, however, he was in London, engrossed in debates over repeal of the Stamp Act. From his position in the gallery of the House of Commons, the Virginian was thrilled by the oratory of

49. John W. Blassingame, "American Nationalism and Other Loyalties in the Southern Colonies, 1763–1776," *Journal of Southern History,* XXXIV (February, 1968), 54–55; Oscar Wegelin, *Early American Poetry* (New York, 1930), 126; Arthur M. Schlesinger, *Prelude to Independence: The Newspaper War on Britain, 1764–1776* (New York, 1958), 39; Moses C. Tyler, *The Literary History of the American Revolution* (2 vols.; New York, 1971), I, 115–120.

50. Arthur Lee to Richard Henry Lee, March 20, 1765, in Hoffman and Molyneaux (eds.), *Lee Family Papers,* I, 326–28.

51. Arthur Lee to Richard Henry Lee, June 27, 1765, in Arthur Lee Papers, Box 1; Richard Henry Lee, *Life of Arthur Lee,* I, 243.

William Pitt. According to Pitt, the Americans were correct in asserting that taxation without representation was contrary to the British constitution. Lee, believing the colonial resisters had acted manfully, legally, and correctly, welcomed Pitt's confirmation of legitimacy. Yet when the Stamp Act was repealed in March by the newly selected Rockingham ministry, Lee did not record his impressions. Later with historical hindsight he asserted, "Though the obnoxious act was repealed, yet . . . the spirit which dictated it and was still resting near the throne, was not changed." [52] The malignant presence of Bute is implied.

It was during the debates on repeal of the Stamp Act that Arthur struck up a friendship with the enigmatic earl of Shelburne, member of the cabinet. He saw in Shelburne a model worthy of emulation and a politico worthy of cultivation. Here was a gentleman politician who catered to the empire's intelligentsia. Arthur informed his brother, "Lord Shelburne has often assured me that he would do anything to serve me; and I sincerely believe him to be an honest man and sincere." He hinted that through Shelburne, Richard Henry might gain the favor of imperial bureaucrats. He did not perceive that he was to be numbered amongst "a salon of second-rate philosophes" who, as one historian put it, flocked around Shelburne, the "ideological magpie." [53]

Lady Shelburne's diary shows that Lee breakfasted with the earl on January 12, 1766, at a time when Shelburne and Pitt were in consultation over the repeal of the Stamp Act.[54] Little trusted and much used by all factions in British politics, Shelburne was of Lee's age and temperament. Looking past the peer's reputation as a treacherous conniver and former minion of Bute, the Virginian was attracted by the libertarian posturing of the politician. That the peer was willing to listen to Arthur's talk concerning affairs in the colonies and defects in the ministry doubtlessly made Lee his protégé. Through Shelburne, the colonist gained his first intimate view of the machinations of British politics—no doubt a disillusioning

52. Richard Henry Lee, *Life of Arthur Lee*, I, 243.
53. Arthur Lee to Richard Henry Lee [December, 1766?], in Arthur Lee Papers, Box 1; Eugene C. Black, review of John Norris, *Shelburne and Reform*, in *William and Mary Quarterly*, 3rd ser., XXI (October, 1964), 611; Esmond Wright, *Fabric of Freedom, 1673–1800* (Rev. ed.; New York, 1978), 25–26, 60.
54. Lord Fitzmaurice, *Life of William Earl Shelburne Afterwards First Marquess of Lansdowne with Extracts from His Papers and Correspondence* (2 vols.; London, 1912), I, 269.

experience. When he returned to Virginia later in 1766, Arthur campaigned to have a statue of Shelburne erected in Williamsburg. Not only would this gesture have served as a public recognition of Shelburne's patriotic role in the repeal, but it could also have further secured the peer's friendship for the Lee family. The statue was never erected, but Arthur later recognized Shelburne's amity by naming his own place of retirement, Lansdowne, after the peer's seat.

Arthur left Shelburne and returned to Virginia on the demand of Richard Henry, who used the promulgation of the Stamp Act to press his brother to return to the homeland. He lamented with Arthur the "loss of American liberty," and the "Egyptian bondage" inflicted by the mother country, "an arbitrary, cruel, and oppressive stepdame." In Richard Henry's view, the Stamp Act should instruct every American that liberty could never be supported without educated leaders. If America did not possess such an elite, she "must fall into barbarous ignorance, and of course become a fit subject for tyrannical natures to impose arbitrary and injurious acts." However, if colonial learning kept pace with America's burgeoning population, "despotism will quickly learn" that American connections could be obtained only "by a free intercourse and equal participation of good offices, liberty and free constitution of government." Having won Arthur's attention and sympathy with such whiggish thoughts, Richard Henry added the concluding thrust to his letter: "America, then, has a parent's claim to her descendents, and a right to insist that they not fix in any place, where, by so doing, they may add strength to cruel and tyrannical oppression." The argument, on ideological, psychological, and nationalistic levels, was unanswerable for Arthur.[55] He dared not withstand the claims of his dear and affectionate brother and mentor.

Before he departed from England, Arthur sought a final mark of recognition, membership in the Royal Society of London. An F.R.S. would be quite a laurel to cap his decade and a half of studies in Britain. It would also enhance his self-esteem both as a patron of science and as a Britisher. He had attended society meetings and read a paper on his experiments

55. Richard Henry Lee to Arthur Lee, July 4, 1765, in James C. Ballagh (ed.), *The Letters of Richard Henry Lee* (2 vols.; New York, 1911–14), I, 10–11; Edwin G. Burrows and Michael Wallace, "The American Revolution: The Ideology and Psychology of National Liberation," *Perspectives in American History*, VI (1972), 167–308.

with Peruvian bark. However, because of "an indespensible call to my own country," he left a complete history of the drug unwritten. Nevertheless, in February, 1766, he was recommended for election to the society. His sponsor, Benjamin Franklin, cited him as "a Gentleman of Virginia now residing in London whom we esteem for his Learning, Ingenuity, and Knowledge in Natural Philosophy." Franklin, Dr. John Fothergill, Lord Cardross, and Israel Mauduit were among those who endorsed the promising intellectual for membership. He was elected on May 15, 1766, although he did not then appear for formal admission, probably because he had departed for Virginia. At the conclusion of the year Franklin came forward to sign a bond covering Arthur's contributions and paid the young man's admission fee. It was not until November, 1768, that Lee returned to assume his obligations and privileges as an F.R.S.[56]

Perhaps Arthur Lee turned to an assessment of himself and the world he knew as he returned home across the Atlantic in 1766. After all, the Lee family motto was: "Not unmindful of the future." He might have contemplated how his own needs and capabilities could enable him to adapt to the opportunities that lay before him. If he had canvassed his dispositions and impulses, he might have listed boundless energy and a catholic mind as his assets. He might not have recognized deep mistrust of others and haunting doubt of himself as his chief liabilities. Pride in himself, his family, and his homeland had been repeatedly undermined by the actions of his parents, some of his siblings, and his peers.

He had no anticipation of tranquility. Rather, he saw himself and his heroes as animated by "patriotism" and embattled by "the prevalence of faction and corrupt influence." [57] To be a patriot meant both to love one's homeland and to be free from reliance on connections. Adherence to and advocacy of such ideals was, for Arthur Lee, a reaction to recurrent episodes of subordination and uncertainty in his upbringing. Book learning,

56. Royal Society of London, *Philosophical Transactions*, LVI (1766), 47–51; C[harles] Morton to Arthur Lee, May 1, 1766, in Arthur Lee Papers, Box 1; "Notes and Queries," *Virginia Magazine of History and Biography*, XVI (October, 1908), 206; Raymond P. Stearns, "Colonial Fellows of the Royal Society of London, 1661–1788," *William and Mary Quarterly*, 2nd ser., XX (January, 1940), 85–89.

57. Arthur Lee to Richard Henry Lee, [n.d. 1765?], in Hoffman and Molyneaux (eds.), *Lee Family Papers*, I, 510.

letters traded with Richard Henry, and his own seasoning at Edinburgh coalesced. He might hope for success both in his vocation as a physician and in his calling as a man of affairs, but question whether life in provincial Virginia could fulfill such expectations.

CHAPTER II

Liberty Is the
Very Idol of My Soul

A notice in the *Virginia Gazette* of July 4, 1766, announced the arrival of Dr. Arthur Lee at Williamsburg. The youthful physician—not yet twenty-six years of age—had returned to his native colony after spending half of his lifetime in British schools. As the scholarly and intense scion of the Stratford Lees, veteran of the Continental tour, companion to Samuel Johnson, Adam Smith, and the earl of Shelburne, Arthur doubtless appeared out of place at the provincial capital. Tall and erect, he could match any Virginian in elegance and grace, perhaps to the point of being overbearing. His defiantly poised yet delicately oval face, brooding blue eyes, large nose, and pointed chin reflected his mother. Perhaps his hair was blond or reddish hued like Richard Henry's.[1] The well-schooled gentleman had arrived to establish his profession as provincial physician.

Williamsburg was the metropolis of baronial Virginia in 1766. Encompassing 1,500 citizens and 230 buildings, the town would double in size during the political season. Lee's credentials made him eminently qualified to minister to the ills of the townspeople. Yet it was a very competitive situation. From 1766 to 1768 there were at least eight other M.D.'s, as well as untold amateurs in Williamsburg. Even more unsettling to the neophyte was the general practice of patients to refuse to pay doctor's fees.[2]

Arthur did not last long as a doctor, nor did Williamsburg contain him. He was still searching for his calling. It might have been the competition or the provincial aspects of the town. He later reflected, "Perseverance, of which I have very little, is absolutely requisite for a physician."

1. Alexander Purdie and John Dixon (eds.), *Virginia Gazette*, July 4, 1766; Hendrick, *The Lees*, 145–46.
2. Carl Bridenbaugh, *Seat of Empire: The Political Role of Eighteenth Century Williamsburg* (Williamsburg, 1950), 30–36; Richard Henry Lee, *Life of Arthur Lee*, I, 14; Richard Shryock, *Medicine and Society in America, 1660–1860* (New York, 1960), 2–6, 15; Blanton, *Medicine in Virginia*, 207–208, 316–24.

It might have been that his European training proved impractical or that he rebelled against the profession chosen for him by his father and oldest brother. He seems to have had a bout with melancholy, and he cast his sorrow in romantic prose to Richard Henry:

> In the path of life, along which I am doomed to travel, many are the thorns and numerous the hills among which toil and circumspection must conduct me; very thinly are its flowers scattered, or opening meads delightful to the eye; difficulty and danger will attend the gathering one, or indulging in the other. So circumstanced, what can administer happiness to me but that of those I love; what can animate me, through this tedious journey, but the comfortable reflection, that my friends are happy.[3]

Such personal brooding coincided with the politics of confrontation that pulsed in Williamsburg and other colonial centers at this time. Lee soon foresook his medical practice and leaped into the public debates, remonstrances, and disturbances which culminated in the War for Independence. He turned away from the healing profession toward more contentious pursuits—those of lawyer and polemicist—and found his true callings.

Political turmoil in eighteenth century Virginia inevitably atttracted one or more of the Lees: historical moment coincided with personal need. It can be argued that Arthur was attracted to political agitation as a means to enhance his self-esteem. It appears that his political impulse was a form of compensatory behavior: he needed to convince himself and others that he was someone to be reckoned with. The role of agitator could be a means to gain as much prominence as his older brothers had.

When Arthur returned to Virginia in the summer of 1766, Richard Henry, his idol, was embroiled in the controversy over the Stamp Act. The previous year the older brother had fomented popular agitation in the Northern Neck. A Lee creation, the Westmoreland Association, arose as a vehicle of popular resistance to British taxation and issued a fiery manifesto, the Westmoreland Resolutions of February 27, 1766, which was signed by a hundred Virginians. These liberty-conscious citizens— including all of Arthur's brothers save Philip Ludwell—compacted to "exert every faculty to prevent the execution of the Stamp Act, in every instance whatever, in the colony of Virginia; and every abandoned

3. Arthur Lee to [?], August 4, 1769, in Richard Henry Lee, *Life of Arthur Lee*, I, 204–205; Arthur Lee to Richard Henry Lee [December, 1766?], in Hoffman and Molyneaux (eds.), *Lee Family Papers*, I, 439–43.

wretch, who shall be so lost to virtue and public good, as wickedly to contribute to introduce the said act in this colony, by using stamp paper, or by any other means, will, with the utmost expedition, be convinced that immediate danger and disgrace shall attend his prostitute purpose."[4]

An "abandoned wretch" singled out by the Lees was George Mercer, the stamp distributor appointed for Virginia. In July, 1765, Richard Henry saw to it that Mercer, a local hero in the French and Indian War, was burned in effigy in Westmoreland County. The Lee-Mercer antagonism was as much rooted in local as imperial politics. In addition to the dispute over imperial prerogative, their ill will was linked to rivalry over American lands. In 1747 the Ohio Company, a speculative effort of Virginia planters, spearheaded by Thomas Lee, had sought 200,000 acres from the Crown. John Mercer had come to the fore of this enterprise in 1750, following the death of Thomas Lee. In 1763 George Mercer had been dispatched to England to revive petitions for land grants but had failed. He had, however, gained the stamp distributorship for himself. Lee's sons, chiefly Richard Henry and Arthur, resented the domination of the land scheme by the Mercers. In late October of 1765 when George Mercer arrived in Williamsburg, he was greeted by a hostile crowd, doubtless incited by Richard Henry. When confronted by the angry colonists, Mercer resigned as stamp distributor and prudently took passage back to England.[5]

Three weeks after Arthur's arrival in Virginia, the Mercer clan struck back against the Lees. John and James Mercer, father and brother of the stamp distributor, revealed to the public that Richard Henry Lee was not the altruistic patriot he appeared to be. The Mercers disclosed that Richard Henry, in November, 1764, had applied for the very office that George Mercer's well-meaning but misguided friends had secured for him: the stamp distributorship! The Mercers alleged that personal resent-

4. Hendrick, *The Lees*, 134–36; Westmoreland Resolutions, February 27, 1766, in Hoffman and Molyneaux (eds.), *Lee Family Papers*, I, 347–48; John C. Matthews, "Two Men on a Tax: Richard Henry Lee, Archibald Ritchie, and the Stamp Act," in Darrett B. Rutman (ed.), *The Old Dominion: Essays for Thomas Perkins Abernethy* (Charlottesville, 1964), 96–108.

5. Paul G. Bowers, "Richard Henry Lee and the Continental Congress, 1774–1779," (Ph.D. dissertation, Duke Univeristy, 1965), 20–28; Joseph Royle (ed.), Supplement Extraordinary to the *Virginia Gazette*, October 25, 1765; Bridenbaugh, *Seat of Empire*, 65–67; Alfred P. James, *The Ohio Company: Its Inner History* (Pittsburgh, 1959), 5–144.

ment, not constitutional or moral principle, prompted Lee's attack on the Stamp Act. Richard Henry could not deny the accusations. He took his defense to the public via the press, publishing a less than persuasive letter, which conceded he had actively sought the imperial favor at a time when he could not foresee the public reaction to the Stamp Act. Then, he said, when he sensed swelling American resentment, he had changed his mind and rushed to the front to defend American liberties. As one student of the episode phrased it, "Lee's financial position led him to solicit the distributorship, his political ambitions soon brought him to eschew the post." Thus even the Lees were vulnerable. Apparently caught at playing both sides of the controversy, Richard Henry felt that Virginians would honor his most recent patriotic stand in 1766 and forgive his earlier transgressions.[6] Most of them did.

Richard Henry Lee's rationalization was unacceptable to the Mercers. They sought to drive him from public office and continued their harassment in the press through the autumn. First John, then James Mercer blasted Richard Henry and the anonymous "infamous scribblers" who had been recruited to express "the gall of Stratford." In a newspaper war that foreshadowed the innuendo and invective of future confrontations in which the Lees were major combatants during the War for Independence, both sides filled the pages of the *Virginia Gazette* with self-righteous defenses of their champions and rancorous animadversions aimed at their opponents. It was the Mercers' impression that Arthur Lee was "the principal, if not the only assassin under different vizors, and he was so regardless of truth that he invented and published the most infamous lies as indisputable facts." In later times, Arthur did not hesitate to fill the press with vituperation behind a buckler of pseudonyms.[7]

The Lee-Mercer quarrel festered through the winter in 1767, and in late April, Arthur Lee challenged James Mercer to a duel. The confrontation was symptomatic of the struggle for power in provincial Virginia. Although tempers waxed hot in Williamsburg, the *affaire d'honneur* be-

6. Bowers, "Richard Henry Lee," 19–28; Matthews, "Two Men on a Tax," 97; William Rind (ed.), *Virginia Gazette*, July 18, August 8, 1766.

7. Rind (ed.), *Virginia Gazette*, July 18, 23, August 8, 13, 15, 1766; Purdie & Dixon (eds.), *Virginia Gazette*, July 18, August 22, September 26, October 3, 24, 1766; John Mercer to George Mercer, December 22, 1767–January 28, 1768, in Lois Mulkearn (ed.), *George Mercer Papers Relating to the Ohio Company of Virginia* (Pittsburgh, 1954), 203.

tween the physician and attorney never came about. Arthur sent his second, fellow physician Corbin Griffin, to challenge Mercer to a dawn encounter with pistols. It was set for April 28. When Lee appeared at five in the morning on the appointed day, Mercer was not to be found. Arthur expressed his contempt for his opponent and departed the field. Mercer evidently arrived soon after and, failing to encounter his foe, reckoned his obligation had been fulfilled. Both men believed the other had backed down. Both belatedly rendered their versions of the farce in the *Virginia Gazette*.[8]

Arthur expected Mercer to renew the challenge. Haughtily he crowed to Richard Henry, "I am heartily ashamed of having such an antagonist." Never in all his quarrels would Arthur ever find a worthy opponent; Arthur's adversaries were all basely motivated in contradistinction to himself. Assessing the resentment he had aroused, he noted that the colonists "hardly deserve the trouble of interposing to preserve them . . . either from Scotch or English imposition and oppression." His pretentiousness was contradicted by his anxiety over the pending duel though; he closed this letter with a "farewell" rather than his characteristic "adeiu."[9]

Emotions flared again in the summer. Coffeehouse advocates trumpeted the cause of Lee or Mercer. An anonymous "Essay on Honor" (unfortunately missing from extant files of the *Virginia Gazette*) was interpreted by Mercer as a taunt from Lee. The year-long affair then disappeared from the Williamsburg press. In the concluding episode—a most ungentlemanly skirmish—Mercer's friends reportedly took offense at Lee's conduct, burned him in effigy before his own door, and threatened to toss him into the fire. One account declared that James Mercer, "without receiving any damage broke the Doctor's head, and closed his eyes in such a manner as obliged him to keep his house sometime." The Mercers believed they had been vindicated and Arthur properly chastised. Lee's impressions do not exist in the historical record, but for a later remembrance of Williamsburg as "a sink of idleness and vice."[10]

8. Purdie & Dixon (eds.), *Virginia Gazette*, May 28, 1767; Rind (ed.), *Virginia Gazette*, July 27, 1767; Carl Bridenbaugh, "Violence and Virtue, 1766; or, The Importance of the Trivial," *Massachusetts Historical Society Proceedings*, LXXVI (1964), 3–29.

9. Arthur Lee to Richard Henry Lee, May 28, 1767, in Hoffman and Molyneaux (eds.), *Lee Family Papers*, I, 476–78.

10. Purdie & Dixon (eds.), *Virginia Gazette*, August 13, 1767, October 31,

The eldest Mercer predicted that Arthur's "vanity and itch of scribbling" would propel him into other quarrels, an accurate prognosis. Another clash hastened the youthful controversialist from Williamsburg and held him up for ridicule. The point of contention was as close to Lee as family pride had been in the Mercer affair; it was his reputation as a member of the educated elite. Arthur's schooling at Eton, Edinburgh, and Leyden, as well as membership in the Royal Society of London, did not go unnoticed in provincial America. In January, 1768, he was elected to the American Philosophical Society in Philadelphia. The previous year in Williamsburg he had been selected to the Board of Visitors, which supervised the College of William and Mary.[11] Here he did battle with the faculty, composed of clergymen who resisted the anti-British sentiment seething in Virginia in the 1760s.

Friction between the faculty and the board dated from selection of a college president in 1752. The conflict had flared notoriously between 1757 and 1763 over the Two-Penny Act, when the board had ousted some faculty members who had sided with colonial clergy against a move to depreciate clerical salaries. Chief spokesman for the dissidents was the Reverend John Camm, described by the lieutenant governor of Virginia as "a man of abilities but a turbulent man who delights to live in a flame." Camm gained reinstatement on the college faculty in 1763 by personally petitioning the Privy Council. He battled both Richard Bland and Landon Carter in the public press over the celebrated Parsons' Cause, and Lee marked Camm as appropriate prey.[12]

1771; John Mercer to George Mercer, December 22, 1767–January 28, 1768, in Mulkearn (ed.), *George Mercer Papers*, 203–204; Arthur Lee to Richard Henry Lee, September 10, 1770, in Hoffman and Molyneaux (eds.), *Lee Family Papers*, II, 33–34.

11. [Earl G. Swem?], *A Provisional List of Alumni, Grammar School Students, Members of the Faculty, and Members of the Board of Visitors of the College of William and Mary in Virginia from 1693 to 1888* (Richmond, 1941), 53.

12. Richard L. Morton, *Westward Expansion and Prelude to the Revolution, 1710–1763* (Chapel Hill, 1960), Vol. II of Morton, *Colonial Virginia*, 751–90; Bernhard Knollenberg, *Origin of the American Revolution, 1759–1766* (New York, 1965), 57–66; "Sketch of John Camm," *William and Mary Quarterly*, 1st ser., XIX (1910–1911), 28–30; Rhys Isaac, "Religion and Authority: Problems of the Anglican Establishment in Virginia in the Era of the Great Awakening and the Parsons' Cause," *William and Mary Quarterly*, 3rd ser., XXX (January, 1973), 15.

In 1768 Camm was acting director of the older boys at the college where he also was professor of divinity, moral philosophy, natural philosophy, and mathematics. Camm alleged that Lee had written a letter to the college president about "The Coalition" of faculty bent on control of instruction at the institution. Camm, possibly believing Lee was open game in the aftermath of skirmishes with Mercer, rebutted him in the newspaper. He took offense at the insinuation of a conspiracy and demanded that Lee furnish particular evidence or desist. He also ridiculed the young physician for flaunting his learning by quoting Greek, Latin, French, and Italian to the president. Sarcastically, Camm compared Lee's effort to "the pedantic style of the royal schoolmaster who is as distinguished in history for bad taste as for vile politics." The faculty, not terrified by Lee's "few puerile flights and schoolboy maxims," demanded that such antagonistic members of the Board of Visitors keep out of collegiate affairs. When Lee failed to step forward and engage in combat Camm called him "a coward in writing . . . a literary coward."[13]

Lee was as attracted to imperial controversies as to local ones. The execution of the Townshend Acts in 1767, a second attempt by British authorities to reap revenue from the colonists, caught his attention. Americans at first felt mixed emotions toward the various import duties legislated by Parliament at the urging of the erratic chancellor of the exchequer, Charles Townshend. There was not the widespread popular resistance that had greeted the Stamp Act in 1765, which had been instrumental in gaining that measure's repeal. Not until John Dickinson's *Letters from a Farmer in Pennsylvania* appeared did American resistance begin to mount among intellectuals along the Atlantic coastline. Lee was soon engaged.

The *Letters from a Farmer* made their appearance in the colonial press in December, 1767. Dickinson, a respected and cautious articulator of colonial grievances, had become disgruntled with inaction in Pennsylvania in response to the Townshend duties, the Quartering Act of 1767, and the Restraining Act imposed on the legislature of New York. Appealing to historical precedent and the general principles of English constitutional-

13. Purdie & Dixon (eds.), *Virginia Gazette*, April 7, 1768; *A History of the College of William and Mary, from Its Foundation, 1660–1874* (Richmond, 1874), 50; J. A. Osborne, *Williamsburg in Colonial Times* (Richmond, 1935), 48–49.

ism, he challenged imperial administrators to show that the colonists had ever conceded the power of taxation to Parliament. He urged Americans to respond to illegal legislation through petitions of grievances and non-importation agreements. If these tactics should fail, then, Dickinson explained, British history dictated forceful resistance as the next option. His views gained widespread popularity in America; the *Letters* went through repeated editions in the colonial cities and in Europe.[14]

Much impressed by "the late excellent and unanswerable Letters of the Farmer," Arthur Lee sought to amplify Dickinson's call for repeal and redress. Within two months of the initial publication of Dickinson's essays, the first in Lee's series of "Monitor" letters appeared in Rind's *Virginia Gazette*. From February 25 to April 28, 1768, Virginia readers received weekly exhortations from Monitor to resist British encroachments on their liberties.[15] These efforts were less impressive than those of the Farmer, although the initial Monitor letter was reprinted in Boston, New York, Philadelphia, and Charleston. In 1769 Richard Henry Lee edited and financed a pamphlet published by William Rind, which combined the efforts of his brother with those of Dickinson. One reader, Thomas Jefferson, was never impressed by the Lee style. He accused Monitor of seeking profit and fame by fastening to the highly regarded Farmer.[16]

Much of what Monitor wished to say merely rephrased Dickinson's thoughts, although Lee was more fervid and strident. Both campaigned for orderly resistance founded upon precedent from English and colonial history. Lee's debt to Dickinson was twofold: Dickinson's essays stimulated Lee to contribute to the newspaper campaign against British author-

14. David L. Jacobson, *John Dickinson and the Revolution in Pennsylvania, 1764–1776* (Berkeley, 1965), 1, 38–50.

15. Usually assigned the prestigious position of page one, column one, the first series of "Monitor" letters appeared in Rind's *Virginia Gazette* as follows: I, February 25, II, March 3, III, March 10, IV, March 17, V, March 24, VI, March 31, VII, assumed to be April 7, VIII, April 14, IX, April 21, X, April 28, 1768. Arthur composed numbers XI (June 1) and XIII (June 8, 1769) in England and sent them to Richard Henry for publication in Virginia. Alvin R. Riggs, "Arthur Lee and the Radical Whigs, 1768–1776," (Ph.D. dissertation, Yale University 1967), 51–52. Citations of "Monitor" are from *The Farmer's and Monitor's Letters to the Inhabitants of the British Colonies* (Williamsburg, 1769).

16. Riggs, "Arthur Lee and the Radical Whigs," 51–52; Richard Henry Lee to Arthur Lee, April 5, 1770, in Ballagh (ed.), *Letters of Richard Henry Lee*, I, 42; Thomas Jefferson to John Adams, August 22, 1813, in Lester J. Cappon (ed.), *The Adams-Jefferson Letters* (3 vols.; Chapel Hill, 1959), II, 369–370.

ity and also served as a model for fashioning his arguments. Lee aspired to "add my feeble voice" to Dickinson's in the effort to arouse the colonists to defend their rights from parliamentary encroachments. He used a metaphor from his training as a physician to exhort his colleagues "to suppress the disease in its infancy; lest it arrive to a degree of violence dangerous in its effects, and uncertain in its remedy." [17]

Like the Farmer, Monitor believed there were men in power in Britain who did not want the colonials to be as free as Englishmen. Such "enemies to our liberties," particularly George Grenville, connived to "sap, not to storm, our freedom," by dividing the colonies first from each other and then from their friends in Britain. To rally Americans, Lee gushed, "Shall we not be grieved to the heart? Will not our jurisdictions, liberties, and privileges be totally violated? Shall we not sink into slaves? O liberty! O virtue! O my country." [18] Indeed, Monitor was an avid guardian of liberty; one of his letters opened with Sallust's epigram: "Liberty procured with danger, seemed preferable to slavery with ease." This conviction was reinforced by examples from both classical and English history. Lee exclaimed that "liberty is the very idol of my soul, the parent of virtue, the nurse of heroes, the dispenser of general happiness. . . . slavery is the monstrous mother of every abominable vice, and every atrocious ill." Whereas the colonies had maintained a "virtuous government," he perceived that "a system of corruption, which is now arrived at so dangerous a height" threatened the British constitution.[19] Lee's focus on moral and civic regeneration encompassed two main ideas. He emphasized that the colonials were increasingly alienated from the corruption-ridden British. Further, an apocalyptic imperative dictated that traditional values be more fervently guarded against the onslaught of new imperial designs.

The dichotomy between virtue and corruption was a familiar theme in the pamphlet literature of the American Revolution. Corruption was a double-barreled charge leveled at the patriot's opponents; those who placed their private lusts above civic goals and who utilized illicit means to influence policy. Whenever Lee failed, he attributed his reversals not to chance or inertia, but to the machinations of corrupt opponents. The

17. "Monitor" VI, in *Farmer's and Monitor's Letters*, 83.
18. "Monitor," I, III, both in *Farmer's and Monitor's Letters*, 61, 70.
19. "Monitor," IV, II, VI, IV, all in *Farmer's and Monitor's Letters*, 72, 63–64, 80, 74.

opposite of corruption was virtue and its cognates: honor, reason, simplicity, benevolence, and public spirit. In Lee's polemics, virtue meant the source of vitality or soul of the individual and the nation. His focus on virtue was revealing of his political thought and his psyche. It exhibited his concern for the people and thus was a clue to his republicanism. Each time he used the term he reminded himself of his self-esteem and self-control, he reaffirmed his sense of autonomy. If he and his countrymen lacked virtue, they would no longer control their own affairs and would become slaves—a shameful destiny. It was *the* keystone to his ideology.

Virtue, the most resonant word in Lee's vocabulary, had a meaning developed from manifold sources in his learning. From his study of classical humanism, he derived a personal set of attitudes and a repertory of responses: the stances he took in later crises were dictated by images of Roman republicans. From his knowledge of the English revolutions, he acquired political beliefs, perceptions, and tactics, and as a Real Whig he was ever vigilant to protect chartered liberties against tyranny. From his family upbringing, he had assumed the temperament and goals of an evangelical, and throughout life he sought to act as a conscience, to deny his own sense of self, to force his colleagues to be selfless, and to aim at a regeneration of civic virtue in America. This mind-set (now known as the Puritan Ethic), as outlined by historian Edmund Morgan, "called for diligence in a productive calling, beneficial both to society and to the individual. It encouraged frugality and frowned on extravagance. It viewed the merchant with suspicion and speculation with horror. It distrusted prosperity and gathered strength from adversity . . . those who urged it most vigorously always believed it to be on the point of expiring and in need of renewal." [20] Lee exhibited these attitudes in the extreme. Thus for him, the virtuous revolutionary, the three basic Rs of the 1770s would become republicanism, resistance, and regeneration.

Lee's hortatory flourishes over endangered liberties advocated two definite tactics for colonial resisters. First the colonists must frame "a petition of rights to the King and never desist from the solicitation till it be con-

20. Philip Greven, *The Protestant Temperament: Patterns of Child-Rearing, Religious Experience, and the Self in Early America* (New York, 1977), 13, 18, 337–38; Richard L. Bushman, "Corruption and Power in Provincial America," in *The Development of a Revolutionary Mentality* (Washington, D.C., 1972), 63–65; Edmund S. Morgan, "The Puritan Ethic and the American Revolution," *William and Mary Quarterly*, 3rd ser., XXIV (January, 1967), 7.

firmed in a charter of liberty." The fourth letter from Monitor outlined procedures for drafting the petition and instructing colonial agents in Britain. Each American county must, in petitions to George III, decry the billeting of troops in New York, the suspension of that colony's legislature, and the Townshend program. Americans at the local level must reassert that "any impositions whatever laid upon us by the *British* Parliament, which does not and cannot represent us, are absolutely destructive to our liberty." [21]

Lee felt that Britain had learned from the Stamp Act crisis; he believed that British policy makers were better informed of and more sensitive to colonial opinion than before. Moreover, he had already reached the threshold of nationalism. Hence he predicted that if a united stand were taken, "the American petitions will not be again treated so cavalierly." The colonial position could be communicated to Parliament most forcefully if, rather than relying on Britons, the colonists chose their agents "from among ourselves." Lee was already forming plans for his own career as a colonial agent in London, but no matter who was selected to these posts, the colonists should never surrender the "ancient and unalienable right" to instruct their representatives. [22]

Like Dickinson, Lee thoroughly condemned Grenville's assertion that the colonies were virtually represented in Parliament. He also suggested that neither Commons nor Lords reflected the true sentiments of the British nation. The liberties of the colonists were "coeval with the *British* constitution, they are confirmed by various Kings, and recognized by various Parliaments; we then my countrymen are free. And let us tell our brethren in Britain that we are free." [23] Virility must be maintained by those who valued their liberties.

Taxation without representation, according to Monitor, was "absurd, monstrous, stupid, iniquitous, and evil." Tyrants and minions of evil were responsible for promulgation of the Stamp Act and Townshend duties. Whereas Dickinson declared all revenue taxation by Parliament to be illegal but accepted commercial regulation, Lee branded *all* forms of parliamentary taxation invalid because there was no colonial representation in the metropolitan Parliament. "Taxing us against our express will

21. "Monitor" I, IV, both in *Farmer's and Monitor's Letters*, 62, 72–74.
22. "Monitor" IV, in *Farmer's and Monitor's Letters*, 73–74.
23. "Monitor" III, V, both in *Farmer's and Monittor's Letters*, 68–71, 78.

is adding insult to oppression; doing it without our consent is taking from us at once all our property." The proper strategy for the colonists was neither to acquiesce in the Townshend program nor to quarrel with the British nation. The goal was to reestablish "our constitution." He explained, "The bond of union between *Great Britain* and *America*, is *support* from us, *protection* from her." If the mother country sought revenue from the colonies in order to defray imperial defense costs, it could only be gained from the colonial assemblies.[24]

American liberties could be regained not only through petitions reaffirming constitutional rights, but also through measures to readjust the development of provincial society. The characteristics of "frugality and industry" channeled into a program of local manufacturing could, in Monitor's opinion, "convince our adversaries of their mistake in one grand point, that we are under a necessity of using the manufactures of Britain." As in the *Vindication* and in private correspondence with Richard Henry, Arthur again campaigned for the formation of associations to promote manufactures in the colonies. Such proposals, linked with his emphasis on liberty and virtue, indicate that Monitor looked upon the Townshend crisis as an opportunity to assert American autonomy. He was certain the colonies held the power "to work the fall of Britain, by unremitting industry in manufactures," and he believed that the "pernicious sloth" creeping over the colonies could be extinguished by the promotion of American industry.[25] He could see the possibility of regeneration through heroic action.

Monitor did not desire immediate independence from Britain for the colonies. He did believe that independence, the "birthright" of the colonies, would come gradually through the passage of time, but could not now be gained without "impious violence." He urged the colonists not to listen "to those who would incite you (if there be any such) to relinquish your connection with Great Britain," and maintained that Grenville's claims that the Americans wanted independence were untruths circulated to stir resentment in Britain.[26]

"The *question* now is, whether we shall be slaves, or freemen, whether we shall *bequeath* bondage or liberty to our children." This dichotomous

24. "Monitor" VI, in *Farmer's and Monitor's Letters*, 81–84.
25. "Monitor" I, VIII, both in *Farmer's and Monitor's Letters*, 62–63, 89–90.
26. "Monitor" VIII, IX, both in *Farmer's and Monitor's Letters*, 89–90, 92.

and prophetic refrain, repeated in Lee's pamphlets during the next decade, encapsulated three of his basic beliefs: that Americans of his generation were faced with momentous decisions; that certain men sought to subvert liberty "by force or guile," and that anticipations of America's destiny as well as assessments of the present British empire should guide the leaders.

The tenth Monitor letter summarized Lee's advice. If the colonies took a united stand to resist British legislation in which they had no voice, their efforts "will be weighty, and, in all probability successful." Division amongst the colonists would make efforts for redress "feeble and ineffectual." The rights of every colony "rest on the same foundation, and cannot be subverted in one, without being overthrown in all." Monitor pledged to abide by the Roman motto "To tyrants, and to tyranny a foe, I will maintain our liberty at the hazard of my life." [27] His subsequent behavior indicates he meant to uphold the slogan.

The Monitor series was of pivotal importance in Arthur Lee's life: it led to a change in career and embarkation on the path to a new outlook and calling. The Monitor series illustrated Lee's passage from one stage of life to another. His style and world view had been formulated within the private sphere of his education. Now public events would offer opportunities for him to manifest his character in the realm of policy making. His previous experience as a student protestor and polemicist, his reputation as a man with political connections and an educated mind, and his contentious personality propelled him into the forefront of debates in the imperial press. By broadcasting his interpretations of events and proposals for alternative actions, Lee was able to gain a measure of renown. The medium of newspaper warfare also enabled the youthful writer to unleash his anxieties and fears. In contrast to the Farmer, Monitor cried in a shrill voice for action on the part of the Americans. Arthur had discovered his calling for the next eight years—that of penman for the American Revolution.

In his memoirs Arthur later explained that he sensed at this time "a very serious contest was approaching." He decided therefore "to form a correspondence with leading patriotic men in each colony." Friends in England, he hoped, would provide him with "speedy and accurate infor-

27. "Monitor" X, in *Farmer's and Monitor's Letters*, 94–95; Henry Steele Commager, "America and the Enlightenment," in *The Development of a Revolutionary Mentality* (Washington, D.C., 1972), 23–28.

mation of the real designs of the British ministry, which being communicated to leading men in several colonies, might enable them to harmonize in one system of opposition." Thus he aimed to monitor British policy making and to orchestrate colonial reaction. His experience must have told him that these activities would exacerbate rather than mitigate the antagonism between the mother country and the colonies.[28]

Richard Henry believed that Monitor and the Farmer had pointed out "all the invasions of public liberty" inflicted by British policy and shown "the proper methods of obtaining redress." They had spoken with "a force and spirit becoming freemen, English freemen, contending for our just and legal possession of property and freedom." Virginians responded to the exhortations for forceful resistance. On April 8, 1768, before Monitor had concluded, six counties petitioned the Burgesses to denounce the suspension of the New York legislature and to object to the Townshend revenue program as destructive of popular liberties. The truculent citizens of Westmoreland asserted that only the House of Burgesses, as the sole constitutional representative body of Virginia, could impose taxation on the colony. Some of the freeholders of Prince William County, citing the right of all subjects of Great Britain to be taxed only by the consent of their representatives, urged the Burgesses to plead the colonial case before the king. The Old Dominion thus prepared a hostile reception for the Townshend program.[29]

The Burgesses responded. Memorials based on Monitor's ideas and others were dispatched to His Majesty, the Lords, and Commons. Each cited Virginia's constitutional right of representation in questions of taxation, the equation of internal taxation—Richard Bland's distinction—with slavery, and the refutation of the theory of virtual representation. The Virginians were not conciliatory. A new governor, Lord Botetourt, dissolved the house on May 17, 1769, after the Burgesses reiterated their claims that taxation by Parliament was unconstitutional and that the introduction of troops into Boston had augmented unrest.

Undaunted, the Burgesses convened immediately at the home of An-

28. Arthur Lee, "Memoir of the American Revolution," in Hoffman and Molyneaux (eds.), *Lee Family Papers*, VIII, 1–2.

29. *Farmer's and Monitor's Letters*, Preface; Glenn Curtis Smith, "An Era of Non-Importation Associations, 1768–1773," *William and Mary Quarterly*, 2nd ser., XX (January, 1940), 85–89.

thony May in Williamsburg. There, as proposed by George Mason, they created the Virginia Association. The preamble of this pressure group's charter, as enunciated by Monitor, declared the Townshend Acts to be unconstitutional and destructive of liberty. Signers of the agreement pledged not to purchase enumerated goods after September 1, to refrain from buying any items taxed for revenue by Parliament, to halt importation of slaves after November 1, and to encourage colonial frugality. The Farmer and Monitor were among those toasted at a gathering of the Burgesses who signed pledges to the association.[30]

Arthur Lee was not in Virginia to participate in creation of the association. In an effort to coordinate an intercolonial network of resistance to British policy he had commenced a trip northward. There is no evidence that he sought out like spirits in the more southern colonies, although patriots in Charleston were later quick to enlist his pen in their own crusades. It seems he did not communicate with local groups of the Sons of Liberty either. Except for a stop at Mount Vernon to talk with George Washington, the historical record fails to show that Arthur cultivated the leading men in his home colony. Evidently he relied on Richard Henry and other brothers to form the nexus of patriotism in Virginia. He did stop in Maryland to talk with Daniel Dulany, the younger, a theoretician who had gained repute for devastating attacks on the concept of virtual representation. The visit was frustrating, though, for a change had already set in. Alarmed by threats of drastic upheaval in colonial life, the Marylander had become, in comparison to the zealous Virginian, "so cold and distant that it seemed in vain to attempt anything with him."[31]

In Pennsylvania Arthur was reassured when he met John Dickinson. Even before his arrival Lee had intervened in the politics of the key colony. One of his letters, printed in the *Pennsylvania Chronicle* of May 5, 1768, scolded Philadelphians for allowing the spirit of liberty to become "lukewarm in this powerful and important city." Lee joined dissidents who sought to convince the local merchants that a united front on the part of all the colonies in support of nonimportation was the answer.[32] In

30. Smith, "Era of Non-Importation," 91–93; Purdie & Dixon (eds.), *Virginia Gazette*, May 18, 1769.
31. Arthur Lee, "Memoir of the American Revolution," in Hoffman and Molyneaux (eds.), *Lee Family Papers*, VIII, 2–3; John C. Fitzpatrick (ed.), *The Diaries of George Washington* (4 vols.; New York, 1925), I, 276.
32. Paul L. Ford (ed.), *Political Writings, 1764–1774* (Philadelphia, 1895),

an effort to ease local suspicions of the goals of Massachusetts and other colonies, Lee and Dickinson tried their hand as lyricists. Their collaborative venture, "The Liberty Song," initially was deemed "too bold" by Dickinson, but a revision gained acclaim throughout the colonies. The sixth verse and chorus voiced the central plea:

> Then join hand in hand brave Americans all
> By uniting, we stand, by dividing we fall;
> *In so righteous a cause*, we must surely succeed,
> For heaven approves of each generous deed.
> > In Freedom we're born, and in freedom we'll live
> > Our money is ready
> > Steady, boys, steady.
> > Let's give it as Freemen, but never as Slaves.[33]

Dickinson credited Lee with eight unidentified lines of the composition. Later Arthur's brother-in-law, the Philadelphia physician William Shippen, Jr., observed of the Pennsylvania politician: "I have never quite forgiven his stealing the Liberty Song from Dr. Lee as he did very vainly and palpably; 'twas a small matter, but discovered his greediness for applause." Arthur never made such an accusation; his association with Dickinson was one of the few relationships wherein the Virginian honored the thoughts of someone with a different perspective from his own.[34] Lee respected Dickinson.

Assured of the friendship of the celebrated Farmer and armed with Dickinson's pledge to correspond, Lee proceeded to New York where he hoped to confer with William Livingston, another noted colonial propagandist. The meeting failed to materialize for Livingston was called away by a death in his family, and in late July, Lee departed for England. Evidently he did not yet contemplate forming a liaison with radicals in New England, but ironically, despite the barrier of the Atlantic Ocean, in the next eight years his perspective and career would become intimately inter-

---

Vol. I of Ford (ed.), *The Writings of John Dickinson*, 435–45; Riggs, "Arthur Lee and the Radical Whigs," 20–22.

33. Colbourn, *Lamp of Experience*, 136–38; Richard Henry Lee, *Life of Arthur Lee*, I, 244; Paul L. Ford (ed.), *Writings of Dickinson*, I, 421–22, 431–32; Arthur M. Schlesinger, "A Note on Songs as Patriot Propaganda, 1765–1776," *William and Mary Quarterly*, 3rd ser., XI (January, 1954), 79–83.

34. William Shippen, Jr., to Richard Henry Lee, August 25, 1770, in Hoffman and Molyneaux (eds.), *Lee Family Papers*, II, 29.

twined with those of Samuel Adams.[35] There is nothing in his letters of this time that indicates he foresaw such a turn of events, nor did he concede his failure at centralizing colonial resistance.

Arthur returned to Britain in 1768, as he had in 1751 and 1760, to enhance his personal opportunities and to further his learning. This time he would not pursue a formal course of study like those at Eton and Edinburgh, but would learn the nature of metropolitan radicalism and the inner politics of running the British empire from living in London. What he saw in England and how he interpreted his observations were integrated into his previous frame of reference. Lee brought his ideology—what Bernard Bailyn has described as "those shifting patterns of values, attitudes, hopes, fears, and opinions through which people perceive the world and by which they are led to impose themselves upon it"—into focus.[36] His notions of the world and his sense of meaning and identity caused him much anxiety at this period of his life. He relished being close to powerful men and the shaping of history, and he could bask in the pleasures offered by Georgian society, but he would not be distracted from his crusade. From England, Monitor assured his readers he was resuming his role "of laying before you the intentions of those, who would by fraud or force annihilate our free constitution."[37] Privately, Arthur lectured his brother, "So circumstanced here, the cause of American liberty would be desperate indeed, if it find not a firm support in the virtuous and determined resolution of the people of America." He assigned the

35. Arthur Lee, "Memoir of the American Revolution," in Hoffman and Molyneaux (eds.), *Lee Family Papers*, VIII, 3; Cazenove G. Lee, Jr., *Lee Chronicle*, 195.

36. Bernard Bailyn, "The Central Themes of the American Revolution: An Interpretation," in Stephen G. Kurtz and James H. Hutson (eds.), *Essays on the American Revolution* (New York, 1973), 11; Erik H. Erikson, *Young Man Luther: A Study in Psychoanalysis and History* (New York, 1962), 22, defines ideology as "an unconscious tendency underlying religious and scientific as well as political thought: the tendency at a given time to make facts amenable to ideas, and ideas to facts, in order to create a world image convincing enough to support the collective and individual sense of identity."

37. Quoted in Riggs, "Arthur Lee and the Radical Whigs," 26; Arthur Lee to [Richard Henry Lee?], [1767?], in Richard Henry Lee, *Life of Arthur Lee*, I, 186–88. J. G. A. Pocock, "Virtue and Commerce in the Eighteenth Century," *Journal of Interdisciplinary History*, III (Summer, 1972), 122, notes, "The country ideology did not of course cause the Revolution; it characterized it. Men cannot do what they have no means of saying they have done; and what they do must in part be what they say and conceive that it is."

Lees the task of quickening the American spirit. No confidence could be placed in the British. "American liberty must be entirely of American fabric," rang the call for autonomy.

Arthur Lee's ideology, which had developed out of his experiences from childhood through young adulthood and his formal schooling in the classics, would be leavened by the rhetoric of the Real Whigs, molded by prevalent Opposition tactics, and brought to fruition in the bloody confrontation between Massachusetts militiamen and British redcoats. Although subject to ambivalence and vacillation, Lee's course through the critical period between 1768 and 1776 traced the path from resistance to revolution. For Lee, an avid contributor to the literature of the "Great Debate," this was primarily an "affair of the mind," an articulation and attempted realization of his intentions. Yet emotion counted, too. His intense personal rivalries and fellowships and his responses to unfolding events also shaped his actions. Lee's personal frustrations interacted with his visions of American grandeur. Like other men, he was "involved in a complicated web of phenomena, ideas, and situations, from which in retrospect escape seems impossible."[38] The further he progressed in life the more deeply he was entrapped by his own characteristic views and pattterns of behavior, by his inherently tragic role as ideologue. That Arthur was following Richard Henry as a disciple of classical and Whig history was evident in the Monitor essays. Arthur wrote a letter representative of his perspective to Richard Henry:

In short to trust in the uprightness and integrity of ruling powers is a chimera that will infallably [*sic*] lead us to ruin and slavery. Such is the insatiable thirst of men after dominion uncontrolled that it has in every age overleapt every bar which the wisest and firmest friends to liberty could raise against it and this by the baneful influence of money. For instances of this I appeal to the athenian state overthrown by the money of Philip, the spartan republic by the Money introduced by Lysander, the roman people subjugated by the largess of Caesar, and lastly the British Constitution totally vitiated by the corrupt measures and influence commenced by King W[illiam] and brought to a diabolical perfection by Sir R[obert] W[alpole] and Mr. Pelham.[39]

38. Gordon S. Wood, "Rhetoric and Reality in the American Revolution," *William and Mary Quarterly*, 3rd ser., XXIII (January, 1966), 3–32.

39. Colbourn, *Lamp of Experience*, 50–56; Arthur Lee to Richard Henry Lee [1765?], in Hoffman and Molyneaux (eds.), *Lee Family Papers*, I, 510–512.

Since Arthur lived in Britain for the bulk of the period between 1760 and 1776, he was especially influenced by currents of Opposition, dissenting, and radical thought. The major assumptions of his "country ideology" were the imperfect and lustful nature of man, the corrupting influence of power, and faith in the vigilant mechanisms of constitutions. Lee thought highly of such writers as James Burgh, who conveyed such interpretations of contemporary Britain, and he sought them out. He was convinced that behind British policy lurked conspirators bent on subverting liberty, and his own experiences with British politicians confirmed his belief.[40]

Within the British ministry Lee sought the favor of Wills Hill, the earl of Hillsborough, who had assumed the post of secretary of state for the American department. The Virginian was initially acting on behalf of the Mississippi Company, an offshoot of the earlier Ohio Company, which was an aggregation of Virginia and Maryland planters dating from 1763. These land speculation companies, in which the Lee family played major roles, sought to explore and settle at the confluence of the Ohio and Mississippi rivers. Previous solicitations for a royal grant of 2.5 million acres were unsuccessful. Nevertheless, Arthur Lee's brothers, Thomas Ludwell, Richard Henry, Francis Lightfoot, and William led a renewed effort to obtain a grant.[41] Although not initially part of the company, Arthur later had a share in the venture and in turn persuaded his London cronies, Edmund Jenings and Stephen Sayre to invest. This endeavor, one of a number of competing schemes fostered by Americans, threw Arthur into the vortex of imperial policy. The experience taught him to distrust men in power and was also the beginning of his envy and suspicion of Benjamin Franklin, his chief competitor.

Arthur Lee was blind to his own nonvirtuous behavior in this and subsequent episodes. He constantly nourished the self-image of an austere and altruistic practitioner of self-denial and was never conscious of his own persistent ambitions for himself and his family. Arthur might believe himself an ascetic, but his personal correspondence shows clearly his con-

40. Jack P. Greene, "Changing Interpretations of Early American Politics," in Ray A. Billington (ed.), *The Reinterpretation of Early American History* (San Marino, 1966), 151–84; Bernard Bailyn, *The Origins of American Politics* (New York, 1968), 3–58; Gordon S. Wood, "Rhetoric and Reality," 31.

41. Clarence W. Alvord and Clarence E. Carter (eds.), *The Critical Period, 1763–1765* (Springfield, 1915), vol. X of the *Collections of the Illinois State Library*, 19–29.

cern with office, wealth, position, and power. Only prominence and the approbation of his peers could silence his inner qualms over self-sufficiency.

Lee confronted Hillsborough with a memorial on behalf of the Mississippi Company. He found the earl to be impervious to his arguments and later characterized him as "affable and plausible" but unwilling to listen. The Virginian judged him "to be extremely shallow, and he is detested in Ireland for his arbitrary principles." In appears that Lee spent much of his time disputing the earl's claim that the colonials wanted independence. Here, as in later diplomatic endeavors, Arthur proved tactless. Temperamentally unsuited for missions that called for delicacy, discretion, and expedience, he lacked caution, circumspection, and calculation, and he was unable to cultivate relationships in the hope that they would later be useful. The minister explained to his petitioner that settlement in the interior of North America was not to be endorsed: that "no lands would be granted" west of a line that ran from the Kanawha River to Chiswell's Mines on the Virginia-North Carolina border.[42] Lee, therefore, formulated a second request, for a grant to be located between thirty-eight and forty-two degrees north latitude and eastward to the Alleghenies from the boundary laid down by the Board of Trade. In an effort to strengthen his lobbying he offered shares in the Mississippi Company to John Pownall, secretary of the Board, and to John Blair, clerk of the Council of Virginia, for he had readily discovered that the levers of power did not always lie at the top level of administration. Yet both men rejected the bait. Lee's petition, read in the Privy Council on December 16, 1768 was referred to the board, where it sat for eighteen months while other petitioners seemingly moved ahead. From experiences like this, wherein his personal aims were thwarted by the maneuverings of the ministry, Lee's dissatisfaction with the so-called private constitution of Great Britain mounted. In reaction, his adherence to and advocacy of the "public" constitution, which emphasized not influence, but the virtues of a mixed and balanced government, grew more vehement.[43]

42. Arthur Lee to [Richard Henry Lee, 1769?], in Richard Henry Lee, *Life of Arthur Lee*, I, 189–190; Arthur Lee to earl of Hillsborough, November 13, 1768, in Arthur Lee Papers, Box 14; Thomas P. Abernethy, *Western Lands and the American Revolution* (New York, 1937), 34; Clarence W. Alvord, *The Mississippi Valley in British Politics* (2 vols.; Cleveland, 1917), II, frontispiece.

43. Arthur Lee to Richard Henry Lee and Richard Parker, December 23, 1768, in Hoffman and Molyneaux (eds.), *Lee Family Papers*, I, 550–552; Alvord, *Mis-*

Disgruntled by failure in his first bid in imperial politics, Lee lashed out at the source of his frustrations. The current ministry, because of its policy against land grants, he judged to be "truly antiamerican." Fortunately, it was also "in tottering condition." Prospects for the Mississippi Company would brighten considerably if the earl of Shelburne could gain control of American affairs. Lee, who had seen Shelburne's plans to establish colonies in the interior of America, gravitated to the Shelburne country seat, Bowood, and the "small and sociable circle of Bath," where he hoped to form "useful acquaintances" to promote his schemes. Such pleasurable confines, he hoped, would be more productive than the "extended, busy and crowded stage of London" where he had failed.[44]

Because Shelburne was the keystone of his scheme to make American discontent a part of the Opposition in British politics, Arthur reestablished his friendship with the earl. Lee was attracted by the earl's aristocratic views and lifestyle anyway. Perhaps there was a resonance between Lee's self-image and Shelburne's reputation as a maverick, who had been victimized by the vagaries of British politics. The American was quick to adopt the perspective of his benefactor but not to trust him totally. His letters to Virginia voiced fears of new policies to be inflicted upon the colonies by either the present ministry or its rumored successors, bent on "subverting the constitution of America."[45] Lee noted how policy directed at America rested solely on maneuverings at the personal and local levels in English politics. He trusted neither those in power nor those out. From his viewpoint only Shelburne exhibited both the cosmopolitan perspective and the sympathy for America necessary for a benevolent imperial policy and the fulfillment of Lee family ambitions along the Ohio River.

The English hostility to the American clamor shook Lee. Arthur published two pieces in the London *Gazetteer* and the *Gentleman's Magazine* in support of Boston's outcry against the Townshend duties. He sensed, however, that such efforts were fruitless for "the load of prejudice seems

---

sissippi Valley, II, 93–94; Purdie & Dixon (eds.), *Virginia Gazette*, March 9, 1769; Bernard Bailyn *et al.*, *Great Republic*, 234, 192.

44. Arthur Lee to Richard Henry Lee, December 27, 1768, in Hoffman and Molyneaux (eds.), *Lee Family Papers*, I, 553–55; Arthur Lee to Richard Henry Lee, August 4, 1769, in Richard Henry Lee, *Life of Arthur Lee*, I, 205.

45. Arthur Lee to Richard Henry Lee, December 27, 1768, in Hoffman and Molyneaux (eds.), *Lee Family Papers*, I, 553–55.

almost immovable and pours despair with every attempt to bring this country to reason." Privately, Lee reminded his brother that "no confidence is to be reposed in the justice or mercy of Britain; and that American liberty must be entirely of American fabric." He repeated this theme in a letter to Dickinson printed in the *South Carolina Gazette and Country Journal*, which included his first suggestion that an appeal to arms was justifiable in the cause of liberty. After only three months in England, Lee no longer believed it to be the paradise of liberty he had spoken of in 1766.[46] Disenchantment and disillusionment would mount.

Never one for thoughtful meditation or patient cultivation of men, Lee had become accustomed to the politics of confrontation. He found an archetype in the London agitator John Wilkes. This cross-eyed demagogue had first gained notoriety in 1763 for his outspoken attacks upon the establishment published in the *North Briton*. He exasperated both the crown and the ministry from his seat in Commons and his newspaper. In late 1763 an issue of the *North Briton* was condemned as seditious libel and Wilkes was forced to flee to Europe as an outlaw. He returned to England in 1768 and, amidst riot, won election to the Commons from Middlesex. In April he was tried at Westminster and committed to prison. Further mob action ultimately led to the Massacre of St. George's Field, where the army attacked a crowd seeking Wilkes's release. Casualties numbered six dead and twelve wounded. In June, Wilkes was fined one thousand pounds and sentenced to twenty-two months' imprisonment.[47]

John Wilkes and Arthur Lee formed a partnership. The Englishman would later refer to the American politician and theorist as "one of the greatest this century ever saw . . . his *first* and *best* friend." Arthur returned the adulation. The Wilkes-Lee association was another relationship wherein the young colonial groped for a sense of personal identity and public renown. From his earlier associations within his basic family as well as the identifications Arthur had made with British characters such as Samuel Johnson, Adam Smith, and the earl of Shelburne, Lee devel-

46. Arthur Lee to John Dickinson, December 28, 1768, quoted in the *South Carolina Gazette and Country Journal*, May 2, 1769, in Arthur Lee Papers, Box 13.

47. James T. Boulton, *The Language of Politics in the Age of Wilkes and Burke* (London, 1963), 1; George Rudé, "Wilkes and Liberty," *History Today*, VII (September, 1957), 571–79.

oped a sense of self. With Wilkes he saw the chance to test his attributes in intimate partnership. It was not enough for Arthur to be conscious of his own ideology; he must make Anglo-American politicians aware of and appreciative of his code. The first recorded meeting between Wilkes and Lee occurred December 14, 1768, while the Englishman was in prison. Soon the American was telling his correspondents that Wilkes was a true friend of the cause of freedom and an admirer of American resistance to the Townshend duties. Lee painted Wilkes as "a thorn in the Side of the Ministry; his party is strong"; and his attachment to Wilkes grew warm. In January, 1769, the Virginian escorted Benjamin Rush on a visit to the imprisoned instigator. Rush was impressed by Lee's intimacy with Wilkes and by Wilkes's enthusiasm for American liberties. Both Americans were much attracted by Wilkes's pose as an advocate of reform, and neither of them was put off by his reputation for personal insolvency and libertine habits. Although Arthur might have been expected to see Wilkes as the epitome of immorality, he later described him as the possessor of "courage, calm and intrepid, of a flowing wit, accommodating in his temper, of manners convivial and conversible, an elegant scholar."[48] He had found a hero; perhaps he vicariously described himself.

Not all Americans in England agreed with Lee and Rush in their identification of John Wilkes with the colonial resistance movement. Benjamin Franklin was particularly shaken by the violence of the Wilkesites. To Franklin, the foremost colonial in London, Wilkes appeared "an outlaw and an exile, of bad personal character, not worth a farthing." He was uncertain where the Wilkes agitation would lead but issued a report that "some punishment seems preparing for a people who are ungratefully abusing the best constitution, and the best King, any nation was ever blest with." Wilkes's success in gaining a following was to Franklin evidence of the deterioration of Britain, but to Lee the popular turmoil

48. Riggs, "Arthur Lee and the Radical Whigs," 246, 94–96; Arthur Lee to Richard Henry Lee, December 27, 1768, in Hoffman and Molyneaux (eds.), *Lee Family Papers*, I, 553–55; Pauline Maier, *From Resistance to Revolution: Colonial Radicals and the Development of American Opposition to Britain, 1765–1776* (New York, 1974), 166; Corner (ed.), *Autobiography of Benjamin Rush*, 61–62; Benjamin Rush to [?], January 19, 1769, in Butterfield *et al.* (eds.), *Letters of Benjamin Rush*, I, 72–73; Arthur Lee, "Memoir of the American Revolution," in Hoffman and Molyneaux (eds.), *Lee Family Papers*, VIII, 3.

seemed a means to salvage the British constitution and American liberties. The conciliatory Franklin preferred drawing-room negotiations; the excitable Lee favored mass demonstrations and coffeehouse remonstrances. The rituals and gestures of the Wilkesite rallies thrilled him, for they gave him the chance to act out the moral code of valor in action, which had been inculcated during his childhood. He was one of the few American leaders whose roles on both sides of the Atlantic included advocacy in both word and deed.[49]

The Wilkes movement was centered in London and its outlying boroughs, an area with traditions of corporate solidarity and political independence. Frequently the city's freeholders served as a vital base of strength for parliamentary opposition. A sense of separation led to continual differences between metropolitan politicians and the men who ruled Britain. Wilkes's appeal particularly gained the support of the "middling sort" and lesser freeholders, many of whom harbored personal and class hostility toward aristocrats and the monarch.[50]

London, in the era of Wilkes and Lee, encompassed a population of 750,000, of which 150,000 were qualified voters. Political power within the city was lodged in the remnants of medieval trade guilds—69 city companies, comprising a total of 12,000 freemen who maintained the privileges of full citizenship that had been gained by birth or purchase. The freemen of London elected a common council of 236 and a court of 26 aldermen to govern the city. Liverymen, who numbered 8,000 in the 1760s, met annually in Common Hall to select the lord mayor, the sheriffs, and the city chamberlain. The four seats in the House of Commons accorded to London were also filled by selections of Common Hall.[51]

---

49. Benjamin Franklin to William Franklin, April 15, 1768, Benjamin Franklin to John Ross, May 14, 1768, in Smyth (ed.), *Writings of Benjamin Franklin*, V, 121–22, 132–34; Rhys Isaac, "Dramatizing the Ideology of Revolution: Popular Mobilization in Virginia, 1774 to 1776," *William and Mary Quarterly*, 3rd ser., XXXIII (July, 1976), 358–68.

50. Lucy S. Sutherland, *The City of London and Opposition to Government, 1768–1774* (London, 1959), 8; Sutherland, "The City of London in Eighteenth Century Politics," in Richard Pares and A. J. P. Taylor (eds.), *Essays Presented to Sir Lewis Namier* (London, 1956), 60, 70; George Rudé, *Wilkes and Liberty: A Social Study of 1763 to 1774* (Oxford, 1962), 81, 84, 145.

51. Dorothy Marshall, *Dr. Johnson's London* (New York, 1968), 79–81; Riggs, "Arthur Lee and the Radical Whigs," 76.

John Wilkes's pose as the individual battling for liberty against the tyranny of the crown was widely applauded in the colonies. Readers of the *Virginia Gazette* were treated to numerous accounts of the champion's travails. Boston and Charleston endorsed the Wilkesite agitation and sustained the agitator with funds. In turn Wilkes warmly advocated American resistance to the Townshend legislation. The British demagogue proclaimed to the Bostonians in 1768, "The cause of liberty in America as well as here shall always have in me a zealous advocate, and where my little influence extends it shall be employed in the promotion of it." He assured American resistors, "You have many warm friends here, who will never give up your cause, nor rest till the *declaratory bill* as well as *all the late duties*, are absolutely repealed. I am proud to be one of the foremost in that cause." In Wilkes's persecution and reversals Arthur Lee and other Americans believed they were glimpsing foreshadowings of their own destiny in the British empire.[52]

The American enlisted in the Wilkesite movement largely out of shared convictions and a sense of persecution. Lee became alarmed when the House of Commons refused to acknowledge Wilkes as the representative of the voters of Middlesex. His letters indicted each ministerial outrage and charted every move against Wilkes and the popular spirit. In March, 1769, he wrote, "We are here in very great confusion, parties run so high, Mr. Wilkes is expelled a third time, and will be re-chosen."[53] Despite endemic mob violence in London and a national petition in support of Wilkes, the ministry refused to allow him to enter Commons. By this time the Virginian had enlisted in this third force in British politics, a popular movement independent of crown and Opposition.

On February 20, 1769, at the London Tavern, the Society of Supporters for the Bill of Rights was established. This organization was an outgrowth of a previous effort by the Reverend John Horne to raise a

52. Stella F. Duff, "The Case Against the King: The *Virginia Gazettes* Indict George III," *William and Mary Quarterly*, 3rd ser., VI (July, 1949), 383–390; John Wilkes to William Palfrey, April 14, September 27, 1769, in George W. Elsey (ed.), "John Wilkes and William Palfrey," *Publications of the Colonial Society of Massachusetts*, XXXIV (February, 1941), 431, 415; Pauline Maier, "John Wilkes and American Disillusionment with Britain," *William and Mary Quarterly*, 3rd ser., XX (July, 1963), 373–74.

53. Arthur Lee to [Francis Lightfoot Lee], March 23, 1769, in Hoffman and Molyneaux (eds.), *Lee Family Papers*, I, 582–83.

subscription in support of Wilkes. Horne, who later added the surname Tooke, was a former parson who preferred directing Wilkes's campaigns to ministering to a congregation. Other original members of the society came from anticourt circles in London and Middlesex. All possessed some education, considerable social standing, and strong interests in metropolitan affairs. All claimed to have a wider interest in promoting agitation than the issue of Wilkes's seat in Commons. The professed goals of the society were "to promote the principles of the constitution" and to pay Wilkes's creditors. The latter task proved prodigious, for in the next two years the society apportioned £12,000 for Wilkes's debts, £1000 for fines, £3000 for election expenses, and £2000 toward the agitator's living expenses. This aid still fell short, by £7000, of keeping Wilkes solvent.[54]

At first participation in the society revived Arthur's flagging spirits. Its very label—centering on the Bill of Rights—appealed to his sense of English history and Anglo-American destiny. It was compatible with *Monitor's* commands to take up the petitionary tactics of the seventeenth century. Lee applauded the society's intention of making Wilkes independent by paying his debts and could only lament that "my purse is not equal to my inclination" in support of the society's aims. Nonetheless, he joined the society in its efforts to rally all of Britain behind Wilkes. Soon the organization undertook a range of functions: selecting candidates for elections who were pledged to specific principles of the group, choosing speakers to harangue public rallies, drawing up petitions and remonstrances, and establishing cells in other urban areas. Despite its efforts, no widespread call for parliamentary reform materialized, though. Lee was disheartened to realize that only in the British trade centers were American grievances linked to the efforts to reform Parliament and to seat Wilkes.[55]

54. Simon Maccoby, *English Radicalism, 1762–1785: The Origins* (London, 1955), 105–106; Eugene C. Black, *The Association: British Extra Parliamentary Political Organization, 1769–1793* (Cambridge, 1963), 11; Sutherland, "City of London," 19; Riggs, "Arthur Lee and the Radical Whigs," 109; Charles Chevenix Trench, *Portrait of a Patriot: A Biography of John Wilkes* (Edinburgh, 1962), 253–54.
55. Arthur Lee to [Francis Lightfoot Lee], March 23, 1769, in Hoffman and Molyneaux (eds.), *Lee Family Papers*, I, 582–83; Riggs, "Arthur Lee and the Radical Whigs," 111–12; Rudé, *Wilkes and Liberty*, 104–105; Sutherland, *City of London*, 22–26.

The Virginian labored industriously through the society and in Middlesex to use the petitionary movement as a vehicle to express colonial grievances. Lee's appreciation for the Wilkesites centered on his sense of historic precedent. In Wilkes and the society, he saw worthy successors to the seventeenth-century Whigs he had studied. A petition in May, 1769, from the aggrieved borough included a clause that was Lee's handiwork, which cited the similarity of injustices suffered in England and in America. It was deprecated by some leaders of the agitation, but Arthur had won his point. He reinforced his plea by submitting a piece, published in both the London *Chronicle* and the *Public Advertiser*, that provided a detailed list of eleven American grievances. In his attempt to prove the congruence between the demands of Middlesex and those of the colonists, his targets were "evil-minded persons" who offered malignant advice to the king and who wielded power arbitrarily. In the summer Arthur journeyed to Bath and Bristol to gather signatures on petitions and, at the same time, seek the patronage of Dr. John Fothergill to further his own medical career in Britain. He must have begun to realize that his desire to treat the ills of the British constitution took priority over his wish to administer to the maladies of well-born tourists in Bath.[56]

Lee's experiences in the petitionary movement—frustrating though they may have been—gave him a degree of expertise in British politics. He was neither slow nor cautious in dispatching his assessments of politicians and policies to his correspondents in America, and his fervor was appropriate to his active involvement in British agitation. (In later roles—such as a diplomat in Europe—the same zeal would be out of place.) As the vital sensor for radicals in the colonies, Arthur was playing a critical role. His reports strongly influenced the pictures that Samuel Adams, John Dickinson, Richard Henry Lee, and others formed of the situation in London, and he added to the cohesion of the colonial opposition by introducing his colonial correspondents to each other. Thus he worked at his mission to be the nexus of both intercolonial and imperial opposition.[57]

56. Arthur Lee to Richard Henry Lee, August 15, 1769, in Hoffman and Molyneaux (eds.), *Lee Family Papers*, I, 621–24; Riggs, "Arthur Lee and the Radical Whigs," 105–108; Richard Henry Lee, *Life of Arthur Lee*, I, 245; *The Annual Register; or, A View of the History, Politics, and Literature for the Year 1769* (London, 1806), XII, 197–200; William Shippen, Jr., to Richard Henry Lee, March 29, 1770, in Hoffman and Molyneaux (eds.), *Lee Family Papers*, II, 10.
57. Maier, *From Resistance to Revolution*, 222–23. Samuel Adams later recalled

Between 1768 and 1776 Arthur Lee served as a prime source of information on British affairs pertinent to the American resistance. He identified the priority of issues, categorized the dramatis personae, and scanned alternative strategies. The messages he broadcast mirrored his disillusionment. In August, 1769, for the benefit of Richard Henry, Arthur offered the following analysis: The Lords Holland, Bute, Bedford and Grafton formed a disparate "court party," while George Grenville, Lords Temple, Chatham, and Rockingham led the Opposition.[58] According to Arthur, American interests were incompatible with those held by the latter group, which was "desirous of changing men only and not measures." The "constitutionalists" offered the only hope of reform, "for appealing to the people at large, and effecting a change of measures as well as men." Wilkes and the independent city politicians formed the core of this aggregation, and Lee included Shelburne in it, although he did not have total confidence in him. Arthur believed that the court party was splintering; "could they agree I do not see what would prevent them, with a corrupt house of commons, vast influence from places and money, with a powerful army, from absolutely subverting the constitution." The disease had spread; not only the ministry but Parliament was stricken as well, although the king still remained immune. Only the activities in America, where "the spirit of liberty seems now so truly and universally diffused," bolstered Lee's enthusiasm. He came to feel that reform could not emanate from within England, but would have to be perfected in the colonies and then injected into the political system of the mother country. As his experience deepened, he developed the notion that the crucial colonial role for his cohorts and himself was nothing less than to revitalize the empire.

Arthur Lee's moods vacillated throughout the summer of 1769. Disgruntled by the lack of success of the society and of Wilkes in British politics and dissatisfied by his own attempts to ease tension between Britain and the colonies, he suffered fits of melancholy and homesickness.

---

that Lee's letters were "written with that Freedom as well as Zeal which would have exposed him to the Risque even of his Life from the Resentment of an unprincipled and nefarious Court, if any of them by Accident of Design had fallen into their hands." Adams to Samuel Copper, January 3, 1779, in Harry Alonzo Cushing (ed.), *The Writings of Samuel Adams* (4 vols.; New York, 1904–1908), IV, 113.

58. Arthur Lee to Richard Henry Lee, August 15, 1769, in Hoffman and Molyneaux (eds.), *Lee Family Papers*, I, 621–24.

His personal life was also unsatisfactory. The marriage of his brother William in London in the spring and Richard Henry's second marriage reminded Arthur of his celibacy. He apologized for his status: "I am now the only unhappy or single person of the family; nor have I prospect of being otherwise." He had, in fact, been jilted in Bath. His career gave him as much anxiety as his celibacy. At the age of thirty, after investing the bulk of his previous life in training to be a physician, as his family expected, he had lost his enthusiasm for medicine. To escape his personal worries, he plunged into politics.[59]

Whenever the Virginian visited Shelburne his hopes and self-confidence revived. As he sat talking of American affairs to Shelburne at Bowood, he was fashioning two key postulates: that Shelburne was his sole entrée and hope in the higher levels of British politics, and that the misinformation and misperceptions that the ministry was receiving from appointed officials and army officers in America were exacerbating imperial difficulties. Therefore Arthur saw to it that Shelburne received copies of Pennsylvania newspapers and reports from Richard Henry of Virginia's affairs. In July, Lee concocted a scheme which anticipated the Rhodes scholarship program of the twentieth century. Shelburne wished that a a group of scholars from American colleges be sent to Britain for further study. Lee suggested that candidates enter an essay competition on the topic of the mututal interests of Great Britain and her colonies, but the plan never got past the initial conversations.[60]

Rumors of a change in ministry whetted Lee's desire for Shelburne's return to office. While other aspirants for power were categorized as an "abandoned crew," the earl was "the only one attached to us from principle; from policy there are many arguments opposing us; as Lord Chatham, Richmond and Rockingham." This peculiar distinction in a letter posted at Shelburne's estate indicates that Lee had a very personal and embittered approach to British politics. Under the nominal leadership of Lord Grafton—"the primeval profligate, arbitrary and contemptible"— the ministry resorted to the use of force in execution of its irrational and

59. Arthur Lee to Richard Henry Lee, August 4, 1769, in Richard Henry Lee, *Life of Arthur Lee*, I, 204–205; John Berkenhout to Arthur Lee, May 1, 1770, Arthur Lee to Richard Henry Lee, August 15, 1769, both in Hoffman and Molyneaux (eds.), *Lee Family Papers*, II, 19, I, 623.

60. Arthur Lee to William Shippen, Jr., February 1, 1769, Arthur Lee to earl of Shelburne July 3, 1769, in Arthur Lee Papers, Box 2, 17.

unjust policy. By the end of the year, however, the Virginian reported sanguine hopes that Shelburne and other leaders of the Opposition were uniting behind the cause of America to undo the "weak and wicked Administration."[61]

Lee was meanwhile eyeing positions of power and influence for himself. In his view a major cause of the controversy between Britain and America, in addition to ill-suited and ill-informed politicians, was the ineffectiveness of colonial agents in Britain. Acting on behalf of the governors or of either house of the colonial legislature or of all three, British lawyers, merchants, and M.P.'s functioned as lobbyists for American interests. This informal and unstable mode of representation, aptly styled by historian Michael Kammen "a rope of sand," was one of the bonds of union that secured the colonies to Britain. In the Stamp Act the institution of the colonial agency had proved successful in effecting the critical cooperation of British merchants to repeal the revenue taxation. The agencies, as later employed by Lee, contributed to a rending rather than cementing of the empire.[62]

As Arthur was most sensitive to the true representation of popular opinion, he looked upon the colonial agency as an institution in need of reform. It might also have appeared as a means to an end he coveted—a seat in Parliament. As early as December, 1768, he had identified the colonial agency as a prospective base of operations. Richard Henry was recruited to keep a watchful eye in Virginia in the event the position of agent for either the council or Burgesses should be vacated. Arthur believed either post would be "opportune" for him. However, neither James Abercromby, who acted as agent for the governor and council of the Old Dominion, nor Edward Montague, a barrister and M.P. who lobbied on behalf of the Burgesses, wished to give up his position. Both had lengthy tenures and, although they failed to cooperate, were deemed more diligent than the average colonial agent.[63]

Lee's ambition to become the agent for Virginia was rekindled in the autumn of 1769, as he took stock of his life. Using his private correspon-

61. Arthur Lee to [Richard Henry Lee], September 18, October, December 3, 1769, in Hoffman and Molyneaux (eds.), *Lee Family Papers*, I, 627, 632–34, 641–43.

62. Michael G. Kammen, *A Rope of Sand: The Colonial Agents, British Politics, and the American Revolution* (Ithaca, 1968), *passim*.

63. Arthur Lee to Richard Henry Lee, December 27, 1768, in Hoffman and

dence and the press, Arthur began trying to unseat Montague. He corresponded with Richard Henry and Robert Nicholas to push his bid in the Old Dominion. He plumed himself as being "much honored in the name Virginian" and applauded the "noble spirit" Virginians showed in the "cause of Liberty." Abercromby and Montague, he reported, had not endorsed the Wilkesites nor had they zealously lobbied on Virginia's behalf before the ministry. Further, the agents had refused to act in unison. Lee found such displays of indifference and faulty priorities to be common failings among colonial agents. Exhibiting all the signs of deep frustration, he lamented, "What reason has America to expect anything farther, when by far the greater number of her agents are unknown here, of no abilities, no rank, and if of any, of bad character; some of them menials, all of them servile expectants." [64]

The accusations leveled at Montague originated in London politics. Lee was piqued that he had opposed John Wilkes's election by Middlesex and felt that such conduct indicated that Montague was a minion of the the administration. Lee was also disturbed at Montague's refusal to oppose the Townshend program. Arthur reported Montague's disloyalty to the colonial patriots and assured Richard Henry that if a Lee had the agency, the interests of Virginia, America, and Middlesex would all be well served. Yet even though he was fortified by an inexhaustible reservoir of self-righteousness, Arthur would sporadically confess to his esteemed brother his "own deficiency in judgement," his penchant to "act in the integrity of my heart," and his tendency to permit "my suspicions to influence my actions." [65] Historians have tended to spotlight these flaws in Arthur's character, neglecting his patriotism.

Arthur took to the press on both sides of the Atlantic to assail Montague. Calling himself "Junius Americanus"—a pseudonym that indicated his admiration for the English penman, "Junius," who was then taking British policy-makers to task—Lee repeated his charges against Montague

---

Molyneaux (eds.), *Lee Family Papers*, I, 553–55; Jack M. Sosin, *Agents and Merchants: British Colonial Policy and the Origins of the American Revolution, 1763–1775* (Lincoln, 1965), 15, 62; Ella Lonn, *The Colonial Agents of the Southern Colonies* (Chapel Hill, 1945), 63–66, 393.

64. Arthur Lee to Richard Henry Lee, September 18, December 3, 1769, in Hoffman and Molyneaux (eds.), *Lee Family Papers*, I, 627–28, 641.

65. Arthur Lee to Richard Henry Lee, November 15, 1769, in *Ibid.*, I, 635–37.

in the *Gazetteer* of September 29, 1769. Junius Americanus abused and accused Montague: "By infinite art, you have for many years succeeded in imposing on their [Virginians] unsuspecting temper; accident has discovered your principles and connections . . . you are in close union with their enemies, their unrelenting persecutors! . . . How little did they think that you would see with indifference, chains forged to enslave them." Montague was specifically charged with assenting to the Stamp Act in return for appointments of his friends as stamp distributors. He had been party to the "wicked counsellors" who sought to trick the king into despotic policies.[66]

Lee's campaign proved abortive. After 1770 Montague was not selected again to represent the Burgesses, but neither was Arthur. The House of Burgesses considered Montague, Lee, and Thomas Adams, a Virginia merchant in London, but since they could not agree on any of the three, after 1770 no agent was named. Reportedly very few members of the Burgesses believed that Arthur Lee was well suited to be their representative. Lee had only the later satisfaction of knowing he had pegged his man: Montague disowned the American cause as it moved toward independence.[67]

By age thirty Lee's career had not yet come into focus. Adolescent anxieties over a career choice, an extended latency period during lengthy schooling, plus distractions and false starts as a young adult had combined to draw out the period of his education. At this stage of his life the unorthodox role of popular political agitator did not appear to be a suitable profession, although it is apparent that Lee was concerned about sovereignty, authority, liberty, and other elements of contemporary political discussion. His sensitivities and convictions impelled him to a political career. Arthur, with his ultra senses of mistrust, autonomy, and initiative was an archetype of American radicalism. As early as 1769 he had exclaimed to Richard Henry, "O how my soul swells with the great idea!

66. Arthur Lee to Richard Henry Lee, December 3, 1769, in *Ibid.*, I, 641. This "Junius Americanus" letter was reprinted by Rind (ed.), *Virginia Gazette*, December 14, 1769, and the *Maryland Gazette*, January 25, 1770.

67. Lonn, *Colonial Agents*, 175–76, 389; Riggs, "Arthur Lee and the Radical Whigs," 178–79; Sosin, *Agents and Merchants*, 142; Colonel Richard Bland to Thomas Adams, August 1, 1771, Richard Adams to Thomas Adams, March 24, 1772, both in *Virginia Magazine of History and Biography*, VI, (October, 1898), 133–34, 389–91.

methinks I could smile in the very pangs of death, and pity the insulting tyrant. Should such a trial come, and my weak flesh shrink from the nobler purpose of my soul, to what contempt would it reduce me." [68] He vowed that his virtue would be equal to the coming struggle over American liberty.

By 1770 Arthur Lee was in the vanguard of American radicalism. During his brief stay in Virginia he had readily adopted the rhetoric of resistance. In his personal correspondence and in the Monitor series, he often exceeded Dulany, Dickinson, and other pamphleteers in insistence on American dominion over all forms of taxation, in reliance upon a united stand by all the colonies, and in faith in petitions and other constitutional mechanisms of redress. His frequent calls for virtue (selflessness) and his alarms concerning liberties (self-determination) had already suggested independence and the possibility of war within the British empire to him. Yet he had no lust for separation. Instead, he once again traveled to England to establish himself close to the center of London radicalism and within the Opposition.

Those American patriots who were informed on English politics in the explosive era of 1768–1776 came to rely on the analyses and prognoses offered in Lee's voluminous writings. Despite his academic training and in-depth reading, Lee was more emotional than his fellow pamphleteers. He combined rational argument with nonrational perceptions and, at the same time, confronted his own personal anxieties and conscious fears. [69] Although he did not fully realize it, Arthur Lee was to play a pivotal role in history.

---

68. Arthur Lee to Richard Henry Lee, October, 1769, in Hoffman and Molyneaux (eds.), *Lee Family Papers*, I, 632–33.
69. Greven, *Protestant Temperament*, 346–49.

★ CHAPTER III ★

That America May Be Free

In his later years Arthur Lee looked back at the period 1770–1774, with fondness, for he saw it as one of the few happy times in his life. He had thrived in the swirl of Georgian society. From chambers at No. 2 Garden Court in the Middle Temple he had had convenient access to the Royal Society, and the playhouses and coffeehouses that he frequented. He associated with leading Opposition spokesmen, and of that time, he later wrote, "I was so well with several of the nobility and gentry that I could spend all my leisure time at their country seats." Much of his time was taken up in learning the law, a profession that he hoped would hold "the prospect of rising to place and profit."[1] Yet, as a defender of the constitutional rights of Anglo-Americans, Lee's personal aims became secondary to his public role. Rather than enjoy the life of law student and man-about-town, he channeled his energies into three interlocking arenas of conflict: the press on both sides of the Atlantic, the agitation bubbling around the English radical John Wilkes and the Society for the Bill of Rights, and the post in Britain as colonial agent for the Massachusetts House of Representatives in its struggle against the ministry. Although he claimed to have been happy, his experiences in these three endeavors were largely negative. Despite his passionate and uncompromising activity, the movement for reform yielded only frustrations.

In the latter half of 1769 Lee took up his pen to alert British subjects in England and America to the grave danger he saw. During the following seven years, under ten identifiable pen names, Lee contributed a stream of publications to the debate over the imperial connection: nine pamphlets, 170 essays, 17 petitions, and 50 anonymous letters in the press.[2] Assigning himself the role of imperial conscience, he sought a re-

1. Arthur Lee, "Memoir of the American Revolution," in Richard Henry Lee, *Life of Arthur Lee*, II, 391–92.
2. Riggs, "Arthur Lee and the Radical Whigs," 269; Stanley Joel Moore, "The Character of Arthur Lee," (M.A. thesis, University of South Florida, 1977), 18.

dress of American grievances and a reform of Parliament. As Monitor he spotlighted "the intentions of those who would by fraud or force annihilate our free constitution." In London he tried to act as internuncio, representing the cause of aggrieved Americans to the British and analyzing the local meaning of Parliamentary debates for the colonists. He took up such tasks "at this dangerous period" when "the most fatal measures" were planned for America.

Lee's published writings echoed his private correspondence. The bulk of British politicians were despicable and bent on suppressing colonial liberties. Neither merchants nor the court seemed sensitive to the American cause. Only Shelburne's following was courageous enough to assert that "Parliament has no right to tax us." Lee was no devotee of the Chathamites. Resolute support of economic boycott appeared to be a solution. Monitor exhorted his readers, "That the *means of vindicating your insulted liberties*, are in your power, cannot be *doubted*." A year later he repeated his grim rendition of British politics and concluded that "the Royal breast has been impressed with an unfavorable opinion of the colonies."[3]

Lee was convinced that George III was receiving false and misleading information from colonial governors and members of the ministry and that the rift in the empire was not caused by impersonal forces, but was traceable to specific malefactors. These beliefs were reinforced by his own experiences and friendships in London. Through his brother William, who had settled into prosperity as a merchant in the city, Arthur met Dennys DeBerdt and Stephen Sayre, two traders in American commerce. Sayre, a charming and volatile adventurer, was following a path parallel to Arthur's. A Princeton graduate, Sayre had attached himself to William Pitt while engaging in city political struggles and far-fetched commercial schemes. Sayre's partner, DeBerdt, was an aged Flemish Protestant, bankrupted by Sayre's recklessness and his own engrossing concern for the colonies. As agent for the House of Representatives of Massachusetts, DeBerdt, like Lee, had sought the friendship of Shelburne.[4]

3. Rind (ed.), *Virginia Gazette*, June 1, 1769, May 31, 1770; Riggs, "Arthur Lee and the Radical Whigs," 50–63.

4. Cazenove G. Lee, Jr., *Lee Chronicle*, 197; William B. Reed, *The Life of Esther DeBerdt, Afterwards Esther Reed of Pennsylvania* (Philadephia, 1853), 42–44; Albert Mathews (ed.), "Letters of Dennys DeBerdt, 1757–1770," *Publications of the Colonial Society of Massachusetts*, XIII (March, 1911), 316–29.

A small circle of Americans frequented DeBerdt's London home in Artillery Court. Arthur Lee and Sayre eagerly assisted the old man in his tasks as colonial agent while Joseph Reed of Pennsylvania courted De-Berdt's daughter, Esther. Lee likewise was attracted by this charmer and solicited her advice in his own affairs of the heart. Once, confessing that his advances had been repulsed by a Miss Palmer, Arthur altered his course and begged Esther to mediate between him and a Miss Talbot. He hoped his go-between could express his florid sentiments "that I live on the idea of her, and of her excellence in all, that in her lovely sex is good, soft, amiable, and sweet. Lay at her feet, the humblest but the truest vassal to her beauty, to live or die as her bright eyes decree." Fired sporadically by what he termed "ill-starred passion" throughout his life, Arthur never succeeded as a suitor. His reliance on the system of indirect courting may have been his downfall. Later, at the age of forty-five, he again dispatched female diplomats to objects of his love. Although certainly Lee was sensitive to never consummating courtship in marriage, it is not evident how deep his anxieties over sexuality or matrimony ran. Perhaps because his mother had distanced herself from him, he had not learned how to approach intimacy with women.[5]

Historians, however, find animosity, not love, to have been dominant at Artillery Court. It is possible that the notorious Lee-Franklin vendetta originated in the gossip at DeBerdt's. Franklin and DeBerdt had been feuding since 1765 because DeBerdt found fault with Franklin's neutrality in the Stamp Act crisis. DeBerdt, whom Lee described as "an upright, spirited, and independent old man," increased imperial friction by venting his spleen on Lord Hillsborough. He traced most of the turmoil in the Bay Colony to misinformation emanating from Governor Francis Bernard. DeBerdt used his metropolitan friendships to stir British support for colonal rights.[6] In short, DeBerdt shared Lee's aims, attitudes, and prejudices.

DeBerdt both encouraged and subsidized Arthur Lee's essays published under the pen name "Junius Americanus." In February, 1771, he ad-

5. Reed, *Life of Esther DeBerdt*, 19–25; Arthur Lee to Esther DeBerdt, [n.d.], in Arthur Lee Papers, Box 14; Philip Greven, *Protestant Temperament*, 126–33.
6. Verner W. Crane (ed.), *Franklin's Letters to the Press, 1758–1775* (Chapel Hill, 1950), 125–26; Kammen, *Rope of Sand*, 129–30, 148; Arthur Lee to [Richard Henry Lee?], November 9, 1769, in Richard Henry Lee, *Life of Arthur Lee*, I, 194; Maier, *From Resistance to Revolution*, 153.

vanced £16.10.6 for publication of five hundred copies of a pamphlet by Junius Americanus. Lee's essays were highly esteemed by Americans although later reviewers have criticized him for openly mimicking Junius, who was then deriding the ministry in the press. Later critics have also faulted Lee for mingling the malicious gossip of city politics with American issues. Lee, to whom both causes were intimately intertwined, acknowledged mixing his subjects but explained that the ploy was intended to gain the attention of British readers: "to make what was written in the defense of the colonies acceptable, it was necessary to give now and then a stroke to the characters obnoxious here." As soon as he had secured a popular following Lee hoped he would concentrate on American affairs. His writings, like those of the colonial press, were "apt to be personal, incendiary, and strident." [7]

The first letter from Junius Americanus appeared in the July 17, 1769, issue of the Evening Post, but Lee soon switched to the Gazetteer, edited by Charles Say. The Gazetteer, a morning paper with a circulation of five thousand, used Lee's screeds as competition for the efforts of Junius appearing in H. S. Woodfall's Public Advertiser. Lee's first series of articles, comprising fifty-six essays, was concluded on January 6, 1772. The second flurry appeared in fourteen issues of the Public Advertiser, between June, 1772, and March, 1774. Then Lee switched to other pseudonyms and lengthier contributions in pamphlet form. Most of his Junius Americanus efforts were given the prestigious position of page one, column one. Foremost among colonial newspapers to reprint these messages was the Boston Evening Post.[8]

Junius Americanus, at the prompting of Artillery Court, focused on politicians and policies concerned with Massachusetts. His initial targets were Hillsborough, secretary of state for the colonies, and Francis Bernard, governor of Massachusetts. Lee contended that these men, bent on stifling rather than aiding the colonies, had overreacted to the unrest

7. Mathews (ed.), "Letters of DeBerdt," 302n; Alvar Ellëgard, Who Was Junius? (Stockholm, 1962), identifies Sir Philip Francis as Junius; James T. Boulton, Language of Politics, offers pertinent criticism; Crane (ed.), Franklin's Letters, xxiv; Arthur Lee to Richard Henry Lee, November 15, December 3, 1769, in Hoffman and Molyneaux (eds.), Lee Family Papers, I, 635–37, 641–43; Esmond Wright, Fabric of Freedom, 95.

8. Riggs, "Arthur Lee and the Radical Whigs," 7, 28–30, 53–57; Crane (ed.), Franklin's Letters, xvi–xvii.

brought on by the Townshend duties. It was the introduction of troops into Boston, "a plan of folly and inequity," that provoked the American mobs. Lee derided and discredited the policy makers in London, and portrayed Americans as liberty-minded and orderly people, who were only resisting provocative policy. He also linked the agitation in America with that in Britain.

Junius Americanus heaped contempt on Hillsborough, finding him to be the prime example of a man in power disrupting imperial harmony. The earl had gained power, according to Junius Americanus, despite early blunders in Ireland, because he was the tool of Lord Bute. His earlier tenure of only eighteen months on the Board of Trade had "destroyed that necessary mutual love and confidence" that had tied the American colonies to Britain "to the unspeakable advantage of Both." Junius Americanus called for Hillsborough's resignation.

Lee believed the root of the discontent in Boston was Hillsborough's support for Governor Bernard, "the avowed incendiary of America," and for the customs commissioners, "objects of universal abhorrence and contempt," who he called "tools, the enemies of all constitutional liberty." Fortified by copies of the Bernard-Hillsborough correspondence, Lee indicted colonial officials. He adjudged them guilty of sending prejudicial misinformation to Britain. It was not surprising to Junius Americanus that the people of Massachusetts arose against such perfidious bureaucrats. When "the temper of the times called for conciliatory measures," Hillsborough and the cabinet chose to use force to crush the complaints. Determinations to stifle Massachusetts by placing troops in Boston were so "rank, they smell to heaven." Junius Americanus threatened Hillsborough: "Your crimes are great, the proofs are pregnant, and vengeance will pursue you even under the protection of your Thane [Bute]."[9]

Lee's attacks on Bernard were even more vituperative. The governor, having his fill of mob agitation, departed from Boston in August, 1769, after calling in the military. Meanwhile the Suffolk County Grand Jury indicted Bernard, General Thomas Gage, and others for libeling the inhabitants of Massachusetts. DeBerdt had sent copies of Bernard's corre-

9. To the Earl of H[illsboroug]h, July 19, August 20, October 9, 12, 1769, in [Arthur Lee], *The Political Detection; or, The Treachery and Tyranny of Administration, both at Home and Abroad; Displayed in a Series of Letters, Signed Junius Americanus* (London, 1770), 1–7, 8–10, 12, 15–18.

spondence to Samuel Adams who, in turn, used the letters to raise a public storm. When Bernard set foot in England, DeBerdt, Lee, and others, on behalf of the Massachusetts House, were petitioning for his dismissal. Despite these efforts Bernard was warmly received in England, gained a sympathetic hearing, and was rewarded with a baronetcy.[10]

Junius Americanus was outraged, and he demanded that the governor be brought before a tribunal of the people to answer charges that he had misrepresented American complaints and misled Parliament. Lee challenged Bernard: "You flatter yourself with having an early prejudice against the just representatives of the people, and an unsurmountable bar to the redress of their grievances." He credited Bernard with having a hand in every provocative measure and repressive policy from the Stamp Act of 1765 through the seizure of John Hancock's ship *Liberty* in June, 1768. Like those who directed *"the arbitrary and inhuman business"* of killing Wilkesites in Saint George's Field, Bernard seemed bent on militarism. Lee reminded the governor of the lessons of English history: "Empson was a tool, Dudley was a tool. Think of their fate, and tremble at your prospect."[11]

Lee's efforts to gain the support of the English people were predicated on the assumption that if they were fully informed of the true conditions in the colonies, they would join the call for redress. Instead, his own credibility was challenged in the British press when "Veritas" asserted that false reports of events in Boston were being circulated. Lee promptly identified this antagonist as John Mein, a tool of Bernard, who had been run out of Boston for publishing claims that certain patriot leaders were less than sincere in upholding the intercolonial economic boycott known as the Association. Lee retorted that Mein, Bernard, and others had attempted to falsify reports of the events in Boston so as to provoke the city to riot. As for Lee personally, so for the groups he represented: the cause of tumult was always traced to an external source. Patriots were blameless. Junius Americanus quipped that Bernard should be appointed "Riot-Maker-General" and Mein sent back to Boston to meet his fate. "The vio-

10. John C. Miller, *Sam Adams: Pioneer in Propaganda* (Boston, 1936), 172–73; Arthur Lee to Richard Henry Lee, November 9, 1769, in Richard Henry Lee, *Life of Arthur Lee,* I, 193–94.

11. To Sir F[ranci]s B[ernar]d, October 25, November 3, 19, 1769, in [Arthur Lee], *Political Detection,* 24–25, 29, 35–40.

lated right of representation" could be restored for all friends of liberty only if American and British resistance were knit together. The policies of Bute, Grafton, and Grenville must be reversed.[12]

In later addresses, Junius Americanus was more lucid. He reemphasized the prime American grievance: "the having of their property granted to the Crown, in an Assembly wherein they are not represented; contrary to the most ancient and most important principles of constitutional liberty." This complaint was plainly the result of parliamentary innovation since 1763 in the revenue taxation of America. The propagandist appealed to all British freeholders to reflect how they would feel if their property were subject to legislation by a group of men other than their own representatives. "The consideration of this," Lee remarked, "will bring home to every man's breast, the feelings of the people of America at the invasion of a right" long cherished by all Britons. Lee became the victim of thinking in analogues, and he repeatedly likened the present situation to the arbitrary despotism of Charles I. From his Whiggish vantage point America appeared to be the "nursery of British Liberty" where "the British constitution may arise anew, like a Phoenix from her parental ashes, to glory, strength, and happiness." Recurrent reliance on this rebirth simile indicates Lee had reached another stage along the path from resistance to revolution. His disenchantment with British politicians and procedures mounted, as did his faith in American sufficiency to meet the challenge. The only concession he was then willing to make was John Dickinson's distinction of sovereignty: Britain would reserve the supreme regulation of trade, while the colonies must retain the rights to dispose of their property and to follow common law, "untouched."[13]

The newspaper campaign against Francis Bernard had little effect on members of the Privy Council and Parliament. DeBerdt's hearing on the Massachusetts indictments before the Privy Council on February 20, 1770, proved disastrous to the American agitators. No instructions and no evidence had been sent to the colonial agent from Massachusetts. When DeBerdt, Lee, and Sayre presented their charges, they were belit-

12. To the People of England, January 3, 1770, in *Ibid.*, 64–68.

13. To the People of England, January 24, 25, 31, February 3, 1770 in *Ibid.*, 71–72, 79–81, 84, 88–89, 98; Lloyd deMause, "The Formation of the American Character through Psychospeciation," *Journal of Psychohistory*, IV (Summer, 1976), 1–30.

tled by defense counsel. Junius Americanus was also condemned for his abuse of the governor. On March 14, shortly after repeal of the bulk of the Townshend duties, the Privy Council reported to George III that accusations leveled at Bernard were "Groundless, Vexatious, and Scandalous." The "Nettleham Baronet," as Lee called Bernard, retired to Aylesbury, the former residence of John Wilkes. Lee and his cronies sulked. They had been dealt the short and iniquitous hand they had come to anticipate from the administration.[14]

The conclusion of the Privy Council's investigation of the charges against Bernard coincided with the remodeling of American taxation in early 1770. Both topics had demanded Arthur Lee's attention for more than a year, and he had labored tirelessly to broadcast colonial views on both issues. Meanwhile he kept brother Richard Henry and John Dickinson informed of the drift of the ministry. In reply his correspondents reported the wavering course of resistance in the colonies. All three agreed there was little hope that the existing administration would change its policy, but they believed that a unified American persistence in nonimportation and nonconsumption would ultimately result in redress of colonial grievances. Dickinson, the moderate Pennsylvanian, called this movement a "holy War" and prayed that Arthur "be blest with the health to assert on the spot, against the weak and the wicked, the cause of our country, and of that liberty which I know you so dearly love, and are so capable of defending."[15] Such pleas spurred the zealot in his tasks in London.

When Parliament convened in October, 1769, Arthur could see little hope. Repression of the colonies was the ministerial policy under the Bedfordites, whom Lee believed were then in control. No element of the Opposition possessed laudable credentials either: "it is rather a scuffle who shall enjoy the power and wealth of office, than who shall administer peace and welfare to the nation." Amidst such diffracted politics, Lee perceived that the king held the reins of power, and that, to the Virginian, meant the nefarious Bute was at the controls of policy. (In fact, Bute had completely withdrawn from politics years earlier.) He deemed further British talk of conciliatory measures a device to cause disharmony among

14. John C. Miller, *Sam Adams*, 174; Riggs, "Arthur Lee and the Radical Whigs," 123–27; Kammen, *Rope of Sand*, 182.

15. John Dickinson to Arthur Lee, April 20, 1769, March 31, 1770, in Richard Henry Lee, *Life of Arthur Lee*, II, 295, 300.

the colonies and to shatter the boycott. Parliamentary endorsement of the use of troops in Boston was made "in heat," Arthur reported. He still trusted that "Better information and more dispassionate deliberation" would lead to the dismissal of Bernard and the repeal of the Townshend duties. As the new year approached and a change in leadership seemed imminent, Junius Americanus thumped the drum for Lord Chatham. He declared that British supporters of America would not tolerate a political alliance with the followers of Grenville who had advocated quelling colonial disorders by force. The penman warned British politicians that "the more force you use the more fatal will be the recoil upon yourselves."[16]

Grafton resigned January 18, 1770, but Lord North, not Chatham, became first minister. Again Lee and DeBerdt matched writing talents and financial resources to influence imperial policy. The result was a brief pamphlet distributed to members of Parliament. Free from the emotionalism of Junius Americanus, this effort from Lee's pen was a call to return to the tranquil days before 1763. All obnoxious measures relative to the colonies enacted by Parliament since that date should be repealed. Again Lee argued the idea of the Farmer when he asserted, "Our wise forefathers drew a line between the supreme legislative power of the Mother-Country and the constitutional rights of her Colonies, as freeborn English subjects." That line divided commercial regulation from internal legislation. Regression to the conditions that existed prior to 1764 was seen as an adequate solution to Lee—"Remove the cause, and the effects will cease"—for he believed that domestic disorder in the colonies was solely a response to treachery and repression carried on by malignant policy and malefic office-holders. He cited eight specific acts, all tending to "the total subversion of every right and security," that should immediately be repealed. "*Americans* are content to be *subordinate*; but they never will submit to be *enslaved*." It was not characteristic of Lee to recognize any such subtlety in the division of sovereignty, and in fact, he concluded here that "*Submission* and *Slavery* are the same."[17]

16. Arthur Lee to Richard Henry Lee, October, 1769, October 3, 1769, in Hoffman and Molyneaux (eds.), *Lee Family Papers*, I, 632–34, 641–43; Arthur Lee to Richard Henry Lee, December 3, 1769, in Richard Henry Lee, *Life of Arthur Lee*, I, 202–204; to the Right Honorable Author of a late Speech [George Grenville], December 12, 1769, in [Arthur Lee], *Political Detection*, 130, 132.

17. Riggs, "Arthur Lee and the Radical Whigs," 7, 31–34, 124; *Extract of a Letter from the House of Representatives of the Massachusetts Bay, to Their*

On March 5, 1770, Lord North moved for repeal of all Townshend taxes except the duty on tea, a strategy prompted, he said, by concern for imperial commerce and not pressured by American protests. Retaining the tax on tea was equivalent to an assertion of the supremacy of Parliament over the colonies and of its right to tax for revenue. Junius Americanus rejected such thinking, blasted partial repeal, and sought to revive the alliance between British merchants and colonial agitators. As "what the Americans really complain of, is the raising of a Revenue upon them without their consent," he predicted that colonial discontent would not be allayed by North's program. Lee recognized that the partial repeal would neither aid British commerce nor completely redress colonial complaints. The sole effect would be a decrease in tax revenues from £13,000 to £9,000.[18]

Stubbornly, Lee clung to the tactic of economic boycott. He urged the colonists to remain loyal to plans of economic coercion and to threaten London merchants with curtailment of trade. As Monitor he lectured, "America must *work her own salvation*, and put no trust in great men here for giving her relief from any other motive but *necessity*."[19] The emphasis, as before, was on colonial autonomy, but Lee's rhetoric was not sufficient to maintain cohesion in colonial resistance. News of the Boston Massacre crushed all hope of further softening of British policy. Although Lee industriously propagated the American version of that fatal encounter, he must have been disheartened. Introduction of redcoats into the colonial cities had yielded the strife and bloodshed Junius Americanus had long anticipated. Tragically, his prophecies were being fulfilled.

Throughout his tenure in London, dexterity—some might say duplicity —was demanded of Arthur Lee. While filling the press with clamor against colonial policy, he was privately courting the favor of administrators at Whitehall. He saw no contradiction in such activities. In 1770

Agent Dennys DeBerdt, Esq., with Some Remarks, in Mathews (ed.), "Letters of DeBerdt," 455–61. Selections from this pamphlet were reprinted in Rind (ed.), *Virginia Gazette,* May 31, June 7, 14, 1770.

18. Charles R. Ritcheson, *British Politics and the American Revolution* (Norman, 1954), 136–37; To the American Merchants, February, 1770, To the People of England, March 12, 1770, in [Arthur Lee], *Political Detection,* 122, 100–101.

19. "Monitor," in Rind (ed.), *Virginia Gazette,* May 31, 1770; Riggs, "Arthur Lee and the Radical Whigs," 36.

various land schemes for the interior of North America were revitalized despite Hillsborough's adamant rejections. It was rumored that the Walpole Associates, an enterprise headed by energetic lobbyist Samuel Wharton and composed of British politicians and American investors, had prevailed over the colonial secretary. As representative for the Mississippi Company, whose request predated Wharton's, Lee solicited the Board of Trade for a grant to southern colonial speculators, but Arthur told Richard Henry his request was hopeless. The Wharton scheme, including "adventurers headed by the mercenary and infamous Lord Hertford," had the upper hand. Later he reported that the old Lee nemesis, George Mercer of the Virginia Company, and an emerging opponent, Benjamin Franklin, plus "other such ministerial tools" had been recruited by Wharton. Arthur bitterly charged that Franklin was protecting the Walpole Company, now known as the Grand Ohio Company, from investigation by the Board of Trade. To Lee "there are not a greater set of knaves under the Sun" than Franklin and his friends who threatened to usurp the claims the Lees made for western lands. Personal, family, and intercolonial rivalries boiled up in the competition, and Lee's frustration fed his wrath and his conspiratorial perspective.[20]

While Lee's petitions and remonstrances failed to gain the Mississippi Company a grant, Franklin and Wharton's projects also languished. Lee's notoriety as a scribbler in the press may have influenced the outcome, but primarily it was Hillsborough's procrastination coupled with the inertia of British bureaucracy that stymied his efforts. Wharton was finally able to muster sufficient influence to force a showdown in the Privy Council in August, 1772, and Hillsborough resigned rather than approve colonization of the interior of America. Lord North's half brother William Legge, earl of Dartmouth, was then named colonial secretary and the Wharton plan approved. It was a short-lived success, however, for drafting the form of government for the proposed colony—to be known as Vandalia—

20. Jack M. Sosin, *Whitehall and the Wilderness: The Middle West in British Colonial Policy, 1760–1775* (Lincoln, 1961), 182–190; [Arthur Lee], "To the Right Hon[ora]ble, the Lords Commissioner, of Trade and Plantations, The Petition of Arthur Lee for Certain Inhabitants of Great Britain, Virginia, and Maryland," [January 24, 1770?], Arthur Lee to Richard Henry Lee, February 15, July 12, 1770, all in Hoffman and Molyneaux (eds.), *Lee Family Papers*, II, 45, 3–4, 24–27.

stalled the project until the land grant was permanently sidetracked by the American crisis of 1774.[21] Lee, held at arm's length by the Board of Trade, suspected his rivals of graft.

Perhaps Arthur Lee's familiarity with governmental transactions, formal and informal, interested him in the law, or perhaps he thought the legal profession would provide him with a means to gain a seat in Parliament. Possibly, he saw from the example of John Dickinson that the study of British statutes could bolster his advocacy of the American cause. It was somewhat ironic that he now chose to follow the paths of his two eldest brothers, his original guardians, who had received training at the Inner Temple. Whatever the motive, in the spring of 1770 he conceded that neither his disposition nor his interests were compatible with the life of a physician. Following the advice of his distant cousin, Edmund Jenings, he enrolled as a student at Lincoln's Inn on March 1, 1770, in the hope that the study of law would prove "more honorable and profitable" than medicine. Undaunted by the prospect of five more years of schooling, Arthur believed he could gain a law degree if he bridled his energy and "unless I shall be diverted by some thing very tempting or discouraging." In fact, academic regulations were lax, the Inns' real value being their libraries, their proximity to Westminster, and their intellectual atmosphere. Lee followed an independent course of study that enabled him to maintain interest in cultural events and political currents in London. He frequented the weekly meetings of the Royal Society, was named a member of the Society of Arts and Agriculture, and subscribed to Bach's and Abel's concerts. Lee thrived amidst such manifestations of high culture.[22]

Arthur's decision to take up the study of law served as a reminder of his dependent status. As had been the case with his previous schooling,

21. Sosin, *Whitehall and the Wilderness*, 192–208; Alvord, *Mississippi Valley*, II, 106–125.

22. E. Alfred Jones, *American Members of the Inns of Court* (London, 1924), 122–24; Sir Henry F. Macgeagh (ed.), *Register of Admissions to the Honorable Society of the Middle Temple, from the Fifteenth Century to the Year 1944* (London, 1949), I, 337; Arthur Lee to Richard Henry Lee, May 20, September 10, 23, 1770, all in Hoffman and Molyneaux (eds.), *Lee Family Papers*, II, 22, 33–34, 114; H. Trevor Colbourn, "A Pennsylvania Farmer at the Court of King George: John Dickinson's London Letters, 1754–1756," *Pennsylvania Magazine of History and Biography*, LXXXVI (July, 1962), 244–45; Richard Henry Lee, *Life of Arthur Lee*, II, 392.

he turned to his brothers for financial support, and his distrust revived. To pursue a law degree, he needed two hundred pounds per year, some of which he got from the sale of his horses and a chaise in Virginia. He was also supposed to receive some money from Philip Ludwell, who promised to pay the interest due Arthur on his inheritance. When these plans failed, reliable Richard Henry, reaffirming the bond between himself and Arthur, stepped into the breach to bear the burden of this latest endeavor. Soon after, when Richard Henry sent his two sons to Britain, Arthur supervised their schooling. The two Lees looked out for each other: Arthur trying unsuccessfully to ease his brother onto the government payroll, Richard Henry continuing efforts to make Arthur agent for the House of Burgesses.[23]

Arthur became friends during the period with three radical thinkers of London, Catharine Macaulay, Joseph Priestley, and Richard Price. Lee was particularly spellbound by the female historian, whose works endorsed classical republicanism and whose political activities were affiliated with those of the Wilkesites through her brother, Alderman John Sawbridge. He probably met Priestley and Price through Shelburne. Arthur urged Priestley to become Shelburne's confidant and librarian, posts the freethinker accepted in 1772. Lee later encouraged Price to migrate to America in order to remedy the economic chaos that plagued the American states during the War for Independence.[24] From these acquaintances Lee acquired certainty that the empire was teetering on the brink of tyranny and disaster. Not above name-dropping, Lee also used this comradeship to enhance the authoritativeness of his reports to his colonial correspondents.

It was fortunate that his law studies were not demanding, for city poli-

23. Richard Henry Lee to Arthur Lee, April 5, 1770, Richard Henry Lee to William Lee, July 4, 1773, May 10, 1775, all in Ballagh (ed.), *Letters of Richard Henry Lee*, I, 41–45, 90–96, 135; William Lee to Philip Lee, April 7, 1770, in Arthur Lee Papers, Box 13; Arthur Lee to Richard Henry Lee, October 20, 1770, June 11, September 23, 1771, in Hoffman and Molyneaux (eds.), *Lee Family Papers*, II, 43, 66–68, 114–17.

24. Arthur Lee to Richard Henry Lee, November 15, 1769, in Hoffman and Molyneaux (eds.), *Lee Family Papers*, I, 635–37; Richard Henry Lee to Arthur Lee, April 5, 1770, in Ballagh (ed.), *Letters of Richard Henry Lee*, I, 41–44; Lucy Martin Donnelly "The Celebrated Mrs. Macaulay," *William and Mary Quarterly*, 3rd ser., VI (April, 1949), 173–207; Arthur Lee to Joseph Priestley, October 25, 1772, Richard Price to Arthur Lee, June 15, 1777, in Richard Henry Lee, *Life of Arthur Lee*, I, 255–56, II, 347–38.

tics engrossed Lee's interest late in 1770. In November, Brass Crosby was elected lord mayor of London as a compromise candidate supported by the Wilkes and Shelburne factions then contending for control of the Society of Supporters for the Bill of Rights. Four mainstays of the society, John Sawbridge, Richard Oliver, James Townshend, and John Horne, challenged Wilkes's leadership. A dispute over payment of the demagogue's debts almost resulted in a duel in December. The following two months were filled with debate over apportionment of the society's resources.

Meanwhile Arthur Lee enlisted his pen in a potentially pivotal squabble over whether city printers should publish the debates of the Commons and whether the society should subsidize such publications. He saw the issue as critical because the people "have an essential and unalienable right to inquire into the conduct of their representatives." This episode was evidence to Lee that not only the cabinet, but also the Parliament was guilty of arbitrary and unconstitutional behavior. The ringing conclusion to his pronouncement on this affair dripped with emotion: "The fabric of english [sic] liberty, has been cemented by the blood of Englishmen; and should it be necessary, we trust there is yet patriotism enough, to furnish blood for its reparation." [25] He looked forward to martyrdom.

The question of priorities rent the society. The decision was made to support Wilkes. After an unsuccessful attempt to dissolve the organization, Horne and other dissenters withdrew to form a rival Constitutional Society. Arthur Lee subsequently persuaded the remaining members to alter restrictions on new subscriptions, thereby making the society an international enterprise open to patriots in the colonies. Throughout the strife Lee sided with Wilkes, a stand that temporarily cost him Shelburne's friendship and contradicted his own primary quest for redress of American grievances. He defended himself by claiming, "The public cause, and particularly that of America, which induced me to engage in the society, was the mover of my conduct." [26] Yet he chose to narrow the

25. Riggs "Arthur Lee and the Radical Whigs," 128–38; Minnie Clare Yarborough, *John Horne Tooke* (New York, 1926), 54–55; [Arthur Lee], "Members of the Bill of Rights Society to the Lord Mayor of London," [March, 1771], in Hoffman and Molyneaux (eds.), *Lee Family Papers*, II, 64.
26. Riggs, "Arthur Lee and the Radical Whigs," 141–43; Trench, *Portrait of a*

society's immediate aims to Wilkes's personal cause rather than follow Horne, who advocated a broader program of agitation.

Perhaps Arthur Lee was captivated by the demagogue, perhaps he simply wished to climb higher in the power structure of the society, or perhaps he clung devotedly to the society's prime tactic of petitions. Certainly Lee interpreted this episode as he did politicking at other levels: evil-minded and ambitious connivers were attempting to seduce patriots. He turned his wrath on the secessionists and their supporter. "Townshend is an opinionated, over-grown schoolboy; Horne is a malevolent, vain, petulant, impudent priest. The former, in his conceit and folly, thought he could lead the City; the other, in his vanity and knavery, conceived that his abilities were equal to Townshend's ambition, and that he would be rewarded. . . . Lord Shelburne suffers from all their follies, and has therefore lost his popularity in the City." Lee's interpretations of political factionalism were, as usual, intensely personal. He had a quick temper and thin skin to go along with his quenchless energy. Convinced he had made the right choice, he founded his conduct in faith in Wilkes's ability to rally popular support. Arthur explained to Richard Henry, "Expecting redress only from the people, I am determined to stand with them, however my particular interest might advise a different course." He did not consider that the deeper he immersed himself in city agitation and Opposition factionalism, the more tenuous became his ties with colonial affairs. He banked on his personal correspondence with American agitators to maintain this field of interest.[27]

In May, 1771, when Wilkes announced his candidacy for the post of sheriff of London, his quarrel with Horne burst upon the public. In a violent and unrestrained exchange of letters in the *Public Advertiser* the two antagonists hurled accusations and insults at each other. Junius entered the fray on the side of Wilkes in an effort to heal the wounds in the Opposition camp. Although no victor could be declared in the newspaper warfare, Wilkes did triumph in the city election in June. In the autumn, however, a candidate of the court was elected lord mayor, and the follow-

---

Patriot, 277–96; Yarborough, *John Horne Tooke*, 55–59; Arthur Lee to Richard Henry Lee [1771?] in Richard Henry Lee, *Life of Arthur Lee*, I, 185–90.

27. Fragment of an Arthur Lee paper on Wilkes and Bill of Rights [1771?], in Hoffman and Molyneaux (eds.), *Lee Family Papers*, II, 82.

ing year James Townshend gained that post. Dissension within the society had proved costly. It was not until September, 1773, that a Wilkesite, Frederick Bull, attained the mayoralty and, in turn, passed it to John Wilkes himself the following year.[28]

Arthur Lee officiously attempted to regroup the followers of Wilkes in 1771. The society altered its name to the Society of the Bill of Rights (S.B.R.), and the younger radicals acquired positions of leadership within the movement. Lee, serving as Wilkes's penman and political theorist through his role as secretary to the society, made notable contributions to S.B.R. strategy and tactics. He recommended a set of instructions—including American and Irish grievances—that each electoral unit should direct to their representatives at the next general election. In June he proposed a broad platform for the society and advocated proselytism of the cause throughout Britain. Hoping to revitalize the manly defense of rights, he envisioned the S.B.R. as a powerful machine endorsing the candidacy of all radical candidates.[29]

The culminating article in the Virginian's program for city radicals called for the redress of American grievances. Lee wanted all S.B.R.-sponsored candidates to pledge to "restore to the Americans the violated right of taxation; by repealing the Declaratory Law and the revenue Acts, which are as fruitless as unconstitutional." A committee of the society revised his proposals and clarified this last instruction to read: "You shall endeavor to restore to America the essential right of taxation, by representation of their own free election; repealing the acts passed in violation of that right since the year 1763 and the universal excise, so notoriously incompatible with every principle of British liberty, which has been lately substituted, in the colonies, for the laws of customs." The society's program for radicalism in 1771 gained short-range triumphs but failed in the long run. The plan led to a temporarily solvent Wilkes. Yet the suspicion it evoked among old Whigs, its failure to recruit new adherents, and

28. Yarborough, *John Horne Tooke*, 59; Minnie C. Yarborough, "John Horne Tooke, Champion of the American Colonies," *South Atlantic Quarterly*, XXXV (October, 1936), 378–79; Trench, *Portrait of a Patriot*, 227–308; Riggs, "Arthur Lee and the Radical Whigs," 153–160.

29. Riggs, "Arthur Lee and the Radical Whigs," 142–45; Arthur Lee to Richard Henry Lee, June 11, 1771, in Hoffman and Molyneaux (eds.), *Lee Family Papers*, II, 66; John Sainsbury, "The Pro-Americans of London, 1769 to 1782," *William and Mary Quarterly*, 3rd ser., XXXV (July, 1978), 426–27.

continued internal discord kept the S.B.R. from attaining its goal of a new constitutional order.[30]

Lee's proposals for the S.B.R. brought the American organizer into conflict with Junius in September. The British satirist offered a critique of the S.B.R. program and particularly found fault with the article on American grievances. Junius, in a letter addressed to Wilkes, claimed that no internal taxes had been laid on America since the Stamp Act. He also found that the tax on tea "Ought to be repealed as an impolitic act, not as an oppressive one. It preserves the contention between the mother country and the colonies, when everything worth contending for is in reality given up." When Junius labeled the S.B.R. proposals verbose, Wilkes disavowed their authorship and introduced Lee, as Junius Americanus, as their originator.[31]

Arthur replied to Junius both at the S.B.R. and in the public press. The American polemicist challenged his British counterpart to prove that Parliament had the right to tax the colonies. Junius refused further contention over the issue and withdrew. The British controversialist acknowledged privately to Wilkes, "My American namesake is plainly a man of abilities" but "a little unreasonable" in seeking complete redress of grievances. To the British disputant the colonists had sacrificed the right of representation when they migrated across the Atlantic. He had no sympathy for de facto rights grown out of imperial neglect and hoped that, rather than bickering, he and Lee could unite in attacking targets in the present ministry.[32]

His hopes were not fulfilled. As the petitionary movement of 1769–1770 had been brushed aside by the crown, so too the S.B.R. program of 1771–1772 met with failure. The electorate was not stirred; a political calm settled over the English countryside following Wilkes's release from prison and his triumph over the ministry in a lawsuit concerning his arrest. Lord North warily avoided provocation of the Wilkesites as he simultaneously sought to pacify the Americans. Arthur Lee could do little but return to his studies. The historical annals are almost barren of his

30. Riggs, "Arthur Lee and the Radical Whigs," 144–45; John Wade (ed.), *Junius* (2 vols.; London, 1850–1855), II, 71–74; Black, *The Association*, 13–14.

31. Junius to John Wilkes, September 7, 1771, Wilkes to Junius, September 12, 1771, in Wade (ed.), *Junius*, II, 80–81, 83–87.

32. Riggs, "Arthur Lee and the Radical Whigs," 40–41; Junius to John Wilkes, November 6, 1771, in Wade (ed.), *Junius*, II, 102–103.

correspondence from June, 1771, to July, 1772. It is recorded that he did purchase the freedom and livery of London, which gave him the right to vote in city elections.[33] His attention also turned to developing connections with agitators in Massachusetts, the hotbed of colonial patriotism.

Since his arrival in England in the autumn of 1768 Arthur had defended the Massachusetts resistance movement. It was not until two years later, however, that he established private correspondence with the embattled patriots of Boston. True, he had formed an alliance with Dennys DeBerdt, the London merchant who acted as agent for the Massachusetts House of Representatives. True, reprintings in the Boston *Evening Post* and Essex *Gazette* of Junius Americanus essays had broadcast his opinions in the Bay Colony. But when DeBerdt died in April, 1770, Lee had no personal contacts to advance his candidacy for a post he coveted.

Chief among the candidates seeking to succeed DeBerdt was Benjamin Franklin. The renowned printer-scientist, then serving as agent for Pennsylvania, Georgia, and New Jersey, wished to add another laurel to his cap. DeBerdt had frequently expressed suspicion of Franklin, claiming he had withheld judgment on the Stamp Act until he had seen what the public reaction would be in America. DeBerdt had aired his misgivings to Lee and other Americans who frequented his home. The reports from DeBerdt reinforced Lee's jealousy and suspicion of Franklin's success at outmaneuvering him to gain favor for the Vandalia land scheme. Nonetheless, Franklin's preeminence in the political and social circles of London made him the first choice of many Massachusetts legislators.[34]

The DeBerdt clique, chiefly Stephen Sayre and Joseph Reed, enlisted James Otis, Samuel Adams, and William Palfrey of the Bay Colony in Arthur Lee's behalf. Adams found Junius Americanus' polemic much to his liking. He told Sayre, "The Author has served the American Cause in a manner in which I have long wished some able pen would have undertaken to do it by appealing to the good Sense of the Body of the Nation." He eagerly accepted Sayre's invitation to correspond with Lee. Palfrey

33. Riggs, "Arthur Lee and the Radical Whigs," 150–151.
34. Esther DeBerdt to Joseph Reed, December 12, 1766, in Mathews (ed.), "Letters of DeBerdt," 306. Verner Crane, depicting Lee as "Impatient and pathologically suspicious," was convinced that the Lee-Franklin feud dated from Arthur's acquaintance with DeBerdt. Verner W. Crane, *Benjamin Franklin and a Rising People* (Boston, 1954), 135.

went even further, believing his colony's gratitude to Junius Americanus should lead to Lee's appointment as agent.[35]

Lee's supporters comprised approximately one-third of the Massachusetts House, but Franklin's popularity was overwhelming, and thus he was selected agent on October 24, 1770. A week later as a sop to Adams and Palfrey, Lee was chosen as Franklin's substitute in the event of death or absence of the philosopher.[36] Mismanagement was one reason for Arthur's defeat. Palfrey believed Franklin should have been disqualified because of his retention of the lucrative post of deputy postmaster and the placement of his son as royal governor of New Jersey. Esther DeBerdt felt that enough was known in Massachusetts of Lee's patriotic efforts in England; she looked forward to his selection as agent in the future. Arthur realized that he had not mustered his forces correctly; he had not sought the recommendations of such paragons of patriotism as Catharine Macaulay and Colonel Isaac Barré. Belatedly, he recognized the extraordinary abilities and pervasive prestige of his rival and lamented that the role of substitute was rather meaningless. Envy and distrust festered in Lee.[37]

Franklin's shadow loomed over Lee the rest of his life and perpetually in history. The relationship between the two men was never warm; a combination of personal differences and political aims led to ill will. Franklin's age—he was thirty-four years older than Lee—made him a potent authority figure over the younger man. Lee was unable to match Franklin's successes either; the sage was a consummate politician. Although both were multifaceted products of the Enlightenment, Franklin was self-taught and practical-minded, while Lee considered himself a substantial and superbly trained member of the intelligentsia. In England, not only did they represent competing colonial companies in quest of grants for

35. Samuel Adams to Stephen Sayre, November 16, 23, 1770, in Cushing (ed.), *Writings of Samuel Adams*, II, 56–61, 66–69; William Palfrey to John Wilkes, October 23–30, 1770, in Elsey (ed.), "John Wilkes and William Palfrey," 424.

36. Samuel Adams to Stephen Sayre, November 16, 1770, in Cushing (ed.), *Writings of Samuel Adams*, II, 59; "Resolution of the House of Representatives of Massachusetts," October 24, 1770, in Hoffman and Molyneaux (eds.), *Lee Family Papers*, II, 40–41; Rind (ed.), *Virginia Gazette*, November 29, 1770.

37. William Palfrey to John Wilkes, October 25, 1770, in Elsey (ed.), "John Wilkes and William Palfrey," 424; Esther Reed to Dennys DeBerdt, December 27, 1770, January 17, 1771, in Reed, *Life of Esther DeBerdt*, 160–163, 164–66; Arthur Lee to Joseph Reed, January 18, 1771, in Arthur Lee Papers, Box 2.

land in the Ohio River Valley, they also differed on city politics—Lee embracing, Franklin rejecting the tactics of mobs. Lastly the pair disagreed over the relaitonship of colonial turmoil to the international scene. Where Franklin counseled conciliation and trust in economic coercion, Lee increasingly sought to aggravate the Anglo-American crisis, came to welcome open hostilities, and was quick to solicit foreign assistance for the patriot cause. Lee's impetuosity frequently proved fruitless; Franklin's cautious cultivation of affairs was relatively successful. Franklin was cordial and conciliatory, Lee uncompromising and combative. They would always pursue dichotomous paths in their diplomatic assignments.[38]

As political rebellion fermented, Arthur Lee formulated an ideology and a self-image. Trying to integrate his readings in past history with relationships in his own life, Lee struggled to wrest a sense of identity from the various roles he played, the prime patterns of behavior he relied on, and the cardinal theorems of his personal philosophy. In 1770 at the age of thirty, he was still struggling. Then Franklin intervened, and Lee used his presence to ameliorate his own personal crisis. Franklin, Lee's antithesis, personified those traits and values that Lee had forbidden in his own makeup. Arthur used devices at his disposal—the press, his private correspondence, and political discussions—to depict Franklin as despicable and to denounce him vehemently. Through Samuel Adams, the Virginian was soon circulating reports that Franklin was "not the dupe but the instrument of Lord Hillsborough's treachery." He catalogued the sage's liabilities: "possession of a profitable office at will," placement of his son as royal governor, concentration on Pennsylvania's concerns ("for which administration must be cultivated and courted"), "the temporising conduct he has always held in American affairs."[39] Franklin's diplomatic

38. Thomas P. Abernethy, "The Origins of the Franklin-Lee Imbroglio," *North Carolina Historical Review*, XV (January, 1938), 1-12; Maier, *From Resistance to Revolution*, 253-54; Herbert James Henderson, Jr., "Political Factions in the Continental Congress, 1774-1783," (Ph.D. dissertation, Columbia University, 1962), *passim*; Wonyung Hyun Oh, "Opinions of Continental American Leaders on International Relations, 1763-1775," (Ph.D. dissertation, University of Washington, 1963), 39; Richard L. Bushman, "On the Use of Psychology: Conflict and Conciliation in Benjamin Franklin," *History and Theory*, V (1968), 225-40.

39. Erik H. Erikson, *Life History and the Historical Moment* (New York, 1975), 20-21; Arthur Lee to Samuel Adams, June 10, 1771, Samuel Cooper to Benjamin Franklin, August 23, 1771, in Labaree *et al.* (eds.), *Papers of Franklin*, XVIII, 127-29, 213.

successes only confirmed Lee's assumption that his wiles were basely motivated. It provided great satisfaction to Lee to be known as Franklin's opponent and opposite, for by this the Virginian knew he *was* someone and what he was *not*.

Although they did not like it, Franklin and Lee were yoked together in the agency of the Massachusetts House. Franklin observed that their selections "have not been at all agreeable" to Hillsborough in the colonial office. Lee masked his resentment in a profusion of thanks to the Bay Colony patriots. He was flattered to be chosen by "a representative body, who have uniformly asserted the constitutional rights of their constituents and eventually of all America, against the insidious and incendiary arts of government with a dignity, discernment and wisdom which have forced the applause of the present, and will secure to them the veneration of all future times."[40] This characteristic flourish was followed by a litany to American liberty and exposition of his views: strive to be self-reliant; oppose the tyrannous foe, the ministry bent on "perfect slavery" for the colonists; trust in God rather than British politicians; seek a redress of grievances. Freemen must be eternally watchful of their unalienable rights.

The Virginian promised to cooperate with "the abler hands" of Franklin in the Massachusetts agency should the need arise, but the older man sought out the younger's assistance only infrequently. Lee's jealousy and his desire for the post mounted, while both men saw the potency of the colonial agency dwindle. The lack of cooperation between the two was typical of agents for the colonies in Britain.[41] Neither the institution of the agency nor the individual agents proved capable at this time of maintaining the bonds of empire. In Lee's case, especially, there was no advocacy for tightening the imperial system.

The ardent alliance Arthur Lee formed with the leadership of American resistance reassured him; it resuscitated his patriotism and self-esteem. Following the twin failures of the colonial boycott and the English petitionary movement in 1770, the Virginian began to express his disillusion-

40. Franklin to Thomas Cushing, February 5, 1771 in Labaree *et al.* (eds.), *Papers of Franklin*, XVIII, 28; Arthur Lee to Cushing, January 6, 1771, in Richard Henry Lee, *Life of Arthur Lee*, I, 246–48.

41. Kammen, *Rope of Sand*, 145–46; Sosin, *Agents and Merchants*, 187–88; Michael G. Kammen, "The Colonial Agents, English Politics, and the American Revolution," *William and Mary Quarterly*, 3rd ser., XXII (April, 1965), 244–63.

ment. The colonies were falling victim to the "luxury and corruption" at work in Britain. His bitterness over placemen—a symptom of the cancerous growth of corruption—was heightened when he failed to secure a governmental position and pension for Richard Henry.[42] John Dickinson and Richard Henry combined their efforts to convince Arthur that Americans did retain enough forthrightness to persevere in the struggle to preserve their rights. Arthur remained the most passionate, as well as the most prone to disenchantment, of these writers.

In 1771 Arthur reported rumors of impending war with Spain over the Falkland Islands. Dickinson agreed with Arthur that war between Britain and Spain might be a good thing, but he did not endorse Arthur's immoderate strategy. In the event of war, Lee proposed that colonial assemblies "harmonize in three things: Refusing supplies without redress of grievances; repeating their resolve of rights; and sending over petitions for redress at that crucial and alarming period when the value of our affection and assistance will appear in its highest lustre." Arthur was willing to flirt with war and the weapon of passive resistance to further the colonial cause. From his viewpoint it appeared that "the more symptoms we show of discontent and alienated affections the more sure will be the attainment of our end."[43] This adamant and inverted stance was characteristic for Lee through 1776. He conceived of the situation as one of simple, direct reciprocity: each British affront to American rights must be met with equal resistance.

Such notions found a congenial recipient in Samuel Adams. Between December 31, 1770, and December 10, 1775, Adams and Lee developed a crucial correspondence. In this period Lee dispatched at least thirty-one letters to Adams who in turn wrote at least twenty-six replies. In sum the writings manifested a synergistic relationship between the two radicals: each correspondent fed on the tactics, impressions, and exhortations emanating from his counterpart. They came to think alike in this process of cross-fertilization. The correspondence was bound together by the extreme sarcasm both penmen aimed at their antagonists and by the reverberating

42. Arthur Lee to Richard Henry Lee, September 10, October 20, 1770, in Hoffman and Molyneaux (eds.), *Lee Family Papers*, II, 33–34, 43.

43. Arthur Lee to Richard Henry Lee, September 23, 1771 [?], in *Ibid.*, II, 114; John Dickinson to Arthur Lee, September 23, 1771, Lee to Dickinson, January 10, 1771, in Richard Henry Lee, *Life of Arthur Lee*, II, 303–304, I, 252–55.

clarions for manly or virtuous conduct from the resisters. So frequent are such comments that it may be suspected that both Lee and Adams used the correspondence to mask vulnerabilities traceable to personal failures. Lee found catharsis in the ideas and doctrines he shared with Adams. Their common perspectives included a dualistic approach to fellow man, a distrust for contemporary institutions, an abhorrence of compromise, totalistic aspirations toward the ordering of society, and a wish to create an idealized past in the future. Lee and Adams were brothers in ideology.[44] Their jaundiced correspondence corroded their attachment to the Anglo-American connection. Over the course of it they came to articulate, point by point, a comprehensive plan to preserve American liberty. Ultimately, they fomented rebellion because they saw that the attitudes and actions of the crown and Parliament imperiled both their hopes of personal stature and the realization of a reconstituted American society.[45] While these anxieties might be pronounced in the personalities of Lee and Adams, they were also present throughout colonial society. Therefore, the spirit of resistance spread to rebellion; a movement led by a handful of ideologues struck a responsive chord in the populace, and a revolution, which deviated from Lee's designs, resulted.[46]

Through the tranquil period of 1771–1773 the spirit of agitation thrived in their letters. Then Adams led Lee through the decision—really the narrowing of alternatives—to join in rebellion. By the outbreak of the War for Independence, Lee's views on British politics and his renditions of events in America, as seen through the eyes of Samuel Adams, contributed to the breakup of the British empire. The Lee-Adams correspondence was a highly moralistic reciprocating engine pulsating at the core of American resistance.

Lee and Adams shared common hates and passions. They were in ac-

44. Clifford Geertz, "Ideology as a Cultural System," in David E. Apter (ed.), *Ideology and Discontent* (New York, 1964), 47–76.

45. Bailyn, *Ideological Origins*, 19, 160–161; Herbert James Henderson, *Party Politics in the Continental Congress* (New York, 1974), 84. Erikson, *Life History and the Historical Moment*, 21, offers: "a historical period may (as, for example the American Revolution did) present a singular chance for a collective renewal which opens up unlimited identities for those who, by a combination of unruliness, giftedness, and competence, represent a new leadership, a new elite, and new types rising to dominance in a new people."

46. Harry S. Stout, "Religion, Communications, and the Ideological Origins of the American Revolution," *William and Mary Quarterly*, 3rd ser., XXXIV (Oc-

cord in their fervid crusade to resist British threats to American liberties. They shared an admiration for classical heroes, believed that American virtue and self-reliance must triumph over British corruption, and utilized every opportunity to manipulate public opinion. Both men had a dogmatic attachment to belief systems and a sense of alienation from society, and both maintained a posture of the guardian of inner rectitude. Mere physical distance played a part in developing Lee's affection for Adams. Just as Arthur, as a schoolboy in England, came to idolize Richard Henry in the House of Burgesses, so he came to imagine Adams as a heroic Boston patriot. Distance was a common denominator in Arthur's friendships. Whenever he was forced to work closely with colleagues he grew intolerant of their faults and insensitive to their virtues, and he vexed them to an extreme. Lee's life record is replete with relationships turned sour. He projected the image of a haughty and self-righteous soul and apparently never tried to understand the reasons for his failed relationships, but one wonders if he did not induge in occasional sessions of self-accounting. Perhaps the unidentified physical maladies that affected Lee in middle-age were induced by anxiety originating from dissatisfaction with himself.[47]

In hindsight it appears odd that Adams and Lee did not commence correspondence until 1770 and never met before 1780, for both men had gained notoriety between 1765 and 1768 in American resistance in the Stamp and Townshend crises. Adams was in the core of the Caucus Club, which through the Boston town meeting and the Sons of Liberty, fanned the fires of antiauthoritarianism. A graduate of Harvard in 1740, Adams had failed in one profession after another, including those of brewer and tax collector, until the 1760s when he came to the forefront of Boston's popular faction in its struggle against British tyranny. The path to his calling was as circuitous as Lee's had been. Perhaps their affinity was traceable to the resonance of their personalities as well as their ideology: the principal chord of their correspondence was the need to maintain virtue. This term was applied to the moral health of governments as well as indi-

---

tober, 1977), 524; Joyce Appleby, "The Social Origins of American Revolutionary Ideology," *Journal of American History*, LXIV (March, 1978), 935–58.

47. Pauline Maier, "Coming to Terms with Samuel Adams," *American Historical Review*, LXXXI (February, 1976), 12–36; Edmund Jenings to Richard Henry Lee, August 17, 1771, in Hoffman and Molyneaux (eds.), *Lee Family Papers*, II, 80.

viduals. States were virtuous if their constitutions were mixed and balanced, if each subunit were independent. Citizens were virtuous if they
remained independent from governmental or social superiors in financial
and political relationships.[48] At the interpersonal level Adams and Lee
proclaimed in a repetitious chant that all comrades in the patriot camp
must exhibit the self-discpline of ascetics and an altruistic devotion to
public welfare. Thus the political liturgy of the revolution reflected the
inner personal needs of Adams and Lee. The movement for national liberation was simultaneously a drive to overcome dependence and a quest
for recognition of personal autonomy.[49]

Whatever the relationship became, the Lee-Adams correspondence had
originated in Arthur's aspiration to the position as agent for the Massachusetts House of Representatives. Adams, acting on the advice of Stephen
Sayre, had supported the candidacy and welcomed the opportunity to con-
fide in someone who was "anxiously concerned for the publick Liberty at
so alarming a crisis." Adams' frame of mind was most evident in this initial epistle as he announced, "Perhaps there never was a time when the
political Affairs of America were in a more dangerous State; Such is the
Indolence of Men in general, or their Inattention to the real Importance
of things, that a steady & animated perseverance in the rugged path of
Virtue at the hazard of trifles is hardly to be expected." Adams sounded
his customary clarion that the true and selfless patriots should jealously
guard their freedoms and that few men truly perceived what was happen-
ing beneath the façade of current events. His jeremiads also enunciated
three further themes: that "so many separate Communities as there are in
all the Colonies" led to lack of "one consistent plan of Opposition"; that
"a Design has been on foot to render ineffectual the Democratical part of
this government [the House of Representatives], a scheme traceable to a
Corrupt Administration," headed by the governor of Massachusetts; and
that faulty information of colonial affairs was being transmitted to Britain.[50] His fears were shared by Lee.

48. Pocock "Virtue and Commerce in the Eighteenth Century," 121; Jack P.
Greene, "An Uneasy Connection: An Analysis of the Preconditions of the American Revolution," in Stephen G. Kurtz and James H. Hutson (eds.), *Essays on
the American Revolution* (New York, 1973), 59.
49. Burrows and Wallace, "The American Revolution," 274–89.
50. Samuel Adams to Arthur Lee, April 19, 1771, in Cushing (ed.), *Writings
of Samuel Adams*, II, 164–67.

Arthur's first letter to Adams concurs in both tone and doctrine. He too took a frank and demonstrative approach to the correspondence. He too trumpeted self-righteously: "It will always make me happy to submit my sentiments on the present state of politics so very alarming to public liberty, to one, with whom I flatter myself I shall entirely harmonize in views of public good. It will be particularly unfortunate when the foes of liberty and virtue are conspiring together manifestly to subvert the constitution, if the friends of freedom should stand single and un-united, to fall unpitied sacrifices in an unavailing struggle." Though he sensed little support for the American cause in Britain, Lee was not then as pessimistic as Adams. A fertile suggestion he made at this time was to establish a "correspondence among the leading men of each province, that might harmonize in any future measure for the general good in the several assemblies." Such a unified stance, he predicted, would render the colonies "formidable and respectable" in British eyes. He concluded that his hobbyhorse, a petition for a bill of rights, would be the most effective means to regain the rights formerly enjoyed by the Americans.[51]

The impressions that eighteenth-century American radicals formed and then acted upon now "appear partial, skewed, inaccurate," as historian Pauline Maier has remarked. At times, though perceiving political processes correctly, these agitators "judged them by standards far different from the modern historians or influential Englishmen of their own era."[52] Activists like Lee and Adams, as well as their antagonists, developed an image of the world and standards for human conduct through the integration of three simultaneous approaches to life. At the basic level of factuality, they were concerned with the data their cognitive processes could comprehend and meaningfully arrange. The Lee-Adams correspondence is replete with reports of current events that had occurred or were rumored or anticipated. At the second level the two zealots concentrated on development of a sense of reality, a belief that they knew the path of history and what role they were to take in it. Here impressions and information became "psychologically true," whatever their factual basis, when they confirmed ideological predispositions. This knowledge, molded as much by belief as disbelief, was value oriented. It possessed visionary

51. Arthur Lee to Samuel Adams, December 31, 1770, in Arthur Lee Papers, Box 2.
52. Maier, *From Resistance to Revolution*, xiii–xiv.

qualities that spurred the American radicals in their revivalistic quest. Symbolism—the virtuous patriot, the corrupt cabinet, malignant standing armies—and ritualization—oaths of allegiance, petition drives, wearing of homespun—appealed to emotions. This led to the third level of understanding, that of actuality, wherein fanatics such as Lee and Adams related to each other, identified themselves first with the cause of resistance and then with rebellion, and willed themselves to act. Personal intentions were subsumed under common utopian goals. They sought to unify action at a critical moment in history, and luck was with them.[53]

The prism formed by factuality, reality, and actuality refracted the authentic world for the minds of members of the British empire in the eighteenth century. For Lee, Adams, and other American radicals, the main product of this process of observation and comprehension was a conspiratorial mind-set. They perceived a pattern of tyranny lurking behind British policy. Although this became an obsession, it was not, as Gordon Wood has pointed out, irrational. "The belief in a conspiracy grew naturally out of the enlightened need to find the human purposes behind the multitude of phenomena, to find the causes for what happened in the social world just as the natural scientist was discovering the causes for what happened in the physical world."[54]

In the summer of 1771 Adams, in clarifying his views of this conspiracy, sensed the "designs of a restless faction to oppress the nation." He feared that the plan was aimed at unseating the Hanoverian monarchy, "which has heretofore supported the rights of the nation, its happiness and grandeur." Around him he saw "luxury and splendour" rampant throughout colonial society and redcoat regiments encamped in Boston. Both phenomena were symptoms of arbitrary power. Thus his Whiggish catechism predicted bondage for Massachusetts under Governor Thomas Hutchinson, his "sycophants and hirelings." Lee, with personal ambition

53. Erik H. Erikson, "Psychological Reality and Historical Actuality," in Erikson, *Insight and Responsibility* (New York, 1964), 159–216; Erik H. Erikson, *Dimensions of a New Identity* (New York, 1974), 33–34; Gordon S. Wood, "Rhetoric and Reality," 31; Jack P. Greene, "Changing Interpretations of Early American Politics," in Ray A. Billington (ed.), *The Reinterpretation of Early American History* (San Marino, 1966), 175; Kenneth E. Boulding, *The Image: Knowledge in Life and Society* (Ann Arbor, 1961), 3–63; Robert Middlekauff, "The Ritualization of the American Revolution," in Robert Middlekauff and Lawrence W. Levine (eds.), *The National Temper* (New York, 1972), 100–110.
54. Gordon S. Wood, "Rhetoric and Reality," 17, 25.

to fulfill and grudges to grind, chimed in with an attack on Franklin. The elder American agent, it appeared to his younger rival, was guilty of "temporising conduct," namely, acting according to the desires of the ministry, "not to the interests of the province." [55] Americans ought not be lulled by conciliatory speeches in Parliament: their rights must be defended at all times.

To Lee, Americans and Britons suffered in common at the hands of the same wicked ministers and corrupt House of Commons. Adams' reply echoed that the root of the dilemma lay in a "corrupt ministerial Influence [which] has been gradually & too insensibly increasing" since the Glorious Revolution.[56] Early in the correspondence Adams began to wean Lee away from his attachment to the mechanical apparatus of constitutional change drawn from British history. The Bostonian had diminishing hope for a remedy in the form of impeachments, elections, or petitions from bill of rights societies on either side of the Atlantic. Lee fitfully followed Adams in narrowing the options.

The bond between Adams and Lee consolidated in the autumn of 1771. A flurry of screeds from Junius Americanus had irritated the Hutchinson-Oliver clique in Massachusetts. When the colony's council condemned the essays as scandalous—Lee had labelled Andrew Oliver "a perjured traitor"—Adams rushed to Lee's aid. Although posing as wounded by the censure, Lee replied unapologetically, "While I have a hand to act, or tongue to speak, it shall be religion in me to resist every attempt to injure the province of Massachusetts Bay, or to extend arbitrary dominion over America." Adams broadcast Lee's heroic sentiments throughout the colony, causing Peter Oliver to muse that Lee's pen, "dipped in the Gall of Asps," must be a most profitable instrument.[57]

As early as October, 1771, Adams was nurturing in Lee a spirit for rebellion. The Bostonian began to write of the approach of the "ultima

55. Samuel Adams to Arthur Lee, July 31, 1771, in Cushing (ed.), *Writings of Samuel Adams*, II, 189–93; Arthur Lee to Samuel Adams, June 10, 14, 1771, in Arthur Lee Papers, Box 2.

56. Samuel Adams to Arthur Lee, September 27, 1771, in *Cushing* (ed.), *Writings of Samuel Adams*, II, 230–37.

57. Samuel Adams to Arthur Lee, October 31, 1771, in *Ibid.*, II, 264–67; Junius Americanus letter in *London Public Advertiser*, October 29, 1771, quoted in Riggs, "Arthur Lee and the Radical Whigs," 39–40; Douglas Adair and John A. Schutz (eds.), *Peter Oliver's Origin and Progress of the American Revolution: A Tory View* (San Marino, 1961), 78.

Ratio," a reference to *ultima ratio regnum*, the final argument or reckoning of kings: war. He asked what steps could be taken by a people abused by rulers who "neither fear God nor regard Man," and he warned Lee to resist intimidation and flattery, the favorite tactics of corrupters. He confessed he had "long been of Opinion that America herself under God must finally work out her own salvation," for the British people apparently were "willing to submit and be enslaved." Lee should lose no opportunity to keep him informed. He feared Whiggish vigilance was "much out of fashion" amidst tranquil times. Indeed, Adams felt that the "grand design of our adversaries" was "to lull us into security, and make us easy while the acts remain in force, which would prove fatal to us." [58]

From 1771 to 1773 Adams and Lee struggled against the prevailing placidity. Both men feared that the lull portended ill for the cause of liberty. Lee wanted to keep the spark of resistance aflame in Massachusetts by means of continuous petitions to the British throne. The Virginian believed that, despite Parliamentary revocation of the bulk of the revenue taxes the colonists still had ample reasons for protest against British oppression. In his mind, "If ever we had cause of complaint; that cause still remains." Although the Adams-Lee correspondence slackened in 1772, the writers' ardor for the resistance movement did not. Of British tax schemes, for example, Adams exclaimed, "The Tribute, the Tribute is the Indignity which I hope in God will never be patiently borne by a People who of all the people on the Earth deserve most to be Free." [59] Lee's energy was invested in polemical broadsides fired in the English press at targets in the colonial office, while Adams turned to establishment of committees of correspondence throughout the colonies.

In an effort to stir the colonists and their supporters in Britain, Junius Americanus renewed his attack on Lord Hillsborough. William Samuel Johnson, who served as agent for Connecticut and frequently attended Parliamentary debates with Lee at this time, thought his colleague "a sensible but very sanguine" man who "delights in the fire and fury of

58. Samuel Adams to Arthur Lee, September 27, October 3, November 13, 1771, January 14, 1772, in Cushing (ed.), *Writings of Samuel Adams*, II, 231–36, 264–67, 274–76, 310–313.

59. Arthur Lee to Samuel Adams, April 7, 1772, in Arthur Lee Papers, Box 2; Samuel Adams to Arthur Lee, November 3, 1772, in Cushing (ed.), *Writings of Samuel Adams*, II, 345.

parties." It was his impression that Lee had assailed Hillsborough to please Shelburne. The revived discussion of land grants may have provided another motive. Lee knew that Hillsborough opposed the petition of Samuel Wharton's Grand Ohio Company, but the Virginian also feared that a cunning distribution of money within the administration could "go a great way" to gain favor. Hillsborough seemed to be "universally hated." In 1772 Lee correctly anticipated that he would soon be relieved of his post. His successor, the earl of Dartmouth, at Lee's first glance appeared "a man of good principles, of a fair character, of exemplary life and a friend of America." Nevertheless, Lee sensed that, whatever the new secretary's character, he was not then the key to colonial policy.[60]

Lee's initial dealings with Dartmouth were amicable. The American was impressed by the secretary's piety and sincerity. Yet in Arthur's analysis, Lord North was Dartmouth's mentor and North, in turn, usually reflected the wishes of George III. It appeared to Lee that North's primary concern was maintaining office. He would, therefore, not be likely to redress American grievances, for that would displease the king. Lee's analysis was correct: North's was a conciliatory nature and the king was obstinate. By June, 1773, Lee had dropped the idea that George III was a dupe of his advisers; rather, the Virginian claimed, "There is not an action of his reign, some few treacherous ones excepted, but what manifest it to be his sole wish to be the tyrant of his people."[61] The king was implicated in the plot to subvert liberties.

When Dartmouth replaced Hillsborough, Lee began writing as "Raleigh" instead of Junius Americanus. From December, 1772, to February, 1774, fifteen "Raleigh" essays directed at Dartmouth appeared in the Public Advertiser. Most of Lee's information was obtained in London through John Temple, a former customs officer from Boston who carried a grudge against Thomas Hutchinson and other placemen in Massachu-

60. William Samuel Johnson to Jared Ingersoll, June 15, 1772, in "Jared Ingersoll Papers," Papers of the New Haven Colony Historical Society, IX (1918), 435–36; Arthur Lee to Richard Henry Lee, July 17, 1772, in Hoffman and Molyneaux (eds.), Lee Family Papers, II, 102–103; Arthur Lee to Samuel Adams, July 20, 1772, in Arthur Lee Papers, Box 2; Arthur Lee to Richard Henry Lee [August 7, 1772], in Hoffman and Molyneaux (eds.), Lee Family Papers, II, 107–108.

61. Arthur Lee to Samuel Adams, December 24, 1772, in Arthur Lee Papers, Box 2; Arthur Lee to Samuel Adams, June 11, 1773, in Richard Henry Lee, Life of Arthur Lee, I, 229–32.

setts. Temple was a well-connected personage on both sides of the Atlantic who, like Lee, was disaffected with the British system.[62] Their joint attempt to unseat Dartmouth proved fruitless.

Arthur Lee lapsed into despondency in early 1773. He believed himself to be "the most determined supporter of the cause of America" then residing in Britain. Although he might glory in his own sense of patriotism, his reputation closed many doors to him. He confided to Richard Henry, "Were my fortune independent, this would not give me one moment's concern. I certainly feel that virtue is its own reward. But at the same time I cannot but be sensible, that narrowness of circumstances is a very great obstacle." He was haunted by his financial dependence, a status that made him susceptible to corrupting influences. Later he would scream, "Good God what trouble does the not having been born to a fortune give me—how much has the reverse fatigued the possessor of Stratford." His pangs of deprivation surfaced whenever Arthur thought of Philip Ludwell. Meanwhile, his personal frustrations were mounting. Although he was getting some fees for his work in the chancery courts, his law studies were only at midpoint. The Mississippi Company had been stymied, as had his quest for a colonial agency from Virginia or Massachusetts. Imperial affairs looked no better: "The Court and Ministry, are as hostile to America as ever." Men like the Lees, he decided, must "wrap ourselves in our own virtue and be contented."[63]

Arthur's concern about his dependent status is apparent in the positions he took in imperial affairs. He admired the Bostonians, who would not submit to British power, because he was familiar with the situation in his own personal life. Similarly, he manifested an interest at this time in the legal status of the slave trade. Of this practice he remarked, "Such is the influence of a few African merchants, that our Assembly cannot obtain the King's consent to prohibit so pernicious and inhuman a trade in Virginia. This is one instance in which we feel the galling yoke of dependence."[64] His immediate concern was for the whites rather than the blacks.

62. Arthur Lee to Samuel Adams, January 24, 1773, in Arthur Lee Papers, Box 2; Riggs, "Arthur Lee and the Radical Whigs," 42–43; Bernard Bailyn, *The Ordeal of Thomas Hutchinson* (Cambridge, 1974), 125, 222.
63. Arthur Lee to Richard Henry Lee, February 14, 1773, in Hoffman and Molyneaux (eds.), *Lee Family Papers*, II, 130–31; Arthur Lee to Richard Henry Lee, October 20, 1773, in Arthur Lee Papers, Box 14.
64. Arthur Lee to Joseph Reed, February 18, 1773, in Arthur Lee Papers, Box 2.

Lee's personal mood influenced his outlook on Anglo-American affairs. This may be seen in his reaction to the burning of the revenue cutter *Gaspee* by Rhode Island patriots in June, 1772. Initially he was much pleased by the action. Then when the ministry reacted by dispatching an investigative commission and invoked an ancient statute authorizing transportation of suspects to England for trial, Arthur was aghast. Such actions would bring "things to that ultimate issue, which cannot be warded off, for our advantage too long." More than two years before a clash of arms, Arthur Lee foresaw the path that Anglo-American affairs were to take. He would not plunge headlong into war. Watchful waiting was the policy Arthur counseled for Richard Henry and other defenders of liberty: "To keep alive just sense of our Rights, and of these invasions of them, yet preventing things from coming to an extremity, till increased strength or a favorable moment shall render the issue certainly favorable, seems to be the best patriotism on our part. An unsuccessful struggle now, might perhaps rivet our chains forever." Lee confessed that perhaps "The northern Colonies, are precipitating matters too much," but he assured Richard Henry that the New Englanders "have had more than their proportion of insult and oppression." [65]

The policy of waiting and watching was predicated on Arthur Lee's sense of history. The record of man, as he saw it, was cyclical. Thus as he felt corruption infesting English institutions, he could trumpet to Samuel Adams, "Yes, my friend, like a young phoenix [liberty] will rise plumed and glorious from her mother's ashes. . . . America in her turn will be imperial mistress of the world." The American sun was dawning as that of the English set. These refrains of renewal became frequent literary conceits in Lee's correspondence as did emphasis that America's burgeoning population was symptomatic of progress.[66] Rebirth and births were intimately linked in his thought patterns.

The wish to avoid provoking Britain prompted Arthur to contradict

65. Arthur Lee to Samuel Adams, July 20, 1772, in Arthur Lee Papers, Box 2; Arthur Lee to Richard Henry Lee, February 14, 1773, in Hoffman and Molyneaux (eds.), *Lee Family Papers*, II, 130–131.
66. Arthur Lee to Samuel Adams, December 24, 1772, Arthur Lee to Joseph Reed, February 18, 1773, in Arthur Lee Papers, Box 2; Commager, "America and the Enlightenment," 23–29; deMause, "Formation of the American Personality," 1–30.

previous ideas. His correspondence with Adams had continually harped on themes of centralizing and popularizing the resistance movement in America. Yet when the Masachusetts agitator proposed a general colonial congress be called for 1773, Lee initially opposed the move. From his post in London the Virginian reasoned that such a move would "rouse this country, and perhaps incense her to some hostile measure. The only contention in which we are unequal to her, is in that of arms. It is not wise policy therefore to provoke the issue of the dispute, if our purpose can be compassed without it. For all her ill usage Britain is still our mother country. We are growing stronger every day, and she weaker. Therefore the more we procrastinate any desperate decision, if it must end in that, the fairer will be our prospect of success." [67] Lee preferred to rely on petitions for redress, but warfare had arisen as a persistent alternative.

Two weeks later, under pressure from Adams, Lee made a major turn in thinking. Adams had questioned, "How many Regiments will be thought necessary to penetrate the Heart of a populous Country & subdue a sensible enlightened and brave people to the ignominious terms of slavery." In a confessional reply Arthur explained his position. He affirmed that since the beginning of the dispute between Britain and the colonies he had been motivated by "a general zeal for liberty." He had been sure that, if the colonies were "firmly united," they could "maintain our rights against the power of this country." "No position" seemed clearer to Lee "than that a free people could not be bound by laws not made or assented to by themselves. In so far as they were bound, they are not free." [68] Here was the either/or refrain repetitious in Lee's private and public writings. He also made, with Dickinson, Franklin, and others, the distinction between internal and external legislation as an expedient for imperial cooperation.

The impact of Adams' preachings and his London experiences on Arthur Lee is pivotal in the letter. Independence and violence were now etched in his mind. He had hoped that the Americans could follow an evolutionary path to "the full enjoyment of liberty by inheritance." He

67. Arthur Lee to Samuel Adams, June 11, 1773, in Arthur Lee Papers, Box 2.
68. Samuel Adams to Arthur Lee, April 8, 12, 1773, in Cushing (ed.), *Writings of Samuel Adams*, III, 18–22, 22–25; Arthur Lee to Samuel Adams, June 23, 1773, in Arthur Lee Papers, Box 2.

now feared that if the colonists were forced to resort to violence to defend themselves, their action would precipitate the fall of Britain. He sensed the growing divisiveness in his own Anglo-American status: "The first wish of my heart is that America may be free—the second is, that we may ever be united with this country." A union of the colonies and mother country must be on fair and honorable terms, but these were not forthcoming in British policy. Hence, he predicted, "Their view was to enfeeble and enslave us. . . . From charging us with aiming at independency, they have brought us to consider, and then to claim, and I think in God they will bring us to confirm it." [69] His anticipation became a self-fulfilling prophecy for Lee: the colonies and Britain were on separate courses. He was a member of a crusade with moral as well as political overtones. The cause was preservative as well as preventive in its liberty-consciousness. Lee's goal as an individual was the same as his goal for the colonies. Independence meant freedom. The only other option was dependence and slavery. The imperative was to rebel.

69. Arthur Lee to Samuel Adams, June 23, 1773, in Arthur Lee Papers, Box 2.

CHAPTER IV

Extraordinary Crisis of the Times

The Lee family manuscripts for 1774–1775 reveal distinct changes. Arthur's two brothers in Virginia, Richard Henry and Francis Lightfoot, expanded their network of intercolonial letter writing, strengthening the bond between the Lees and Samuel Adams. Secondly, William Lee, from his position as a merchant in London, emerged as a link between American agitators and their counterparts in the British metropolis. As William gained the offices of alderman and sheriff in city politics, his letters became more captious in their interpretation of the political scene. He was not as confident of reform as Arthur, and he particularly distrusted Shelburne. Thirdly, Arthur Lee's personal correspondence was relatively infrequent, for the bulk of his energy was devoted to negotiating alliances among British factions and to producing essays for public consumption in Britain. His contributions to the press altered in form and tone. He turned away from serialized pieces to more sustained efforts in pamphleteering, and his viewpoint increasingly defended the use of violence on the part of the colonists. More and more colonial resisters sought him out as their contact in London. He became the recipient of communications from pockets of resistance: colonial assemblies, committees of correspondence, and the Continental Congress. These transformations indicate a major turn in the Lees' thinking. These writings reveal the Lees' role in fomenting the drive for independence.

Yet it is difficult to point to a conscious decision by Arthur Lee for a break. The narrowing of options necessitated a negative process of rejecting various imperial bonds and discrediting conciliation, as well as the positive process of learning to envision a separate status for America. Arthur, as an Anglo-American Whig, unquestionably was tormented by the idea of cutting ties with the mother country. In the end he overrode his personal qualms and devoted his energies to charting prospects for an American republic. He was certain a violent struggle would ensue, that the colonists had full justification for their revolt, and that the last hopes for reconciliation had vanished. His polestar in the maelstrom was his belief that America, free of European corruption, was the inevitable seat of liberties.

Letters exchanged between Arthur Lee and Samuel Adams in 1773 focus on a theme they deemed critical to the uneasy Anglo-American connection. The system's major failing in their eyes was that misinformation about conditions and attitudes in the colonies had been transmitted to policy makers in Britain by malignant placemen in America. The chief target for Adams, and thus for Lee too, was Thomas Hutchinson, governor of Massachusetts, a man passionately detested by the American agitators. A possible means to unseat Hutchinson, and thus to reform the imperial connection, came into the hands of the radicals in 1772. Hutchinson's correspondence with British officials in 1768–1769 had been restrained and candid. It contained no sentiment he had not previously proclaimed. Yet when six letters addressed to Thomas Whately fell into the hands of the radicals and were published in Boston in the summer of 1773, their impact, intermeshed with the events of the Tea Crisis, sent a thunderous wave reverberating across the Atlantic Ocean. This potent resource was manipulated by the radicals of the Massachusetts House to destroy Hutchinson. It convinced untold Americans that Whig fears about the subversion of rights were well founded, it led to Franklin's and Lee's commitment to the cause of independence, and it permitted British leaders to implement a policy of coercion. The Hutchinson affair raised the Anglo-American controversy to a level of explosive enmity.[1]

In London, Arthur Lee acted as spokesman for the radicals of Massachusetts. His pen was the transatlantic outlet for Adams' philippics. As Raleigh, Lee aimed his denunciations at Hutchinson and his lieutenant, Andrew Oliver, archexamples of the malignant colonial administrators. Lee explicated, "We have put the most treacherous, worthless, and obnoxious of their fellow subjects in authority" over the colonists. Junius Americanus leveled a second barrel of abuse at British colonial policy. "To condemn a whole People not only unheard, but unapprized of the Accusation, upon the private Representations of a few interested Individ-

---

1. Bailyn, *Ordeal of Thomas Hutchinson*, 225–27, 245.

uals notoriously their Enemies" was, the polemicist judged, a most excessive injustice.[2]

Acquisition of the Hutchinson-Whately correspondence proved fruitful to the designs of Adams and Lee, yet how they were procured remains a mystery. Franklin was certainly the link between the donor and the Boston radicals. Adams, Thomas Cushing, and other leaders of the House evaded Franklin's restrictions and published the letters. Lee was party to the procurement in London and in favor of their transmission to America, yet hesitant about ultimate publication. His role in this episode is clearly that of an accessory. Unfortunately his writings do not pinpoint the source of the information. Contemporaries pointed to John Temple; recent analysis suspects Thomas Pownall.[3] Whatever the source of the leak, the letters exposed Hutchinson's beliefs that constitutional changes necessary for colonial governments included abridgment of British liberties in America. The governor had advocated these changes in the hope of more effectively bonding the colonies to the mother country, but fate had it that his letters would have the opposite effect.

It was Samuel Adams who used the Hutchinson correspondence to fan the flames of crisis. In the spring of 1773, the Boston agitator wrote his counterpart in London to correct false impressions of Boston then circulating in Britain. He asked Lee to broadcast reports of unity within the camp of resistance and of refusal of the Massachusetts House to concede that supreme legislative power lay in the hands of Parliament. Adams joyously reported that the governor had inadvertently aroused the people from their tranquility. The nature of government in the colony and the connection of the colonies to Britain were now spiritedly debated. Fortunately, Adams found at his disposal the Hutchinson letters sent from London by Franklin. In June he reported his triumph—the House brushed aside Franklin's restriction against circulation. Having scrutinized the epistles, the House, by a 101-to-5 vote, found "that the design and tendency of them is to subvert the constitution and introduce arbitrary

2. Raleigh to the Earl of Dartmouth, in Rind (ed.), *Virginia Gazette*, July 8, 1773; Junius Americanus to Dartmouth, in Purdie & Dixon (eds.), *Virginia Gazette*, October 21, 1773.

3. Cecil B. Currey, *Road to Revolution: Benjamin Franklin in England, 1765–1775* (Garden City, 1968), 308–309; Bailyn, *Ordeal of Thomas Hutchinson*, 230–36.

power ino the province." Adams was rapturous: "there is now a full discovery of a combination of persons who have been the principal movers, in all the disturbances, misery, and bloodshed, which has befallen this unhappy country." He sent copies to Lee. Soon the Boston *Gazette* and other colonial newspapers were publishing the notorious letters. Adams pushed his case through the House. George III was petitioned to remove Hutchinson and Oliver. Franklin was instructed to handle the petition. Arthur Lee, it was hoped, would act as legal counsel. Adams trusted that Lee's enthusiasm for liberty, if not his legal training, would prove advantageous in the impeachment proceeding.[4]

The events in Boston remained outside Arthur Lee's control. He was ambivalent about the value of the Hutchinson letters. Like Franklin, Lee felt that publication should be prohibited. He added his pen to the Pennsylvanian's to explain to the Boston radicals, "The letters you have, were obtained by a very singular accident; and you may guess it will not be easy to procure any more at least in a short time. I shall try however to get from Lord D[artmouth] some general idea of the character Hutchinson has given him of the province. No doubt he will for the future be extremely guarded, though perhaps no human circumspection could have prevented the present detection. May providence thus always interfere to confound the politics of wicked men; and teach even the worst of them that honesty is the best policy." When Samuel Adams evaded this cautious advice, Lee altered his position to join in the public denunciation of Hutchinson and Oliver for their "malignant censure against the proceedings of the People, and Invectives against Individuals."[5]

Lee stirred various pools of discontent in 1773. He was engaged in transmission of the Hutchinson letters and pushed the petition for the governor's ouster. Simultaneously, in London he was immersed in debate over the plight of the East India Company. Not surprisingly these affairs merged in his mind. Lee had qualified as a proprietor of the beleaguered

4. Samuel Adams to Arthur Lee, April 22, May 6, 17, June 14, 1773, in Cushing (ed.), *Writings of Samuel Adams*, III, 36–41; John C. Miller *Sam Adams*, 282–83; Samuel Adams to Arthur Lee, June 21, 28, 1773, in Cushing (ed.), *Writings of Samuel Adams*, III, 44–45, 48–49.

5. Bailyn, *Ordeal of Thomas Hutchinson*, 238–39; Arthur Lee to Samuel Adams, July 21, 1773, in Richard Henry Lee, *Life of Arthur Lee*, I, 232–34; Junius Americanus· to the Earl of Dartmouth, in Purdie & Dixon (eds.), *Virginia Gazette*, October 21, 1773.

company, presumably through the purchase of five hundred pounds' worth of stock. Soon he joined in opposition to governmental plans to tighten control of affairs in India and within the company's structure. Because the company had failed to reform itself from within, Lord North moved to remedy its ills from without. Lee interpreted intervention as a further attempt to extend ministerial corruption and a violation of the company's charter. His opposition to the ministry's regulation of voting on company affairs soon won him added notoriety, but Lee quickly withdrew from the limelight. He refused to carry his testimony to Commons, giving as his excuse a lack of confidence based on "being little conversant in public speaking." This retrospective apology marks a personal shortcoming. As a debater in the public press, he appeared profuse and prolix if not persuasive, but his oratorical skills, unlike brother Richard Henry's, proved unremarkable. Perhaps he found face-to-face dialogue threatening to his sense of self-esteem. Despite his imperfections, however, Arthur continued to resist governmental regulation of the East India Company, unfortunately to no avail. He later drew on the experience to buttress his vision of the empire. He saw that riches from India would corrupt Parliament and lead to imperial demise. "In this prospect," he projected, "there is but one consolation. That Liberty, when she abandons this country, will not like Astraea, relinquish us forever; but will fix her favorite seat in the rising regions of America." The statement bares Lee's view of history as cyclical.[6]

As the year 1773 advanced, Lee's mood followed Adams' lead. In one reply to Adams, Lee denounced Hutchinson and Oliver in an attempt to surpass his counterpart in vehemence as a test of patriotism. Then followed a lament that "disunion should be thus sown between two brave people, who united are proof against the world in arms, by men who have neither worth nor wisdom." Although he offered a prayer to God for guidance, efforts to remove Hutchinson were not moving smoothly. Lee would be unable to act as legal counsel in the case because he was at least a year away from being admitted to the bar. Another problem was that the petition of the Massachusetts House could not be delivered until Dartmouth returned from Ireland. Colonial affairs moved slowly. Further

6. Lucy S. Sutherland, *The East India Company in Eighteenth Century Politics* (Oxford, 1952), 217–90; Arthur Lee to Samuel Adams, December 6, 1773, in Richard Henry Lee, *Life of Arthur Lee*, I, 258–61.

delays, in Lee's analysis, could be expected from the corruptible Lord North who would shy away from momentous questions. Nevertheless, his procrastination might work to America's avail: "Every day gives us new light and new strength." Contemplating America's growing population, Lee foresaw "decided victory dwell[s] upon our side."[7]

By the end of 1773 Lee's moral fervor had quickened in his correspondence with Adams. His perception of America's promising mission was coming into focus. The apocalypse was approaching, and Lee believed that God sided with the Americans in their opposition to British policy. They were engaged in a cause whose trinity was "virtue, Liberty and truth." He prostrated himself before Adams, exclaiming, "At first it was a tender point to question the authority of Parliament over us *in any case* whatsoever—time and you have proved that their right is equally questionable *in all cases* whatsover. It was certainly a great stroke, & has succeeded most happily." The ironic twist that Lee gave to the phrase from the Declaratory Act of 1766 was not lost on Adams. That the younger man was now demanding, "This proud usurping Parliament must humble itself before us, and acknowledge the Liberties of America and England to have the same sacred foundation," also brightened the Bostonian's countenance.[8] Under Adams' tutelage Arthur Lee had edged closer to choosing rebellion as the means to assert autonomy for both his native land and himself.

Lee continued in his roles of intelligence source for the Boston radicals and exhorter of American resistance. In October, 1773, he warned of the scheme to send East India Company tea to the colonies and predicted that, if this project succeeded, the company would be corrupted and would therefore never support American petitions for redress. A "thousand other artful ways of enslaving us" would follow if the landing of the tea were not opposed. The Tea Act of May permitted the company a rebate of taxes, lifted a prohibition on direct shipment to America, and established a monopolistic distribution scheme in the colonies. The ministry hoped that prices would be lowered, sales increased, and the surplus of 17 million pounds of tea be decreased. Lord North's sponsorship of

7. Arthur Lee to Samuel Adams, August 23, October 13, December 6, 1773, all in Richard Henry Lee, *Life of Arthur Lee*, I, 234–36, 236–38, 258–61.
8. Arthur Lee to Samuel Adams, October 13, 1773, in Arthur Lee Papers, Box 2.

this legislation and of a bill regulating the internal affairs of the company were apparently well meant, but Lee did not see it that way. North, in the Virginian's eye, was "treachery himself," and his scheme was a "ministerial trick." Lee believed that the first minister was attempting to stir up violence in the colonies in order to perpetuate "the present impositions by coercive means." Arthur's mind functioned in its customary convoluted channel: if North appeared conciliatory, he must really have coercion in mind. North inadvertently made tea a magnified symbol of confrontation for Lee and other zealots guarding constitutional principles and sensitive to American autonomy.[9] Men like Lee—who feared for the colonies as well as the East India Company—made a crisis out of North's program for 1773.

Samuel Adams and his Boston cohorts did not need Arthur Lee to point out the implication of the tea shipments. In early November, before the arrival of the first chests of tea, Adams hinted of impending confrontation: "One cannot foresee events, but from all observation I am able to make, my next letter will not be upon a trifling subject." Adams was true to his word, for his letter of December 31 recounted the Boston Tea Party, "as remarkable an event as has yet happened since the commencement of our struggle for American liberty." The Bostonian dispatched enclosures for Lee so he might impress upon Britons that the colonists were provoked into destroying property in defense of their rights. Adams beamed in satisfaction that the colonists were again aroused and Hutchinson disconcerted.[10]

News of the Boston Tea Party reached London in late January, 1774. Already British sentiment against Massachusetts had been stirred by the effort to unseat Governor Hutchinson. Lee, utilizing the Hutchinson-Whately correspondence and writing as Junius Americanus, failed to persuade London readers that Boston had legitimate grievances. No sympathy swelled for the colonists; the British supported the administration. It did not help that Franklin had become involved in a scandal over procurement of the Hutchinson correspondence. William Whately, brother of

9. Arthur Lee to Samuel Adams, December 22, 1773, in Arthur Lee Papers, Box 2; Lawrence Henry Gipson, *The Coming of the Revolution, 1763–1775* (New York, 1954), 217–19; Darrett B. Rutman, *The Morning of America, 1603–1789* (Boston, 1971), 169.

10. Samuel Adams to Arthur Lee, November 9, December 25, 31, 1773, in Cushing (ed.), *Writings of Samuel Adams,* III, 70–71, 73–77.

the late colonial official who had received the notorious letters, accused John Temple of pilfering the papers. A duel involving swords and pistols failed to settle the issue but prompted Franklin to declare that he had been the party who gained the letters. Hence, by the time Franklin was finally able to testify before the Privy Council on the colony's petition against Hutchinson, opinion was openly hostile to the Americans. Letters written by Lee and Franklin had fallen into the hands of the ministry, which pondered whether both men should be charged with treason for attempting to incite Massachusetts against Britain.[11]

As subagent for the Massachusetts House, Arthur Lee was as deeply immersed in the turmoil as Franklin. Lee had rallied on the side of John Temple when William Whately accused him of dishonorable dueling practices. Although the Virginian never explicitly stated that Temple was the actual source of the Hutchinson letters, he did consider the former customs officer "our valuable friend" and believed that "there is no man more obnoxious to Hillsborough, Bernard, Knox, and all that tribe of determined enemies to truth, to virtue, liberty and America than Temple."[12] This was high praise for a member of the Grenville faction.

Lee had previously taken his position on the Hutchinson correspondence in his Raleigh series directed at Dartmouth. He demanded that Hutchinson be removed. The notorious letters, by Lee's reading, confirmed his preconception that Hutchinson and Oliver were attempting to "subvert the charter rights of the colony; to subject the people to arbitrary government; and to subdue them by military force." To enhance their designs, the conspirators "painted the proceedings of the people in the most false and odious colors, forging falsehoods where misrepresentations would not suffice." The scheme was the "atrocious and . . . Treasonable conspiracy against the constitution." Boston Whigs had just cause. They should be lauded for their patient resolve to trust in impeachment proceedings rather than take the law into their own hands. Yet if the indicted escaped punishment—or worse, were promoted according to British custom—Raleigh predicted "the greatest degree of discontent" would sweep Massachusetts.[13]

11. Bailyn, *Ordeal of Thomas Hutchinson*, 254; Currey, *Road to Revolution*, 324–25; Sosin, *Agents and Merchants*, 154–55, 179–80.
12. Arthur Lee to Samuel Adams, December 22, 1773 in Arthur Lee Papers, Box 2; Richard Henry Lee, *Life of Arthur Lee*, I, 239–40, 270–72.
13. Raleigh to the Earl of Dartmouth, in Rind (ed.), *Virginia Gazette*, May

Although Franklin and Lee agreed on the effort to displace Hutchinson, they were not on the best of terms. Lee was still itching to be a colonial agent in his own right. Through Richard Henry, he continued his quest for the Burgesses' agency. Meanwhile Franklin's "cunning" kept Arthur from the prestigious post with the Massachusetts House. To Samuel Adams, Arthur lamented, "Dr. Franklin frequently assures me that he shall sail for Philadelphia in a few weeks; but I believe he will not quit us until he is gathered to his fathers." The aspirant was probably little salved by Adams' reply that the Massachusetts radicals considered him their most zealous and able advocate in London. Franklin sensed that Lee coveted his place and credited the Virginian's impatience and animosity to Lee's early alliance with Dennys DeBerdt.[14]

In 1774 Franklin and Lee, as objects of ministerial abuse, were bound more tightly than ever. In early January when Franklin received word that he would soon be permitted to present the Massachusetts petition to the Privy Council, he sought out Lee for legal advice. When the Virginian could not be located, Franklin turned to William Bollan, the agent for the Massachusetts Council. Bollan correctly judged that Lee was not qualified to represent Franklin, and Franklin decided not to employ any legal assistance. Tension mounted throughout the month. Rumors flourished that Franklin would be the target of court rancor at the hearing. Franklin perceived that the "torrent of clamor against us increased" as reports of the Tea Party circulated in London. Arthur Lee suddenly returned from Bath, "entered heartily into the business," and persuaded John Dunning, a retired solicitor general, and John Glynn, who would later hold that post, to act as counsel for Franklin. Dunning, Franklin, and Lee then prepared a brief to be used at the inquiry.[15]

The much awaited hearing took place January 29, 1774, in the Cockpit, a large room adjacent to the chamber of the Privy Council. Before a crowded audience that included Arthur Lee, Benjamin Franklin silently

---

19, 1774; Raleigh letter [undated, 1773?], in Richard Henry Lee, *Life of Arthur Lee*, I, 267–69.

14. Arthur Lee to Samuel Adams, June 11, 1773, in Richard Henry Lee, *Life of Arthur Lee*, I, 229–32; Samuel Adams to Arthur Lee, December 25, 1773, in Cushing (ed.), *Writings of Samuel Adams*, III, 73; Franklin to Cushing, July 7, 1773, in Smyth (ed.), *Writings of Franklin*, VI, 81–85.

15. Franklin to Cushing, February 15, 1774, in Smyth (ed.), *Writings of Franklin*, VI, 182–93; Currey, *Road to Revolution*, 325–26.

endured the vile attack of Solicitor General Alexander Wedderburn. Lee believed that the case had been prejudged, that the governor would be acquitted and Franklin and the Massachusetts patriots be besmirched. Even these expectations were exceeded, however, as Wedderburn praised Hutchinson, condemned riotous conditions in Boston, discounted the Hutchinson-Whately letters, and charged Franklin with plotting American independence. Lee dashed off word to Adams of the humiliation inflicted on Franklin and the Massachusetts House. He was moved to praise Franklin, the martyr who, he confided, "cannot be too much commended. The resentment that was brought against him is excessive. . . . These sufferings will, I trust, raise him, as they ought, in the opinion of the People for whom they were incurred." Lee intended to show his newfound affection for Franklin by chastising Wedderburn in the British press. He wanted to share in the illustrious cause and in the suffering, which for Lee was symbolic of redemption. Virtue would be tested.[16]

The Cockpit affair was decisive for both Franklin and Lee. Franklin not only suffered public humiliation at the hand of Wedderburn, but also lost his position and salary as deputy postmaster general for the colonies. Soon after, his hopes for the Grand Ohio Company also fell through. He determined to return to America and align himself with radicalism. Lee could not laud Franklin enough for what he took to be a metamorphosis in sentiment. Arthur reiterated to Adams that Franklin had suffered grave insult "with a firmness & equanimity, which conscious integrity alone can inspire." He welcomed Franklin into the camp of virtuous patriots who stood up for their rights. Wedderburn's scurrilous attack and its affirmation by the Privy Council confirmed "the meanness & malignity" of the administration. Proudly bearing the buckler of "Bostonian," Lee ventured into the press to tilt with the foe. His savage counterattack on Wedderburn and Hutchinson was, perhaps, a tactic intended to divert public attention from reports of the Tea Party.[17] He could little hope to detour Parliament.

By February 8, Arthur Lee was convinced that a flood tide of resentment would result in a new oppressive policy. Starkly he forewarned

16. Arthur Lee to Samuel Adams, January 31, 1774, in Arthur Lee Papers, Box 2; Currey, *Road to Revolution*, 326–32.

17. Arthur Lee to Samuel Adams, February 8, 16, 1774, in Arthur Lee Papers, Box 2; Riggs, "Arthur Lee and the Radical Whigs," 46–48.

Adams, "From the prevailing view here, I think you ought to be prepared for the worst." Parliament would, no doubt, attempt some sort of retaliation for the Tea Party, and Bostonians, although unable to prevent it, should organize to frustrate it. A week later a second letter reported that George III intended to make the Massachusetts Council appointive rather than elective. Lee transmitted the news that the Privy Council had labeled the House petition against Hutchinson "groundless, vexatious and scandalous, and calculated only for the seditious purpose of keeping up a spirit of clamor and discontent" in Massachusetts. Lee credited the absolution of the governor and lieutenant governor to Dartmouth. He feared, not without reason, that the hand of repression was about to strike at patriots like Adams and himself: "It is impossible for me to describe the rancor and sanguinary sentiments which prevail here. I vow to God, I believe they will make no ceremony of taking some of our Lives." Apparently, Dartmouth was ferreting out correspondence among Franklin, Lee, and the speaker of the Massachusetts House with the object of incriminating them as ringleaders of rebellion.[18]

Parliament acted as Lee had predicted. Neither his polemical version of the Tea Party as a reaction to Hutchinson's provocations, nor Franklin's suggestion to have Boston reimburse the East India Company made much impact. Likewise, Dartmouth's effort to prosecute the incendiaries through the ministry was rejected. Rather, it was decided that parliamentary measures, not crown prerogative, should be wielded against the insolent Bostonians. This decision, Arthur alerted Richard Henry, would challenge the moral wherewithal of American patriotism, for the cause of Boston was that of all the colonies. Behind this policy Arthur saw North and George III operating in tandem in "the accursed designs of deliberately destroying the Liberty of his Country," treasonous ideas for an Anglo-American residing in Britain.[19]

Armageddon was approaching. Lee recommended that the colonists stand resolute and united, and he continued to put his trust in petitions. Firm and temperate manifestos should be carefully drafted, "prefaced

18. Arthur Lee to Samuel Adams, February 8, 16, 1774, in Arthur Lee Papers, Box 2; Bailyn, *Ordeal of Thomas Hutchinson*, 256–57, 298.

19. Bernard Donoughue, *British Politics and the American Revolution: The Path to War, 1773–1775* (London, 1964), 37–65; Arthur Lee to Richard Henry Lee, March 18, 1774, in Hoffman and Molyneaux (eds.), *Lee Family Papers*, II, 201–202.

with the strongest professions of respect and attachment to this country; of reluctance to enter into any dispute with her; of the readiness you have always shown, and still wish to show, of contributing according to your ability, and in a constitutional way, to her support; and of your determination to undergo every extremity rather than submit to be enslaved." This was the familiar argument and tactic Lee had relied upon for a decade, but it was now part of a different strategy that Arthur was developing. The petitions should now be composed not only to appeal to moderate men in Britain, but also with European observers in mind. Arthur had come to see, in March, 1774, that it could be Europe "to whose interposition *America* may yet owe her salvation, should the contest be serious and lasting"—uncommonly prescient thoughts.[20]

Lee was not yet moved to endorse overt rebellion. Again he adopted the familiar ploy: "In short, as we are the weaker, it becomes us to be *suaviter in modo*, however we may be determined to act *fortiter in re*." The most useful option was resumption of a colonial boycott of all commercial intercourse with Britain, which, although it might strain colonial purses, would be triply advantageous: Americans would save their money, free themselves from British merchants—"these petty tyrants"—and secure their "general liberties." The policy of economic coercion was implicit in the letter of March 16 from Junius Americanus to the printer of the *Public Advertiser*, a piece widely reprinted in the colonial press. The American propagandist affirmed that Britain was dependent upon American commerce and that the colonists would resort to an "irresistible Mode of Opposition" to counter British coercion.[21]

A flurry of legislation, labeled the Intolerable Acts by American radicals, began to appear the last week of March, 1774. First out was a bill to close the port of Boston, a measure little opposed in either Commons or Lords. Efforts by all three agents of Massachusetts failed to affect the measure. William Bollan was not permitted to read petitions in Parliament. Benjamin Franklin conferred privately with certain M.P.'s in vain. Arthur Lee cranked out separate addresses to the king, Lords, and Commons. These round robins were signed by as many natives of the colonies

---

20. Arthur Lee to Richard Henry Lee, March 18, 1774, in Hoffman and Molyneaux (eds.), *Lee Family Papers*, II, 201–202.

21. Riggs, "Arthur Lee and the Radical Whigs," 57; Junius Americanus to [?], March 16, 1774, in Arthur Lee Papers, Box 13.

as Lee could recruit in London. Franklin considered such protests "ably drawn" but unfortunately ineffective.[22]

Lee's petition to the House of Lords was published in the London *Evening Post* on March 25 and read to the peers by Shelburne three days later. The piece was mainly a plea that Parliament hear the colonial version of the Tea Party before condemning Boston. Lee hoped that Americans were "entitled to the rights of natural justice, and to the common law of England, as their unalienable birthright." He depicted the bill to close Boston harbor as an act that would punish the innocent. He asked that Parliament rely on colonial law for restitution to the East India Company and argued that Parliamentary intervention in the due course of colonial law was "as unnecessary as it is arbitrary and unjust."[23]

This petition met the same fate as Lee's previous efforts had. The Lords, unswayed by his rhetoric, ordered the remonstrance to lay on the table. George III likewise proved obdurate when Lee's effort was read March 31, the day the Boston Port Act took effect. Lee believed the legislation to be the first step to force explicit recognition from America of parliamentary right to taxation. More drastic measures, including the dispatch of General Thomas Gage and three regiments to reduce Boston to "entire obedience," were in the wind. "The storm," Arthur signaled Francis Lightfoot, "runs high; and it will require great prudence, wisdom, and resolution, to save our liberties from shipwreck." Recalling the suggestion of Samuel Adams, Arthur recommended "a general Congress of the Colonies" be called, preferably for Annapolis. There the meeting might be safe from military or naval interference on the part of the British. He persisted in his belief that if the Congress sanctioned nonexportation and nonimportation, redress would follow: 'If you have virtue enough to resolve to stop, and to execute the resolution of stopping your efforts and imports for one year, this country must do you justice." He

22. Riggs, "Arthur Lee and the Radical Whigs," 183–90; Franklin to Cushing, April 2, 1774, in Smyth (ed.), *Writings of Franklin*, VI, 224–26.

23. "The Petition to the House of Lords, from Several Natives of America, read March 28, 1774," in Peter Force (ed.), *American Archives, Fourth Series: Containing a Documentary History of the English Colonies in North America, from the King's Message to Parliament of March 7, 1774, to the Declaration of Independence by the United States* (6 vols.; Washington, D.C., 1837–46), I, 58–59. Among the signers were Arthur Lee, William Lee, Edward Bancroft, and Henry Laurens. Rind (ed.), *Virginia Gazette*, May 26, 1774, reprinted the petition.

emphasized Britain's dependence on tobacco and naval stores from the southern colonies. But the tandem tactics of petitions and boycotts were ineffective, and he could conceive of no alternative. If America did not resist the closing of Boston harbor, Lee foresaw further repression by British politicians. The haunting fear returned: "For you may depend upon it, that if they find the chains can be easily imposed, they will make them heavy, and rivet them fast." [24]

Following an Easter recess Parliament returned to consider further punishment for Massachusets. By May 20 the Massachusetts Bay Regulating Act and the Impartial Administration of Justice Act had been passed overwhelmingly and signed by the king. Together with a revised Quartering Act to sustain military rule, this program was sent to General Gage, the new governor, on June 3. Arthur Lee and other American symphathizers had protested in vain against this coercive policy. They had hoped that the king did not share the anti-American animosity. On May 14, William Lee and Stephen Sayre, in their capacities as sheriffs of London, presented yet another petition from Arthur's pen, which pleaded that the king withhold signature from the baleful legislation. The previously warm attachment the colonials had shown the royal family would be in jeopardy if George III imposed "absolute power and laws of extreme rigor" on America. When these appeals were cast aside, Arthur privately pronounced that Parliament was "under a very scandalous & undue influence of the King and his ministers." Passage of the Coercive Acts convinced Arthur Lee that George III, the cabinet, and both houses of Parliament all wanted to oppress the colonies.[25]

In the 1760s Arthur had thought that evil or ignorant individuals in Parliament and the colonial service had spawned the anti-American measures. In the 1770s he began to believe that the disease emanated from the monarchy and spread outward to include M.P.'s and colonial officials. The change in his thinking about causes meant a change in his ideas about American resistance. Remonstrances and lawsuits were suitable means to change specific laws or personnel, but if anti-Americanism pervaded Brit-

24. Force (ed.), *American Archives*, I, 58–61; Arthur Lee to [Francis Lightfoot Lee], April 2, 1774, in Hoffman and Molyneaux (eds.), *Lee Family Papers*, II, 205–207.

25. Donoughue, *British Politics*, 87–102; Force (ed.), *American Archives*, I, 96; Riggs, "Arthur Lee and the Radical Whigs," 188–92; Arthur Lee to [Richard Henry Lee], July 30, 1774, Arthur Lee Papers, Box 2.

ish governing circles, there were only two options: a complete overthrow of the malignant politicians by Anglos and Americans or a break in the empire.

Arthur Lee's moods rose and fell according to the fortunes of the movements he joined. Thus in the spring of 1774, as Parliament was considering punishments for Massachusetts, he lapsed into a personal depression. This despondency, characteristically, was revealed in a letter to brother Francis Lightfoot rather than to Samuel Adams or even Richard Henry Lee. To these more fanatical correspondents Arthur could not or would not admit to possessing a sense of self. He was thus presented with a quandary. From his reading of Montesquieu and others, he had readily adopted a differentiation between virtue and honor. The former was the main support of republics; the latter was at the core of free monarchies. Virtue called for selflessness; honor indicated self-assertion and recognition of the individual. Lee's self-image was increasingly toward virtue and hence republicanism. Yet he was not insensitive of his own personal ambition and the role he sought within the British empire. As he now paused to reflect on the course of his life amidst tumult, Arthur revealed a struggle between his inner and outer worlds. He lamented to Francis Lightfoot "that my fortune & my temperament are perpetually combatting against my inclination & my judgement." Longing to retreat to a blissful and tranquil retirement—his idealized image of Virginia squirearchy—Arthur found instead that fate had thrown him "into public life, and the impatience of my nature makes me embark in it, with an impetuosity and imprudence which increase the evils to which it is necessarily subject." Was this a sincere self appraisal or mere posturing? Arthur claimed to have found public life an endless pursuit, "turbulent and deceitful. One bubble is no sooner burst than another arises, with something new to engage, and irritate its deluded pursuers." He reached, he faltered, he suffered, and he persisted.[26]

His unhappiness with life could be traced to Lee's frustrated efforts to operate within the British political milieu. Mounting personal frustra-

26. Arthur Lee to [Francis Lightfoot Lee], April 2, 1774, in Hoffman and Molyneaux (eds.), *Lee Family Papers*, II, 205–207; Robert R. Palmer, *The Challenge* (Princeton, 1959), Vol. I of Palmer, *The Age of Democratic Revolutions: A Political History of Europe and America, 1760–1800* (2 vols.; Princeton, 1959), 58.

tions made him an easy victim of the conviction that corruption ruled all of life. He observed, "The busy haunts of men furnish more to lament than to rejoice in; to censure, than to praise. They are filled with scenes of false happiness, and real misery, variety of vice and wretchedness." [27] This theme of disillusionment was an increasingly critical component of the Virginian's world view.

Lee believed, however, that part of the world had escaped the cancerous growth of corruption. America was the land of newborn optimism. Perhaps in defiance of the Scottish rationalism heaped on him throughout his formal education, he retained a persistent streak of romanticism, namely an idealized image of America and its prospects. In contrast to life as he knew it in London, he cherished the belief that "it is rural retirement only, rural innocence, rural tranquility, which excite an uninterrupted flow of ideas, amiable and delightful. In these passing scenes, the perturbed spirits settle into a calm, productive of more real happiness than all the splendor of fortune, all the pomp of power can bestow." Such images were not uncommon to this generation of Virginia gentry. Paradoxically, ten years later when he contemplated this era of his career, Arthur mused that the circumstances of his personal situation in England in the 1770s were promising "but the peculiar and extraordinary crisis of the times prevented me from being entirely happy, and pursuing the fortune which sat with golden plumes within my reach." [28] Did he ever realize that a theme common to his contemporary observations and later reflections was his wish for "fortune," the badge of personal independence and of the self-interest he found so damnable in others?

The soul-searching and disillusionment evinced in Lee's correspondence in the spring of 1774 together with his public pronouncements indicated a ripeness for rebellion. His confidence in existing authority had eroded; his loyalty to the ideals of liberty and America outshone older attachments. Membership in the British empire had grown burdensome. Men like Hutchinson and Dartmouth were undeserving of the power and prestige they commanded. Most importantly the government was, as analyst Robert R. Palmer has noted, "sensed as distant, apart from the governed

27. Arthur Lee to [Francis Lightfoot Lee], April 2, 1774, in Hoffman and Molyneaux (eds.), *Lee Family Papers*, II, 205–207.
28. *Ibid.*; "Arthur Lee's Indian Journal," [December 24, 1784?], in Richard Henry Lee, *Life of Arthur Lee*, II, 392.

and not really 'representing' them." In this situation of alienation Lee's sense of community lay with America and "the liberties of my country-men," despite his station in London.[29]

Lee's anomie, rooted as it was in the political context, was subject to rapid alteration. In the period 1770 to 1773, he frequently voiced despair over colonial slippage into luxury and corruption. In 1774 as an atmos-phere of crisis intensified, his sagging verve was renewed and fortified by letters from kindred spirits in the colonies. Samuel Adams wrote that if Britain did not return "to the principles of moderation and equity . . . *the entire separation and independence of the colonies*" would soon come to pass. Adams reassured his correspondent that he yearned for "permanent union with the mother country, but only on the principles of liberty and truth. No advantage that can accrue to America from such a union can compensate for the loss of liberty." Adams emphasized, as had his cor-respondence from Richard Henry Lee, that "we make one uniform, steady effort to secure an explicit bill of rights for British America." The British empire must be founded on "the principles of moderation and equity."[30] A return to the imperial relationship of 1763 seemed to Adams, the proper reform. Arthur Lee and Adams agreed that all revenue legislation passed during the last decade was both unconstitutional and the source of unrest.

Not all of Lee's correspondents in America were as bellicose as Sam-uel Adams. Arthur's acquaintance from 1768, Daniel Dulany, Jr., agreed that "every efficient measure, should be taken against the British Parlia-ment in their designs to tax America," but he cautioned Americans to use moderation in their resolves in order to avoid British charges of injustice. Philadelphians, according to Benjamin Rush, were growing "more san-guine daily from the success of our opposition to the measures of the court." The careful colonist John Dickinson doubted that intelligent En-glishmen could seriously think "of sheathing their swords in bosoms so affectionate to them" or contemplate a war destined to ruin Britain. He posited the idea that Lord North intended to dethrone George III "by the calamities and convulsions." Dickinson had not yet endorsed Arthur's

29. Palmer, *The Challenge*, 21; Arthur Lee to [Francis Lightfoot Lee], April 2, 1774, in Hoffman and Molyneaux (eds.), *Lee Family Papers*, II, 205–207.

30. Samuel Adams to Arthur Lee, April 4, 1774, in Cushing (ed.); *Writings of Samuel Adams*, III, 97–102.

conviction that the king was leading rather than following his advisers. His cautious views contrasted sharply with the harangues flowing from Richard Henry, who could not overemphasize the grave danger to America "when the dirty Ministerial Stomach is daily ejecting its foul contents upon us." This outburst was followed by the Lee litany praying for a united and manly stand of the colonies in defense of their rights.[31]

In the spring of 1774 Arthur Lee again enlisted his pen in the colonial cause. As was his custom, he lashed out at British policy and politicians in pseudonymous newspapers screeds. This time the signature was "Bostonian." The series aimed at Alexander Wedderburn's mistreatment of Benjamin Franklin and condemned British coercion of Massachusetts, but Lee was not tied narrowly to this issue. In April a 140-page pamphlet entitled *Answer to the Considerations on Certain Political Transactions of the Province of South Carolina* was published in London. The essay, reflecting concern for sovereignty in so critical a period, was written by Lee for Henry Laurens and Ralph Izard, two South Carolinians then residing in London, who wanted to refute an earlier pamphlet written by Sir Egerton Leigh, attorney general of the colony and a bitter foe of Laurens. Leigh had championed the cause of the Council of South Carolina in its dispute with the House of Assembly over money bills. This controversy dated from December, 1769, when the lower house, without consent from the council or royal governor, had boldly voted £1,500 to the Bill of Rights Society to pay John Wilkes's debts. The action touched off a most disruptive explosion. The House refused to cooperate with the council. In the colony no tax bill was passed between 1769 and 1774, and no legislation at all gained the approval of both bodies after February, 1771. In Charleston as well as London bitter arguments focused on which side in the Wilkes fund controversy had the best constitutional foundation.[32] Laurens found Lee's brand of patriotism to his liking, supplied the penman

31. Daniel Dulany, Jr., to Arthur Lee, May, 1774, in Force (ed.), *American Archives*, I, 354; Benjamin Rush to Arthur Lee, May 14, 1774, in Butterfield *et al.* (eds.), *Letters of Benjamin Rush*, I, 85; John Dickinson to Arthur Lee, August 24, 1774, quoted in Colbourn, *Lamp of Experience*, 116; Richard Henry Lee to [Arthur Lee], June 26, 1774, in Ballagh (ed.), *Letters of Richard Henry Lee*, I, 114–18.

32. Riggs, "Arthur Lee and the Radical Whigs," 58–70; Jack P. Greene (ed.), *The Nature of Colony Constitutions: Two Pamphlets on the Wilkes Fund Controversy in South Carolina By Sir Egerton Leigh and Arthur Lee* (Columbia, 1970), 37–42.

with a subsidy, and awaited the essay justifying the stance of the House. Lee's work was done by February but not published until later, perhaps because events—such as the Coercive Acts—now pushed aside the arguments from the adversaries Leigh and Lee. Neither author's work was widely purchased.

The key point of contention for the pamphleteers was what roles the crown and local custom would take in the government of South Carolina. Stumbling into historical error and misconstruing the rival argument, Lee answered Leigh's argument point by point. Leigh had contended that the lower house owed its existence to the king's pleasure, that innovations by the representatives had unbalanced the constitution. Lee countered by exclaiming, "The Rights of Privileges of the House of Commons spring from the Rights and Privileges of *British* Subjects, and are coeval with the Constitution. They are neither created, nor can they be abolished by the Crown."[33] The Virginian argued for a degree of self-government for South Carolinians. Actual practices in government in the colony since its establishment—especially the evolution of representative government—gave shape and content to the constitution. Customs and usages had been integrated into colonial law. Law, in turn, harnessed the will of policy makers. It is apparent that colonial views of the nature of the British empire were becoming increasingly divergent. The ultimate implication of Lee's argument was autonomy for the Americans.

Disturbed, perhaps even harassed, by animosity manifested toward "every active friend of America," Lee thought it best to leave England temporarily. At about the time *Answer to Considerations* was published, Arthur accepted the invitation of Ralph Izard and his wife to visit Rome. Little could be done in England until American radicals at home developed a program to counter the Coercive Acts. Nonetheless, at Franklin's behest, Lee tried his hand at another pamphlet, *A True State of the Proceedings in the Parliament of Great Britain and in the Province of Massachusetts Bay.* A rebuttal to reports of colonial violence, this work was drawn from materials gathered by Franklin, published through Franklin's connections, and financed by the Massachusetts House.[34]

33. Greene (ed.), *Nature of Colony Constitutions*, 46–55.
34. Arthur Lee to [Francis Lightfoot Lee], April 2, 1774, in Hoffman and Molyneaux (eds.), *Lee Family Papers*, II, 205–207; Franklin to Cushing, June 1, 1774, in Smyth (ed.), *Writings of Franklin*, VI, 231–32; Thomas R. Adams,

A True State, Lee's fifth pamphlet on imperial affairs within a decade, was uncharacteristically straightforward. Perhaps Franklin's documentation or his counsel had helped purge Lee of his customary virulence and cavil. Perhaps the temperateness of his essay illustrated Arthur's recognition of the explosive atmosphere. Again the propagandist attempted to prove that the British had provoked the people of Massachusetts in the crisis over tea. Proceeding from numerous accounts of the colony's exertions in the French and Indian War, Lee catalogued the injustices inflicted by a stream of officials including Bernard, Hutchinson, and Hillsborough. Since 1764, in this interpretation, the Massachusetts House had resisted any tax. Since that date repeated affirmations of loyalty to the king and Parliament had been dispatched by the colonists. Popular petitions for redress went unread in Britain, while malignant men had been rewarded in direct proportion to the misinformation they had transmitted. Within the colony, although the popular faction had tried to pacify less orderly elements of society, the attempt was foredoomed, for "Every Species of Insult and Outrage was, as if purposely, practiced to drive the People into some violent Acts, which should justify the letting loose the Military upon them." Under such conditions, neither restraint nor relief was possible.[35]

Thomas Hutchinson was portrayed as the archprovocateur, a cunning bureaucrat who in 1773 had sought to ensnare the colonists by forcing the Massachusetts Council and House to consider the question of the supreme legislative authority of Parliament. The representatives, according to Lee, "had never ventured to agitate," this question and they answered reluctantly that Parliamentary authority did not extend "to the levying of Taxes in any form on His Majesty's Subjects in this Province."[36]

Less a pamphlet than a compilation, *A True State* was replete with lengthy quotes from House petitions, colonial dispatches, and private correspondence. Lee used these sources to recount the explosions of 1773—

American Independence: The Growth of An Idea (Providence, 1965), 94; Richard Henry Lee, *Life of Arthur Lee*, I, 269; Kammen, *Rope of Sand*, 212.

35. [Arthur Lee], *A True State of the Proceedings in the Parliament of Great Britain, and in the Province of Massachusetts Bay, Relative to the Giving and Granting the Money of the People of that Province, and of all America, in the House of Commons, in Which They Are Not Represented* (London, 1774), 16.
36. *Ibid.*, 24.

Hutchinson's letters, Wedderburn's abuse of Franklin, the Tea Party— then artfully asked his readers to form their own judgment of the reasons for colonial discontent. The cause lay in the stimulus. Lee besought the British to imagine themselves in the place of the colonists. He concluded that, though manifold grievances existed, the crucial complaint was "the having their money taken from them without their consent." All Americans wished "to return to the state in which they were" before taxation for revenue commenced. They wanted not independence, but only a full and open hearing. The current policy of coercion, the answer to seven years of supplication on the part of the colonists, must be reversed.[37]

Possibly *A True State* did not sell well in Britain, for when a companion piece, *An Appeal*, dispatched by Lee as he passed through Paris in early summer, arrived in London, minor difficulties arose. At least one printer rejected the essay before Franklin approached John Almon, predicting that publication would be profitable, for the pamphlet was well written and the public receptive. Almon wisely accepted the proposition, and indeed, the piece proved so popular that thousands of copies were run off. Four editions appeared in London, one in New York, and it was eventually serialized in Purdie's *Virginia Gazette*. Evidently this lucrative endeavor created a fissure in American solidarity in London: both Franklin and William Lee later claimed credit for supervising the publication.[38] Almon, familiar with Arthur Lee through Junius Americanus writings, found the assocation to his liking. Lee favored him with two more pamphlets in 1775.

Posing as an old member of Parliament—a role he fantasized about— Lee presented a temperate and well-organized argument in *An Appeal*.[39] This effort at persuasion indicates a twofold transformation in Lee's rhetoric. He now aimed at a wider audience for his pamphleteering than simply the gentleman ruling class of Britain. In tone he sought to be less

37. *Ibid.*, 37–39.
38. Kammen, *Rope of Sand*, 212–13; Franklin to Jane Mecom, July 28, 1774, in Carl Van Doren (ed.), *The Letters of Benjamin Franklin and Jane Mecom* (Princeton, 1950), 145–46; Richard Henry Lee, *Life of Arthur Lee*, I, 262.
39. [Arthur Lee], *An Appeal to the Justice and Interests of the People of Great Britain in the Present Disputes with America. By an Old Member of Parliament* (London, 1775); Gordon S. Wood, "The Democratization of Mind in the American Revolution," in *Leadership in the American Revolution* (Washington, D.C., 1974), 70.

emotional and to depersonalize the Anglo-American rift. Demonology was replaced by political science. Devoid of personal rancor and concerned with exposition of American rights, this essay drew on Arthur's recent law studies, his previous command of the classical heritage, and a sampling of Lockean history. He depicted the gravity of the situation dramatically: the disharmony between Great Britain and the colonies dating from 1764, if not rectified, would lead to American independence. With uncharacteristic lucidity Lee progressed through consideration of two separate crucial questions for Britons: "Whether we have a right to tax the colonies? and, Whether it be expedient to exercise that right." [40] Both queries were answered resoundingly in the negative after a lengthy discourse on theory and practice of taxation and a farsighted prediction of the course of a war between Great Britain and America.

Founding the statement not only on English practice and Lockean theory, but on "an eternal law of nature," *An Appeal* posited that "taxation and representation are constitutionally inseparable." Lee used examples from English and European history to support a second point, that the consent of the governed was necessary to appropriation of the people's property. A survey of the relations between Britain and other parts of the empire, such as Ireland, convinced Lee that this right of consent had been upheld. A review of the history of the American colonies showed "that this right of their giving money by their own consent alone, has been always claimed, asserted, and exercised by Americans; and that the crown and parliament has constantly recognized the exercise of it, til the year 1764." Further, there was no truth to the contention that emigration to America divested Englishmen of their rights.[41]

The right of property was the prerequisite for all rights. In *An Appeal* Lee, for once, specified the imperial connection. Perhaps he was sincere; perhaps he was merely propagandizing. He escaped his usual Manichean conception to make a distinction: "The Americans are subordinate, when we control them for our advantages, in the means of acquiring property; when we add to that the practice of taking the property so acquired, at our pleasure, they are slaves." At this time and in this piece, Lee argued that the proper colonial roles were subordinate to and dependent on Britain. As there was no delegation of Americans in Parliament, that

40. [Arthur Lee], *An Appeal*, 3.
41. *Ibid.*, 4–5, 11.

body possessed no right to legislate taxation over the colonists. Parliament's unconstitutional practice over the past decade had reduced the people of America to "a state of absolute villeinage."[42]

The second part of *An Appeal* pointed out that taxation was both impractical and profitless. If a coercive policy were maintained, Lee prophesied a war between Britain and the Bourbons and a revolt of America within five years. If British-American strife arose, France would intervene, Americans would not meekly succumb, and Britain would be hard pressed. Even if Britain were victorious, war would prove fatal to her schemes of empire: "If we succeed, we are ruined. If we do not succeed . . . we should be repulsed, to what a State of humiliation shall we be reduced." Lee found the latter fate more probable, and he suspected treachery. "Is it that a serious system of slavery has ascended the back stairs, the first line of which is to subjugate America?" he asked. "One would be very apt to suspect this, had we not the royal assurances that his majesty has no interest, can have no interest, separate from that of his people." Although he could only imply that he suspected George III, Lee flatly contended, "There is no feeling for their [the people's] interests either in the cabinet or in parliament; their representatives sacrifice every thing to their own pride and profit."[43] British government had lost its virtue.

Lee still believed that disharmony in the empire would vanish if the relationship reverted to what it had been in 1763. The second edition of the pamphlet endorsed the stand of the Continental Congress as "the fairest ground for reconciliation." In summarizing his argument Lee could not restrain his pen. The House of Commons, he mocked, had as much right to dispose of property in America "as the Divan at Constantinople has in England." Passage of the Coercive Acts stirred him to call out, "Spirit of the Stuarts, look down and wonder! This single transaction will put all your merits to blush!" If the British people did not intervene in formulation of colonial policy, Lee predicted, "a great revolution will ensue."[44]

Possibly Arthur appealed to the electorate rather than to Parliament or the court because he sensed that there would soon be an election. It is

42. *Ibid.*, 30–31, 35.
43. *Ibid.*, 42–44, 48.
44. *Ibid.*, 49, 54, 57–58.

more probable, though, that he was simply disillusioned by the fate of previous petitions addressed to men in power. For whatever reason, *An Appeal* emphasized that the British nation at large must be convinced that America had suffered, that her grievances were real, and that justice was mandatory. Britons must disregard the interpretations offered by colonial officials, for these were prompted by "Prejudice and imaginary interests" and showed the situation in America "through a false medium." Patriot leaders, the British should understand, had come to see "an invasion of their rights and liberties, as convinced them there was a design in his majesty's ministers to enslave them." No chimera, this conspiracy "of the crown'" would subvert English liberties if it were successful against the colonists.[45]

The writing of *An Appeal* probably took up a large part of Arthur Lee's time in Paris. He later revealed his pride in its popularity but did not record the impact it made. Lee could at best remind himself that he had again done what he could to inform the British of the colonial contentions in the crisis. Whenever the American question had come before Parliament, he had busily propagated the radical perspective in the London press. Reprintings of *An Appeal* can serve as a gauge of the influence of Lee's essays. One close student of his publications asserts that *An Appeal* was the most successful pamphlet published between John Dickinson's *Letters from a Farmer* in 1768 and Thomas Paine's *Common Sense* in 1776.[46] The piece little impressed M.P.'s and other Britons, though, for moderation in tone and regression of policy were not then in style.

Lee may have breathed easier as he journeyed over Europe in the summer of 1774. He was heartened by European admiration for the patriot cause. On August 22 he and the Izards were in Geneva where they made an unsuccessful bid to see Voltaire. By November 15 they had made their way to Rome, where Arthur, learning that George III had called for the election of a new Parliament, cut short his stay and hastened back to London alone. Thwarted by ice and snow along the route, Lee did not arrive in London in time to participate in city and parliamentary elections. The latter event he later catalogued as "a ministerial maneuver, for the purpose of carrying on the war against America."[47]

45. *Ibid.*, 61–63.
46. Riggs, "Arthur Lee and the Radical Whigs," 67.
47. Ralph Izard to Henry Laurens, August 22, 1774, in Anne Izard Deas (ed.),

The general election of 1774 was a key test for Anglo-American radicalism. Lee was most surprised by the results; the Bill of Rights Society less so. Whereas city radicals avoided the disaster of 1771, there was yet little to console them. In September, John Wilkes had finally attained his goal of becoming Lord Mayor of London. He and John Glynn, Arthur's acquaintance and occasional employer, then ran unopposed for the Middlesex seats in Commons, pledging to repeal the Coercive Acts. City candidates Frederick Bull, George Hayley, John Sawbridge, and Richard Oliver also were selected as M.P.'s, but radicalism was frustrated elsewhere in Britain. Lee's brother William lost in a bid at Southwark as did his crony Stephen Sayre at Seaford. Perhaps Arthur had wished to contend for office himself. Twelve Wilkesites, only two of whom came from outside the city, won seats in Commons. This faction, no matter how vocal or strategically placed, stood little chance of either bringing about parliamentary reform or moderating colonial policy. The timing and conduct of the election resulted in deep harmony between crown and Parliament on the American issue. Any hope Lee had had for an alliance between city radicals and the Opposition was overwhelmed by the pervasively repressive tone of the new Parliament.[48] In his absence, Lee's cause had faltered again.

Arthur Lee was back in London by December 1, soon after the new Parliament had been opened by George III. His brother William quickly brought him up to date on events of the past half year. Doubtless William's jaundiced view of American affairs affected Arthur. The brothers agreed war was in the offing and the bond of allegiance between king and colonial subjects had been shattered, but Arthur refused to share William's complete disgust for Shelburne and other luminaries of the Opposition. Immediately Arthur alerted Richard Henry to the gravity of the situation. The king was bent on divesting Americans of their liberties, and the patriots must prepare for armed conflict. The crisis confronted

Correspondence of Mr. Ralph Izard, of South Carolina, from the year 1774 to 1804, with a Short Memoir (New York, 1844), 12–14, 29; "Arthur Lee's Memoir on the American Revolution," in Richard Henry Lee, *Life of Arthur Lee*, I, 262–63.

48. Riggs, "Arthur Lee and the Radical Whigs," 198–203; Ian R. Christie, "The Wilkites and the General Election of 1774," *Guildhall Miscellany*, XI, (October, 1962), 155–64; Donoughue, *British Politics*, 155–64; Maier, *From Resistance to Revolution*, 234–36.

the Lees with two simple alternatives: "arms or submission must decide the controversy." Arthur knew the nonimportation and nonconsumption agreements brought forth by the Continental Congress would make little impact within a year. He urged Richard Henry to convince Virginians "that nothing but a hearty struggle will preserve their civil and religious liberties." The contest would demand a total effort. Arthur therefore directed that corn and grain be planted in place of tobacco in order to provide sustenance for the embattled colonists. Likewise, cotton should be cultivated and sheep withheld from slaughter to provide clothing for the crusaders. Arthur also listed rye and barley as necessities to be grown to fortify the rebellious spirit in America.[49]

Arthur sounded the clarion in public as well as in private writings. He exhorted Americans to resist British military rule in the summer of 1774. Junius Americanus directed a series of thrusts at the new governor of Massachusetts General Thomas Gage, in which he claimed that Gage was part of the ministerial malevolence being worked "by some invisible hands, to destroy the British constitution in America." Initially, Lee asked Gage to renounce his commission, but later he turned, by means of a characteristically convoluted thought pattern, to proclaim, "The liberties of America will be safe, while you are held up as an epitome of the military spirit and generosity of the British nation."[50]

Newspaper warfare also heated up in Britain. "Sagittarius" and "Minos" disputed in the *Public Ledger* whether the Boston agitators and their agent, Franklin, were innocent. There was unproven conjecture that Minos was "That Pitiful Fellow," Arthur Lee. It is likewise uncertain whether Lee wrote the "Tribunus" introduction for the London publication of Thomas Jefferson's *A Summary View of the Rights of British America*. Although these pieces are in harmony with Lee's thoughts and tone, his authorship is problematical since he was absent from England when they appeared. He never claimed them as his own. The ten pieces signed "Vespucius" that appeared in the winter of 1774–1775 are more certainly attributable to Arthur Lee, for the pieces rely heavily on his

49. William Lee to Richard Henry Lee, September 10, 1774, in Worthington C. Ford (ed.), *Letters of William Lee* (3 vols.; New York, 1968), I, 87–94; Arthur Lee to Richard Henry Lee, December 6, 1774, in Arthur Lee Papers, Box 14; Force (ed.), *American Archives*, I, 1040–1041.
50. Junius Americanus to General Gage, in Rind (ed.), *Virginia Gazette*, September 1, 1774; Pinckney (ed.), *Virginia Gazette*, October 27, December 15, 1777.

previous works and they are imbued with his forebodings of war. In these pieces though, Lee chose a new target, Lord George Germain, then a leading advocate of coercion.[51]

So prolific was Lee's pen whenever the American issue loomed in British politics that his contributions might be deprecated as merely the product of personal compulsion. Such an appraisal depreciates both the sincerity with which he approached his task and the impact his efforts made in Britain. Hindsight also leads to the unfortunate suspicion that his repeated premonitions of war were made in increasingly welcome tones. Warnings of an impending revolution and war and lists of preparations for them indicate Lee's ideological commitment and his limitation; he was entranced by the bifocal vision of a corrupt Britain and an American millenium. His daily personal concerns with finding funds for law training and with his imminent call to the bar provided occasional distractions.[52]

In December, 1774, while tirelessly producing Cassandralike warnings of catastrophe, Arthur Lee was also working with Benjamin Franklin and William Bollan to bring about a reconciliation between the colonies and the mother country. This effort was neither foredoomed nor hypocritical in their eyes. These three, the only agents who wished to represent the First Continental Congress in Britain, presented the king with an American petition in mid-December. Lord Dartmouth, who received the petition, promised to lay it before Parliament after the lengthy holiday recess. To Lee, who had spent the last six years advocating such tactics, a dramatic turnabout appeared possible. His initial reaction to the petition, the Declaration of Rights, and the Continental Association fashioned by the Congress was one of respect. "The proceedings of the Congress meet with universal approbation here, and have operated like an electrical

51. Crane (ed.), *Franklin's Letters*, xxvii–xxviii; John E. Alden, "John Mein: Scourge of the Patriots," *Publications of the Colonial Society of Massachusetts*, XXXIV (February, 1942), 571–99; Riggs, "Arthur Lee and the Radical Whigs," 9, 49, 60, 204; Paul L. Ford (ed.), *The Writings of Thomas Jefferson* (10 vols.; New York, 1892–99), I, 423; Thomas P. Abernethy (ed.), *A Summary View of the Rights of British America* (New York, 1943), vi, xvi; Julian Boyd *et al.* (eds.), *The Papers of Thomas Jefferson* (19 vols.; Princeton, 1950–), I, 672–75; Peter O. Hutchinson (ed.), *The Diary and Letters of His Excellency Thomas Hutchinson, Esq.* (2 vols.; London, 1883–86), II, 398, 416.

52. Arthur Lee to Richard Henry Lee, December 13, 1774, in Force (ed.), *American Archives*, I, 1040–1041.

shock upon the ministry and their Dependents," Arthur told Richard Henry. At the brink he was swept by a flurry of optimism. The London merchants, notorious for their previous reserve, seemed on the verge of endorsing colonial grievances, and hopes for a "speedy accommodation" surfaced. Arthur would not modify American claims: "Your demands are made with great moderation; and should not, nay I think cannot be receded from a single Iota. Depend upon it the same firmness and unanimity which have compelled a conciliatory disposition will enforce a full redress." Nonetheless, he saw fit to inject another dosage of fortitude. He forewarned his compatriots "that he who sheathes the sword before the peace is concluded, exposes himself to a shameful defeat."[53]

The source of Arthur's buoyancy lay in the illusion that he was to play a crucial role at this point in history. The crisis beckoned to his theatrical impulses, and he reveled in the role he had designated for himself, keystone of Anglo-American opposition. A union of all the out-groups of British politics now seemed feasible. He ventured forth to enlist Chatham, Shelburne, and other nobles in the dramatic cause. Conversations on Christmas day with Chatham boosted his spirits. According to the Virginian, Chatham praised the moves by the American Congress and believed a settlement was within reach if Parliament would but renounce its right to tax the colonies, and the colonials but acknowledge the supremacy of Parliament. The position was not unlike the situation in 1766 after the repeal of the Stamp Act and the enunciation of the Declaratory Act. Lee did not indicate whether he agreed with Chatham or not, but his previous writings had diverged from the earl's position.

Buoyed by Chatham's observations, Lee believed he could single-handedly ally the disparate elements of the Opposition and the Wilkesites to bring about an abrupt change of policy. Access to Chatham, whom he revered, had made him heady. He overestimated his own influence and the popularity of his cause. Between talks with Chatham and Shelburne he trumpeted to Ralph Izard, "The Rockinghams will of course come in; and we shall form an opposition, which, supported by the popular voice and petitions of the merchants, etc., will be irresistible." It seemed to Lee that efforts to operate within the British system were finally to succeed. He badly wanted reality to fit his fantasy. Excitedly, he for-

53. Arthur Lee to Richard Henry Lee, December 22, 24, 26, 1774, in Arthur Lee Papers, Box 2.

warded a rumor that "the Resolution of the Court is to repeal all the acts except the Declaratory Act and Admiralty Act, that Lords North and Dartmouth are to give place to the Lords Gower and Hillsborough, who are to commence their Administration with these conciliatory measures." He fervidly hoped these reports were founded in fact, but his experiences with British ministers caused him to add, "The utter inconsistancy of this plan is no objection to the probability of it, for these men have been long disciplined to turn and turn, and turn again." In conclusion he told the colonists to doubt such reports and remain resolute. Meanwhile, he closeted himself with Shelburne, Lord Temple, and other Opposition luminaries. All the while the ministry was apparently kept informed of the bustling American's machinations by Lee's apartment-mate, Paul Wentworth.[54]

Lee's optimism was quickly shattered when Parliament considered the American question in January, 1775. As Lee had predicted, Chatham delivered an impassioned speech in praise of American resistance, and the Rockingham faction did support Chatham's resolution to recall troops from Boston. But it did no good. The recommendation was defeated in Lords by a vote of sixty-eight to eighteen. Last-minute efforts by Chatham and Dartmouth in league with Franklin were of no avail either. On February 5, the Massachusetts triumvirate of Franklin, Bollan, and Lee reported their failure to all the colonies: "the Ministry have declared in both Houses the Determination to enforce Obedience to all late laws." More troops were on the way. The cause of virtue, though endorsed by "a considerable Number of good and wise Men in both Houses of Parliament" had suffered another reversal. Coercion, not reconciliation, reigned.[55]

This was the ultimate letdown for Arthur Lee. The first act in the tragedy of his life history had come to a climax. The tactic—the petition-

---

54. Arthur Lee to Ralph Izard, December 24, 1774, in Deas (ed.) *Correspondence of Izard*, I, 35–37; Mark A. DeWolfe Howe, "The English Journal of Josiah Quincy, Junior, 1774–1775," *Massachusetts Historical Society Proceedings*, L (June, 1917), 445–53; Peter O. Hutchinson (ed.), *Diary and Letters of Hutchinson*, II, 339.

55. Alden, *History of the American Revolution*, 162–63; "William Bollan, Benjamin Franklin, and Arthur Lee to the Honorable Speaker of the House of Representatives of the respective colonies," February 5, 1775, in Arthur Lee Papers, Box 2.

ary movement—that had engrossed his energy for more than six years had failed, bitterly disillusioning him. From February, 1775, Arthur Lee looked upon war as inevitable, and he readily adopted the new role of spy. For the next twenty months while he remained in Britain, he continually dispatched reports of troop movements, diagnosed parliamentary development of further coercive legislation, and exhorted the colonists to resist. He was inspired. In February he warned Samuel Adams that ten thousand troops and three generals were headed for Boston. He urged America to hold out in the forthcoming clash: "If the war is protracted and America resists for two years, it is believed here, that the Army will be enfeebled, and this Country in such distress and confusion, if not insurrection, as to compel an alternation of measures." The Virginian's vision was not then of a war for independence between American mainland colonies and the British empire. Rather, he foresaw an upheaval which would have repercussions throughout the empire. He anticipated domestic disruptions in England and advocated the cultivation of the Irish resentment against the English. With crusading zeal, he admonished Adams, "You are therefore to consider your present struggle as of so desperate a temper, that you are neither to expect or give quarter. Whatever blow is struck should from its magnitude and violence be worthy the dignity and desperation of our cause."[56] Thus he welcomed the fires that would test American patriotism.

Although Arthur's faith in American resistance was deep, his suspicious nature made him question the intensity of his compatriots. He was particularly attentive to rumors that the British were planning to subvert the cause by bribing the less ardent leaders. Because the patriots in the middle colonies, strategically placed between the hotbeds of resistance in New England and the South, were susceptible to temptation, Lee kept his correspondents informed of such doubtful men as Joseph Reed and Joseph Galloway of Pennsylvania. Lee categorically condemned Reed, his friend from DeBerdt's circle, as "a man of deep dissimulation and cunning, with whom self alone is sacred."[57] Lee's notions were frequently

56. Arthur Lee to [Samuel Adams], February 2, March 4, 1775, in Arthur Lee Papers, Box 2. That Arthur and William Lee shared these thoughts is evident in William Lee to Landon Carter, March 10, 1775, in Worthington C. Ford (ed.), *Letters of William Lee*, I, 147.
57. Arthur Lee to Samuel Adams, February 24, 1775, in Arthur Lee Papers,

wide of the mark and often appear irresponsible and paranoiac, but in this case, they had some foundation. Galloway did become a Tory leader; Reed was at the time corresponding privately with Dartmouth. John Jay, another patriot Lee accused, seems blameless. Lee and Jay were subsequently personal and political opponents perhaps because of this early incaution.

That the British would attempt to buy off Americans was no fantasy conjured up by an abnormal mind. Arthur Lee knew it firsthand. In London circles he had risen to prominence as a leading agitator for the American cause. Virginians were told by their *Gazette* that "the amiable doctor Lee, admired by all for his literary abilities, and excellent pieces in vindication of the colonies, shines conspicuous as one of the first patriots of the age." This note, probably planted by the Lees, did not indicate Arthur's vulnerability to ministerial attempts to suppress him. His mail was being intercepted, and he was under surveillance. Then in the spring of 1775 Paul Wentworth was commissioned to tempt the ardent American. Wentworth reportedly offered Lee £300, ostensibly to finance another European excursion. Arthur was also told that Richard Henry could be appointed to the council in Virginia and that he himself could receive ministerial support for his bid to become recorder of London. When Lee rejected the enticements, the ministry considered other means of quieting him. It was later rumored in the London press that Arthur Lee was being held in Newgate Prison as a purveyor of sedition.[58]

Lee's eminence as a leading American in England was heightened in March, 1775, by the departure of Benjamin Franklin for America. So harassed were the two that no time was taken to transfer the agencies of the Massachusetts House and Assembly of New Jersey. Franklin simply sent Lee the pertinent papers; he had no time to map out strategy with his successor. The personal differences between the two still festered but since the Cockpit affair, Lee and Franklin had interpreted British policy and calculated American alternatives together. The only notable differ-

---

Box 2; Arthur Lee to [Richard Henry Lee], April 7, 1775, in Hoffman and Molyneaux (eds.), *Lee Family Papers*, II, 366–67; B. D. Bargar, *Lord Dartmouth and the American Revolution* (Columbia, 1965), 100–107.

58. Pinckney (ed.), *Virginia Gazette*, March 15, 1775; Peter O. Hutchinson (ed.), *Diary and Letters of Hutchinson*, I, 434–35; Sosin, *Agents and Merchants*, 222; Riggs, "Arthur Lee and the Radical Whigs," 208.

ence between the two was Lee's conviction that open hostilities were inevitable while Franklin persisted in hopes of economic coercion.[59] When Franklin withdrew from Britain, Lee assumed the post he had coveted for six years. Perhaps Arthur gave no pause to record his impressions of this new role because he recognized the present futility of the colonial agency. The affairs of any particular colony were subsumed by larger concerns.

As 1775 dawned, Arthur Lee returned to city agitation and pamphleteering to voice American views. The S.B.R. resolved, "That the liberties, franchises and chartered rights of our fellow subjects in America, are so nearly connected with those of Great Britain, that the subversion of either must prove equally fatal to both." If this was not Lee's rhetoric, it certainly expressed his position. Likewise he advocated that the S.B.R. beseech its contingent in Parliament to seek justice for America. In February and March tension mounted over the Coercive Acts. Petitions on behalf of repeal were dispatched to the king, crowds swarmed through the streets in protest, and the S.B.R. voted £500 to the distressed inhabitants of Boston.[60] Lee doubtless had a hand in these demonstrations, although only the composition of city remonstrances can be credited to him with any certainty.

In an effort to get the British to look at the crisis from an American point of view, Arthur reworked *An Appeal* into yet another pamphlet, *A Speech*, which was published in March and serialized in April by the London *Chronicle*. In sixty-seven pages Lee listed fourteen "real, dangerous, and alarming" grievances that threatened the "property, personal liberty, and life" of all subjects of George III. He charted the path of British oppression and American complaint since 1763. Central to his argument were two points: Americans should have constitutional parity with the British, and taxation without representation was unconstitutional. Of the first Arthur remarked, "If you consider the Americans as endued with the same feelings, and vested with the same human rights by the God who is our common Maker, you will then perceive, nay feel, that a violation of those rights must be atrocious to them as to you. But if you

59. Howe, "Journal of Josiah Quincy," 468–69; Maier, *From Resistance to Revolution*, 250–55.

60. Force (ed.), *American Archives*, I, 1145; Riggs, "Arthur Lee and the Radical Whigs," 223–26.

deny them this common nature and these common rights, it is time they should look to themselves, and appeal to the Almighty Being to protect them in what he gave." [61] This argument illustrated Lee's altered position. No longer would he contend against specific evils. He now reflected the increased emphasis on natural rights that would be crystallized in the Declaration of Independence.

Although the bulk of the bill of particulars dealt with the implementation of law by the redcoats, the Royal Navy, and customs commissioners in America, Lee pinpointed the "greatest source of the disturbances" to be "the giving and granting the property of the People of America" by Parliament "where they are not represented." He challenged the M.P.'s to produce "one avowedly legal or constitutional instance of taxation without representation." Cuttingly he observed, "There is no magic in the word of Parliament, which makes it necessarily compatible with freedom to be bound by its law in all cases whatsoever. It is the part that the People have in the Constitution of Parliament which renders it protective of liberty, gives security to the subject, and makes them happy in living under the Laws only to which they have consented. Take away this intervention of the People, and Parliament will become only a plausible instrument of Tyranny." [62] Lee's growing defiance of British rule was founded on his quest for colonial self-determination. Unfortunately, the concept of divided sovereignty had not yet been articulated. Neither parliamentary spokesmen nor American resisters could yet fathom protodominion status. Instead, the former became entrenched in a policy of coercion, while the latter gravitated toward independence.

The diagnosis offered in *A Speech* was as familiar as the remedy. The "dangerous and designing men" attempting to separate Britain and America must be removed. These malignant and selfish men, who misrepresented the colonies and misled the mother country, had brought about the Coercive Acts. The panacea was to rout these sycophants from office and return to the system of voluntary requisition. "Peace, prosperity, and reconciliation attend on retraction—division, desolation, and ruin on

---

61. [Arthur Lee], *A Speech, Intended to Have Been Delivered in the House of Commons, in Support of the Petition from the General Congress at Philadelphia, by the Author of an Appeal to the Justice and Interest of Great Britain* (London, 1775, I, 3.

62. *Ibid.*, 22–24.

perseverence" in schemes of taxation for revenue. He reminded the Brittish that "the only band of peace and order among British Subjects is Liberty." Since Parliament had provoked the confrontation, Lee asserted, Parliament should initiate redress. He exhorted the British representatives to rise to the call of the Continental Congress to be "an inquiring, avenging, redressing, reforming House of Commons."[63] Arthur Lee's remonstrance written for the London livery reinforced the latest petition from Congress. Like *A Speech*, the London protest of April 10, although supported by public demonstration, failed to have any effect on George III. Nonetheless the Common Hall produced a second remonstrance in June, thus affirming the city's support for American resistance. The petitioners asked for the removal of the crown advisors inimical to liberties and the dissolution of a Parliament deemed to be persecutory. The king, however, would not be swayed by either city agitation or rhetoric from the pen of Arthur Lee.[64]

Lee's activities in city politics took up a great part of his time in the spring of 1775. Following completion of his law studies on May 5, Arthur turned to managing William Lee's successful campaign for alderman of Aldgate Ward in London. This bid provided the Lee brothers an outlet for further enunciation of their brand of patriotism. William posed as a defender of constitutional liberties who would teach "the Tories of this day, as their ancestors had been happily taught, how vain a thing it is to attempt wresting their liberties from a people determined to protect them." Both Lees had come to see that, as defenders of the "good old cause," they must oppose George III as the Whigs had rebelled against James II.[65] History provided an imperative for action and a model to adopt.

That the path of crisis was determined as much by events in America as by occurrences in Britain, Arthur Lee well knew. In April he wrote,

63. *Ibid.*, 34–40, 52.
64. Riggs, "Arthur Lee and the Radical Whigs," 223–34; Arthur Lee's draft of a remonstrance, in Hoffman and Molyneaux (eds.), *Lee Family Papers*, II, 523; Force (ed.), *American Archives*, II, 1073–1074.
65. William Lee quoted by the London *Chronicle* of June 14, 1775, in Worthington C. Ford (ed.), *Letters of William Lee*, II, 26–27; Earl of Buchan to Arthur Lee, January 5, 1775, in Hoffman and Molyneaux (eds.), *Lee Family Papers*, II, 322; Junius Americanus to Lord Chatham [1775] in Richard Henry Lee, *Life of Arthur Lee*, II, 20–21.

"There is a silence in the New England provinces, which argues an approaching storm." This premonition was soon confirmed by John Dickinson and other colonials who rushed accounts of the battles at Lexington and Concord to Lee. The traumatic events caused the Farmer to lament, "The *immedicable vulnus* is struck. The rescript to our petition is written in blood. The impious war of tyranny against innocence, has commenced in the neighborhood of Boston." Dickinson assured his compatriot in London "that the continent is preparing most assiduously for a vigorous resistance" and that Americans would struggle valiantly for "freedom or an honorable death."[66]

News of the military engagements cast Lee in his familiar role as press agent for American patriots. He made affidavits concerning the encounters available at the Mansion House, residence of the Lord Mayor of London, John Wilkes. Under four pseudonyms—Memento, Raleigh, Junius Americanus, and a Bostonian—Arthur hurled accusations at Lord North and General Gage and defended the colonials. He also issued a pamphlet that charted *The Rise, Progress, and Present State of the Dispute Between the People of America and the Administration.* Privately he rejoiced that open warfare had commenced. Joyfully he assured fellow Puritan Samuel Adams, "Heaven chose to try us with afflictions, that we might try our resources, Know our strength, and prize our liberties the more. . . . The trial may be severe, the interval may be filled up with honors and distresses; but the end will be American liberty and glory." Anticipating that America was on the verge of one of the "Revolutions of Great Empires," Lee was not repelled by the prospect. Not only did he believe "an overriding Providence" was on his side, but he also convinced himself that the petitionary movement, an orderly and legal procedure, would climax in revolution if not acceded to by British rulers. Evidently, Lee did not yet foresee total independence, for he asked that Bostonians furnish him with petitions of grievances from all the colonies. He anticipated a time when redress could be demanded and gained. There was still hope that the empire could be reordered.[67]

66. Arthur Lee to Ralph Izard, April 23, 1775, in Deas (ed.), *Correspondence of Izard,* I, 67–76; John Dickinson to Arthur Lee, April 29, 1775, in Richard Henry Lee, *Life of Arthur Lee,* II, 307–311.

67. Force (ed.), *American Archives,* II, 848–49; affidavits in Hoffman and Molyneaux (eds.), *Lee Family Papers,* II, 370–95; Riggs, "Arthur Lee and the Radical Whigs," 46–61, 227–30; Arthur Lee to Samuel Adams, July 8, 1775, in

Lee's private sentiments conflicted with his public posture in the summer of 1775. Although convinced that war was mandatory, he found himself obliged to transmit one more conciliatory plea, the Olive Branch Petition, from the Second Continental Congress to George III. In the piece, drafted by Dickinson in July, the "dutiful subjects" in America beseeched the king "to direct some mode by which the united applications of your faithful colonies to the throne . . . may be improved into a happy and permanent reconciliation."[68] Congress made no concessions and mentioned no rights, as Dickinson explained to Lee, because such specifications had been made before to no avail. Dickinson thought the mild and humble Olive Branch the final test of British policy. If it were rejected, Americans would assuredly side with the advocates of rebellion.[69]

The petition, carried by Richard Penn, reached London in mid-August. Arthur Lee had just returned from arguing cases before a circuit of the Court of King's Bench. If he thought the petition futile and hypocritical he did not say so. Rather, with characteristic energy he tried to find British sponsors for this American plea. His efforts were rebuffed, however. Shelburne had departed for Ireland to avoid melancholy politics. Edmund Burke, though he privately endorsed the petition, explained to Lee that he had not been directed by New York, whose agent he was, to participate in this attempt at reconciliation.[70]

Unable to recruit an imposing delegation, Penn and Lee sent Lord Dartmouth a copy of the Olive Branch on August 21. It was spurned. The colonial secretary departed London, leaving only an assurance he would discuss affairs with the two Americans upon his return. After a

Arthur Lee Papers, Box 2; Arthur Lee to Benjamin Franklin, July 6, 1775, in Benjamin Franklin Papers, American Philosophical Society, Philadelphia; Gary Wills, *Inventing America: Jefferson's Declaration of Independence* (Garden City, 1978), 51–64.

68. Cornelius W. Wickersham and Gilbert H. Montague (eds.), *The Olive Branch Petition* (New York, 1954), n.p.

69. John Dickinson to Arthur Lee, July 7, 1775, quoted in Wickersham and Montague (eds.), *Olive Branch Petition*, 33–34.

70. Ralph Izard to Arthur Lee, August 21, 1775, in Deas (ed.), *Correspondence of Izard*, I, 117–19; Riggs, "Arthur Lee and the Radical Whigs," 234; Lord Shelburne to Arthur Lee, July 31, 1775, in Force (ed.), *American Archives*, II 1756; Edmund Burke to Arthur Lee, August 22, 1775, in Hoffman and Molyneaux (eds.), *Lee Family Papers*, II, 438.

week of waiting Lee grew apprehensive. He anticipated that the petition would not be accepted and that the moderate Dartmouth would resign if harsh steps were taken. In fact, on August 23 George III had proclaimed the colonies to be in rebellion. Lee envisioned French intervention and a general war. The dispute, he predicted, "will operate to *hasten the independence of America*, at least a century." It was ironic that Americans had been pushed to this positive action by malignant British leaders.[71]

Lee's expectations were realized. By September 2, after conferring with Dartmouth, Penn and Lee learned that George III had refused to receive the Olive Branch and that "no answer would be given" to this last American plea for reconciliation. Efforts by Opposition and city forces to call a halt to hostilities in America were also repulsed. Lee was personally vexed. He believed that Dartmouth had ridiculed Penn and himself before the Commons. Arthur contemplated challenging the secretary, but Richard Penn persuaded his ardent colleague to reconsider. Lee's quarrel was not with Dartmouth.[72]

Despite news of bloodshed at Bunker Hill, in late November Lee made one final exertion for peace in his pamphlet, *A Second Appeal*.[73] This piece, priced at one shilling and sixpence like his previous ones, was aimed at neither the governmental officials nor the people at large. Rather, Lee directed his plea to the merchants of Britain. He posed, for the last time, as an Englishman, even though his true identity was readily apparent. The fatalistic essay was composed of three sections: a condemnation of ministerial and parliamentary policy, a discourse on the economic havoc war would cause Britain, and a reiteration that only a return to the status of 1763 would solve the Anglo-American crisis.

The imperial relationship had worsened in the past year. Chatham in

71. Arthur Lee to [Massachusetts House of Representatives?], August 28, 1775, in Wickersham and Montague (eds.), *Olive Branch Petition*, 22–28.

72. Arthur Lee and Richard Penn to the President of the General Congress, September 2, 1775, in Hoffman and Molynaux (eds.), *Lee Family Papers*, II, 450–452; Parliamentary proceedings, October 26, 1775, in Force (ed.), *American Archives*, VI, 3, 69; Richard Henry Lee, *Life of Arthur Lee*, I, 44–45; Richard Penn to Arthur Lee, November 12, 1775, in Sol Feinstone Collection, American Philosophical Society, Philadelphia.

73. [Arthur Lee], *A Second Appeal to the Justice and Interests of the People, on the Measures Respecting America by the Author of the First* (London, 1775).

Lords and Edmund Burke and David Hartley in Commons had failed to enlighten Parliament on the merits of conciliation. Petitions from America and London and other English cities had gone unanswered or were rejected. Lee lashed out at Lord North and other advisors to the king who had "secret motives of thus urging on a war with the colonies." Tories, Jacobites, and Scots were blamed for directing the "ministerial war" against Whig principles in America. Warily avoiding outright condemnation of George III, Lee insisted that pernicious counselors had "put into his Majesty's mouth" many provocative and duplicitous speeches.[74]

If the British nation would not be persuaded by moral or constitutional arguments, Lee hoped that the economic consequences of war would stir the potent commercial interests of Britain. Much was at hazard. He estimated that 40,000 soldiers and 10,000 sailors at a cost of £470,000 would be necessary to open a campaign of conquest in America. An additional £2,500,000 would cover existing debts and civil lists. Adding export and import losses, Lee calculated total costs for 1776 at £19,120,000. His review of the logistical costs of an English force in America brought him to proclaim, "It is insanity to suppose our [British] funds and our credit will survive the shock . . . it is a war of absurdity and madness. We shall sooner pluck the moon from her sphere, than conquer such a country." It was a war that could not be won. The colonies would be lost, and Spain, France, and the Netherlands would have the lucrative American trade.[75]

Lee's plan to settle the dispute between Britain and America comprised the final segment of *A Second Appeal*. The design was to return to the era when Americans were "subject to our supremacy, and subordinate in everything but—taxation." Policy from 1763 to 1775 aimed at enslaving the colonists must be repudiated. There could be no compromise, for in Lee's eyes the British were totally in the wrong. He denied that the colonials wanted independence and cited the debate between Governor Hutchinson and the Massachusetts House between 1770 and 1773. Lee preferred to emphasize the immediate cause of the present strife, the Coercive Acts. The fundamental grievance remained taxation without representation.[76]

It was clear that time was short. Lee offered the last version of his im-

74. *Ibid.*, 8–12.
75. *Ibid.*, 31–37, 40–47, 53.
76. *Ibid.*, 70–78.

perial corrective. All "obnoxious acts" and "the animosity those acts have produced" must be purged. The armed forces must be recalled, an act of oblivion passed, respectable men appointed as governors who would co-operate with colonial assemblies in a review of trade regulations, reliance restored in the system of requisitions. "Confidence and affection" were the bonds of empire. The colonists "must be cultivated, not coerced. From conciliation we may expect everything—from compulsion nothing." There was no middle ground. Britain should not begrudge the loss of revenues; she should value more the productive resources of America. Lee concluded pessimistically, "I am afraid the die is thrown, and we must stand the hazard. I am afraid that good men have nothing to do, but to weep over what they can not prevent—the ruin of their country."[77] This was the result of eight years of personal and colonial disgruntlement.

It must have been apparent to Arthur Lee that his hopes for alteration of either mood or policy in Britain were illusory. Was he so addicted to pamphleteering and petition-writing that he could not see their futility? Or was he a hypocritical propagandist, insincere in his arguments? Certainly he had difficulty keeping pace with events. In November of 1775 the ministry proposed to hire Hanoverian mercenaries to aid in suppressing American resistance. Edmund Burke's plan for conciliation was rejected by a two-to-one ratio in Commons. Lord George Germain, an ardent advocate of repression and hence a prominent target of Lee's, replaced Dartmouth as colonial secretary.[78]

Doubtless he feared for his life when Stephen Sayre was arrested for conspiring to kidnap George III. With John Dunning, Sergeant Adair and other lawyers, Lee was able to effect Sayre's release from the Tower of London, but he knew he could not thwart the animosity mounting in England against Americans.[79] By his readings, personal suffering was a concomitant of the patriotic cause. It was ironic that the attempt to bind the colonies more tightly to the mother country had precipitated American consideration of independence.

Arthur Lee shared with his fellow leaders of American resistance two

77. *Ibid.*, 81–84, 90.
78. Arthur Lee to Franklin, July 6, 1775, in Franklin Papers, American Philosophical Society.
79. Force (ed.), *American Archives*, III, 1142–143; *Dictionary of American Biography*, XVI, 406; *The Annual Register, 1775*, XVIII, 239–43; Riggs, "Arthur Lee and the Radical Whigs," 241–42.

common roles. Through the 1760s and 1770s, these statesmen developed a common consciousness and a distinctive role for the emerging nation in America. Lee's writings through 1776 were a major contribution to that development. Casting his eye on the future, he outlined criteria for the new government: guarantees of the right to bear arms, prohibitions of hereditary titles, annual elections. The American revolt must bequeath a republic. Lee's brand of republicanism, an outgrowth of his nature and aspirations, was founded upon distrust of authority and looked forward to a wider career for someone with his talents. Lee, for himself and his readers, had endowed the cause with high moral purpose. He would soon be called upon to carry this message to the courts of Europe.[80]

80. Arthur Lee to Samuel Adams, December 10, 1775, in Arthur Lee Papers, Box 2; Bailyn, *Ideological Origins*, 319; Bernard Bailyn, "Political Experience and Enlightenment Ideas in Eighteenth-Century America," *American Historical Review*, LXVII (January, 1962), 351.

Stratford Hall, shrine and symbol of the Lee family of Virginia.

In this Cartoon of 1775, Europe, flanked by Africa and Asia, ponders the American rebellion as displayed by Father Time's magic lantern. The French cock stands near the flames engulfing the Tea Tax and Stamp Act, while British Redcoats and lions recoil. On the right the Indian who personifies America reaches for the cap of liberty. In the left foreground of the cartoon, America sits awaiting world reaction to the tempest. The cartoon displays the sense of British diplomatic isolation and American opportunity as armed strife was just beginning.

Richard Henry Lee, the older brother whom Arthur idealized, was the most prominent political figure among the Stratford Lees. This portrait is the work of Charles Willson Peale.

The commission of Benjamin Franklin, Silas Deane, and Arthur Lee to the court of Louis XVI, issued in 1776. The trio of fanatic (Lee), deist (Franklin), and dunce (Deane) had widely divergent aims and expectations.

Miniature of Silas Deane attributed to Charles Willson Peale. Lee despised this ambitious Yankee, collaborator in Beaumarchais' schemes, and dupe of British agents. The Lee-Deane feud eventually led to revision of American foreign policy.

déssé par C. N: Cochin Chev. de l'Ordre du Roi a Paris 1777.

D. BENIAMIN FRÆNCKLIN.

Grand Comissaire plenipotentiaire du Congres d'Amerique en France
né a Boston 1706. en 17. Janvier.

Se vend a Londres chez Thom Hart.

A cult arose around Benjamin Franklin soon after his arrival in Europe. This 1777 engraving by Charles Nicholas Cochin, in which Franklin, the public relations man *par excellence*, is shown as a simple, natural American, was widely distributed. In reality, as Lee discovered, Benjamin Franklin was cunning, resourceful, and powerful.

Portrait of Charles Gravier de Vergennes by Charles Willson Peale. As foreign minister, Vergennes persuaded Louis XVI to subsidize the American rebellion in hopes of restructuring the European balance of power. He came to distrust Lee.

Conrad Alexandre Gérard by Charles Willson Peale. Gérard negotiated the Franco-American Alliances of 1778 and served as the first ambassador from France to the Continental Congress, from which vantage point he participated in the traduction of Arthur Lee.

This popular cartoon satirized the Franco-American Alliance. While the British lion sleeps and the Howes dally in Philadelphia, the cow that represents British commerce, is dehorned by America and milked by the Dutch, who pass the milk on to the Bourbons. The cartoon is concerned with loss of trade, not with the possibility of European war.

Franklin Urging the Claims of the American Colonies Before Louis XVI, a mid-nineteenth-century painting by George P. A. Healy, emphasizes the splendor of the French court and Franklin's role in American diplomacy. The two men standing behind Franklin do not resemble Silas Deane, John Adams, or Arthur Lee. Actually, all Franco-American negotiations before March, 1778, took place outside the court and were carried on between the American commissioners and Gérard or Beaumarchais.

★ CHAPTER V ★

To Hazard Everything

The three commissioners plenipotentiary who assembled in Paris in late 1776 were a disparate lot. As representatives of the rebellion in America their upbringings, careers, and perspectives illustrated the diversity of the movement. Noting the divergence of the delegation a Loyalist wag, Jonathan Odell, quipped,

> When it became the high United States
> To send their Envoys to Versailles' proud gates
> Were not three ministers, produced at once?—
> Delicious group, fanatic, deist, dunce![1]

The fanatic was Arthur Lee, at thirty-six the youngest of the trio. His prominence as physician, polemicist, and colonial agent had perhaps been undercut by a transatlantic career. Not so for the deist, seventy-year-old Benjamin Franklin, the foremost cosmopolite in the British realm. His continental conspicuousness had been an outgrowth of his intellectual achievements and his propensity as a publicist for a mélange of causes, foremost of which was his own welfare. Silas Deane, the dunce of the group, was a more provincial character, once having been a Connecticut schoolteacher. His penchant for commercial dealings cast him into the orbit of Robert Morris at Philadelphia and led him subsequently to the French court to seek foreign aid for the American cause and personal profit for himself and enterprising associates. The lack of unity in the commission would hamper the American diplomatic effort for the next three years.[2] The source of the disagreement and disruption, according to his colleagues, was the petulant, paranoid Lee.

1. Quoted in Moses C. Tyler, *Literary History of the American Revolution*, II, 112.
2. Cecil B. Currey, "Ben Franklin in France: A Maker of American Diplomacy," in Frank J. Merli and Theodore A. Wilson (eds.), *Makers of American Diplomacy* (2 vols; New York, 1974), I, 7.

The choice of American emissaries to the French court was not wholly rooted in sectional bargaining within the Continental Congress. A welter of factors—cultural, economic, ideological, and political—affected the American outlook in the formulation of foreign policy and the conduct of diplomacy. Selection of the commission in 1776 illustrated the abilities of rival groupings within Congress: the constructive group focused on the establishment of intercolonial governmental institutions to harness the revolutionary movement, while the radical group aimed primarily at extinguishing of the connection with Britain. Silas Deane, after failing to be reelected by Connecticut to Congress, had attached himself to the fortunes of Robert Morris, the Pennsylvania merchant prince and early congressional kingpin. Morris was a member of the Committee of Correspondence (later called the Committee of Secret Correspondence), the largely autonomous body that developed and directed foreign policy for Congress, and through his influence Deane was appointed emissary.[3] In March, 1776, he had been dispatched to France on a dual mission. In his public capacity he was to solicit arms, aid, and a commercial pact with France for the rebellious Americans. In private he was operating on commission from Morris in quest of goods to funnel into speculative trade with the Indians.[4] Benjamin Franklin, the most experienced of Americans in the ways and byways of European negotiations, was also a member of the Secret Committee and a partisan of the constructive party. In September when Congress decided to create a commission to treat with the French, he willingly returned to Europe.

The original third nominee for the negotiating team was Thomas Jefferson. However, when he refused the appointment in order to remain close to his own affairs, both domestic and political, Arthur Lee was selected. His choice may be credited to the Adams-Lee axis in Congress, an affiliation of radicals first spawned in Arthur Lee's transatlantic correspondence before hostilities erupted. That Arthur was already in Britain as an agent for Congress was also a consideration. The *Journal* of the Congress, however, gives no clue as to the extent and nature of the debate

3. George C. Wood, *Congressional Control of Foreign Relations During the American Revolution, 1774–1789* (Allentown, 1919), 42–48.

4. Silas Deane to Elizabeth Deane, March, 1776, in *The Deane Papers: Correspondence Between Silas Deane, His Brothers and Their Business and Political Associates* (Hartford, 1870, 1930), vols. 2 and 22 of the Connecticut Historical Society, *Collections*, II, 360–64.

over Lee's selection. Morris, writing on behalf of the Secret Committee to inform him of his appoinment, politely observed that the Congress "flatter ourselves from assurances of your friends here, that you will cheerfully undertake the important business and that our country will greatly benefit from those abilities and that detachment you have already maintained" as a secret agent. The flattery was meant to camouflage the fact that Arthur was a substitute.[5]

These three men would create American diplomacy. No matter what goals, manifestos, and instructions for foreign policy might emanate from the Continental Congress, the Revolution's representatives on the European stage were crucial in two respects. On the one hand they selected and supplied information for the policy deliberations in Philadelphia; on the other hand they interpreted and implemented the policy guidelines. As recent analysis has reminded us, "Issues of foreign policy and the forces that produce them transcend the purposes and preoccupations of individual statesmen; nevertheless, they can only find expression through the marvelously unpredictable, chaotic realm of human motivations and the decisions of fallible men."[6] The difficulties that afflicted the American commission in France may be traced to personal differences as well as to the inadequacies of the Continental Congress, where policy-making by committee was hamstrung by "factionalism, inefficiency, and lack of direction." The committee approach led to the lamentable spectacle of this triad of American diplomats in France and others wandering over Europe, uncertain of their assignments and jealous of their colleagues.[7]

Arthur Lee came to feel particularly victimized as a diplomat. An analysis of his contributions to the diplomacy of the American Revolution

5. Oliver P. Chitwood, *Richard Henry Lee: Statesman of the Revolution* (Morgantown, 1967), 104–105; Samuel Adams to Richard Henry Lee, July 15, 1776, in Cushing (ed.), *Writings of Samuel Adams*, III, 298; Herbert James Henderson, Jr., "Political Factions," 164; Worthington C. Ford (ed.), *Journals of the Continental Congress, 1774–1789* (34 vols.; Washington, D.C., 1904–1937), VI, 879; Robert Morris to Arthur Lee and Franklin, October 23, 1776, in Hoffman and Molyneaux (eds.), *Lee Family Papers*, II, 704. Richard Henry Lee, *Life of Arthur Lee*, I, 181, notes another factor: Lee's alleged fluency in Italian, Spanish, and French, as well as Latin and Greek.

6. Merli and Wilson (eds.), *Makers of American Diplomacy*, I, xv.

7. Lawrence S. Kaplan, *Colonies into Nation: American Diplomacy, 1763–1801* (New York, 1972), 101; Jennings B. Sanders, *Evolution of Executive Departments of the Continental Congress, 1774–1789* (Gloucester, 1971), 38–39.

yields three paradoxes. Although he was a Whig patriot, and thus technically a victor in the war, he emerged from the contest without a sense of fulfillment. Although American foreign policy was successful on the whole, he repeatedly was haunted by failure in his own assignments. Although a Virginian by birth, he found his outlook and approach to foreign affairs repeatedly condemned by southerners throughout the War for Independence. His years on diplomatic assignment, 1775–1780, proved as adverse as his previous experience with the radicalism of Wilkes and Shelburne.

Sensitivity to foreign policy had grown as Anglo-American relations deteriorated in the 1770s. It is evident from Arthur Lee's writings that Americans were conscious of the international ramifications of their struggle with Britain. In the spring of 1774, Arthur had confided to Richard Henry that America might ultimately owe her salvation to European intervention. Publicly, in *An Appeal*, he pointed out, "There is not a part of the world upon which France looks with a more attentive eye than upon America. There is not the smallest event, relative to our proceedings towards the colonies of which they are not minutely informed."[8] Possibly, he made the European tour that year because of a change in his priorities. His absence from Britain made it impossible for him to participate in the agitation against the Coercive Acts and in city and parliamentary elections, causes in which he had previously invested much energy. Instead, he made a reconnaissance of Europe, sampling opinion toward America and observing the mechanisms of European policy makers. His vision became international in scope.

The principles of American foreign policy predated the Continental Congress.[9] The key components synthesized from the colonial experience included the belief that the New World was different from and better than the Old World, the goals of intensified international commerce and freedom of the seas, and the realization that foreign aid would be critical in the contest against Britain. Discussion of these factors rent the Conti-

8. Arthur Lee to Richard Henry Lee, March 18, 1774, in Hoffman and Molyneaux (eds.), *Lee Family Papers*, I, 201; [Arthur Lee], *An Appeal*, 22.

9. Max Savelle, "Colonial Origins of American Diplomatic Principles," *Pacific Historical Review*, III (September, 1934), 334–50; Felix Gilbert, *To the Farewell Address: Ideas of Early American Foreign Policy* (Princeton, 1970), 16–18; James H. Hutson, "Early American Diplomacy: A Reappraisal," in Lawrence S. Kaplan (ed.), *The American Revolution and "A Candid World"* (Kent, 1977), 42.

nental Congress both before and after the Declaration of Independence. Lee, as one of those who looked upon war as a means to civic regeneration within America, likewise believed that Americans would purify international affairs. His self-righteous and uncompromising approach to negotiations, based on the belief that the American revolutionaries held the balance of power in the western world and heralded a new day for international law, endangered negotiations abroad and harmony at home. In the midst of controversies Arthur Lee raised, the mission of the Revolution was brought into focus.

Europe did not wait passively for the Americans to make the first diplomatic move. The entire continent was eyeing the Anglo-American crisis with ambitious, but cautious, self-interest. France, under dissolute Louis XV and plodding Louis XVI, had cultivated tension within the British empire since 1765. Charles Gravier de Vergennes, who assumed office as foreign minister in 1774, directed a policy of revenge. He intended to redeem the crushing loss of empire inflicted by the Peace of Paris of 1763 and to rebalance power in Western Europe. "Devoted to duty, gifted with a subtle intellect, unscrupulous when the needs of France seemed to require duplicity, Vergennes hovered on the brink of greatness."[10] Through the Bourbon Family Compact with Spain and a defensive alliance with Austria, Vergennes sought to relieve France of continental worries and permit concentration on the Atlantic turmoil. His policy encountered opposition from Louis XVI, who morally affirmed the peace of 1763, and from Baron de Turgot, the finance minister, who feared the financial implications of a new war effort. Only after much argument was Vergennes able to gain royal approval for his plans to support the struggling American rebellion. The initial mode of attack would be secret assistance to the Americans, the traditional means of subversion that Britain herself had utilized recently in Corsica.[11]

10. Orville T. Murphy, "Charles Gravier de Vergennes: Profile of an Old Regime Diplomat," *Political Science Quarterly*, LXXXIII (September, 1968), 400–418; Jonathan R. Dull, *The French Navy and American Independence: A Study of Arms and Diplomacy, 1774–1787* (Princeton, 1975), 8–11; John R. Alden, *The American Revolution 1775–1783* (New York, 1954), 180.

11. Kaplan, *Colonies into Nation*, 63; Charles H. Van Tyne, "French Aid Before the Alliance of 1778," *American Historical Review*, XXXI (October, 1925), 20–40; Richard D. Harris, "French Finances and the American War, 1777–1778," *Journal of Modern History*, XLVIII (June, 1976), 233–58.

Charles III of Spain did not share the French enthusiasm for the American cause. He feared that creation of a new state in North America would threaten Spanish control of the Mississippi River. Spanish foreign policy was then dominated by the struggle with Portugal in South America. Yet the Spaniards hoped to profit from Britain's troubles by offering Spanish neutrality to the British in return for the pawns of Minorca, Gibraltar, or the Floridas.[12]

Frederick II of Prussia shared the continental animosity toward Britain. His bitterness was rooted in British perfidy during the Seven Years War. Yet the Prussian soldier-monarch prudently resisted becoming an open enemy of the British until he could ascertain whether the American rebels would succeed. Like most sovereigns in Europe, Frederick chose to remain a "tranquil spectator" on the sidelines of the Anglo-American quarrel.[13] Only France was prepared in 1775 to accept overtures from the American patriots.

The leaders of the rebellion knew that foreign aid, especially the supply of gunpowder, would be critical to their cause. On November 29, 1775, the Second Continental Congress appointed the five-man Committee of Secret Correspondence to establish a network of political and commercial agents in Europe. This committee, which kept its business secret from the main body of Congress, was controlled by more conservative insurgents like John Dickinson, Robert Morris, and John Jay, plus the worldly Franklin. Its first action was to create a foreign service by soliciting observations of European affairs from two men. One of these informants was Franklin's friend in Holland, Charles W. F. Dumas, who would faithfully transmit reports throughout the war. The other agent was Arthur Lee, the American zealot in London. The committee informed the Virginian of his appointment in a dispatch dated December 12, 1775, and asked for knowledge of "the disposition of foreign powers to us." They reminded Lee that his task required "great circumspection and impenetrable secrecy." Franklin thoughtfully enclosed £200 for Lee's expenses and confided that "Congress rely on your zeal and abilities to serve them, and will readily compensate you for whatever trouble and expense"

12. Samuel Flagg Bemis, *The Diplomacy of the American Revolution* (Bloomington, 1957), 81–112.

13. Paul L. Haworth, "Frederick the Great and the American Revolution," *American Historical Review*, IX (April, 1904), 460–62.

might be encountered.[14] This trust reflected a number of factors in Arthur Lee's favor: his placement in England in the vanguard of Opposition, his knowledge of European languages and affairs reinforced by a recent continental tour, and his political connections in Congress through the Adamses and Richard Henry Lee. These were eminent qualifications.

Even before Lee received news of his appointment by Congress, he had assumed the role of revolutionary agent. The French chargé d'affaires in England, Monsieur Garnier, reported as early as December 19, 1774, that he had been approached by friends of the American insurgents—probably Arthur and William Lee—who desired secret assistance from the French and, possibly, an alliance with the Bourbons. Vergennes, not ready for open warfare, responded in two ways. He dispatched a French merchant to Philadelphia to probe the resources of the rebels and to hint that covert aid would be forthcoming. At the same time he requested appraisals of the North ministry from his agent in London.[15] Intrigue commenced.

Vergennes' contact in London in 1775 was Pierre Caron de Beaumarchais, an enthusiastic and extraordinary emissary, who had already gained fame as a dramatist and notoriety as a court intriguer. The son of a watchmaker, he had attached himself to the nobilty of France by means of bribes, marriages, and an ability to amuse the sullen daughters of Louis XV. Like Lee, Beaumarchais yearned to be in the center of public excitement. Like Vergennes, he was an early sympathizer with the American cause and was determined to inflict painful wounds on archrival Britain. Indicative of Beaumarchais' stance and inspiration is his declaration of September 21 to his king that America "must be invincible" and that "the English colonies are lost to the mother country."[16]

Following interviews with Louis XVI and Vergennes, Beaumarchais was sent back to London on September 23. He was instructed to maintain

14. Elizabeth S. Kite, "French 'Secret Aid' Precursor to the French American Alliance, 1776–1777," *French-American Review*, IV (April, 1948), 143; Wharton (ed.), *Correspondence*, I, 300–333; Committee of Secret Correspondence to Arthur Lee, December 12, 1775, in Wharton (ed.), *Correspondence*, II 63.

15. Bemis, *Diplomacy of the American Revolution*, 19–21; Jared Sparks, "Early Diplomatic History of the United States," in James B. Scott (ed.), *The United States and France, 1778–1783: Some Opinions of International Gratitude* (New York, 1926), 15.

16. Arnold Whitridge, "Beaumarchais and the American Revolution," *History*

conversations with the discontented elements within British politics and to initiate parleys with American rebels. He soon encountered a man well versed in both fields, Arthur Lee, at one of the convivial affairs at Mansion House, the residence of London's lord mayor, John Wilkes. Lee and Beaumarchais plunged into fervid and fantastic discussions of French support for the American rebellion. Neither man could be a passive observer, for both wanted to make policy. At secret parleys conducted at Lee's residence, No. 2 Garden Court in the Middle Temple, the two agents enthusiastically exceeded their official instructions in their efforts to encourage each other. They were joined by a third zealot, Comte de Lauraguais, a Frenchman characterized by the caustic Horace Walpole as "a wild, dissolute man, of a head not very strong but of some parts." These three formed the foundation of the Franco-American attachment.[17]

Though frenzied, the discussions were not fraternal. Beaumarchais, proudly fancying himself the personal emissary of Louis XVI, considered Lauraguais a rival. Perhaps Vergennes wanted to use the comte as a check on the dealings of Beaumarchais, not an uncommon practice. Beaumarchais found Lauraguais' presence a hindrance to negotations with Lee. He therefore reported to Versailles that Lauraguais, like Lee, was associated with Shelburne and other English Whigs. From this seed grew the later antipathy between Lee and the French diplomats. Henceforth, the French ministry could not conceive that Arthur Lee would separate himself totally from English political acquaintances, while Lee could not comprehend that his loyalty to the rebellion might be so questioned. Within a year, Vergennes transmitted reports to Congress that Lauraguais was well-meaning but indiscreet. This news cast a shadow of suspicion and doubt over Lee's early dealings with Beaumarchais in London.[18]

Today, XVII (1967), 98–105; [Beaumarchais] For the King Alone [February 29, 1776?], in Louis de Lomenie, *Beaumarchais and His Time* (4 vols.; London, 1856), III, 107–133.

17. Henri Doniol, *Histoire de la participation de la France à l'établissement des Etats-Unis d'Amerique: Correspondance diplomatique et documents* (5 vols.; Paris, 1886–92), I, 133–38; Van Tyne, "French Aid," 38–39; Arthur Lee to the Secret Committee, April 20, 1779, in Wharton (ed.), *Correspondence*, III, 119; A. Francis Steuart (ed.), *The Last Journals of Horace Walpole During the Reign of George III from 1771–1783* (25 vols.; New York, 1889–1910), I, 38.

18. Doniol, *Participation de la France*, III, 379; Silas Deane to Committee of Secret Correspondence, August 18, 1776, in Wharton (ed.), *Correspondence*, II, 48.

Lee was a most dynamic diplomat, dispatching reports of British troop movements and poltical maneuverings to the American audience and try- ing to radicalize the Committee of Secret Correspondence. The appoint- ments of Franklin and Jay, two men who had only recently endorsed the rebellion, vexed him. Arthur reportedly declared, "If I am to commit my- self into an unreserved correspondence, they must be left out and L[ees] or A's [Adams] put into their places." He also confided, "From experi- ence I can say (though without any connection or commerce with them) the New England men are fittest to be trusted in any dangerous or im- portant enterprise." He hoped to swing foreign policy into the hands of the more extremist members of Congress headed by Richard Henry Lee and Samuel Adams. Characteristically, his zeal overwhelmed his tact.[19]

While Arthur was exhorting the American patriots and hinting of French aid, Beaumarchais, on February 29, 1776, dispatched a forceful memorial to Louis XVI. This document, "For the King Alone," was most crucial to Lee's cultivation of Franco-American affairs. According to the French agent, his American counterpart in London was pressing the French for assistance. Lee, "quite discouraged by the inability of the ef- forts he has made through me, with the French ministry to obtain assis- tance in the shape of powder and munitions of war," believed France would submit to Britain and not take advantage of the opportunity of- fered. Lee, in the playwright's rendition, offered a secret lucrative com- mercial pact as well as a guarantee of the French West Indies. If France did not come to the aid of the Americans, Lee foresaw that the American colonies would soon be reconciled with Britain and together they would plunder French holdings in the sugar islands. In conclusion, Lee asserted that Congress had received a satisfactory answer to its inquiries for sup- port from Spain.[20] This memorial had a paradoxical impact: French aid

19. Various copies of this letter, addressed to either Cadwallader Colden [a cover] or Benjamin Franklin and dated February 13 or 14, 1776, are found in Wharton (ed.), *Correspondence*, II, 71–78, Arthur Lee Papers, Box 3, Hoffman and Molyneaux (eds.), *Lee Family Papers*, II, 548–59, Force (comp.), *American Archives*, IV, 1125–1126.

20. Bemis, *Diplomacy of American Revolution*, 24; Doniol, *Participation de la France*, I, 402–407; John Durand (ed.), *New Materials for the History of the American Revolution* (New York, 1889), 74–85; [Beaumarchais] For the King Alone, February 29, 1776, in Brian N. Morton (ed.), *Beaumarchais Correspon- dence* (2 vols; Paris, 1969–), II, 171–176.

was soon forthcoming, but it was given at a great personal cost to Lee. Louis XVI agreed to subsidize the American rebellion, but Vergennes, in reaction to Arthur's aggressive and guileful stance, came to distrust him. Whether Lee actually made these statements or Beaumarchais invented them is impossible to ascertain. Both men were after the same goal, the commitment of the Bourbons to a war with Britain. Both possessed sufficient bravura to concoct such threats.

Beaumarchais had argued effectively that the French sugar islands would be plundered by either the British or the Americans, whoever won the war. His main contention was that in order to maintain peace and protect the French empire, intervention must be made on behalf of the American rebels. Yet, he noted, such aid to the Americans should "put their forces in balance with England's but not beyond that." The best French investment was to prolong the Anglo-American conflict so that French blood and more money would not be expended. The essence of the plan to aid the Americans without compromising Louis XVI was "secrecy and speed."[21]

In playing on the fears of an Anglo-American rapprochement and proffering a commercial connection this memorial had affirmed Vergennes' own thoughts. Vergennes might even have dictated the memorandum to Beaumarchais, but when the French foreign minister learned from the Spanish that they had not been approached by solicitous Americans, Vergennes' antipathy toward Lee was aroused: he would not be duped by an upstart American. Furthermore, Vergennes viewed Lee's threat of reconciliation as evidence of the Virginian's bias. The French knew Lord Chatham was then pushing for reconciliations. Thereafter the foreign minister would never be convinced that Lee did not sympathize with the British. Lee was marked as antigallic.[22]

Beaumarchais' essay was complemented by a circumspect scheme to assist the Americans. The intriguer understood that "considerations of state" impelled the king "to extend a helping hand to the Americans," yet caution was necessary lest secret aid become "a brand to kindle strife

21. Morton (ed.), *Beaumarchais*, II, 175.
22. Doniol, *Participation de la France*, I, 307–374, Ralph L. Ketcham, "France and American Politics, 1763–1793," *Political Science Quarterly*, LXXXVIII (June, 1963), 201; Charles H. Van Tyne, "Influences Which Determined the French Government to Make the Treaty with America," *American Historical Review*, XXI (April, 1916), 528–42.

between France and England." He proposed a commercial house to over-see clandestine aid to the rebels. The goal of the assistance was "not so much to terminate the war between America and England, as to sustain and keep it alive to the detriment of the English, our natural and pro-nounced enemies." Through a bogus firm, designated by Beaumarchais as Roderique Hortalez et Cie., the agent would use royal funds to purchase discounted powder from royal arsenals and sell it to the Americans at a profit of 300 percent. Perhaps as a jest, Beaumarchais suggested that Louis XVI enact a tax on English vehicles entering France to furnish capital for Hortalez and Company.[23]

Beaumarchais' scheme was endorsed by Vergennes and circulated among members of the French cabinet in mid-March. Louis XVI ulti-mately yielded to this advice based on the belief, fostered by Arthur Lee, that the British were critically dependent upon American colonies. On May 2 the King directed that one million livres ($2,150,000 purchasing power in 1975 dollars) be signed over to Beaumarchais to finance muni-tions shipments through Hortalez and Company. An additional million livres was procured from Charles III in August to further the plan. Clothes and munitions were soon dispatched in chartered vessels to aid the "insurrectionists." The Bourbons, prodded by Lee and Beaumarchais, embarked on a program of subsidizing the American revolutionaries, at last giving factual basis to year-old rumors in England of French aid to the rebels.[24]

Lee and Beaumarchais had previously discussed how transactions would be handled by Hortalez via Cap François in the West Indies. In late April they were conferring busily in London. Beaumarchais reported that Lee was pressing for outright assistance and threatening to journey to France.

23. Memorial of Beaumarchais to the King of France, February, 1776, in Charles Isham (ed.), *The Deane Papers* (New York, 1887–91), vols. XIX–XXIII of New York Historical Society, *Collections*, XIX, 108–115; John J. Meng, "A Footnote to Secret Aid in the American Revolution," *American Historical Review*, XLIII (July, 1938), 791–95; Dull, *French Navy*, 32.

24. *Time—Special 1776 Issue: Educational Edition* (Boston, 1975), 3, 34–35. Conversion scale: £1 (1776) = $50 (1975); $1 (1776) = $11 (1975); £1 (1776) = 23.3 (1776) livres; 1 livre (1776) = $2 (1975); Dull, *French Navy*, xiv, 31–37; Bemis, *Diplomacy of the American Revolution*, 37–38; Helen Augur, *The Secret War of Independence* (New York, 1955), 65; Lord North to the King, January 5, 1776, in Sir John Fortescue (ed.), *The Correspondence of King George the Third from 1760 to December, 1783* (6 vols.; London, 1927–28), III, 327.

Vergennes, replying to the impatient intriguers, observed, "with all due respect for your fiery qualifications, all sleep is not lethargical . . . consider the matter well and you will find me nearer to you than you think." The foreign minister revealed that Beaumarchais "will be authorized to begin sending gold coin; but rather long credit would be wanted" from the Americans. To Beaumarchais, then worried that the rebels "will make an advantageous peace against us," this was most welcome news.[25] The opportunity to wound Britain would not be missed.

In a series of letters addressed to "Hortalez" and signed "Mary Johnston," Lee impatiently exhorted the French agent to hasten aid to America. Arthur tried to persuade Beaumarchais not to worry about payment in tobacco in exchange for war material. He also discounted the reappearance of Lauraguais as a threat to their dealings. By early June, Arthur was able to assure Congress that, "The desire of the Court of France to assist may be depended on; but they are yet timid and the ministry unsettled. . . . Spain is more reserved and her minister here an old woman, but assuredly when France moves Spain will cooperate." Buoyed up by his negotiations, Lee urged the rebels to take a crucial step: "Independency is essential to your dignity, essential to your present safety, and essential to your future prosperity and peace."[26] A declaration of independence would reassure the French of an investment in the rebellion. It was apparent to Lee that, once armed strife commenced, American self-determination was no longer possible within the British empire, but was now entwined with the foreign policies of European powers.

The nature of French covert support for the American cause became most controversial in later years. What Beaumarchais had said and what Lee had heard in these early negotiations diverged. The historical record reveals little, for much of the bargaining was face to face, and in fear for his life Lee wisely kept no memoranda. Beaumarchais, citing his own personal investment in the scheme, later claimed the proffered assistance had been in the nature of a loan and that he should be reimbursed. Lee re-

25. Beaumarchais to Vergennes, April 26, May 8, 1776, in Benjamin F. Stevens (ed.), *Facsimiles of Manuscripts in European Archives Relating to America, 1773–1783* (25 vols.; London, 1889–98), nos. 1328, 864.

26. Mary Johnston to Roderique Hortalez et Cie., May 23, 1776, Arthur Lee to Committee of Secret Correspondence, June 3, 1776, both in Wharton (ed.), *Correspondence*, II, 94, 95–96.

plied that he had understood all the aid to be a royal gift. He came to believe that Beaumarchais wanted the windfall profits for himself. Their claims and counterclaims were further poisoned by personal antipathies that developed later. Yet Lee was not the only one to find initial French assistance something other than a straightforward commercial transaction. A jealous Lauraguais later testified that Beaumarchais' early promise of 200,000 livres had not stipulated whether it was a gift, a loan, or a contract. Members of Congress ambiguously noted the offers of a "loan and succors." 27

Lee's zeal kept him from approaching Beaumarchais' offers cautiously. In his eagerness for French support, he tried to persuade the French agent not to adhere to regular commercial practices. Rather, Lee admonished Beaumarchais that they must "do all in our power, without insisting on a certain and immediate return." From the American's point of view the agents were "not transacting a mere mercantile business" for "politics is greatly concerned with this affair." In reply the French intriguer reiterated that American payments would be expected at the exchange point in the West Indies.28 Lee could not understand why Beaumarchais insisted on operating as a profiteer. Lee thought Roderique Hortalez et Cie. a pretense; Beaumarchais did not.

As Hortalez was established, Congress selected Silas Deane to venture to France. The post was a plum for the former lawyer-shopkeeper who had been dropped from Connecticut's congressional delegation. His new tasks were manifold and somewhat contradictory. In search of material assistance and recognition of the rebellion, Deane combined political and commercial missions. In his private capacity he had formed a partnership with Robert Morris and others to procure goods, at a 5 percent commission, for an Indian trade scheme. Further, it appears that Deane had become embittered by his fall from political office; he saw his opponents as actuated by "low, envious, jealous, and sordid motives." He felt he had suffered censure when the governor had asserted he lacked "politeness

27. Kaplan, *Colonies into Nation*, 92; Arthur Lee to Secret Committee, April 20, 1779, in Wharton (ed.), *Correspondence*, III, 119; Lauraguais' testimony, February 8, 15, 1778, in Arthur Lee Papers, Box 14; Memorandum of Benjamin Franklin and Robert Morris, October 1, 1776, in Wharton (ed.), *Correspondence*, III, 151–52; Morton (ed.), *Beaumarchais*, II, 210–215.

28. Mary Johnston to Roderique Hortalez et Cie., June 14, 1776, Hortalez to Johnston, June 26, 1776, both in Wharton (ed.), *Correspondence*, II, 97–98.

and gentility," and he contemplated calling for a public hearing. Deane had been attracted to the French post, he confessed, because he was susceptible to becoming "involved in one scheme and adventure after another." That Morris advanced him £500 and promised £500 more in six months also appealed to him.[29]

In the transparent guise of a Bermuda merchant, Deane arrived in Paris, July 7, 1776. Vergennes offered little encouragement, and only one dealer, Beaumarchais, was willing to send supplies on credit to Congress. Impressed by Deane's official credentials and his offer to pay handsomely for war stores, Beaumarchais forsook his arrangements with Arthur Lee. He proposed to Deane that Hortalez "begin anew, in a manner more certain and more regular, a negotiation which was before touched upon." Deane and Beaumarchais spoke the same tongue—that of profit. The American talked of repayment in six to twelve months and of considerable remittances, while the Frenchman promised to keep an exact account of the advances he made to the "virtuous people," the Americans. Restitution would cover not only the value of goods shipped but also insurance, a commission, and other attendant costs. Though he might write of his patriotism, the prospect of a 10 percent commission was also among Beaumarchais' motives. The two entered into a working partnership with Beaumarchais procuring arms from the royal arsenal while Deane prepared shipping arrangements. By November, a ship laden with twelve thousand muskets and sixty cannons had departed L'Orient, destined for American battlegrounds. The profit would fall into the pockets of Deane and Beaumarchais.[30]

Lee, whose initial negotiations with the French had prepared the agreements that Deane concluded, was not content to sit idle in London. He wrote Deane that he was coming to Paris to discuss their different understandings with the proprietor of Hortalez in order to settle on a single plan for providing French assistance to America. Always wary of British spies, Lee enclosed a cipher for further correspondence and a list of

29. Silas Deane to Elizabeth Deane, November 26, 1775, March, 1776, in *The Deane Papers*, II, 323–25, 360–64; John Trumbull to Deane, October 20, 1775, in Isham (ed.), *Deane Papers*, XIX, 87.

30. Beaumarchais to Deane, July 22, 1776, in Morton (ed.), *Beaumarchais*, II, 230; Deane to Committee of Secret Correspondence, August 18, 1776, Beaumarchais to Deane, July 28, 1776, both in Wharton (ed.), *Correspondence*, II, 112–27, 99–100.

Americans whose allegiance to the rebellion was doubtful. He lectured Deane, "In these times it is necessary to abstain from trusting those of whom there is the least suspicion. The scale is coming so near to a balance, that a little treachery may turn it to our destruction, and the ruin of public Liberty." Deane did not heed the advice. He refused to relay Lee's list of suspects to Congress, claiming that Lee lacked proof of their perfidy. Yet within two months he was warning Congress of disloyal individuals who were probably British agents.[31]

Deane had been primed by Beaucarchais to disregard Lee. The French distrusted Arthur because of his friendships with the flamboyant Lauraguais and the hostile Shelburne, although, in fact, he had severed his ties with Lauraguais after receiving Deane's warning that the Frenchman was suspect. Deane himself maintained correspondence with Shelburne, Thomas Walpole, and other British politicians. Further, it was Deane, not Lee, who was indiscreet, for immediately upon his arrival he fell in with a cunning double agent, Dr. Edward Bancroft. A native of Massachusetts, perhaps a schoolboy student of Deane, and a friend of Franklin, Bancroft offered his services to the American agent in Paris. Deane, always trusting toward those who were his mental superiors, found the good doctor to be a source of intelligence on British affairs. In reality, Bancroft was operating in concert with Britain's chief of spies, William Eden, and with Eden's confidant, Paul Wentworth.[32]

31. Arthur Lee to Deane, July 28, 1776, in Stevens (ed.), *Facsimiles*, no. 467; Deane to Arthur Lee, August 19, 1776, in Isham (ed.), *Deane Papers*, XX, 226–27; Deane to the Committee of Secret Correspondence, October 1, 1777, in Wharton (ed.), *Correspondence*, II, 153–57.

32. Beaumarchais to Vergennes, April 26, 1776, in Morton (ed.), *Beaumarchais*, II, 350, is the first record of Lee's distrust for Deane. Joseph Hopkins to Vergennes, August 16, 1776, Barbeau Dubourg to Vergennes, July 28, 1776, both in Stevens (ed.), *Facsimiles*, no. 1348, 892; Silas Deane to Committee of Secret Correspondence, August 18, 1776, in Wharton (ed.), *Correspondence*, II, 118; Lord Shelburne to Deane, October 20, 1776, in Isham (ed.), *Deane Papers*, XIX, 330–31; Richard W. Van Alstyne, "Thomas Walpole's Letters to the Duke of Grafton on American Affairs, 1776–1778," *Huntington Library Quarterly*, XXX (November, 1960), 17–20; Julian Boyd, "Silas Deane: Death By A Kindly Teacher of Treason?" *William and Mary Quarterly*, 3rd ser., XVI (April–October, 1959), 176–81; Deane to Secret Committee of Congress, August 18, 1776, in Isham (ed.), *Deane Papers*, XIX, 204–210; Samuel F. Bemis, "British Secret Service and the French-American Alliance," *American Historical Review*, XXIX (April, 1924), 474–95.

Bancroft cleverly avoided Deane's early conferences with Vergennes, but he pumped information from him after every interview. He then returned to London, just before Arthur Lee arrived in Paris, and reported to Lords Weymouth and Suffolk, secretaries of state. For his information Bancroft was rewarded with an annual pension of £200, for the good doctor, through Deane, had opened a direct line from the secret parleys in Versailles to the British ministry at Whitehall. It was an invaluable connection! Deane's intimacy with Bancroft covered a plethora of commercial schemes, including the fitting out of privateers, purchasing supplies for Congress, and speculating on London war stocks. Either Deane knew Bancroft to be a British agent, or he must be considered chronically negligent in revealing critical information to a man known to frequent the governing circles of Britain.³³

Much to Deane's dismay, Lee appeared in Paris on August 23, to discover the status of commercial affairs with Hortalez. Deane had already plunged into commitments for over three million livres worth of clothing and arms. He had promised Beaumarchais full payment—he hoped within a year. Evidently, Deane was not deterred by the communications problem that had supposedly hindered Lee's earlier affairs with Beaumarchais.³⁴ Deane had also accepted the offer by Donatien Le Ray de Chaumont, clothier for the French army, of one million livres credit, putting him, he felt, well along in his negotiations to furnish arms, clothing, and accoutrements for a force of twenty-five thousand. Although he had been promised credit, Deane advised Congress that the supplies "must be paid for, the sooner the better, if to be done without too great a risk." Except for Beaumarchais' demand that Hortalez be granted a monopoly on all American shipments to France, Deane was fully satisfied with him.³⁵

33. Edward Bancroft, "Narrative of Deane's Mission," August 14, 1776, in Stevens (ed.), *Facsimiles*, no. 890; Lewis Einstein, *Divided Loyalties: Americans in England During the War of Independence* (Boston, 1933), 6–14; Boyd, "Silas Deane," 168, 187; Edward Bancroft to Deane, November 8, 1776, in Isham (ed.), *Deane Papers*, XIX, 350; Bancroft to Deane, December 13, 1776, in *The Deane Papers*, XXIII, 56–68.

34. Deane to Beaumarchais, July 20, 24, 1776, in Wharton (ed.), *Correspondence*, II, 102–106. An interpreter, Gérard de Rayneval, was supplied by Vergennes to enhance the Deane-Beaumarchais parleys. Morton (ed.), *Beaumarchais*, II, 234–35.

35. Deane to Committee of Secret Correspondence, August 18, 1776, Roderique

Deane resented Lee's intrusion into his affairs. He dashed off a note to Vergennes, expressing surprise at Lee's arrival, "as I know of no particular affair" that would call him to Paris. Ostensibly Deane was afraid that Lee's visit would alert British spies and thwart his business with Hortalez. Evidently Deane wanted to keep all commercial matters—then in "as favorable a course as the situation of the times will admit"—to himself. He wanted no fellow agent of Congress scrutinizing his transactions with Beaumarchais. Unfortunately the historical record yields few clues as to the extent and nature of the initial encounter between the two American agents. Lee, after perhaps a month in France, returned to London in mid-September to resume his station as observer of British politics and his role as lawyer. He did not indicate to anyone disharmony with his fellow agent. Deane, meanwhile, went his separate way, spurning Lee.[36]

Taking advantage of his position as American agent, Deane furthered his private schemes. He faithfully followed the advice of his mentor and partner, Robert Morris, who counseled, "It seems to me the present opportunity of improving our fortunes ought not to be lost, especially as the very means of doing it will contribute to the service of our country at the same time." The Philadelphia merchant offered Deane a third of the profits gained from international trade by the firm of Willing, Morris, and Company. The merchant confided to his protégé, "You may depend that the pursuit of this plan deserves your utmost Exertion and Attention so far as your mind is engaged in making money." Deane accepted the proposal and advice. By the end of September he promised Morris that £100,000 worth of French consumer goods would be dispatched to America for sale by the Philadelphia profiteers.[37]

Deane's confusion of his private accounts with public funds was inevitable. At first he purchased linens and calicoes, which would reap handsome profits in America, which was suffering from a self-imposed

Hortalez et Cie. to Committee of Secret Correspondence, August 18, 1776, Deane to Vergennes, August 22, 1776, all in Wharton (ed.), *Correspondence*, II, 112–27, 129–31, 132–33.

36. Riggs, "Arthur Lee and the Radical Whigs," 249; Arthur Lee to C. W. F. Dumas, September 23, November 15, 1776, both in Wharton (ed.), *Correspondence*, II, 148–49, 192–94.

37. Morris to Deane, August 11, 1776, Deane to Morris, September 30, 1776, Deane to Messrs. Delap, November 13, 1776, all in Isham (ed.), *Deane Papers*, XIX, 172, 786–87, 354–57.

embargo and the British blockade. Later, seeking to profit at the expense of Congress, Deane split up saltpeter and powder shipments between himself and the New York firm of Livingston, Lewis, and Alsop. He advised French adventurers to ship silks, ribbons, brandy, and window glass to America to be sold to the highest bidder. In one deal Deane and Chaumont financed a £20,000 cargo for such speculation. In turn Chaumont furnished Deane with a house in the suburbs of Paris. British spies reported Deane was partner in a giant international venture. Deane, Chaumont, the firm of Delaps at Bordeaux, and Thomas Walpole, a friendly speculator in London, concocted a scheme to operate on the spectacular capital of £400,000. Although the sum appears exaggerated, the scheme, involving British goods shipped to America through France, was feasible. Historians are unsure, however, whether the plan was ever tried.[38]

Deane's initial ventures were handicapped by lack of capital. By 1778, however, he had set up his brother Simeon as a prosperous commercial agent in Virginia. The costs of shipping private cargoes were reduced by using American warships in convoys. Prizes taken by American privateers or naval vessels frequently fell into Deane's hands to be disposed of at his discretion and, it happened, for his profit. Losses incurred by the Connecticut merchant in private ventures were often placed on the accounts of Congress.

The mixing of private and public accounts did not lead to Deane's undoing. Rather, he alienated Congress when he exceeded instructions and signed contracts with French soldiers of fortune who desired commands and high rank in the American army. Arthur Lee had proposed that French engineers and artillerymen be recruited to fill voids on Washington's staff. Deane, however, indiscriminately hired French officers, like Transon du Coudray and Thomas Conway, who harassed Congress and the commander in chief with outlandish demands. Ultimately Congress

38. Samuel Beall to Deane, August 5, 1776, in *The Deane Papers*, XXIII, 34–35; Deane to Messrs. Delap, September 7, November 13, 1776, Deane to Morris, January 6, 1777, in Isham (ed.), *Deane Papers*, XIX, 224–46, 354–57, 448–51; Paul Wentworth to Earl of Suffolk [received November 23, 1776], in Stevens (ed.), *Facsimiles*, no. 131; E. James Ferguson, *The Power of the Purse: A History of American Public Finance, 1776–1780* (Chapel Hill, 1961), 70–105; Thomas P. Abernethy, "Commercial Activities of Silas Deane in France," *American Historical Review*, XXXIX (April, 1938), 477–85.

came to question Deane's judgment in this and other concerns, and his re-call resulted.[39]

Benjamin Franklin arrived on the coast of France on December 4, 1776. He was armed with the appointments of himself, Deane, and Lee (in Jefferson's stead) as joint commissioners to "communicate, treat, agree, and conclude with his Most Christian Majesty the King of France . . . upon a true and sincere friendship and a firm inviolable and uni-versal peace" between France and the United States. It remained to be seen whether the French would openly treat with American envoys. Franklin recognized that France might be embarrassed by such a proposal. Surely the British ambassador, Lord Stormont, would heartily protest. Franklin did not want to jeopardize the patriot cause by hazarding "a disgraceful refusal" from Vergennes.[40] He was ready to match wits with the wily French.

By December 16 Arthur Lee in London had received word of Frank-lin's arrival and his own appointment. Since the conference with Deane, Lee had busied himself in his law practice and in furnishing intelligence to the Americans of British troop movements. He dispatched continuous reports, along with exhortations to Congress and occasionally to George Washington. The commander in chief was often perplexed by these mes-sages. Following a warning from Lee that the British were to attack Bos-ton in early 1777, Washington observed, "Doctor Lee's opinion on the propriety of attacking the enemy upon their first arrival, under a suppo-sition of their being raw and undisciplined is certainly well-founded, if our circumstances will admit of it; but the Doctor little apprehended, I believe, that we ourselves should have an army to raise, at this late hour, of men equally raw, and officers probably much more so." It was evident to Washington that Lee's patriotic zeal often distorted reality. His ardor, of course, had made Lee a marked man in British eyes. He confided to one correspondent, "I flatter myself with being as much within the eye of their enmity as any man can be. But I think that the enmity of bad men is the most desirable testimony of virtuous merit."[41] Appointment as Com-

39. Beaumarchais to Deane, July 26, 1776, in Isham (ed.), *Deane Papers*, XIX, 164–65; Augur, *Secret War*, 144–45; Sparks, "Early Diplomatic History," 23–24.

40. Commission from the Continental Congress, October 23, 1776, in *The Deane Papers*, XXIII, 44–45; Franklin to John Hancock, December 8, 1776, in Smyth (ed.), *Writings of Franklin*, VI, 474–75.

41. Washington to Richard Henry Lee, April 27, 1777, in John C. Fitzpatrick

missioner to France enabled Lee to escape from an increasingly perilous situation in England.

The American Commissioners assembled in Paris by December 22. Vergennes warily avoided open recognition of their official role and forestalled discussions of an alliance. According to British spies, Vergennes received the credentials of the Americans, offered general promises of French friendship, and complimented each commissioner: "to Dr. F. on his celebrity, his knowledge, and the honor of seeing so distinguished a person, on an Errand of the first consequence,—to Mr. Deane, on his ability to engage the court in his country's interests . . . and his discretion in maintaining the confidence of the trusts,—to Mr. Lee—on the distinguished reward for the well-known hand he had exerted in England in his country's cause, and ended with wishes he might yet be useful *there.*" The "trembling hesitation" of the French was apparent to Lee. Immediately he noted that Beaumarchais and Deane had changed "the mode of conveying" the secret assistance via Hortalez et Cie., but he did not elaborate. Perhaps Lee had convinced himself at last that what had previously been cast as a gift was now a speculative venture. No doubt he was chagrined to find that Deane had assumed complete control of all commercial affairs. Franklin, however, was pleased by the arrangement, for he claimed to be deficient in business acumen and preferred to reap the advantages of the social prominence accorded him at Paris and Versailles.[42] This was not Lee's idea of sharing responsibilities.

The first report from the commissioners to Congress revealed the mixed reception they met in France. By January 17, 1777, they had been advanced only 500,000 livres of a 2-million-livre loan from Louis XVI's treasury, but the French ministry refused to be pushed. The diplomats observed, "The hearts of the French are universally for us, and the cry is strong for immediate War with Britain . . . but the Court has its reasons for postponing it a little longer. In the meantime, preparations for it are making." Arthur Lee was wary of such sanguine hopes. He privately

---

(ed.), *The Writings of George Washington* (39 vols.; Washington, D.C., 1931–44), VII, 462–65; Arthur Lee to C. W. F. Dumas, November 15, 1776, in Force (ed.), *American Archives,* III, 692.

42. Paul Wentworth to Earl of Suffolk, January 25, 1777, in Stevens (ed.), *Facsimiles,* no. 7 (my italics); Arthur Lee to Committee of Secret Correspondence, December 31, 1776, in Wharton (ed.), *Correspondence,* II, 242–44.

warned Richard Henry that he was doing his best to obtain foreign assistance for the patriots. "Two things, however, I wish to impress on your minds; to look forward and prepare for the worst event, and to search for every resource within yourselves so as to have as little external dependence as possible."[43] The French interpreted Arthur's insistence on self-reliance—a cardinal principle of the Lees—as antigallicism. In truth, Arthur Lee was not so much against dependency on the Bourbons as for total American independence.

There was a degree of coordination but little cooperation within the American Commission in France. Deane closeted himself with Beaumarchais and other commercial-minded Frenchmen. Franklin at first permitted Deane to dominate discussions with Vergennes' first secretary, Conrad Alexandre Gérard, whose assignment was to appease the Americans without committing France to an alliance. Franklin quickly sensed the delicacy of his mission and the presence of both British and French spies. He set about to charm rather than intrigue, making the most of his role, wherein he found himself "treated with great civility and respect by all orders of people."[44] With little formal procedure to follow, the commission went its own way. Deane increasingly looked after his own affairs and subordinated himself to French schemers. Franklin polished his public image and permitted formal negotiations to languish. Lee, by nature hyperactive, was left without any set duties and dissociated from his colleagues.

Perhaps Lee's recent connections in England had led to his ostracism, even though he had severed all correspondence with Britons. He was anxious over his separation. Immediately upon his arrival in Paris he informed Shelburne of the cutting of ties. Arthur bid adieu to England, where "I had fixed my fortunes, and to a people whom I respected and could have loved." He explained that patriotism compelled him to cast off his British friends: "the first object of my life is my country; the first wish of my heart is public liberty. I must see, therefore, the liberties of my country established, or perish in her last struggle." It was Lee's aim

---

43. Franklin, Deane, and Arthur Lee to Secret Committee of Congress, January 17, 1777, in Arthur Lee Papers, Box 3; Arthur Lee to Richard Henry Lee, January 4, 1777, in Hoffman and Molyneaux (eds.), *Lee Family Papers*, III, 1–2.

44. Franklin to Samuel Cooper, May 1, 1777, in Smyth (ed.), *Writings of Franklin*, VII, 55.

that virtuous Americans, "with a sort of filial piety," reanimate the expiring English constitution in a new nation. Ironically, the French did not believe Lee had cut his ties in England and they continued to suspect him. Meanwhile Franklin and Deane were working cheek to jowl with Bancroft and other English agents.[45]

At the root of the French distrust of Lee was his attitude toward them. Lee followed the tactics of militia diplomacy, an impetuous approach to foreign affairs that defied the ageless codes of Old World diplomacy and relied on an image of virtuous plain-dealing. The "notion that it was beneath the dignity of the United States to resort to traditional diplomatic measures to obtain a hearing from European courts was a fundamental principle of the anti-Gallicans. American diplomats were simply to appear at selected courts, outline the commercial advantages to be reaped from relations with the United States, and enter into negotiations for treaties of alliance and commerce."[46] Militia diplomats resisted the subordination of American to French interests. No doubt Lee's attitude evinced the sentiments he broadcast to American radicals through Samuel Adams: "It is well to cultivate Europe but not to depend upon it . . . probably the more dearly we purchase our liberties, the more we shall prize them." Thus Lee expressed a cardinal tenet of virtuous diplomacy. The statement is revelatory of Lee's familiar self-image as defender of American virtue, a role applauded by his two mentors, Richard Henry and Samuel Adams. Unfortunately, it clashed with the ideas of the diplomats of the *ancien régime*, who looked upon the Americans as ingenuous and weak negotiators.[47]

Lee should not have been the chief suspect of the French, for the real culprit was Edward Bancroft, who crossed the English Channel in February to take a position as secretary to the American commission. Both Wil-

45. Arthur Lee to Lord Shelburne, December 23, 1776, in Wharton (ed.), *Correspondence*, II, 239–40; Cecil Currey, *Code Number 72 / Ben Franklin: Patriot or Spy?* (Englewood Cliffs, 1972), 112–17.
46. David M. Griffiths, "American Commercial Diplomacy in Russia, 1780 to 1783," *William and Mary Quarterly*, 3rd ser., XXVII (July, 1970), 391, 383–84; Bemis, *Diplomacy of the American Revolution*, 114; Marshall Smelser, *The Winning of Independence* (New York, 1973), 167–68.
47. William Stinchcombe, *The American Revolution and the French Alliance* (Syracuse, 1969), 33–34; Arthur Lee to Samuel Adams, January 21, 1777, in Arthur Lee Papers, Box 3.

liam and Arthur Lee accused Bancroft of leaking information, but not even the suspicious Virginians could then imagine the depth to which Bancroft's intrigues ran. He had signed a contract with Paul Wentworth to steal commission correspondence, which would be passed to the British embassy in France. Stormont, the British ambassador, could use the information to harass Vergennes to halt French shipments to the American rebels, and the British ministry could remain abreast of negotiations between the Bourbons and the Americans. Bancroft won himself a £500 bonus and a £400 annual pension for his work. Although the British did not totally trust Bancroft—like Arthur Lee, George III recognized the spy's penchant for stock speculations—other spies confirmed his reports.[48] Meanwhile, Deane and Franklin smiled upon Bancroft.

Arthur Lee grew restless with inactivity in Paris. His presence made his colleagues uneasy. Vergennes' policy of watchful waiting was prolonged by news of the British capture of New York. Louis XVI remained determined that France would enter no war without a commitment from Charles III of Spain. The American trio therefore would have to convince Charles III to support their rebellion before Louis XVI would act. On January 23, perhaps as an effort to cut costs in Paris or perhaps as an attempt by Deane and Franklin to rid themselves of a pest, it was decided that Lee would venture to Spain and Deane to Holland in quest of foreign assistance. In fact, Deane never began his mission, but Lee gained a degree of success in his.[49]

The Americans had been encouraged by the Spanish ambassador in Paris, Conde de Aranda. Yet Aranda was out of touch and favor with his own government because he was promoting a Bourbon war on Great Britain in the hope of reasserting himself in Spanish politics. Vergennes, in fact, had intervened once to prevent Aranda's recall. Somewhat an outcast at his post in Paris, Aranda nonetheless helped Lee to plot his secret venture to Madrid. The Spaniard reportedly told Deane, but not

48. Bancroft to Deane, November 8, 1776, in Isham (ed.), *Deane Papers*, XIX, 345–50; Engagement of Dr. Edwards with Paul Wentworth and Lord Stormont, December, 1776, in Stevens (ed.), *Facsimiles*, no. 235; George III to Lord North, January 16, 1778, in Fortesque (ed.), *Correspondence of King George*, IV, 19.

49. Joint Commissioners to the Committee of Secret Correspondence, February 6, 1777, in Wharton (ed.), *Correspondence*, II, 264; Currey, *Code Number 72*, pp. 113–14; Paul H. Giddens, "Arthur Lee, First United States Envoy to Spain" *Virginia Magazine of History and Biography*, XL (January, 1932), 3–13.

the eager Lee, that he felt himself "a disgraced Man with his court, and any idea known to be suggested by him would suffer from that very circumstance."[50] Lee had little inkling that his mission had been undermined before he crossed the Pyrennes.

Buoyed by Aranda's exhortations, Lee solicited the blessing of his colleagues for the expedition to Madrid. Franklin, who had been empowered by Congress to treat with Spain, readily excused himself in favor of his younger and more vigorous associate. Not only age but principle determined Franklin's demur. He later revealed, "I have never changed the Opinion I gave Congress, that a Virgin State should preserve the Virgin Character, and not go suitoring for Alliances, but wait with decent Dignity for the Application of others. I was overruled; perhaps for the best."[51] Franklin was no militia diplomat.

Before the commissioners went their separate ways, they signed a pledge. If either Bourbon monarchy concluded a treaty of amity and commerce with the Americans and subsequently aided the rebellion with supplies or opened war on Britain, the trio vowed that their government would not conclude a separate peace. Privately, Lee, Franklin, and Deane resolved, "It is further considered that in the present perils of the liberties of our country it is our duty to hazard everything in their support and defense. That if it should be necessary to the attainment of anything in our best judgment essential to the defense and support of the public cause, that we shall pledge our persons, or hazard the censure of Congress, by exceeding our instructions, we will for such purpose most cheerfully resign our personal liberty or life."[52] The ritual reaffirmed Lee's willingness to become entangled in a political pact with the Bourbons.

Persuaded by Aranda and his fellow commissioners, Arthur Lee ventured to Spain in hopes of procuring aid, if not an alliance, from Charles

50. Doniol, *Participation de la France*, I, 49–50, 64–65, 172; George Bancroft, *History of the United States of America From the Discovery of the Continent* (6 vols.; New York, 1883–85), V, 128–29; Richard Herr, *The Eighteenth Century Revolution in Spain* (Princeton, 1958), 11–22, 75; Employment of Lt. Col. Smith, March, 1777, in Stevens (ed.), *Facsimiles*, no. 248.

51. Franklin to Arthur Lee, March 21, 1777, in Smyth (ed.), *Writings of Franklin*, VII, 32–35; Currey, *Code Number 72*, pp. 114–16.

52. Personal Pledge of the Commissioners, February 2, 1777, in Wharton (ed.), *Correspondence*, II, 260.

III. He first journeyed to Nantes, a port on the Loire River in northwestern France. There he discovered the commercial affairs of Congress that had been entrusted to Thomas Morris to be "greatly deranged." More specifically, Arthur informed Richard Henry that Morris, half brother to Robert Morris of the Pennsylvania delegation, was "a sot . . . a man who could not get a month's employment in any counting house in Europe." He recommended that commercial-minded William Lee be appointed supervisor of Congress' European business. Meanwhile Arthur paused to reflect on his Spanish mission. Poor roads and worse weather hampered his progress and gave him forebodings of failure. He promised "my using every diligence to reach my destination in time to make the best advantage of the present situation of affairs" and prepared himself for "some obstacle in the umbrage" that the Spanish court might take to his hasty, unauthorized, and unilateral commission.[53] Though a zealot, Lee was certain to pack his correspondence with pessimism. Thus, should he succeed, his sense of triumph would redouble; should he fail, posterity could recall the odds against him.

As Lee traversed the Pyrenees, a significant change occurred in the ministry of Spain. On February 15, 1777, Count Floridablanca became foreign minister. Narrowly nationalistic, rival to Aranda, esteemed for his common sense, jealous of the French, Floridablanca was just the man to help Charles III cautiously and independently nurture Spanish imperialism. Immediately Don Diego de Gardoqui, a Bilbao merchant experienced in American trade, was instructed to waylay Lee and keep the American out of Madrid, lest the British ambassador be irritated.[54]

Gardoqui caught up with Lee at Burgos, 120 miles from Madrid, where they awaited the arrival of the deposed foreign minister, the Mar-

---

53. Arthur Lee to Committee of Secret Correspondence, February 11, 1777, in Wharton (ed.), *Correspondence*, II, 266–69; Arthur Lee to [Francis Lightfoot Lee?], February 20, 1777, Arthur Lee to [Richard Henry Lee?], March 6, 1777, both in Hoffman and Molyneaux (eds.), *Lee Family Papers*, III, 94–95, 120–121.

54. John J. Meng (ed.), *Despatches and Instructions of Conrad Alexandre Gérard, 1778–1780* (Baltimore, 1939), 73–74; Vera Lee Brown, "Studies in the History of Spain in the Second Half of the Eighteenth Century," *Smith College Studies in History*, XV (October, 1929–January, 1930), 18; Don Diego de Gardoqui to Arthur Lee, February 17, 1777, in Hoffman and Molyneaux (eds.), *Lee Family Papers*, III, 82.

quis de Grimaldi, who had been sent to commence parleys. Lee was still troubled by the lack of specific proposals to make. He confessed his awkward position: "It would grieve me to be put to the alternative of letting a favorable opportunity pass unembraced." Nor did he wish to hazard a commitment based upon his "weak judgment and very limited information" for fear of misplaying his hand.[55] He wanted to avoid personal responsibility for a mission that was looking less and less likely to succeed.

The first interview among Lee, Gardoqui, and Grimaldi took place March 4. Lee remonstrated against the Spanish suggestion that he avoid Madrid and return to the French border. Such conduct, the patriot charged, would only "beget an opinion that Spain had renounced the states of America, in refusing to receive her deputy." This impression would injure American endeavors to establish credit elsewhere in Europe. Disappointed by the "timidity" of the Spaniards, Lee pressed for official recognition of the American Congress. At the least, he suggested, Spain could establish a covert fund in Holland to finance "the most effectual aid" for the rebellion. Stubbornly he awaited at Burgos the decision of the Spanish Court.[56]

Lee used the familiar tactics of militia diplomacy. Styling himself commissioner plenipotentiary from the Congress of the United States of America, he penned a memorial to the Spanish court on March 8. It was as if he were back in London petitioning George III. Reviewing his offer of an alliance of amity and commerce, Lee sketched the alternatives open to Spain just as Beaumarchais had done for Louis XVI. He pushed for a Bourbon commitment before the military campaign of 1777. If Bourbon neutrality persisted for another year, Lee predicted that Britain would either totally destroy the rebellion or else come to an accommodation with the colonists. If Britain triumphed, "America will become a powerful instrument in her hands, to be wielded at her will" against Spain and France. An Anglo-American reconciliation would produce "almost all the same consequences." The Bourbons best not "let slip such an opportunity of humbling her [Britain] as may never return." Lee

<hr/>

55. Arthur Lee to the Commissioners in Paris, February 26, 1777, in Wharton (ed.), *Correspondence*, II, 275.

56. Arthur Lee to Marquis de Grimaldi, March 5, 1777, in Hoffman and Molyneaux (eds.), *Lee Family Papers*, III, 116–17; Arthur Lee to Franklin, March 5, 1777, in Arthur Lee Papers, Box 3.

urged, "Great Britain would endure any insult short of an open and out-
rageous act of hostility rather than engage in a European war during her
contest with America."[57]

The Spaniards were persuaded. They decided to placate the American
envoy and remove him as quickly as possible. By March 8 Lee was able to
report headway in negotiations. Spain refused open recognition of the
revolutionaries, but Gardoqui was permitted to channel secret aid to
America. Free supplies of munitions, blankets, and clothing were to be deposited at New Orleans and Havana "with directions to lend them to such
American vessels as may call for that purpose."[58] Gardoqui's firm in Bilbao was willing to make further transactions. A session with Grimaldi at
Vitoria, closer to the Pyrenees, produced further points of agreement. The
Americans would undertake a joint expedition with Spain against the
British at Pensacola. Spanish accounts in Holland would provide funds,
ultimately 400,000 livres, for American use, a contribution to the American crusade to vindicate "violated rights of human nature." In thanks, Lee
wrote Floridablanca that he understood that succors from Spain came from
"the graciousness" of Charles III's "royal disposition, without stipulating
any return."[59] Lee had secured another diplomatic bridgehead, second
only to his successful intrigue with Beaumarchais.

Lee considered his negotiations with the Spaniards analogous to his initial parleys with the French. Floridablanca, like Vergennes, refused overt
recognition of the American cause, but Gardoqui, like Beaumarchais,
was permitted to funnel covert assistance to the rebels. Lee, perhaps sensitive to French demands, reported to Congress, "I have avoided stipulating any return" on the part of the Americans for Spanish assistance. His

57. Memorial presented to the Spanish court by Arthur Lee, March 8, 1777, in
Wharton (ed.), *Correspondence*, II, 280–83.
58. Arthur Lee to Committee of Secret Correspondence, March 8, 1777, Grimaldi to Arthur Lee, March 8, 1777, both in Wharton (ed.), *Correspondence*, II,
280, 282–83; J. F. Yela Utrilla, *España ante la independencia de los Estados Unidos* (Lerida, 1925), II, 162. Footnotes in Lee's personal journal, possibly added at
a later date, assert, "these aids would be given without demanding any thing of
us in return" and "N. B. The Duke hinted that Spain had contributed part of
what had been given in France." March 4, 1777, "Spanish Journal of Arthur Lee,"
in Arthur Lee Papers, Box 9.
59. Currey, *Code Number 72*, p. 117; Arthur Lee to Floridablanca, March 17,
1777, in Wharton (ed.), *Correspondence*, II, 290–91; Arthur Lee to Franklin and
Deane, March 16, 1777, in Arthur Lee Papers, Box 3.

foray across the Pyrenees would yield a subsidy of 187,500 livres in 1777 and a loan of 187,500 livres in 1778. The contributions of goods funneled by Gardoqui to the American rebels at spots outside Spain cannot be precisely estimated. At least 30,000 blankets were involved. His experience in Spain, notwithstanding his frustrations, did not hamper Lee's zeal for militia diplomacy. He informed his colleagues that he was prepared to propagandize the American cause throughout Europe. He also rationalized that it was probably best that no treaty with Spain was concluded "since our present situation would raise demands, and perhaps enforce concessions of which we might sorely regret hereafter." [60] American autonomy must be preserved.

Upon Lee's return to France there was some confusion about the Spanish connection. Bancroft, having installed himself as the commission's general secretary, informed the British of Arthur's success but confided that "the Court of Spain are prejudiced against Lee." Franklin handled negotiations with Floridablanca for a time, but Congress, being informed that Lee had taken up the mission to Spain, was moved to reconsider its representatives in Europe. On May 1, Arthur Lee was empowered as congressional agent at the court of Spain. Within a week, Ralph Izard was elected commissioner to the court of Tuscany and two days later, William Lee won a similar assignment to Berlin and Vienna. The Adams-Lee junto reached its high-water mark in directing foreign policy of the Continental Congress. When Arthur's commission came up for confirmation on May 31, Congress voted itself into a committee of the whole to consider the state of foreign affairs and guidelines for the new appointees. Deliberations concluded June 5 with approval of Arthur's commission. "Confiding in the prudence and integrity of Arthur Lee, esquire, of Virginia," the Congress deputed him "with full power to communicate, treat and conclude" a treaty of amity and commerce with Charles III. His commission to France was also reaffirmed "so long as he shall remain in, and be present at, the said court." [61] Brothers Richard Henry and Francis

60. Bemis, *Diplomacy of American Revolution*, 93; Arthur Lee to Committee of Secret Correspondence, March 18, 1777, in Wharton (ed.), *Correspondence*, II, 292–96; Ferguson, *Power of the Purse*, 41; Buchanan Parker Thomson, *Spain: Forgotten Ally of the American Revolution* (North Quincy, 1976), 48–56, 241–44; Arthur Lee to Franklin and Deane, March 16, 1777, in Arthur Lee Papers, Box 3.

61. Paul Wentworth to Earl of Suffolk, April 14, 1777, Bancroft to Went-

Lightfoot Lee had piloted Arthur's appointments through tricky currents of Congress.

European situations were not amenable to congressional directions, though. Within two weeks of his arrival back in Paris, the three commissioners decided Lee should try his luck with an expedition to Berlin. The prospects facing this mission resembled those Lee had confronted in Spain.[62] Like Charles III, Frederick the Great was mainly concerned with strengthening power within his country. He did not wish to be encumbered with the demands and desires of an envoy as persistent as Arthur Lee. The Prussian soldier-monarch had little love for the British, but he recognized his vulnerability to blockade by the British fleet if he gave countenance to the American rebels by allowing trade with the colonial insurgents or by opening Prussian ports to American privateers.

The commissioners had been enticed by Prussian representatives in Paris. In February they had proposed to Baron Schulenberg, a minister of state for Frederick II, that discussions over commercial ties be commenced. In drafting a reply to this petition, the monarch instructed his advisor, "to put nothing into your answer to the said plenipotentiaries that can displease their employers, but explain your position toward their offer as favorably as possible, so that the moment events become more propitious there we may be able to take advantage of it." [63]

Lee's assignment to Berlin generated acrimony. He proposed that William Carmichael, Deane's secretary who had been to Berlin in 1776, accompany him. Already a staunch member of the Deane-Bancroft clique as well as a British informer, Carmichael refused. The Lee-Carmichael dispute was but one of the fissures within the American commission; there were others. Deane and Franklin had taken up residence in suburban Passy, while Lee was forced to find lodging three miles away at Chaillot. His colleagues did not see fit to brief Lee on negotiations made during his absence, nor was he permitted a key to the files of the American mission. British spies, fed by Carmichael and Bancroft, depreciated Lee's talents

worth, May, 1777, George Lupton to [William Eden], April 8, 10, 1777, in Stevens (ed.), *Facsimiles*, nos. 250, 151, 681; Worthington C. Ford (ed.), *Journals*, VIII, 318, 334, 343, 409–420, 522–23; Henderson, *Party Politics*, 191.

62. "Spanish Journal of Arthur Lee," March 21–April 18, 1777, in Arthur Lee Papers, Box 3.

63. Quoted in Haworth, "Frederick the Great," 464.

and role. Reports sent to London minimize his part in the conduct of American diplomacy. At most he is mentioned as a hindrance to the schemes of the band of intriguers. Whitehall was informed that "Lee is upon very bad terms with Franklin and Deane," that the French so distrusted Lee because of his English acquaintances that "they deal only in generals [generalities]" in his presence, and that Lee's absence meant "a clear stage" for agents who had infiltrated the American embassy.[64]

Before his departure, Lee addressed a memorial to Gérard to be forwarded to Vergennes. This epistle presages the disputes Lee later had with his colleagues, which sprang from Lee's image of the ideal diplomat. To him, Deane and Franklin lacked both system and patriotism. The mistrustful envoy had learned that, during his absence in Spain, the French had been informed that he had participated with Deane and Franklin in an improper private commercial scheme. Lee forthrightly vowed that "nothing could be more remote from the truth than such a representation." He was stunned that he could ever be suspected of engaging in "so unbecoming an action" as to use official position as a means of attaining private profit. Lee's behavior in this episode is most revealing. The role he played throughout his career in the diplomatic corps was that of the revolutionary ascetic: he devoted himself totally and tirelessly to the cause of American autonomy. Deane meanwhile indulged in personal speculative ventures, and Franklin took a casual and submissive approach to negotiations with the French. Lee's memorial to Gérard exhibits his much acclaimed paranoia also. He felt that he was being persecuted, but was unable to recognize the persecutor or the modes of persecution. Nevertheless, his suspicions were indeed rooted in fact.[65]

Before his suspicions could develop, Lee set off for Vienna and Berlin on May 15. With him went Stephen Sayre as secretary. Sayre, Arthur's London crony, possessed great aspirations, vanity, and wit. He hoped to

64. William Carmichael to Franklin, May 3, 1777, in Benjamin Franklin Papers; Currey, *Code Number 72*, pp. 113–19; Lord Stormont to Earl Weymouth, April 16, 1777, Dr. B[ancroft] to Mr. W[entworth], April 24, 1777, both in Stevens (ed.), *Facsimiles*, nos. 1518, 65.

65. Arthur Lee to M. Gérard, April 30, 1777, in Stevens (ed.), *Facsimiles*, no. 687; Bruce Mazlish, "Leadership in the American Revolution: The Psychological Dimension," in *Leadership in the American Revolution* (Washington, D.C., 1974), 117–19; Morton Schatzman, "Paranoia or Persecution—The Case of Schreber," *History of Childhood Quarterly*, I (Summer, 1973), 82.

continue on to Saint Petersburg to woo aid from Catherine the Great. The two envoys departed in a conspicuous four-wheeled green postchaise with Lee's initials embossed on the doors. After their embarkation Franklin and Deane received a hasty note from Schulenburg, too late to forestall the Americans. The Prussian minister also cautioned Lee that he considered all their previous correspondence merely "preliminaries" rather than any "negotiations from which immediate advantages may be expected." [66] The note boded ill for Lee and Sayre.

The circuitous route via Strasbourg, Munich, and Vienna to the Prussian court tested their enthusiasm. Lee fell ill, travel proved expensive, and the Viennese greeted him coldly. The Americans arrived in Berlin on June 4 and established themselves at an inn, the Auberge de Corsica, under scrutiny of both Prussian and British spies.[67] As in Spain, Lee found his presence embarrassed his hosts. Although the Americans had not been invited, Schulenburg permitted them to remain as long as Frederick's neutrality was unaffected. No official recognition of the rebels was forthcoming.

Lee was repeatedly foiled in Berlin. A series of memorials failed to move Schulenburg and his monarch. The Prussians would not engage in commerce until miltiary campaigns of 1777 had concluded in America. The American could not comprehend why Europe would not open her ports to the rebel merchantmen and privateers. He pleaded, "We are left like Hercules in his cradle, to strangle the serpent that annoys all Europe." His enthusiasm for the revolution did not infect the careful Prussians who remained in a "perfect system of quietism." Nor were his efforts to hawk tobacco for munitions and clothing successful. Schulenburg assured the British ambassador at Berlin that the king of Prussia "had too great a friendship for the King of Great Britain to enter into any connections with his rebellious subjects." [68] It was not Lee's fault he had failed.

Humiliation was heaped on frustration, and Lee became the center of

---

66. Earl of Suffolk to Hugh Elliot, May 30, 1777, Wentworth to Suffolk, May 15, 1777, both in Stevens (ed.), *Facsimiles*, nos. 156, 694; Schulenburg to Arthur Lee, May 20, 1777, in Wharton (ed.), *Correspondence*, II, 321.

67. Arthur Lee to Schulenburg, June 10, 1777, in Wharton (ed.), *Correspondence*, II, 327–30; Arthur Lee to M. Francy, May 23, 1777, in Box 3; Hugh Elliot to Suffolk, June 6, 1777, in Stevens (ed.), *Facsimiles*, no. 1455.

68. Arthur Lee to Schulenburg, June 10, 1777, in Wharton (ed.), *Correspondence*, II, 334; Arthur Lee to Messrs. Francois and Chaumont, June 13, 1777, in

an uproar when it was discovered that Hugh Elliot, the British representative in Berlin, had pilfered the American's daily journal and portfolio of diplomatic correspondence.[69] Elliot realized that Lee's papers would reveal details of militia diplomacy in France, Spain, and Prussia. On June 26, therefore, while Lee and Sayre were away, Elliot dispatched a servant to Lee's lodgings. While the henchman was stealing the dispatches, Elliot visited Prussian officials to establish his personal alibi. When the Americans returned to the inn, Elliot engaged them in conversation while a team of copiers worked over Lee's dispatches. Finally Lee retired to his room to make the daily entry in his journal, discovered the theft, thundered into the lobby shouting that he had been robbed, and sped off with Sayre to recruit assistance of the Prussian authorities.

In an attempt to quiet the uproar, Elliot hastened to his house, gathered together the dispatches, and returned in disguise to place the portfolio outside the entrance of the inn before Lee returned. A maidservant, also in English pay, then took the case to the American. Later a copy of some instructions from Congress, inadvertently left at Elliot's, was also returned. This last piece was the only document Lee thought had actually been stolen, as he imagined the other messages had been abandoned by the thief. When the Prussian investigation of the inn's employees implicated him, Elliot came forward to meekly confess that the theft had been the result of his own imprudent inquisitiveness and his servant's excessive zeal. Meanwhile he had hastened a courier to London with copies of Lee's files.

Elliot's daring and Lee's embarrassment delighted the British. The English envoy was publicly rebuked, recalled from his assignment, and rewarded with £1000. Frederick the Great would not follow Lee's demands to expel the Briton even though he confided, "In truth, the English ought to blush with shame at sending such ministers to foreign courts." Ultimately the purloined material proved of limited value. The British made

---

Hoffman and Molyneaux (eds.), *Lee Family Papers*, III, 294; Hugh Elliot to Earl of Suffolk, June 10, 14, 19, 1777, Stevens (ed.), *Facsimiles*, Nos. 1456, 1457, 1459.

69. The following account relies on the variation offered in William Eden's "Narrative of the Abstraction of Arthur Lee's Papers at Berlin," July 11, 1777, gained by Eden from Elliot's courier in Stevens (ed.), *Facsimiles*, no. 1468. See also an "Account of the Robbery of the Papers of (Arthur) Lee American Agent, at Berlin 26 June 1777," in Hoffman and Molyneaux (eds.), *Lee Family Papers*, VIII, 39–61.

no noticeable addition to intelligence they already possessed. They were merely able to confirm what Bancroft, Carmichael, Wentworth, and others had reported: that Arthur Lee failed to gain an alliance at either Madrid or Berlin and that his colleagues in Paris had made little more headway.[70]

Chagrined by Frederick's stubbornness, frustrated by Schulenburg's hesitancy and embittered further by a quarrel with Sayre, Lee departed Berlin in a fluster July 9. American militia diplomacy in central Europe had proved fruitless. In summarizing his activities, Lee was most pessimistic. Schulenburg had raised objections to every proposal. The only encouragement Lee could find was the somewhat hollow prediction that if the American armies were not annihilated in 1777, the European powers would be forced to decide on recognition in the following year.[71]

Lee's hopes were never realized. In December, 1777, amidst reports of Burgoyne's surrender at Saratoga and rumors of Bourbon alliances with the rebels, the Prussians continued to drag their heels. Schulenburg could only assure Lee that Frederick the Great "will not be the last power to acknowledge your independency; but you must feel yourself that it is not natural that he be the first, and that France, whose commercial and political interests are more immediately connected with you should set the example." Prussian priorities lay on the European continent, not across the Atlantic. Lee's subsequent efforts to open trade between Prussia and America actually widened differences. The Prussians filled Lee's first order for weapons with eight hundred aged muskets. The sharp-eyed Virginian discovered the defective pieces before they were shipped to America, sent them back to Schulenburg, and demanded reimbursement.[72] Lee's suitoring for alliances had not been completely successful, but the odds had

70. Earl of Suffolk to Hugh Elliot, August 1, October 7, 1777, in Stevens (ed.), *Facsimiles*, nos. 1477, 1482; quoted in Haworth, "Frederick the Great," 467; Elliot to Earl of Suffolk, June 29, 1777, William Eden's List of Elliot's theft of Lee's Papers, July 11, 1777, both in Stevens (ed.), *Facsimiles*, nos. 1460, 1469; Wharton (ed.), *Correspondence*, II, 351–54; Lord North to the King, December 31, 1777, in Fortesque (ed.), *Correspondence of King George*, III, 410.

71. Elliot to Suffolk, July 12, 22, 1777, in Stevens (ed.), *Facsimiles*, nos. 1470, 1475; Arthur Lee to Committee on Foreign Affairs, July 29, 1777, in Wharton (ed.), *Correspondence*, II, 369–72.

72. Schulenburg to Arthur Lee, December 18, 1777, in Wharton (ed.), *Correspondence*, II, 457; Haworth, "Frederick the Great," 468–70; Arthur Lee to Schulenburg, December 25, 1777, in Richard Henry Lee, *Life of Arthur Lee*, II, 21–23.

been against him. His successor in Spain, John Jay, had no more success with Charles III and Floridablanca than Arthur Lee had. No American minister was ever recognized or ever gained assistance from Berlin until peace was signed ending the War for American Independence.

★ CHAPTER VI ★

Everything in Their Power to Traduce Me

Arthur Lee was not in the best frame of mind when he returned to Paris in late July, 1777. His efforts at the courts of Charles III and Frederick the Great had proved less than fulfilling for the American rebellion and particularly vexing for the aggressive emissary. A fever had added to the indispositions of his travel back from Berlin. Nor was the situation in France promising. True, brother William Lee had arrived in Paris to add his rancorous comments to those that passed within the American diplomatic colony. But as had been the case when Arthur returned from Spain, both Franklin and Deane were cold toward him. During his absence the commissioners had moved into spacious quarters in suburban Passy owned by the speculator, Le Ray de Chaumont. Lee, meanwhile, was forced to find separate accommodations at Chaillot. Thus dissociated, he grew increasingly disgruntled. For the next half year, his daily journal recorded mounting animosities among the Americans. Lee perceived a cabal of Edward Bancroft, William Carmichael, and Silas Deane scheming against him. In the autumn he warned Richard Henry Lee that this trio "have done everything in their power to traduce me here, and possibly may attempt the same on your side of the water."[1]

This was no fantasy, for the situation was commented upon both in France and England. One of Lee's associates, Lauraguais, charged that Vergennes himself had directed that Lee be isolated. The London *Public Ledger* reported: "Dr. Lee is certainly joined in the Commission, but he understands the business of courts so ill, that not one of the ministers will negotiate with him. He is the straight-laced image of awkward formality. To the preciseness of a Presbyterian he endeavors to add the Jesuitism of a Quaker. The one renders him ridiculous, the other suspect. When he

1. Journal of Arthur Lee, July 9–August 13, 1777, in Arthur Lee Papers, Box 9; Arthur Lee to Richard Henry Lee, September 5, 1777, in Hoffman and Molyneaux (eds.), *Lee Family Papers*, III, 457.

thinks he is imposing on mankind, they are laughing at him."[2] The Lee brothers never ascertained whether the report originated with the American traducers, with English spies who circulated around Passy, or with French informants.

Arthur's "preciseness" demanded in particular that his colleagues account for the disbursement of public funds. He was chagrined to discover that not only had his associates expended their funds (5 million livres) without keeping adequate records, but that they continued to make decisions without consulting him. Deane made "some evasive objection" to Lee's recommendations on systematizing accounts while Franklin remained silent. Lee was appalled to discover that his colleagues were careless in letting documents lie open to any visitor to Passy and that Deane and Franklin meddled in private schemes for profit "so much as to degrade their characters and occupy most of their time." His observations were on target; his fellow commissioners were not selfless patriots.[3]

The Lees had won their reputation for "Jesuitism" by trying to unseat Edward Bancroft as secretary to the commission. William and Arthur rightly charged that Bancroft had leaked information to the British since 1776. The double agent brazenly disavowed the allegations, and apparently, challenged first William and then Arthur to a duel. No duel ever took place, but verbal altercations continued to disrupt the commission.[4] Deane, dependent on Bancroft, bristled at the Lees' accusations.

The Lees had little love for Deane either. Before departing for Berlin, Arthur had warned William, "Mr. Deane you will treat with the respect due his place, but not with confidence; and as he is a man of no inconsiderable art, it will be prudent at least to avoid making him your enemy." William soon caught scent of schemes between Deane and Franklin's grandnephew Jonathan Williams, Jr. For reasons of his own Deane saw fit to appoint Williams commercial agent for the American commission in France. This appointment contradicted a congressional assignment of

2. Lauraguais to Vergennes, March 5, 1778, in Stevens (ed.), *Facsimiles*, no. 799; William Lee to Arthur Lee, August 6, 1777, in Worthington C. Ford (ed.), *Letters of William Lee*, I, 208n.

3. Journal of Arthur Lee, July–September, 1777, in Arthur Lee Papers, Box 9; Cecil Currey, *Code Number 72*, pp. 130–132, 281.

4. [George Lupton] to [William Eden], June 27, 1777, Conversation Between W. I. [J. W.] and Dr. r. [Dr. Ruston], September 27, 1777, in Stevens (ed.), *Facsimiles*, nos. 702, 266.

William Lee to supervise all European business negotiated by American diplomats. At this time, William counseled Arthur to "lie upon your oars quite inoffensively" until he could ferret out more information.[5]

At the Nantes agency chaos and speculation were rife. Thomas Morris had fallen under the influence of alcohol and of a French firm that, Arthur Lee charged, would "plunder the public at pleasure." Arthur's denunciations roiled Robert Morris in America and Silas Deane in France, for Nantes was the linchpin to American schemes of war profiteering. Soon John Ross was dispatched from Philadelphia, and Williams selected by Passy, to contend with William Lee for the Nantes agency. Franklin and Deane disregarded William Lee's congressional commission as chief commercial agent in Europe and funneled business to Williams. To the Lees it appeared that the disorder at Nantes was traceable to "too much attention to private schemes of commerce on public funds and contemptible private jobs." By the employment of Williams, Deane had secured the nodding acquiescence of Franklin.[6] William and Arthur Lee, abetted by Ralph Izard, set about to secure evidence of the misdealings of Deane and his henchmen, Bancroft, Carmichael, and Williams. They accumulated bits and pieces of circumstantial and hearsay testimony that private profits had been made in England, France, and America from public funds meant for the war effort.

Arthur Lee's journal for the autumn of 1777 was filled with laments. "A great deal of money has been expended in my absence, and almost all without consulting me. In consequence, I am utterly incapable of giving any account of expenditures," he deplored. Another time he recorded his colleagues' neglect: "In this determination Mr. L. had no part, but in this, as in many other things, they seemed to like Dr. F's idea, that the majority formed the Commissioners . . . and that therefore it was not necessary to ask my opinion."[7] These notations allowed Lee to vent his spleen and salve his conscience. His accusations were not yet openly hostile because

5. Arthur Lee to William Lee, May 1, 1777, in Hoffman and Molyneaux (eds.), *Lee Family Papers*, III, 208; William Lee to Arthur Lee, August 6, 1777, in Worthington C. Ford (ed.), *Letters of William Lee*, I, 204.

6. Arthur Lee to Richard Henry Lee, October 4, 1777, in Stevens (ed.), *Facsimiles*, no. 269; Abernethy, "Origins of the Franklin-Lee Imbroglio," 1–12; Worthington C. Ford (ed.), *Letters of William Lee*, I, 232–75.

7. Arthur Lee's Journal, November 2, 20, 1777, in Richard Henry Lee, *Life of Arthur Lee*, I, 346–62.

he feared total disruption of the American diplomatic effort. In the long run his disclaimers would substantiate his claims that Franklin and Deane had mismanaged their mission. Lee's journal, that of a lawyer, overflowed with notations of his colleagues' misdeeds.

In early October, 1777, Arthur Lee, for the benefit of Congressmen Richard Henry Lee, Francis Lightfoot Lee, and Samuel Adams, paused to assess the American war effort in general and his own record in particular over the previous two and a half years. As a Whig, he did not look forward to a prolonged war. He hoped if the American rebellion could persist two more years, the hawkish spirit in Britain would be totally dissolved. Yet he also feared that war and its attendant "state of danger, dissipation and corruption of manners" might "kindle the fatal ambition of some Cromwell" in America. From his perspective—styled "old Radical" by historians—Lee's frustrations with militia diplomacy might be understood, for "liberties established by labor and endurance will be more prized and durable than those acquired by foreign interposition." Sensing that Congress was concerned with the nature of previous foreign succor, Arthur reemphasized that Spanish and French aid "hitherto received is given without expectation of any return." [8]

Turning toward the future, Lee called for an overhaul of the American diplomatic corps. He was not happy with his recently received commission to Spain. First and foremost, mercantile affairs should be handled by commercial agents separated from the other American envoys. Then, he suggested, "adapting characters and abilities to places." His experiences in Europe and his assessments of the Americans then in Europe were included in his recommendation: "Dr. F. to Vienna, as the first, most respectable, and quiet; Mr. Deane to Holland; and the Alderman [William Lee] to Berlin, as the commercial department; Mr. Izard where he is [Tuscany]; Mr. [Edmund] Jenings [a cousin of the Lees] at Madrid, his reserve and circumspection being excellently adapted to that court." This arrangement would leave France "the centre of political activity, and here therefore I should choose to be employed." He hoped that these plans could be implemented by his congressional contacts, but his schemes were

8. Arthur Lee to Samuel Adams, October 4, 1777, in Stevens (ed.), *Facsimiles*, no. 1713; Arthur Lee to Richard Henry Lee, October 4, 1777, in Richard Henry Lee, *Life of Arthur Lee*, I, 114–16; Arthur Lee to Francis Lightfoot Lee, October 7, 1777, in Stevens (ed.), *Facsimiles*, no. 481.

never fulfilled, possibly because these letters were among the American dispatches from France stolen by Joseph Hynson, a British agent.[9]

Lee maintained a characteristically self-righteous stance when he informed his correspondents of dissension among the Americans in Paris. Although Deane, Bancroft, and Carmichael were seeking to defame him, he endured "a thousand causes of resentment and dispute," taking care "never to let it break out into a quarrel." Lee did not specify transgressions, but he believed Deane, finding him "a disagreeable check" upon commercial affairs, wanted to displace him. The other two vainly aspired to become Lee's successor as commissioner. He, of course, emphasized that the two subordinates coveted his position but downplayed his own attempt to shoulder Deane and Franklin aside. Later, he informed Samuel Adams, "I have reason to suspect there is jobbing both with you and with us. The public concerns and the public money are perhaps sacrificed to private purposes. Congress should interfere."[10] Adams shared Arthur's fears and suspicions, but by the time he received this missive, he had withdrawn from Congress.

Lee's proposals to dispatch the other American negotiators throughout Europe, leaving only himself in France, "the great wheel that moves them all," caused repercussions in Philadelphia as well as Paris. Historians inimical to Lee's perspective have overreacted to the ambition and suspicion in these letters, giving them undue emphasis. To Lee's contemporaries, his challenge to Beaumarchais' demand to be reimbursed for goods gained by Deane in 1776 was far more controversial.

For the benefit of the Committee of Foreign Affairs, Lee reviewed his understanding of the early negotiations with Hortalez and Gardoqui, both of whom had pestered the commissioners for compensation. Lee, in turn, asked for clarification from Madrid and reported back "that for the supplies already sent no return was expected, but in future that remittances of American produce were expected for supplies through the house of Gardoqui." Suspecting, however, that this exchange was mere camouflage, Lee then questioned "whether they mean this in earnest or only as a cover should the transaction transpire." Although he was "inclined to think the

9. Arthur Lee to Richard Henry Lee, October 4, 1777, in Richard Henry Lee, *Life of Arthur Lee*, II, 114–16.

10. Arthur Lee to Samuel Adams, November 25, 1777, in Arthur Lee Papers, Box 3.

latter," he nonetheless recommended, in an uncharacteristically uncertain tone, that payments be made to the Bilbao merchant.[11]

Lee was more adamant concerning Beaumarchais' claims. He remembered from the London meetings of "Mary Johnston" and "Roderique Hortalez," that colonial tobacco exchanged for French supplies was "for a cover only and not for payment, as the remittance was gratuitous." (Ultimately, this initial aid was shipped to America aboard the *Amphitrite* and two other French vessels.) The Virginian claimed he had told Franklin this "by sundry opportunities," but no extant letter confirms his assertion. Nonetheless, even as he wrote, Lee explained, "[the French] minister has repeatedly assured us, and that in the most explicit terms, that *no return is expected from these subsidies.*"[12] Certainly Vergennes, beset by the howling British ambassador, could not publicly acknowledge underwriting the colonial rebellion while trying to maintain a tenuous peace with Great Britain. Ironically, Lee's letter, intercepted by Hynson, confirmed British suspicions of French involvement.

All of the American commissioners recognized the veneer of the French position. The trio cautioned Congress not to speak of a royal subsidy of 2 million livres from Vergennes "nor the assurances we have received that no payment will ever be required from us for what has already been given us, either in money or military stores. The great desire here seems to be that England should strike first, and not be able to give her allies a good reason."[13] Yet the diplomatists urged the delegates to send remittances to fulfill contracts made "for clothing and arms." Earnest Arthur Lee took the French at their word and also failed to distinguish between military and nonmilitray succor. Later, after France went to war with Britain, Vergennes reversed his stand and supported Beaumarchais. Lee refused to alter his position and tried to block payment to the French merchant and commissions to Deane.[14] Beset by the financial chaos of the

11. Arthur Lee to the Committee of Foreign Affairs, October 6, 1777, in Wharton (ed.), *Correspondence*, II, 402–403. Currey, *Code Number 72*, pp. 154–59, rightly points out that Franklin and Deane also complained to their friends in Congress.

12. Arthur Lee to the Committee of Foreign Affairs, October 6, 1777, in Wharton (ed.), *Correspondence*, II, 402–403.

13. American Commissioners to the Committee of Foreign Affairs, October 7, 1777, in Wharton (ed.), *Correspondence*, II, 404–406.

14. In the autumn of 1777 Vergennes attempted to persuade Floridablanca to

War for Independence, Congress shrewdly followed Lee's interpretation. The controversy was to rage until 1835 when the demands of Beaumarchais' offspring, supported by the French government, were finally settled by the Twentieth Congress for $35,000.[15]

Privateering sponsored by Silas Deane further alienated the Lees. Arthur found the escapades of Captain Gustavus Cunningham to be both disruptive to Franco-American negotiations and a misappropriation of public monies. He feared American privateers, operating out of French ports, would compromise Bourbon neutrality. The Virginian had little proof that Deane, John Ross, and William Hodge were manipulating private and public shares according to Cunningham's success in the English Channel, nor could he yet perceive that Williams and Chaumont had joined Deane in selling prizes taken by privateers for their own profit although the ships had been outfitted at public expense. Such indeed was the case. Whether Arthur's denunciations were overly self-righteous is a point to ponder. It is not known if he was aware of brother William's dealings, which included shipments of private goods on public conveyances and speculation on war stocks in Britain.[16]

Thoroughly embittered and enraged, Arthur penned a screaming missive to America on November 29, copies of which found their way to Richard Henry Lee and Samuel Adams. Arthur reiterated his appraisals of the "total confusion and disgrace" of American affairs in France. Thomas Morris, a shameful emissary, was trumpeting that his powerful

---

cooperate in aiding the Americans. The French proposed a fund of six million livres as "purely gratuitous help." Stevens (ed.), *Facsimiles*, nos. 1704, 1711, 1725; Doniol, *Participation de la France*, II, 598–602.

15. Charles J. Stillé, "Beaumarchais and 'The Lost Million': A Chapter on the Secret History of the American Revolution," *Pennsylvania Magazine of History and Biography*, XI (1887), 1–36. Better versed in the nature of commerce than Arthur, William Lee did perceive that the Americans owed tobacco for a loan of one million livres gained from the French. William Lee to Francis Lightfoot Lee, November 11, 1777, in Hoffman and Molyneaux (eds.), *Lee Family Papers*, III, 598.

16. Arthur Lee to Richard Henry Lee, November 25, 1777, in Arthur Lee Papers, Box 3; Abernethy, "Commercial Activities of Silas Deane," 480–82; E. James Ferguson, *Power of the Purse*, 86–91; William Lee to Francis Lightfoot Lee, November 11, 1777, in Isham (ed.), *Deane Papers*, XX, 213–19; William Lee to Thomas Rogers, December 8, 18, 1777, William Lee to T. Adams [Edward Browne], all in Worthington C. Ford (ed.), *Letters of William Lee*, I, 284–86, 300, 295–98.

half-brother would cashier anyone—such as William Lee—who threatened the Nantes agency. Deane, Arthur again charged, had come to France "with a view and stipulation of trading for himself" as well as for Congress. Between Morris and Deane "three millions of livres have been expended, and near another million of debt incurred" without the public receiving "a livre's worth." Arthur predicted the American revolutionaries would be fortunate to receive "half the value" of the funds that Deane handled. As he had in past letters, Lee advised that commercial affairs be separated from the diplomatic effort and reiterated that Deane mocked and vilified his own patriotic efforts, while Franklin remained closemouthed. Characteristically Lee wrapped himself in the flag: "It is not the personal injury and uneasiness which this conduct of Mr. D. has given that is to be lamented, but the consequences of it to the public." His conclusion that although the French "do not all we wish, they certainly do more than others" was uncharacteristically temperate. Oddly enough, *Affaires Étrangeres*, which apparently was keeping track of Lee's reputed antigallicism, obtained a copy of this sentiment.[17]

The boiling controversy between Deane and Lee was interrupted on December 4 when the commissioners received word from Congress of the British defeat at the battle of Saratoga. Suddenly the gears of diplomacy, which had largely lain inactive, began turning at Versailles. Activity also quickened at Passy. Bancroft dashed off to London to look after his and Deane's war insurance speculations and to report to his true employers. His haste paid twenty thousand livres to Deane.[18] In turn, as Lord North formulated a futile attempt at reconciliation, a series of agents was dispatched from London to sound out the American representatives in Paris. Vergennes simultaneously hastened to convince Louis XVI and the Spanish crown that the time had come to recognize the independence of the United States. Conrad Alexandre Gérard was designated to meet daily with the commissioners to draft treaties. Suddenly, the goal of militia diplomacy appeared within grasp of the Americans in Paris.

17. Arthur Lee to (?), November 29, 1777, in Hoffman and Molyneaux (eds.), *Lee Family Papers*, III, 655; photocopy from *Affaires Étrangeres*, Paris, Arthur Lee Papers, Box 3.
18. E. James Ferguson, "Business, Government, and Congressional Investigation in the Revolution," *William and Mary Quarterly*, 3rd ser., XVI (April, 1959), 306.

Beaumarchais saw an opportunity to even scores with Arthur Lee at this critical moment. Angered by the Virginian's refusal to approve payment for Hortalez shipments, such as the cargo of the *Amphitrite*, Beaumarchais whispered to Vergennes on December 7, "I have always made a great difference between the honest deputy Deane with whom I have had dealings, the insidious politician Lee and the taciturn Dr. Franklin." Vergennes got the message and soon approached the Spanish ambassador, Aranda, with the proposition that if Bourbon-American parleys were to be productive, "it would be very fortunate for us to get rid of that Deputy, who is very troublesome, and English to the marrow of his bones," according to Aranda's version. The plan was to tempt Lee away from Paris by telling him Madrid requested his attendance for weighty negotiations and then, once again, halt him at the Pyrenees. A maverick and outcast somewhat like Lee, the Spanish ambassador would have none of it. He lectured Vergennes, "It is the less to be feared that he would not regard the interests of his country with fitting integrity. If he is to be put out of the way simply because he is troublesome, it seems to be that we must reflect whether a worse result would not follow in case he should perceive the distrust with regard to him." Aranda then persuaded Lee to desist from petitioning to go to Madrid.[19]

Beaumarchais would not restrain his grudge. He persisted in his efforts to undermine or isolate Lee's position on the American team. A whispering campaign broadcast Lee's antigallicism and anglophilia. The basis for these charges was Arthur's correspondence with Lord Shelburne, as well as his previous activities in London politics. Indeed, Lee, at this time, did write Shelburne but the subject was British treatment of American prisoners of war, not reconciliation. The Virginian did reveal his position when he proclaimed, "The necessity which has made us enemies for a time, and separated us forever from the same government, has not altered the esteem I felt for the good and wise in England."[20] Such sentiments were misconstrued by Lee's enemies to indicate that the Virginian's admiration

19. Beaumarchais to Vergennes, December 7, 1777, D'Aranda to Vergennes, December 11, 1777, both in Stevens (ed.), *Facsimiles*, nos. 1763, 1767; D'Aranda to Arthur Lee, December 11, 1777, in Richard Henry Lee, *Life of Arthur Lee*, II, 359.
20. Beaumarchais to Vergennes, December 12, 1777, January 3, 1778, in Stevens (ed.), *Facsimiles*, nos. 1770, 1829; Arthur Lee to Shelburne, December 10,

of British aristocracy bordered on treason. There is absolutely no evidence that Lee ever vacillated from commitment to American independence.

At the turn of the year, the Americans found themselves engaged in simultaneous sets of negotiations. In secret the trio met with Gérard while, in even more covert arrangements, Deane and Franklin weighed the entreaties of English agents. As he had in November, so Lee again in December and January spurned the inquiries of John Berkenhout, a former acquaintance from his days in Edinburgh and London. Lee's approach to this bait was to inform his fellow commissioners of the overtures and to rebuff Berkenhout. Deane and Franklin, however, chose to hear out the blandishments of Paul Wentworth, who was dispatched by the British ministry to woo the Americans away from the Bourbons. Franklin cagily utilized these sessions to pressure the French to hasten their bids, but it is suspected that Deane fell victim to Wentworth's enticements. So unapproachable was Lee that the spy minimized the Virginian's role in parleys with the French and categorized him as "suspicious and insolent."[21]

The progress in negotiations with the French was duly noted in Lee's journal. Almost daily through December and January the three Americans met with Vergennes' deputy, Gérard. The quartet formulated treaties of amity and commerce while Vergennes and Beaumarchais hastened a reminder to the Spaniards that "We must not forget that the power which recognizes the independence of Americans first will gather all the fruits of war." At Passy there was euphoria in the anticipation of an affirmative answer from Madrid within three weeks. By December 18 Arthur Lee could hint to Samuel Adams that a Franco-American alliance was in the offing. His pen followed its customary effusive track: "The last ray of British splendor is passing away, and the American sun is emerging in full glory from the clouds which obscured it. *His most Christian majesty has assured us, in the most explicit terms, that he will enter into a treaty with us as soon* as the courier returns from Spain; and will maintain our independence by arms if necessary."[22] He was chary of the French alli-

---

1777, in Hoffman and Molyneaux (eds.), *Lee Family Papers*, III, 684; Doniol, *Participation de la France*, III, 167–75.

21. Arthur Lee to Franklin, November 16, 1777, in Arthur Lee Papers, Box 3; Lee to John Berkenhout, January 13, 1778, in Richard Henry Lee, *Life of Arthur Lee*, I, 146–47; Paul Wentworth to William Eden, January 1, 4, 7, 1778, all in Stevens (ed.), *Facsimiles*, nos. 327, 769, 489.

22. Elmer Bendiner, *The Virgin Diplomats* (New York, 1976), 86–94; Arthur Lee to Samuel Adams, December 18, 1777, in Arthur Lee Papers, Box 3.

ance, though, for fear that the English, once their ancient rivals, the Bourbons, entered the conflict, would redouble their war effort. The point was not without merit.

Optimism in the American camp was tempered by mounting dissension between Lee and Deane as well as bickering between Lee and Beaumarchais. Lee, this time in association with Franklin, rejected the Frenchman's claims for restitution for the *Amphitrite*'s cargo, thus depriving Deane of a sizable commission. Deane became even more haughty and abusive toward Lee, who, in turn, dispatched a steady stream of denunciations in confessional correspondence to Samuel Adams and Richard Henry Lee. Following a huge blowup over selection of a courier to Nantes, Lee repeated the charges he had made three months earlier: "Things are going on worse and worse everyday among ourselves, and my situation is more painful. I see in every department, neglect, dissipation and private schemes." He disavowed responsibility for the "misdeeds" of his colleagues, called for an audit of commission accounts, and once more broached the scheme of reassigning Americans to other European posts while he retained the Paris station.[23]

Deane, chafed to an extreme by Lee's conduct, could no longer remain "insensible" to the complaints and insinuations issuing from Chaillot, but face-to-face encounters between the antagonists led to no decisive outcome. When Lee questioned him closely concerning Bancroft's hasty scurrying to London and Wentworth's dinners at Passy, Deane let loose, prescribing to Doctor Bancroft, "Mr. A. L. must be shaved or bled, or he will actually be mad for life." Franklin apparently shared in the prognosis, for Deane told Jonathan Williams, "It is very charitable to impute to insanity what proceeds from the malignity of his [Lee's] heart; but the Doctor [Franklin] insists upon it that it is really his case, and I am every day more and more inclined to believe it. I am sure he cannot be far off from it if he pursues the track he is in." That Lee soon learned of such estimations probably caused Deane untold joy. Whether because of Lee's harassment or British bribes, Deane's patriotism was evaporating. He glimpsed his impending downfall at the hands of the Lee forces and

23. Arthur Lee to Richard Henry Lee, December 22, 1777, in Hoffman and Molyneaux (eds.), *Lee Family Papers*, III, 720; Arthur Lee to Richard Henry Lee, January 5, 9, 1778, in Richard Henry Lee, *Life of Arthur Lee*, II, 126–28; Arthur Lee to Samuel Adams, January 5, 1778 in Richard Henry Lee, *Life of Arthur Lee*, II, 125–26.

swore he would get even. Meanwhile, he looked forward to retirement from public office so he might concentrate totally on "private adventures."[24]

Lee's prickliness affected not only his personal relations but also the negotiations between the French and American nations. He would not miss the opportunity to make his impression on an event of historic import, nor would he humble himself or his country in treating with the French. He convinced Franklin, who shared an imperial vision of their newborn nation, to demand that the French disavow any intention of regaining Canada. He also persuaded Franklin that congressional instructions to the commission should not be confided to the French. Arthur brought not only his legal training, but the full thrust of his revolutionary drive to bear when he adamantly demanded that all drafts of the Franco-American pacts expressly acknowledge the sovereignty and independence of the United States. Deane and Franklin conceded the point.[25] Lee correctly perceived that establishment of the alliance would change the entire political and miltary course of the War for American Independence.

Ralph Izard did his best to support Arthur's contentions in the haggling over the alliances. For more than half a year the South Carolinian remained at Paris unable to take up his post in Tuscany as Congress wished. Sharing Lee's passions and suspicions, Izard sought a role in the negotiations but was rebuffed. He, therefore, pumped Arthur about articles of the commercial pact. Specifically, Izard was irate over the threats to the southern states that he saw in articles eleven and twelve.[26] In the original Model Treaty of 1776 drafted by Congress, the Americans proposed they be exempt from all duties on molasses purchased from the French West Indies, a substantial benefit to New England merchants. Gé-

---

24. Deane to Arthur Lee, December 31, 1777, in Isham (ed.), *Deane Papers,* XX, 272–73; William Lee to Deane, December 17, 1777, in Worthington C. Ford (ed.), *Letters of William Lee,* II, 288–95; Deane to Bancroft, January 8, 1778, Deane to Jonathan Williams, January 13, 1778, both in Isham (ed.), *Deane Papers,* XX, 310, 327; William Stevenson to Arthur Lee, February 1, 1778, in Arthur Lee Papers, Box 4; Deane to John Ross, January 3, 1778, Deane to Robert Morris, January 4, 1778, both in Isham (ed.), *Deane Papers,* XX, 303, 307.

25. Richard Henry Lee, *Life of Arthur Lee,* I, 124, 272; Arthur Lee to Theodorick Bland, Jr., December 13, 1778, in Isham (ed.), *Deane Papers,* XXI, 80–81; Currey, *Code Number 72,* pp. 194–96, 272–73.

26. Gerald Stourzh, *Benjamin Franklin and American Foreign Policy* (Chicago, 1954), 150–51; Arthur Lee to Ralph Izard, January 28, 1778, Izard to Franklin, January 28, 1778, in Wharton (ed.), *Correspondence,* II, 477–80.

rard, seeking reciprocity, countered by asking that no duties be placed on merchandise exported from America to the French islands.

Lee and Izard found Gérard's equation "mischievous" in that it was inflexible and perpetual. The rub was that one American import was equated with all French imports. Lee observed that the proposals would tie "both our hands with the expectation of binding one of her fingers." Further, the French might use their islands as a duty-free entrepôt for transshipping American goods to Europe. Too much was being conceded. When Gérard, Franklin, and Deane refused to compromise, Lee submitted and agreed, but he and Izard dispatched critiques to Congress that ultimately led to expungement of the controversial sections.[27] The delegates to Congress were rightly thankful that at least one of their envoys refused to be subordinate to the French in such critical bargainings. Arthur Lee might have been periodically shunted aside in the negotiations and might have been captious of the stances of all the other negotiators, French as well as American, but when he had the opportunity, the bulk of his contributions were constructively critical.

Part and parcel of Lee's faultfinding in the parleys with the French were Arthur's snipings at the Deane camp. He aimed at both Edward Bancroft and William Carmichael, but though his accusations were on target, they were of little avail. For example, he discovered Bancroft was leagued with the Wharton brothers, British stockjobbers. When he brought evidence of this fact before Franklin, and demanded Bancroft's exclusion from the Commission, though, Franklin ignored him. Particularly galling to Lee was his continued belief that Bancroft had originated the all-too-true stories that Lee had been avoided by the other commissioners. Arthur's vendetta was propelled by wounded pride as well as patriotism.[28]

Nor was Lee able to counter Carmichael when that ambitious and

27. Arthur Lee to Franklin and Deane, January 30, 1778, Deane and Franklin to Arthur Lee, February 1, 1778, Gérard to Three Commissioners, February 2, 1778, Ralph Izard to Henry Laurens, February 16, 1778, all in Wharton (ed.), *Correspondence*, II, 481, 484, 485, 498; The Committee of Foreign Affairs to the Commissioners at Paris, May 15, 1778, in Edmund C. Burnett (ed.), *Letters of Members of the Continental Congress* (8 vols.; Washington, D.C., 1921–36), III, 240–42; Currey, *Code Number 72*, pp. 194–96; James H. Hutson, "Intellectual Foundations of Early American Diplomacy," *Diplomatic History*, I (Winter, 1977), 16–17.

28. Boyd, "Silas Deane," 329–33; Joseph P. Wharton to Bancroft, November 10, 1777, in Stevens (ed.), *Facsimiles*, no. 301; John Thornton Attestments, Janu-

amoral Marylander was chosen to carry messages from Passy to Philadelphia. Although Lee was outraged by Carmichael's selection he nonetheless tried to ascertain what verbal reports the messenger would make to Congress. It was rumored that Carmichael was disillusioned with his patron and was threatening to reveal Deane's misdealings to the delegates. Other rumors claimed that Carmichael had opened sealed letters from Arthur Lee to his American correspondents. Lee deputed his nephew, Thomas Lee, and William Stevenson, his own nominee for courier, to interview Carmichael at Nantes before embarkation. When Carmichael refused to return dispatches Lee had written in 1776 (which had questioned the patriotism of some Congressmen) and denied any wrongdoing, Arthur gathered testimony of Carmichael's previous denunciations of Deane. It was evident that Carmichael's arrival at Congress could pop the cork of the Lee-Deane feud.[29]

Despite internecine feuds in the American camp, the deliberations between the commissioners and the French progressed. Even though he had been unable to secure Spanish approval for his enterprise, Vergennes determined to see the project through. The Americans' goal would be consummated amidst their own rancor and Bourbon misgivings. At the office of the ministry for foreign affairs in the Hôtel de Lautrec, Paris, the eventful day came on February 6, 1778. Franklin, wearing the same brown velvet suit he had worn for his trial in the Cockpit at Whitehall in 1774, added to the dramatic symbolism of the moment. After ceremonially exchanging their credentials, Gérard and the three Americans affixed their signatures to a Treaty of Amity and Commerce, a Treaty of Alliance, and an Act Separate and Secret. The first recognized the independence of the United States and affirmed that most-favored-nation privileges would govern commercial transactions between the French monarchy and the American republic. The alliance, which would be brought into effect in the event of a war between Britain and France,

---

ary 5–8, 1778, in Hoffman and Molyneaux (eds.), Lee Family Papers, IV, 27–34; Abernethy, Western Lands and the American Revolution, 205–207.

29. Arthur Lee to William Carmichael, January 27, 1778, Carmichael to Arthur Lee, February 1, 1778, William Stevenson to Arthur Lee, February 1, 1778, all in Hoffman and Molyneaux (eds.), Lee Family Papers, IV, 113, 115, 73–84; Arthur Lee to Committee of Foreign Correspondence, January 27–31, 1778, in Arthur Lee Papers, Box 4.

guaranteed American sovereignty. Both pacts promised not to conclude peace or armistice with the British without consent of the ally. While France renounced claims to the American interior east of the Mississippi River, the United States would permit French seizures of British possessions in the West Indies. Finally, the Secret Act, added perhaps at Vergennes' or Arthur Lee's request, provided for the admittance of Spain, if Charles III so desired, on equal footing with France in all agreements with the American revolutionaries. The American commissioners had forsaken the ideal of the Model Treaty of 1776 that American connections with Europe would only be commercial. Lee, Franklin, and Deane had committed their country to defense of French territory, the West Indies. Not only was American isolation swept aside, but the envoys from the New World had signed a perpetual alliance with the Old World power. Entanglement was certain.[30]

The resentment between Deane and Arthur Lee boiled over at the signings. After Gérard and Franklin had signed the pacts and moved aside to converse, the American antagonists went up to add their names. Jealousy between the two ran so deep that they could not accomplish this simple task without discord. Lee, as his diary recorded, wished to sign twice since he then held commissions to both France and Spain. Deane objected vigorously. Gérard intervened and assured the Virginian that only one endorsement was necessary. Arthur complied, with the added subscript of "Deputy Plenipotentiary for France and Spain."[31]

Thus the American commission to France gained its objective, quite magnanimous treaties of commerce and alliance with Louis XVI. The French had come to recognize that their own international policies temporarily coincided with the goals of the American revolutionaries. Credit lay more with Vergennes' predispositions, especially his fear of an Anglo-American reconciliation, and with the tenacity of patriotic armies than with the strategies of Congress or the tactics of the three commissioners. In the two months of actual negotiations, Deane had been distracted by

30. Bendiner, *Virgin Diplomats*, 93–94; Meng (ed.), *Despatches and Instructions of Gérard*, 84–87; Dull, *French Navy*, 88–97; David Hunter Miller (ed.), *Treaties and Other International Acts of the United States of America* (8 vols.; Washington, D.C., 1931–48), II, 3–47; Lawrence S. Kaplan, "Toward Isolationism: The Rise and Fall of the Franco-American Alliance 1775–1801," in Kaplan (ed.), *The American Revolution and "A Candid World"* (Kent, 1977), 136–39.
31. Richard Henry Lee, *Life of Arthur Lee*, I, 393–94.

his own commercial affairs and captivated by British overtures. Franklin had divided his time between dining with English agents, in order to pressure the French, and cultivating opinion and esteem in the salons. True, he had ready command of American objectives and had largely agreed with Lee's specific recommendations. Arthur Lee's marginal role had only made him more anxious to participate. He later claimed that during the treaty-making Franklin and Deane had furnished him "a kind of half information" and had "secretly counteracted" him. He confessed, "it was very difficult for me to be of any utility whatsoever in these negotiations." His very exclusion from the center of the negotiations had motivated his intense scrutiny of the agreements. Afterward, he hardly paused to congratulate his correspondents on the milestone successfully passed in Paris. The War for Independence would soon entangle the Bourbons and other European powers, and the long-range aspirations of the revolutionaries must be secured.[32] He persisted, unrealistically, in imagining that the American diplomatic service could be revamped according to his specifications.

Congress, indeed, was reconsidering foreign affairs, but its deliberations and actions were largely grounded on hints rather than substance. Since May, 1777, no communications from the commissioners had reached Congress. The delegates, then convened at York, Pennsylvania, did not receive official word of the Franco-American treaties until May 2, 1778. When Congress, perplexed by its own impotence and ignorance, came to consider the fate of Silas Deane, it was not in response to Arthur Lee's malignant reports, which had yet to reach the congressmen. Rather it was traceable to petitions from disgruntled French officers clamoring for the military posts Deane had promised and from Beaumarchais' agent demanding payments. On August 5, 1777, an early motion for Deane's recall was made and then tabled. Six weeks later Congress resolved it would not honor the merchant's contracts with soldiers of fortune. Finally, at the urging of Richard Henry Lee, a unanimous vote of the delegates chose John Adams to replace Deane. His recruitment of foreign officers for the American army, as Deane's recent biographer observes, "caused the single greatest resentment" against him and was "probably the greatest factor

32. Charles H. Van Tyne, "Influences Which Determined," 528–42; Arthur Lee to Francis Lightfoot Lee, February 9, 1778, in Hoffman and Molyneaux (eds.), *Lee Family Papers*, IV, 191; Arthur Lee to Ralph Izard, May 23, 1778, in Arthur Lee Papers, Box 3.

leading to his recall by Congress."[33] His own poor judgment, not Lee's animus, caused Deane's fall.

Deane got word of his recall early in March, 1778. Ostensibly he was requested to return to America quickly in order to brief Congress on European affairs. Although his pride was stung by this vote of nonconfidence, Deane looked forward to devoting himself "solely to my own affairs, which have been for several years neglected." His past schemes, with Chaumont, Beaumarchais, the Delaps of Bordeau, and both Morris brothers had garnered mixed results.[34] He hoped he would get the better of Arthur Lee, who was again tattling to various American correspondents.

Once the treaties had been settled, Lee saw to it that Congress did not associate him with Deane's machinations. Lee's remonstrances to the Committee of Foreign Affairs repeated his former indictments and emphasized the need for separation of diplomatic and commercial duties. He made a special effort to refute the claims of Beaumarchais and Deane concerning the *Amphitrite* shipments. Lee explained that the Bourbons' "balancing conduct" had necessitated the "continual contraditions and disappointments" in the commission's dispatches. Lee and, he claimed, Franklin too had no knowledge of promises to Beaumarchais for remittances. Hence, the commissioners advised Congress to allow them to settle Beaumarchais' claims in France as there was "mixture in it of public and private concern, which you cannot develop." Their accounting was never rendered, but the longer the Lee-Beaumarchais feud boiled, the more adamant Arthur became. Only once did he ever momentarily concede, "I absolutely do not know whether Beaumarchais is right or wrong."[35]

Lee's private postals were more acrimonious than those he sent to Con-

33. Bowers, "Richard Henry Lee," 217, 281, 288; Worthington C. Ford (ed.), *Journals*, VIII, 605, IX, 947; Richard Henry Lee to Samuel Adams, November 23, 1777, in Ballagh (ed.), *Letters of Richard Henry Lee*, I, 355; Coy Hilton James, *Silas Deane: Patriot or Traitor?* (East Lansing, 1975), 26.

34. Deane to Morris, January 4, 1778, Deane to Jonathan Williams, March 15, 1778, Deane to John Ross, March 23, 1778, all in Isham (ed.), *Deane Papers*, XX, 307, 407–408, 422–23; Ferguson, *Power of the Purse*, 89–90.

35. Arthur Lee to the Committee of Foreign Affairs, February 15, 1778, in Wharton (ed.), *Correspondence*, II, 494–95; Arthur Lee to the Chairman of the Committee of Foreign Correspondence, February 28, 1778, Franklin, Deane, and Lee to the Committee of Correspondence, February 16, 1778, both in Richard Henry Lee, *Life of Arthur Lee*, II, 38–40, 35–38; Arthur Lee to Mr. Pringle, July 4, 1779, extract, in Hoffman and Molyneaux (eds.), *Lee Family Papers*, VI, 220.

gress. For the third time in four months, he fervently wrote to congress-men he felt were partial to his perspective. Deane had secured "douceurs" from contractors such as Beaumarchais who brought him, for 100,000 livres, to support the Frenchman's million-livre claim. In some of Deane's other partnerships "the public money and influence" had been made "subservient to private profit." Arthur felt his criticisms of Deane might simply be interpreted as evidence of personal enmity. He denied this, maintaining that his only interest was "public justice." He included Franklin's dalliance in the damnation of his fellow commissioners. Re-treating to familiar terrain, Arthur warned Richard Henry "these are dangerous men, and capable of any wickedness to avenge themselves on" opponents like himself. As Arthur and William had previously counseled, Richard Henry was to utilize "great circumspection" in secur-ing proof of malfeasance before publicly accusing Deane and his co-horts.[36] Following his own advice, Arthur was amassing records of the commission's finances and testimony from heelers around the Americans. Apparently he did not send this evidence until 1779.

Arthur Lee's acrimony could hardly be concealed, but he did try to refurbish his image with the French. Perhaps suspecting that the Bour-bons had access to his mail—which they did—he profusely affirmed his allegiance to the new guarantors of United States independence. Mean-while, he sought a letter of recommendation from Count Lauraguais. He charged Deane and Franklin, who had reverted to ignoring him, as malig-ners. Lee directly put it to his colleagues, "Is there Gentlemen, any public utility to be derived from a conduct, which sets me in the light of an in-capable or a suspected person, and annuls the appointment of Congress. If there were I should submit to it without reluctance." It was particular-ly vexing that Lee had not been privy to the dispatch of the treaties to Congress, nor could he ascertain if Deane, as rumored, had received his recall. Ralph Izard was enlisted to add his interpretation of relations among the commissioners. Although Lee did not escape blame, Izard placed the burden of disunion on the other two.[37] Izard's rendering to

36. Arthur Lee to Richard Henry Lee, February 15, 1778, in Richard Henry Lee, *Life of Arthur Lee*, II, 133–35; Arthur Lee to Samuel Adams, February 17, 1778, in Isham (ed.), *Deane Papers*, XX, 368–69; Arthur Lee to [Henry Lau-rens], February 16, 1778, in Arthur Lee Papers, Box 4.
37. Arthur Lee to Committee of Correspondence, February 28, 1778, in Arthur Lee Papers, Box 4; Count de Lauraguais to Comte de Maurepas, March 5, 1778, in Stevens (ed.), *Facsimiles*, no. 799; Arthur Lee to Deane and Franklin, Febru-

the president of Congress was further stimulus for congressional scrutiny of Deane's affairs.

The feuding Americans assembled on March 20 for the official reception at the French court. This ceremony, fortunately unmarred by incident, was the occasion for Louis XVI to recognize the independence and sovereignty of the United States. After dining with Vergennes, the three plenipotentiaries, as well as William Lee and Ralph Izard, were presented to the king in his antechamber and then met with the cabinet.[38] Arthur Lee was somewhat crestfallen when the formal ritual turned out to be a simple affair. Nonetheless he was impressed with the sincerity of the French officials. Two days later his aristocratic tastes were satisfied when the Americans were presented to Queen Marie Antoinette at a levée attended by a bustling throng of courtiers.

The Lee brothers made Deane's departure a scene of acidulous invective by stirring up the Nantes affair. Following the death of Thomas Morris in January, William Lee had forsaken refuge at Chaillot and, armed with a writ from the Commissioners, had descended on the French port. There he confronted John Ross, henchman of Robert Morris, over claims to the vouchers and commercial papers in the estate. Ross asserted that the materials were the property of the firm of Willing, Morris, and Company. A dispute ensued that almost led to a duel. Both men scurried to their patrons, one to Arthur Lee, the other to Deane. Ultimately, William Lee packed all the Nantes papers into locked trunks, which he hauled to Passy to be impounded by Franklin. Then, having thoroughly antagonized the Deane camp, he embarked on a long-awaited excursion to Prussia. In turn, Deane packed his own trunks and, on the last day of March, 1778, slipped out of Paris for Philadelphia. He took with him certificates of commendation from both Vergennes and Franklin, as well as a gift portrait of Louis XVI set in diamonds, a symbol of French approbation of his conduct and services.[39] Despite almost a month's preparation, though, Deane did not see fit to pack his financial records, an omission that would

---

ary 15, 1778, in Arthur Lee Papers; Box 4; Arthur Lee to Deane and Franklin, February 26, 1778 in Wharton (ed.); *Correspondence*, II, 506; Lee to Franklin, March 13, 1778, in Arthur Lee Papers, Box 4; Izard to Henry Laurens, February 16, 1778, in Wharton (ed.), *Correspondence*, II, 498–99.

38. "Arthur Lee's Journal," March 20–22, 1778, in Richard Henry Lee, *Life of Arthur Lee*, II, 403–404.

39. John Ross to Deane, March 3, 1778, Deane to William Lee, 1778, in Isham (ed.), *Deane Papers*, XX, 385–89, 391–92; Chaumont to Vergennes, March 7,

cost him his post and stain his reputation when he underwent congressional investigation.

Another vitriolic ingredient added at this time was Beaumarchais' renewed discrediting of Arthur Lee. The Virginian had been kept in the dark concerning Deane's return to America. Because Gérard, named French ambassador to the United States, would be traveling with Deane, perhaps Vergennes was the culprit here. Beaumarchais had inclined Vergennes to the belief that Arthur Lee was passing news of Franco-American affairs to Shelburne and others in England. Beaumarchais intimated that his antagonist was a double agent, "a lance with two heads" and confided that Lee's "design has ever been to choose as between England and France the power that would most assuredly promote his future, and he has frequently declared this at his dissolute suppers." Later, Philadelphia newspapers would pick up this false charge and use it against Lee. Ever a Whig, Arthur's counterattack would label his accusers, such as Deane, as "Tories." There is no evidence that Arthur Lee ever contemplated changing sides or leaked word of the alliance.[40] Rather it appears his suspicions of Beaumarchais plus his recalcitrance toward Gérard and Vergennes resulted in his being labeled antigallic and antialliance.

Deane's departure heightened, rather than lessened, Lee's volatility. He soon directed his vitriol toward Franklin, and Izard soon joined in the harassment of the congenial diplomat. If extant correspondence is a true indicator, Franklin and Lee had not been in open conflict during their tenure as commissioners. Their diplomatic spheres of interests had not collided because Franklin had permitted Lee to venture over Europe and had let the commercial affairs fall where they might. When Deane left, however, Lee called Franklin to task for his languor. Although the two lived only ten minutes apart, they avoided a face-to-face confrontation. The aged ambassador was vexed by Lee's self-righteous stance and imputations "whereby superior merit is assumed to yourself . . . and blame is

---

1778 [misdated May 7, 1777], in Stevens (ed.), *Facsimiles*, no. 823; Franklin to Laurens, March 31, 1778, in Smyth (ed.), *Writings of Franklin*, VII, 128.

40. Secret Memoirs of Beaumarchais to Vergennes, March 13, 1778, in Isham (ed.), *Deane Papers*, XX, 399–406; George Genet (ed.), "Beaumarchais' Opinion of Silas Deane, and Arthur Lee: A Secret Memoir for the Ministers of the King Alone," *Magazine of American History*, III (1879), 631–35; Arthur Lee to Richard Henry Lee, April 18, 1778, in Hoffman and Molyneaux (eds.), *Lee Family Papers*, IV, 461–62; Doniol, *Participation de la France*, III, 167–75.

insinuated on your colleagues without making yourself accountable." Vouchers and other commercial papers were available to Lee at his convenience, Franklin asserted, and he added cuttingly, Arthur "had abundantly more leisure" than his colleague to supervise accounts.[41]

Thus provoked, Lee sent a lengthy reply imbued with his feeling of persecution. It was not only Deane's departure at issue but more. "Had you studied to deceive the most distrusted and dangerous enemy of the public, you could not have done it more effectually," he intemperately countered. Lee called on Franklin to act jointly in "consideration and information" on European affairs but then added that he was affronted by Franklin's lack of regard for his talents.[42] In sum, this sudden yet climactic confrontation came about because Lee was conscious of the inferior role he had played in France. He saw an opportunity to reassert himself and his brand of Whiggish patriotism, but he was afraid that Franklin's transcendence would again overwhelm realization of his personal goals.

So roiled was Franklin that he uncharacteristically lost his poise. He drafted a rebuttal that raked Lee's position. The sage admitted failing to answer Lee's "angry Letters" and "Magisterial Snubbings and Rebukes." Such silence, he believed, maintained the security and unity of the American diplomatic mission and was founded on "my love of Peace, my Respect for your good Qualities, and my pity for your Sick Mind, which is forever tormenting itself with Jealousies, Suspicions and Fancies that others mean you ill, wrong you or fail in Respect for you. If you do not cure your self of this Temper it will end in insanity. . . . God preserve you from so terrible an Evil; and for his sake pray suffer me to live in quiet."[43] Each capital letter would have jabbed at Lee's insecurities and fears.

Having vented his anger—and also, incidentally and unintentionally, having furnished an interpretation largely followed by later historians—Franklin then reconsidered. Instead of sending the letter, he put it aside and on the following day dispatched a shrewd, lengthy, and forthright reply. He categorized Lee's "high-sounding charges" as lacking founda-

41. Franklin to Arthur Lee, April 1, 1778, in Wharton (ed.), *Correspondence*, II, 530, 535n.

42. Arthur Lee to Franklin, April 2, 1778, in Smyth (ed.), *Writings of Franklin*, VII, 130.

43. Franklin to Arthur Lee, April 3, 1778, in Smyth (ed.), *Writings of Franklin*, VII, 130.

tion and alluded to "artful" and "unjust Insinuations." Basically Franklin charged that his antagonist was writing with a congressional audience in mind, one that might be sympathetic to Lee's goal of self-enhancement. He considered Arthur's charge of being "inconsistent with my Duty to the Public" as "heavy" and "undeserved," but "it is to the Public that I am accountable and not to you." Mildly he revised his appraisal of Lee's "jealous, suspicious, malignant, and quarrelsome Temper" which caused the Virginian to treat all he met with ill will. Then Franklin extended the palm branch, exclaiming in conclusion, "of all things I hate Altercation." Could not the two remaining commissioners sit down and quietly scrutinize the accounts left behind by the third? If not, then Franklin believed they would each be held accountable separately to Congress.[44]

This rebuke and proposed *modus vivendi* went unanswered. Instead, Arthur vented his spleen in a letter to Richard Henry, as was his custom the first week of every month. The letter was replete with his usual laments and accusations but a little less controlled than before. Gérard was "a politician" under Deane's spell. Franklin was linked by 'some criminality" also to Deane. "Deep designs" against Arthur abounded, and he charged, "they have endeavored to ruin me here, and will attempt the same" in America. Looking forward to combat in Congress, Arthur promised to furnish a substantiated case against Deane, suggested Carmichael be ordered to testify, and hesitantly contemplated approaching Robert Morris to bring his substantial powers to bear against his own colleague. Arthur indicated his wish to bring the feud before Congress when he repeated his plaints to the Committee of Foreign Affairs.[45]

Into the midst of the Lee-Franklin imbroglio came John Adams, Deane's replacement. He tried to remain neutral while each of the rivals sought his ear. Franklin told him that both Lee and Izard were unstable, quarrelsome, and disliked by the French. Lee, it seemed, was "suspected of too much affection in England . . . and has given offense, by an unhappy disposition." Adams' diary reiterated Beaumarchais' stories of Lee corresponding with Shelburne and raging against the French in the

44. Franklin to Arthur Lee, April 4, 1778, in Smyth (ed.), *Writings of Franklin*, VII, 132–37.

45. Arthur Lee to Richard Henry Lee, April 1, 10, 18, 1778, in Arthur Lee Papers, Box 4; Arthur Lee to Committee of Secret Correspondence, April 3, 1778, in Richard Henry Lee, *Life of Arthur Lee*, II, 41–42.

presence of servants and others. Nonetheless, Adams was impressed by the Virginian's habits and values: "His manners were polite, his reading extensive, his Attention to Business was punctual, and his Integrity beyond reproach." Lee and Adams shared the republican mindset that looked upon the War for Independence as an opportunity to create a Christian Sparta in North America. Richard Henry had recommended John Adams as "a wise and worthy Whig," and Samuel Adams had offered his cousin a testimonial to Arthur's "candor as well as inflexible Integrity and Attachment to our Country."[46] Yet Arthur, inexplicably, failed to develop more than a working relationship with Adams. He refused Adams' invitations to live at Passy. All of Adams' patriotic preachments about the necessity for harmony and order in the commission could not overcome Arthur's distaste for Franklin.

Neither Deane nor Franklin lived up to Adams' rigorous standards for diplomats. Although Deane had been surprisingly successful in his mission, Adams predicted that his return to America "in such Splendor" would cause an "Altercation." Franklin's reputation in Europe raised Adams' envy, but the outspoken New Englander judged his older colleague to be too taciturn and benevolent toward the French to negotiate forcefully for America: "He loves his ease, hates to offend, and seldom gives any opinion until obliged to do it. . . . Although he has as determined a soul as any man, yet it is his constant policy never to say yes or no decidedly but when he cannot avoid it."[47] Adams vowed to do his patriotic duty no matter whom it might offend. Whereas Lee complied, Franklin rarely presented himself for business sessions.

Arthur Lee welcomed Adams' intent to bring ardor, order, and honesty to the Commission. For more than half a year Lee had been investigating the misdealings of Americans in Europe. His discoveries, recently rediscovered by historians, correctly pointed out the guilt of Joseph Hynson and Edward Bancroft. The first was a Maryland seafarer in Franklin's

46. Lyman H. Butterfield (ed.), *The Diary and Autobiography of John Adams* (4 vols.; Cambridge, 1961), II, 304–306, IV, 43, 70, 118–19; Richard Henry Lee to Arthur Lee, May 12, 1778, in Burnett (ed.), *Letters*, III, 231; Samuel Adams to John Adams, June 21, 1778, in Cushing (ed.), *Writings of Samuel Adams*, IV, 39–41.

47. Quoted in Carl Van Doren, *Benjamin Franklin* (New York, 1938), 600. Peter Shaw, *The Character of John Adams* (Chapel Hill, 1976), 115–17, posits that Franklin's fame caused Adams much anxiety.

pay, who stole commission dispatches in 1777 for the British. Lee was able to ferret out Hynson's intercourse with the British at Le Havre and also to implicate William Carmichael as an accessory. Bancroft, Lee discovered, was the spy at the center of the American affairs in Europe. Although Lee collected much testimony as to Bancroft's disloyalty and duplicity and made repeated appeals, neither Franklin nor Congress was moved to oust the British agent from his post as commission secretary.[48] Perhaps Lee had too often brought charges of spying, or perhaps Franklin had brought his acumen, agility, and authority to bear in American political circles.

Their efforts to reform American accounts engrossed Adams and Lee through the summer of 1778. Lee used the opportunity to restore parity among the commissioners. He especially demanded that all three signatures be required for drafts on the commission's banker. Further, he requested the envoys jointly scrutinize Deane's affairs. Franklin interpreted his demands as a bid for ascendancy and rejected both recommendations. He recognized that "Mr. Lee is pleased to be very angry with him," and felt that the Virginian was overly curious about Deane's affairs. As was his wont, Franklin sought to withdraw from contention, claiming he little understood commercial dealings.[49]

Deane's records proved perplexing. After an audit Lee and Adams reported to Congress, "All we can find is that millions have been expended, and almost everything remains to be paid for."[50] Deane's henchmen, Jonathan Williams and John Ross, could not or would not account for 1.4 million livres. Lee avowed his own innocence: "I have seen with infinite concern the public money expended without economy and without account. My colleagues excluded me from knowing or advising about the

48. Einstein, *Divided Loyalties*, 51–71; Currey, *Code Number 72*, pp. 131–42; Samuel F. Bemis, "British Secret Service," 480; Attestments of John Thornton, January 8, 1778, and Musco Livingston affidavit, April 11, 1778, in Hoffman and Molyneaux (eds.), *Lee Family Papers*, IV, 43, 434; Arthur Lee to Committee of Correspondence, April 21, 1778, in Richard Henry Lee, *Life of Arthur Lee*, II, 47–48; Arthur Lee to Samuel Adams, April 14–26, 1778, in Arthur Lee Papers, Box 4.
49. Franklin to Arthur Lee, May 17, 1778, in Smyth (ed.), *Writings of Franklin*, VII, 154–55.
50. Arthur Lee to Committee of Foreign Affairs, May 20, June 1, 1778, both in Richard Henry Lee, *Life of Arthur Lee*, II, 49–51, 52–57. Wharton (ed.), *Correspondence*, II, 590, questions whether these messages were ever received by Congress.

manner in which it was expended. They have encouraged our agents to treat me with disrespect so that my interdisposition might be useless." To remedy the "studied confusion" pervading the commission, Lee suggested a reorganization of American foreign service. His reasonable proposals included an annual set stipend for each envoy, assignment of one minister per country, and a differentiation of commercial and political duties under separate men.[51]

While Franklin focused his concern on American privateers in European waters and continued to cultivate French opinion, Adams and Lee tackled the commercial labyrinth at Nantes. Here the Lee brothers were able to record a victory over their aged antagonist. Evidently following brother William's advice, Arthur persuaded Adams to remove Jonathan Williams from the post of American agent at Nantes, and replace him with John Daniel Schweighauser, a Lee compatriot.[52] Arthur's nephew, Thomas Lee, was made second in command. Although Franklin may have been vexed by this assault on his domain, he did not argue at this time. So Arthur and Ralph Izard continued the attack through the summer. Franklin endured the storm while petitioning Congress to separate him from Lee. Later he would remark of the hostility of Lee and Izard: "I deserved the Enmity of the latter, because I might have avoided it by paying him a compliment, which I neglected. That of the former I owe to the people of France, who happened to respect me too much and him too little; which I could bear and he could not."[53]

Even by his own standards of conduct Arthur Lee was unusually frenetic in 1778. The whole Passy entourage—Franklin, William Temple, and Jonathan Williams—were targets of his salvos. Although Deane had been removed, the cancer remained. Arthur reported to Richard Henry

51. Lee became more careful in keeping account of his own disbursements. Expenses calculated for the period of December, 1776 to March, 1778 listed the expenditure of 113,004 livres by Deane, 65,956 livres by Franklin, and 68,846 livres by Arthur Lee. Trips to Spain and Prussia were included in Lee's expenditures. Wharton (ed.), *Correspondence*, II, 573–74. See also Hoffman and Molyneaux (eds.), *Lee Family Papers*, IV, 711–14.

52. Kammen, *Rope of Sand*, 149, traces Lee's enmity toward Jonathan Williams to Franklin's snubbing of the Virginian in 1771. When Franklin toured Great Britain that year Williams, rather than Lee, was entrusted with the affairs of the Massachusetts House.

53. Franklin to James Lovell, July 27, 1778, Franklin to Francis Hopkinson, September 13, 1781, both in Smyth (ed.), *Writings of Franklin*, VII, 78, VIII, 306.

that the elder statesman dominated the commission as "the solon and the Dictator of America." He made no specific accusations except to say that "whatever public business is put into his own hands will either be totally neglected or converted into a private job." Franklin threatened Lee's sense of esteem, autonomy, and ambition. From Lee's point of view, he had earned Franklin's "enmity and maleficence" by refusing to become "his dependent and the avowed slave of his will." Arthur retreated to his accustomed stance as selfless patriot while simultaneously confessing envy of the prestige accorded Franklin.[54]

Jonathan Williams was already contending with William Lee over the Nantes agency when Arthur entered the fray. An ensuing audit by Arthur taxed Williams' patience and tact. Arthur blasted Williams' bookkeeping, unsuccessfully sought details of Deane's affairs, and maneuvered to humble his opponent. Ultimately, however, the accusations sent to Congress were of a general nature and undercut by Arthur's whining that "insult and defiance" had accompanied the standoff. It was pointed out that Williams, Franklin's grandnephew, had gotten overly generous commissions on purchase orders placed in France and had utilized public funds to finance four privateering ventures. The proof, to the Lees, was that Williams had arrived penniless in Europe at the war's commencement and now flaunted his wealth. Ultimately, in 1779 a second audit cleared Williams of charges of embezzlement, not surprising since the examiners then were none other than Edward Bancroft and Samuel Wharton.[55]

The counterattack against the Lees came at two points and utilized the French allies of the Franklin camp to sully the integrity of Arthur and William and their cohorts. The French merchant Chaumont, a patron of Jonathan Williams, accused the house of Schweighauser of mismanagement at Nantes and collusion with the British. The accusations stood and, more embarrassing to Arthur Lee, were augmented by Edward Bancroft's

54. Arthur Lee to Richard Henry Lee, July 15, 1778, in Hoffman and Molyneaux (eds.), *Lee Family Papers*, V, 43; Arthur Lee to Samuel Adams, August 11, 1778, in Arthur Lee Papers, Box 5; Claude-Anne Lopez and Eugenia W. Herbert, *The Private Franklin: The Man and His Family* (New York, 1975), 233–39.

55. Arthur Lee's Report on Jonathan Williams, July 15, 1778, in Hoffman and Molyneaux (eds.), *Lee Family Papers*, V, 44; Arthur Lee to Committee of Correspondence, July 20, August 11, September 9, 1778, in Richard Henry Lee, *Life of Arthur Lee*, II, 64–67, Arthur Lee to Samuel Adams, September 12, 1778, in Arthur Lee Papers, Box 5; Van Doren, *Benjamin Franklin*, 600–601.

charges that his own personal secretary, John Thornton, was in the British pay. Shamefacedly Lee had to confess the charges were true—for £100 a year, Thornton informed the British of movements of the French fleet. Lee's bitterness deepened. He had been framed. It was Franklin who had recommended Thornton to Lee and, more damning, it had been Thornton who had uncovered Bancroft's duplicity and stockjobbing. "Upon the whole," wrote Arthur, "it appears to me that their plan was to reduce my secretary to the very infidelity of which they accuse him." When Thornton did not return from a trip to England it was taken as proof of his guilt. Lee could do little to remove the tarnish from his own reputation. In fact, he blundered further by replacing Thornton with Hezekiah Ford, a southerner who was under suspicion in Virginia.[56] The episode was a three-way disaster for Lee.

Bickering and harassment took their toll on Arthur Lee's fervor for the patriotic cause. In July, he claimed to be "heartily tired" of his assignment, and since American republicanism practiced rotation in office, he anticipated relief soon "from the most tiresome situation I was ever in." Richard Henry tried to bolster his brother's spirits and prescribed perseverance, patience, and "honest patriotism" to see Arthur through the trying times. Bitter resignation pervaded Arthur's response. Pleading with the Committee for Foreign Affairs, he acknowledged "the licentious means . . . employed to injure my character"; predicted another trip to Madrid, where he was assigned, would be "ineffectual"; and awaited not only new instructions, but also a vote of confidence. Arthur confided separately to Congressman James Lovell and Samuel Adams the depths of his grievances against his fellow commissioners and a preference for assignment to France. He reflected that he "was in fact a joint Commissioner, *sine gratia* and *sine potentia.*" Perhaps anticipating the dispute in Congress that his accusations would elicit, he counseled his advocates in America not to contend too vociferously on his behalf. Rather, he asked,

<hr>

56. Schweighauser to William Lee, August 27, 1778, Chaumont to Arthur Lee, September 5, 1778, both in Hoffman and Molyneaux (eds.), *Lee Family Papers,* V, 239, 273; Arthur Lee to Committee of Foreign Correspondence, August 7, 1778, in Wharton (ed.), *Correspondence,* II, 679–80; Currey, *Code Number 72,* p. 192; Arthur Lee to Committee of Foreign Affairs, April 26, 1778, in Wharton (ed.), *Correspondence,* II, 562; Thornton's undated affidavits, James Lovell to Arthur Lee, January 26, 1779, in Hoffman and Molyneaux (eds.), *Lee Family Papers,* IV, 42–43, 565–69, V, 692.

"send me where they judge I can be most useful to the public. This is the first wish of my heart, and my own convenience never was and never will be put in competition with it."[57] Self-denial was always a useful tactic for Lee.

Altruism and asceticism epitomized Arthur Lee's conscious self-image, but even he needed some reward. Later, in reviewing the course of his career for 1777 and 1778, he estimated, "I have experienced more cares and anxieties . . . than in all my life besides." Then, uncharacteristically, he confided that he felt deprived of public recognition.[58] Even such a fervent revolutionary as Lee could not perform perpetually without some emotional reinforcement. When criticism, rather than praise, was heaped upon him, he understandably grew angry and disillusioned.

His criticism of his colleagues' commercial dealings forced Lee to be Argus-eyed in his own forays in the world of business. He undertook a venture on behalf of the state of Virginia to secure a loan of cannon and mortars. Lee prevailed on the French war ministry to ship the requested armaments from depots in Flanders to Dunkirk. Meanwhile he scouted around for a miscellaneous cargo of small arms, drugs, and the casting of a state seal for Virginia. Much haggling ensued over transshipment to Nantes, over his native state's credit, and over waiver of French export duties, but he persisted until May, 1780, when the artillery, valued at £256,633, finally left Nantes. The negotiations continued for a year, and he had to appropriate ten thousand dollars in congressional funds for this Virginia project. It was first-hand experience for him with the intricacies of contracting in Europe. In addition, if Franklin is to be believed, Arthur's contentious temperament alienated co-workers and contractors alike.[59]

57. Arthur Lee to Marquis de Rosignan, July 6, 1778, in Richard Henry Lee, *Life of Arthur Lee*, II, 157–59; Richard Henry Lee to Arthur Lee, May 19, 1778, in Burnett (ed.), *Letters*, III, 257; Arthur Lee to Committee of Foreign Affairs, August 24, 1778, in Wharton (ed.), *Correspondence*, III, 308; Arthur Lee to J[ames] L[ovell], August 6, 1778, Arthur Lee to Samuel Adams, September 12, 1778, both in Arthur Lee Papers, Box 5.

58. Arthur Lee to Theodorick Bland, December 13, 1778, Arthur Lee to Samuel Adams, November 11, 1778, both in Richard Henry Lee, *Life of Arthur Lee*, I, 163, II, 150–152.

59. Arthur Lee to Vergennes, June 14, 1778, in Stevens (ed.), *Facsimiles*, no. 834; see also nos. 835, 831, 833, 842, and Richard Henry Lee, *Life of Arthur Lee*, I, 413–25; Franklin to Patrick Henry, February 26, 1778, Arthur Lee to Committee

Lee's dogged persistence in negotiating with Spain proved more rewarding. Spanish Foreign Minister Floridablanca balked at overt recognition of American independence and at covert loans, but Gardoqui, his agent, hinted that Spain would be more accommodating if the rebels captured Florida and presented the territory to Charles III. This was a ruse to forestall a commitment. The Virginian complained to Vergennes of Spanish hesitancy, which "most certainly gives encouragement to our enemies," and despite French prescriptions of patience, Lee's theatrical bent prodded him to further remonstrances. When it became known that the English had dispatched the Carlisle Commission to America to make a major bid for reconciliation, Arthur saw his opportunity. Using both flattery and fulmination, he called upon Charles III to become "a fit avenger of the common cause of mankind." The "dictates of religion, the laws of God and of nature" were on the side of America in the struggle with Britain. The Spaniards, however, were unmoved by the rhetoric. Although a total of thirteen shipments from Bilbao and Bordeaux may be credited to Lee's wooing of Floridablanca, the Spanish policy was one of demurral, if not deception.[60] For another year they sought to serve as mediators of the world stage. Their eyes were on Gibraltar, not the western hemisphere.

Lee's experience in the world of accounting broadened throughout 1778. Day by day he joined John Adams in surveying and ordering the vouchers left behind by Deane. It was not rewarding labor. By September, the commissioners were forced to solicit Vergennes' aid to make sense of Beaumarchais' claims. The rub was that there were no documents of the Deane-Beaumarchais understandings. Lee evidently persuaded his colleagues to endorse his position "that they were under obligation to his Majesty's good will for the greatest part of the merchandise and warlike stores heretofore furnished under the firm of Roderique Hortalez and Co." The ghost of Hortalez vexed the entire cast at Versailles and Passy. Beaumarchais, Deane, Williams, and perhaps indirectly, Franklin had a

of Foreign Affairs, November 15, 1778, both in Wharton (ed.), *Correspondence*, III, 67–68, 839–41.

60. Gardoqui to Arthur Lee, August 20, 1778, in Wharton (ed.), *Correspondence*, II, 690; Arthur Lee to Vergennes, October 12, 1778, in Richard Henry Lee, *Life of Arthur Lee*, II, 132–34; Arthur Lee to Floridablanca, December 17, 1778, in Wharton (ed.), *Correspondence*, II, 858–60; Worthington C. Ford (ed.), *Journals*, XVII, 466.

concern for their own pocketbooks. Vergennes and, probably, Franklin could not now contradict their previous stances without being labeled liars. Arthur Lee may have had mixed motives. It is certain that he saw a way to publicize Deane's cheating. He also had his own image—and his historicizing of the events of 1776—to protect. Lee perpetually affirmed that the Hortalez contracts were only "to serve as a cover. . . . This I stated originally to the Committee [of Foreign Affairs] so it was stated to me at first and so I always understood it." [61] What had originally been interpretation, Lee now declared as fact.

France, at war with Britain after June, now saw no need to continue the camouflage surrounding Hortalez. Vergennes alerted his man in Philadelphia, Gérard, that the king did not furnish a thing, that Beaumarchais owed for material from the royal arsenals, and that, if necessary, the foreign minister could intervene on behalf of the Americans "in order that they are never pressed on the repayment of the military objects." Evidently nonmilitary articles were definitely to be paid for. Although Vergennes would not recognize Hortalez and Co., he did recognize Beaumarchais' dealings as sanctioned by the king. The commissioners had been unable to obtain a definitive answer from Vergennes. Perhaps Gérard, who had been privy to many of the Deane-Beaumarchais arrangements, could fill in details for Congress.

Any unanimity within the commission was merely superficial. Although Adams might see that economy as well as respectability dictated that all three American representatives live at Passy, Lee would not budge. His mistrust for Franklin was infinite, and he refused to be associated with the "old man" whose life had been "a series of intrigues." Lee lamented that he was "unhappily the object of those intrigues," and party to such disputes as that over the Nantes agency. As was his wont, he wrapped himself protectively in self-righteous denial, claiming he had been "compelled to engage in a contest which I shall regret as long as I exist." [62]

Perhaps Lee's regret originated from an intuition that he could not

61. American Commissioners to Vergennes, September 10, 1778, in John Durand (ed.), *New Materials*, 127–31; David Schoenbrun, *Triumph in Paris: The Exploits of Benjamin Franklin* (New York, 1976), 219–22; Arthur Lee to Samuel Adams, July 5, 1778, Arthur Lee Papers, Box 6.

62. Vergennes to Gérard, September 16, 1778, in Meng (ed.), *Despatches and Instructions of Gérard*, 294–95; John Adams to Arthur Lee, October 10, 1778, in Wharton (ed.), *Correspondence*, II, 760–61; Arthur Lee to Samuel Adams, November 11, 1778, in Arthur Lee Papers, Box 5.

unseat Franklin. Certainly there was much jealousy in his regret, although Lee was able to rationalize it. He convinced himself that Franklin's cultivation of friendship and prestige was rooted in improbity and peculation. He told Samuel Adams that only those who "look for advantages to themselves" appeared to profit from the Revolution. While he labored selflessly, those about him filled their pockets. Lee grieved that it was "not a little unpleasant to be deprived of that praise that constant toil and assiduity in the public service have deserved, and submit to be traduced by those who . . . have made immense private fortunes for themselves and their dependents." Lee averred that Deane had made £60,000, Bancroft lived in elegance, and Williams had risen "from being a clerk in a sugar-bake house in London" to prominence and, doubtless, profit at Nantes. It was Arthur's sense of virtue that was offended for he imagined himself as ascetic even if others saw him in a different light. John Adams, careful to maintain his neutrality amidst his colleagues, depicted Lee as "a man of honor and integrity, yet to be very frank, he cannot easily govern his temper and he has some notions of elegance, rank and dignity that can be carried too far."[63] It was hinted that Arthur's personal liabilities outweighed his assets.

Arthur Lee had two causes for dread at the end of 1778. One was that Deane might be in America reaping credit for the alliance with France. He grew fearful when informed that Deane, Franklin, Robert Morris, and John Holker (agent for the French navy in America) now dominated Congress. "The Junto" of Passy appeared on the verge of triumph. If Deane gained redress from Congress concerning his recall, Lee sensed his own imminent downfall. A second tremor was that Franklin was again colluding with English cronies; the Vandalia land scheme might be reactivated. Patriots were losing the reins of revolution to profiteers and pro-French forces. American liberty was in danger. The struggle of 1775–1776 must be renewed.[64]

Lee's fears were soon to be realized. Although Richard Henry had

63. Arthur Lee to Theodorick Bland, December 12, 1778, in Richard Henry Lee, *Life of Arthur Lee*, II, 161–63; John Adams to James Warren, December 5, 1778, in *Warren-Adams Letters: Chiefly a Correspondence Among John Adams, Samuel Adams, and James Warren* (Cambridge, 1917, 1925), vols. LXXII–LXXIII of the Massachusetts Historical Society, *Collections*, LXXIII, 73–77.

64. Arthur Lee to Richard Henry Lee, December 7, 1778; Arthur Lee to Samuel Adams, September 12, 1778, both in Richard Henry Lee, *Life of Arthur Lee*, II, 128–31.

promised that Congress would investigate, discredit, and punish the "impudence and jugglery of Deane and his associates," his promise was difficult to fulfill. Both Richard Henry and Francis Lightfoot Lee had seen their power eclipsed in Congress. Richard Henry's brand of radicalism had been questioned and then outvoted by moderates in the Virginia delegation. Another Lee associate, Henry Laurens, was even less sanguine. From his position as president of Congress, the volatile South Carolinian perceived that Deane's testimony would prove troublesome. While he minimized disputes among the commissioners as "School Boy jarrings," Laurens feared "the consequences of a heated and injudicious discussion" by a Congress then besieged by rumors of scandals throughout the Continental Army. Yet Congressman James Lovell, the Lee-Adams delegate from Massachusetts who supervised correspondence with the commissioners, anticipated Deane would "return with renewed honor in Commission to Holland," a false prophecy. In the spring of 1778, the clue that an explosive situation was on the horizon was the Committee of Foreign Affairs' note to Arthur Lee that his dispatch of October 6, 1777, was "more explicit than any we had before received" in regard to the Hortalez shipments.[65]

Deane's arrival July 12, 1778, at Philadelphia was overshadowed by the festivities that greeted his companion, Gérard. The city and Congress vied in contests of paying their respects to the first ambassador from the court of Louis XVI. It was not until August 15 that Deane was granted a hearing before Congress, and then debate arose over whether a written or an oral report should be required of the recalled commissioner. By this time Laurens believed the delegates "had as absolutely taken sides as it can be supposed gentlemen are capable of in a purely unbiased assembly." Factionalization took the form of a "second resistance," analogous to the 1775–1776 split in Congress. Around Deane rallied Robert Morris and his commercial-minded cronies, personal opponents of the Lee-Adams bond, those who credited the Franco-American alliance to Deane, and those who coveted assignments in Europe. These were the "Tories," by

---

65. Richard Henry Lee to Arthur Lee, May 19, 1778, in Burnett (ed.), *Letters*, III, 257; Bowers, "Richard Henry Lee," 230–46, 279; Henry Laurens to George Washington, June 8, 1778, in Burnett (ed.), *Letters*, III, 283; Ferguson, *Power of the Purse*, 102; James Lovell to Franklin, May 15, 1778, Committee of Foreign Affairs to Arthur Lee, May 14, 1778, both in Burnett (ed.), *Letters*, III, 242, 238.

the standards of the Whigs like Richard Henry Lee and Samuel Adams. Adams found it ironic that Arthur Lee, "a gentleman whom the leading American Whigs have placed high in their List of Patriots," was under attack. What was more tragic was that Lee's opponents, "wicked men," stood "high in the esteem and confidence of the Congress."[66] Just as independence from Britain had had to be proclaimed earlier, so now autonomy from France must be guarded. The virtuous must struggle to overcome the vice-ridden.

The initial skirmish in the Lee-Deane controversy came in September. Ralph Izard's correspondence rather than Lee's letters from Europe played the major role in provoking debate over personnel in the foreign service. Congress wanted to place its mission in Europe on equal footing with Gérard, the minister plenipotentiary. Thus on September 11 the triumvirate commission system was abandoned, and after two days' debate, Benjamin Franklin was selected sole minister to Versailles. Richard Henry Lee saw to it that Arthur's appointment to Madrid went unchallenged. However, he confided to both his brothers in Europe that "envy, selfishness and Deane's cuts have created a strange spirit among many, and will require on your parts great wisdom and much *caution* in all your *conduct* and *correspondence*." Richard Henry also intimated that Franklin "must soon be *called* to *account* for his *misdeeds*; therefore *bear* with him, if possible."[67] The issue would not be dormant.

The following month emotions dominated, and little headway was made. Congress concluded that "certain dissensions detrimental to the public service are said to have existed" in their European diplomatic mission. When William Carmichael was asked to testify, no further light was shed, although Arthur Lee had put some stock in hopes that Carmichael's

66. Henry Laurens to the President of South Carolina (Rawlins Lowndes), [August 11, 1778?], in Burnett (ed.), *Letters*, III, 368–71; Henderson, *Party Politics*, 186–96; Samuel Adams to James Warren, October 14, 1778, in Burnett (ed.), *Letters*, III, 449.

67. Isham (ed.), *Deane Papers*, XX, 465–85; Bowers, "Richard Henry Lee," 289–95; Richard Henry Lee to Sir James Jay, November 3, 1778, in Ballagh (ed.), *Letters of Richard Henry Lee*, I, 449–50; Izard to Laurens, February 16, 1778, in Wharton (ed.), *Correspondence*, II, 498; Richard Henry Lee to Arthur Lee, September 16, 1778, in Burnett (ed.), *Letters*, III, 414–15. The italicized words were originally in one of four codes used by the Lee brothers that Burnett solved. This variation appears to be keyed to an edition of Entick's *New Spelling Dictionary*. See Burnett (ed.), *Letters*, III, 231.

testimony would damn Deane. He imagined Carmichael to be so base as to turn on his cohort. His testimony could have been confirmed by William Stevenson, whom Arthur dispatched to Philadelphia brimming with the case against Deane.[68] Carmichael evaded the issues, though, and Stevenson apparently made no direct input into the investigation.

Deane was rankled. Unable to present his version to the investigators, he nonetheless let it be known that factionalism and misapprehension existed in the commission. He made Arthur Lee the scapegoat: "I never knew Mr. Lee, from his first coming to Paris, satisfied with any person he did business with, whether of a public or a private nature, and his dealings, whether for trifles or for things of importance, almost constantly ended in a dispute, sometimes in litigious quarrels." This interpretation revived the representations of Lee that had circulated in Philadelphia in August when Carmichael had revealed that Arthur suspected Joseph Reed, a city leader and associate from his days in London, of treachery. Reed had not been overly emotional about Arthur's charges. He felt that Arthur's talents were counteracted by lack of "Candour and common ordinary sense." Newspaper accounts in the autumn emphasized Lee's misanthropy and charged him with carrying on a perfidious correspondence with Britons such as John Berkenhout. The attack aroused the Whig defenders of Lee's reputation. Samuel Adams offered as a testimonial that Arthur's "invariable attachment to the Liberties of our Country never was, and I think cannot be justly suspected." It was a question of the virtuous being pursued by the corrupt. Richard Henry Lee wide-eyedly proclaimed that the "wickedness of Deane and his party exceeds all belief." [69] The battle was joined.

68. Edmund C. Burnett, *The Continental Congress* (New York, 1964), 363; Arthur Lee to Richard Henry Lee, April 10, 1778, in Hoffman and Molyneaux (eds.), *Lee Family Papers,* IV, 425–27; Arthur Lee to Laurens, April 10, 1778, in Arthur Lee Papers, Box 4; Paul Wentworth to [William Eden], January 10, 1778, in Stevens (ed.), *Facsimiles,* no. 335.

69. Deane to the President of Congress, October 12, 1778, in Isham (ed.), *Deane Papers,* XXI, 4–21; Burnett, *Continental Congress,* 362–63; Joseph Reed to Mrs. Reed, August 16, 1778, in Burnett (ed.), *Letters,* III, 375–76; Howard Peckham, "Dr. Berkenhout's Journal, 1778," *Pennsylvania Magazine of History and Biography,* LXV (January, 1941), 79–92; Samuel Adams to James Warren, October 11, 1776, in Cushing (ed.), *Writings of Samuel Adams,* IV, 68–72; Richard Henry Lee to [Arthur Lee], October 27, 1778, in Ballagh (ed.), *Letters of Richard Henry Lee,* I, 445–46.

Gérard was at the core of the controversy. Although he was a career diplomat who had been well trained for the ambassadorial appointment in Philadelphia, Gérard was unable to recognize the plural nature of the revolutionary movement, and he played to the commercial interest group. Nor could he ever conceive of the two countries of the alliance as equals. His handling of the Lee-Deane dispute thus alienated some potent American groups, specifically the old Whigs. It is not overstating the case to say that Gérard's actions generated antigallicism. This was not unanticipated by Arthur Lee. Originally he had recommended Gérard highly as a friend to America, although he knew that Deane had ample opportunity "to fill his mind with very unfavorable impressions of me . . . [such as] a doubt of my attachment to the cause of our country, and a suspicion of my being secretly a favorer of England." Lee saw Gérard as "a politician," against whom the Whigs should be on guard.[70]

The French stance against Arthur Lee and for Silas Deane was not without rationale.[71] Lee's adamant role in the treaty negotiations may have been viewed as obstreperous. Certainly Beaumarchais' rumor mongering had not missed Gérard's ears. Vergennes possibly harbored a grudge from 1776 when Lee, as Mary Johnston to Beaumarchais' Hortalez, had lied about Spanish support for the American rebellion. In sum, there was a French predisposition to distrust, if not detest, Arthur Lee. Delegates of the Lee-Adams persuasion who indicated less than subservience to the wishes of the court of Louis XVI were hence labeled Francophobes and Anglophiles.

For the French, as well as for the American Congress, three major strands were interwoven in the debates between 1778 and 1781 over Silas Deane and Arthur Lee. Deane's recall, and the possible recall of the other commissioners, was linked with subsequent personnel selections for European stations and peace negotiations. The militia diplomacy of Lee and John Adams was contrasted to the less autonomous and more deferential strategy of Deane and Franklin. Frequently the debate was founded on the dichotomous value systems of the revolutionaries. Often delegates

---

70. Kaplan, *Colonies into Nation*, 122–24; Stinchcombe, *American Revolution*, 32–34, 45; Arthur Lee to Richard Henry Lee, April 18, 1778, in Hoffman and Molyneaux (eds.), *Lee Family Papers*, IV, 461; Arthur Lee to Richard Henry Lee, April 1, 1778, in Arthur Lee Papers, Box 4.
71. Henderson, *Party Politics*, 196.

with ambitions of their own tried to unseat the militia diplomats. A second and probably critical vein concerned policy. Gérard and his successor, Luzerne, made major attempts to direct American policy and to order the priorities for settlement of the war, and where Gérard had failed, Luzerne largely succeeded.[72] A tertiary concern, but nonetheless explosive, dealt with the nature of French aid to the Revolution. Congress was harassed by petitions from aggrieved French soldiers of fortune, beseechments and threats from the agents of Beaumarchais, and contradictory or cloudy accounts from Passy and Versailles. It seemed that the French connection would never be clarified.

With Gérard's acquiescence Deane pressed Congress. On December 5 the *Pennsylvania Gazette* published Deane's address, "To the Free and Virtuous Citizens of America," a bombshell that hurled general and specific abuse at the Lees. The Connecticut merchant sought to make good on his threat to pull down Arthur Lee with him. In his version of the commission, he had been "honored with one colleague, and saddled with another." He castigated Lee's failures in Spain and Prussia and said that both Arthur and William Lee, "gave universal disgust" to the French. Arthur's association with Britons had embarrassed the American mission "exceedingly and was of no small prejudice" to Congress' affairs. Not only had Lee corresponded with Shelburne and Berkenhout, but he had also leaked news of the alliance to the British, according to Deane. In a final jab, Deane asserted that Arthur Lee "was dragged into the Treaty with the utmost reluctance." The address was calculated to deflect criticism to Lee and to rouse public opinion against congressional impassivity.[73]

The self-styled "virtuous" adherents of the "great cause" counterattacked. Laurens, not so much rushing to Lee's defense as concerned with the reputation of Congress, was most exercised. Failing to gain vindication of the honor of Congress and a censure of Deane, Laurens furiously resigned as president and returned to the floor to debate. John Jay of New York, an acknowledged Deane supporter, took his place. Mean-

72. Morgan, "Puritan Ethic," 32–33; Stinchcombe, *American Revolution*, 32–45, 65–77.
73. "To the Free and Virtuous Citizens of America," *Pennsylvania Gazette* (Philadelphia), December 5, 1778, in Arthur Lee Papers, Box 5.

while Francis Lightfoot Lee had tried his hand at newspaper polemic only to stir up further animosity against all members of his family. By December 22 he could only report to Richard Henry, then in Virginia, that "Publications still continue in abundance to blacken the Lees and make Deane the greatest man in the world." The gravity of the situation was emphasized by Samuel Adams, who espoused the cause of Arthur Lee for the sake of correspondents in Massachusetts. Adams pronounced that Lee's reputed distrust was actually an asset to the cause: "that jealousy is a good Security of Public Virtue. I have expressed my fears that America is too unsuspecting long to continue free. These I know are the sentiments of Dr. Lee. . . . Publick Liberty will not long survive the loss of Publick Virtue." A fortnight later Adams catalogued Lee's detractors as "a combination of political and commercial men, who may be aiming to get the trade, the wealth, the power and the Government of America into their own hands." [74] The call went out to rally the old Whigs.

Thomas Paine responded to the call for crusaders. Not only was Paine a friend to Henry Laurens and Richard Henry Lee, but he was also drawn into the fray from his position as secretary to the Committee of Foreign Affairs of Congress.[75] From this clerkship he had gained inside information pertaining to the claims of Deane and Beaumarchais. On December 15 he entered into the embittered exchanges in the Philadelphia press as a champion of the Lee position. At least five other penmen shared the battleground with "Common Sense" in a fray that lasted three months. Ultimately Paine was undone by his assertion that supplies from France could not be credited to Deane but, rather, "were promised and engaged, and that as a present, before he ever arrived in France." This statement not only violated Paine's oath as secretary, but, most importantly, provoked Gérard's wrath. Whether it was true or not, the French minister did not debate. He simply insisted that the reputation of his court must be purged of such tarnish. He prodded Congress to disavow Paine's

74. Samuel Adams to Samuel Cooper, December 25, 1778, in Cushing (ed.), *Writings of Samuel Adams*, IV, 106–108; Francis Lightfoot Lee to Richard Henry Lee, December 22, 1778, in Burnett (ed.), *Letters*, III, 545–46; Samuel Adams to Samuel Cooper, December 25, 1778, Samuel Adams to James Warren, January 6, 1779, in Cushing (ed.), *Writings of Samuel Adams*, IV, 105–106, 114–15.

75. David Freeman Hawke, *Paine* (New York, 1974), 83–93; Eric Foner, *Tom Paine and Revolutionary America* (New York, 1976), 158–61.

claims and then, after much debate over discharging the polemicist, reckoned that the acceptance of Paine's resignation from the secretaryship was sufficient. A satirist took a final shot at Paine's pro-Lee posture:

> Hail mighty Thomas! In whose works are seen
> A mangled Morris and distorted Deane;
> Whose splendid periods flash for Lee's defense
> Replete with every thing but common sense.
>
> Thou pupil worthy her attentive care
> By Satan granted to her earnest prayer;
> When on the brink of fate smooth Adams stood
> And saw his Arthur flound'ring in the flood.[76]

Despite such sarcasm, Paine had been able to stir up emotion against war profiteering. In Philadelphia he took a leading role in the movement for price controls. Virginia and Maryland passed statutes prohibiting congressional delegates from being party to contracts with the government.

Deane's publication was successful in that Congress granted him a hearing. During the last week of the year Deane read a narrative of his accomplishments to the delegates. Generally, he shielded himself behind Franklin's reputation, praised French aid, and characterized the Lees as captious and antigallic, but he made only one specific charge against his nemesis: "M. Petrie, a gentleman of character, indeed, showed me a letter from his friend in London in which he sent him an extract of a letter which he had received from Mr. A. Lee, dated the 6th of February, the day the treaty was signed, addressing to him in London informing him generally of the event which had taken place." [77] Congress continued to hold Deane in suspension. Rather than exonerate or condemn him, the delegates voted to inform him that his future would soon be decided. This congressional temporizing was favorable to the Lee camp, but hardly a victory.

Arthur Lee's case was seriously undermined by Richard Henry's absence from Congress. Although aided by information from his brothers in Europe, Richard Henry was limited in the sort of defense he could coordinate from his home. Launching a three-pronged counterattack,

76. "An Epistle," in *Pennsylvania Evening Post* (Philadelphia), July 16, 1779, quoted in Bruce I. Granger, *Political Satire in the American Revolution* (Ithaca, 1960), 245.
77. Isham (ed.), *Deane Papers*, XXI, 175–82.

Richard Henry published replies in the *Virginia Gazette* that were later reprinted in the *Pennsylvania Packet*. He portrayed the Lee brothers as devotees of the true American Cause, rather than malingering discontents. Richard Henry also made an effort to belittle Deane's diplomatic talents and emphasize his personal commercial bent (if not embezzlement) and associations with Robert Morris. He underscored Bancroft's duplicity as *the* security leak at Passy. Richard Henry pleaded with Arthur to supply further evidence on Deane's affairs in Europe and to "take all imaginable pains effectually to vindicate your own [character]." If Arthur failed, not only would he lose his post, but the revolutionary cause would falter.[78]

In the coming year the reputation of Arthur Lee and the struggle in Congress for control of foreign policy would prove most critical to the old Radicals. Republican wailing echoed across the Atlantic. Arthur sensed that the "Junto" composed of Morris, Holker, Deane, and Franklin was on the ascendancy. In Richard Henry's opinion the self-centered "Intriguers" were inflicting "infinitely more injury to the common cause than all the power of the enemy." The revolutionary movement was beseiged by "Toryism," "commercial plunder," and "ambition." The prospects were not encouraging, as Francis Lightfoot Lee foresaw: "If our brothers are not disgraced now, I am sure they will be e'er long; for they always stand in the way of bad men; and no villainy will be left unpracticed to ruin them."[79] His perceptions were shared not only throughout the Lee family, but also with their congressional cohorts, colleagues in the diplomatic corps, and other votaries of American Whiggism. A life-or-death struggle was on the horizon.

---

78. Bowers, "Richard Henry Lee and the Continental Congress," 313–18; Richard Henry Lee to Arthur Lee, February 11, 1779, in Ballagh (ed.), *Letters of Richard Henry Lee*, II, 30–35. Arthur had already noted that Deane "has always been reputed a Tory in the small circle" of Connecticut politics. Arthur Lee to Richard Henry Lee, April 18, 1778, in Hoffman and Molyneaux (eds.), *Lee Family Papers*, IV, 461.

79. Arthur Lee to Richard Henry Lee, December 7, 1778, in Arthur Lee Papers, Box 5; Richard Henry Lee to Arthur Lee, February 11, 1779, in Ballagh (ed.), *Letters of Richard Henry Lee*, II, 30–31; Francis Lightfoot Lee to Richard Henry Lee, December 25, 1778, in Burnett (ed.), *Letters*, III, 551.

★ Chapter VII ★

To Succeed or Perish

The winter of 1778–1779 was Arthur Lee's most trying time. Anxiously he awaited word from Congress as to his diplomatic assignment. Although he may not have realized that his anxiety flowed from his lack of control over his own future, he recognized that he felt "deprived of that praise that constant toil and assiduity in the public service have deserved." He craved reinforcement. His character was under fire, and worse yet, his vision of the Revolution was being challenged. Adams wrote to revive his colleague's flagging spirits: "From our former Correspondence you have known my Sentiments. I have not altered them in a single Point, either with Regard to the great Cause we are engaged in or to you who have been an early, vigilant, and active Supporter of it." All the while, neglect and disapproval mounted. Adversaries like Deane, Franklin, Williams, and Morris contended with the Whigs for control of the revolutionary movement, and it was a painful contest. Not only was Lee cast into despondency, but he also suffered from a protracted illness that kept him confined to bed. Nonetheless, he possessed enough resolve to reject once more Berkenhout's "endeavors to seduce" him into discussions of an Anglo-American peace. In fact, he not only spurned the "offers of emoluments and titles of honor" from this correspondent, but also reported the bid to both Franklin and Vergennes. Perhaps Arthur wanted to contrast his own behavior with the secretive ways of Franklin and to neutralize French distrust of himself.[1] An ideologue like Arthur Lee could only be satisfied by the fulfillment of his vision of an independent American republic.

1. Arthur Lee to Theodorick Bland, December 13, 1778, Arthur Lee to Samuel Adams, February 3, 1779, both in Richard Henry Lee, *Life of Arthur Lee*, II, 161–63, 156–57; Arthur Lee to Samuel Adams, March 6, 1779, in Arthur Lee Papers, Box 6; Samuel Adams to Arthur Lee, October 26, 1778, in Cushing (ed.), *Writings of Samuel Adams*, IV, 82–83; Carl Van Doren, *Secret History of the American Revolution* (New York, 1941), 100–111.

By March of 1779, he had refurbished his determination. In a letter reminiscent of correspondence a decade before, Arthur preached to Samuel Adams that "we have the battle to fight over again against the Tories" and others. Prospects were not encouraging but, drawing from his classical education, Lee proposed "my System is that *numquam desperandum est de republica* [one must never despair about the republic]." As in the early 1770s, Lee patriotically blazoned, "as I entered into the Cause with a predetermined resolution to succeed or perish with it, the worst fortune cannot find me unprepared. . . . I have therefore long prepared my mind to receive both fortune's buffets and rewards with equal temper."[2] His resolve would be severely tested before the war and the Revolution were concluded.

The renewed resistance of the American Whigs and a revival of the Lee-Adams connection coincided. The immediate stimulus for both was the question of Arthur Lee's future as a diplomat, but fundamentally everything was motivated by the radical goals of autonomy and republicanism. Arthur Lee's vision was perhaps best described by a acquaintance from London, Dr. Richard Price. Arthur had been authorized by Congress to invite Price to emigrate to the United States so that the fledgling republic might benefit from his financial prowess. The aged Price rejected the invitation in 1779, but hoped that "America may preserve its liberty, set an example of moderation and magnimity, and establish such forms of government as may render it an asylum for the virtuous and the oppressed in other countries." Here was a restatement of the millennarian dreams shared by Arthur Lee and kindred spirits, which were now being challenged by internal and external foes. As Samuel Adams put it, Lee's "stern Virtue and Republican jealousy" had been vital to the resistance to the British and were as critical in withstanding encroachments from domestic corruption and Bourbon intrusion.[3] The combat over foreign policy was to be waged between the virtuous and the unregenerated.

News in Paris the first week of February, 1779, presaged Lee's fall.

2. Arthur Lee to Samuel Adams, March 6, 1779, in Arthur Lee Papers, Box 6.
3. Richard Henry Lee, *Life of Arthur Lee*, I, 148–49; C. C. Bonwick, "English Dissenters and the American Revolution," in H. C. Allen and Roger Thompson (eds.), *Contrast and Connection: Bicentennial Essays in Anglo-American History* (London, 1976), 88–112; Samuel Adams to Benjamin Austin, March 9, 1779, in Cushing (ed.), *Writings of Samuel Adams*, IV, 132–37; Henderson, *Party Politics*, 193–95, 210–211.

Franklin was named sole minister plenipotentiary to Versailles. Worse, Deane's denunciations published in Philadelphia were accorded space in European newspapers. Arthur's reactions were overshadowed by those of fellow Whig John Adams. His immediate impulse was to petition Vergennes to halt publication of Deane's attack. Adams supported Lee thoroughly. Although perhaps he did not indicate to the Virginian the extent of his support, he denounced Dean's address in his diary as "one of the most wicked and abominable productions that ever sprung from a human heart." Adams made it plain to Franklin and to Bancroft that no matter what Lee's temper was, "he was an honest Man, and held the utmost fidelity towards the United States." If the French sided with Deane, then the alliance should be broken. Adams expressed similar sentiments to Vergennes: the Lees' patriotism was above reproach and Deane's malicious publication raised an "emergency." Vergennes, unswayed, permitted Deane's comments to be made public. Lee, in turn, issued a defense of his conduct that included a counterattack on Deane's liaisons with Britons and his privateering ventures, which had earlier aggravated Franco-American relations.[4]

The Lee-Deane imbroglio vexed John Adams. Although Franklin, Vergennes, and others might write him off as pro-Lee, and therefore anti-gallic, Adams disavowed the labels. True, like Lee, he resented Franklin's prestige and Congress' neglect. Certainly Adams and Lee shared the virtue-mindedness and brash tactics of militia diplomacy. Yet Adams would not be drawn into Lee's party; perhaps he saw in Lee and Izard the last extremities of Whiggish suspicion. In his diary he distinguished himself from all of his colleagues in Paris—Lee, Izard and Franklin— "Virtue is not always amiable. Integrity is sometimes ruined by Prejudices and Passions. There are two Men in the World who are Men of Honour and Integrity, I believe, but whose Prejudices and violent Tempers would raise Quarrels in the Elisian Fields if not in Heaven. On the other Hand there is another, whose Love of Ease and Dissipation will prevent any

4. Arthur Lee to Vergennes, February 7, 1779, in Arthur Lee Papers, Box 6; Entry of February 8, 1779, in Lyman Butterfield (ed.), *Diary and Autobiography of John Adams*, II, 345; John Adams to Vergennes, February 11, 1779, in Wharton (ed.), *Correspondence*, III, 42–44; "Arthur Lee's Memorial," May 1, 1779, in Worthington C. Ford (ed.), *Letters of William Lee*, II, 534n; "Arthur Lee's Defense" (1779 draft), in Hoffman and Molyneaux (eds.), *Lee Family Papers*, V, 560–63.

thorough Reformation of any Thing—and his [cunning and] Silence and Reserve, render it very difficult to do anything with him." Adams, perhaps entranced by Lee's caricature of the virtuous Whig, went on to delineate Arthur's disposition: "He has confidence in no body. He believes all men selfish—And, no Man honest or sincere. This, I fear, is his creed." Adams concluded that he himself had no trust in any of his companions, for he lacked "the Wisdom of Solomon, the Meekness of Moses and the Patience of Job" necessary for the Paris assignment.[5]

Adams wrote to cousin Samuel that Lee's removal, which he felt was imminent, would "give me much pain on many accounts" and "ought to be resisted." Lee was "a faithful man and able and should not be deprived of his assignment to Spain," Adams continued, although leaving Franklin at Passy was "right." He repeated his evaluation a week later to James Lovell, who managed Arthur's cause in the Committee of Foreign Affairs. Knowing he had been relieved of his duties and would soon depart from France, Adams offered an appraisal of Arthur Lee's factious personality that has long endured: "There is an acrimony in his temper, there is a jealousy, there is an obstinacy, and a want of candor at times, and an affection of secrecy, the fruit of jealousy, which renders him disagreeable often to his friends, makes him enemies and gives them infinite advantage over him. That he has had great provocation here I never doubted."[6] His assessment considered as incubi the Whig virtues that Lee had perfected to an extreme. Adams also injected his own envy of Franklin into this diagnosis. Few historians bother to remember Adams' last line; few but John Adams have empathized with the afflicted Lee.

Lee would not knuckle under to critics or compromisers. Rather, his discordant disposition revived. He reopened the attack on Bancroft in one last effort to discredit that agent, who was passing freely between Passy and London. Bancroft's notoriety as "a Stockjobber" and his lifestyle "in open defiance of decency and religion" were reviewed for the benefit of Adams and Franklin. Lee claimed, "I have evidence in my possession, which makes me consider Dr. Bancroft as a criminal with regard to the United States," but he failed to convince his colleagues of the treachery of

5. Shaw, *Character of John Adams*, 117–21, 140–144, 290; entry of February 9, 1779, in Butterfield (ed.), *Diary and Autobiography of John Adams*, II, 346–47.
6. John Adams to Samuel Adams, February 14, 1779, John Adams to James Lovell, February 20, 1779, both in Wharton (ed.), *Correspondence*, III, 47–48, 52–53.

their secretary. Next Franklin felt Lee's sting when he tried to accumulate all diplomatic dispatches at Passy. Lee, claiming he needed the files to fashion a retort to Deane, insolently held out. This skirmish point was not resolved until February, 1780, just before Lee departed France. Meanwhile, the reckoning of Jonathan Williams' accounts plodded on, with Lee making repeated insinuations.[7]

At Nantes in early March of 1779, Lee concluded two tasks: he hastened shipment of supplies to Virginia and fashioned an answer to Deane's accusations. Armaments valued at £219,489—including £3,627 on Arthur's personal credit—were headed to the Old Dominion. Lee retained the seal he had had cast for the commonwealth of Virginia because he could not find a suitable means to ship it. (Only one of the two ships was to escape British patrols.) He also sent three copies of his rebuttal. Although this reply was accompanied by "authenticated vouchers for every material fact" he advanced, Arthur left it to the discretion of his brothers to press his case before Congress. Despite "a long and dangerous illness" that had hampered his endeavor, Arthur proved "incontrovertedly the baseness, falsehood, and wickedness of the accusations" of Deane. He also included a letter of resignation. If Congress "should not have censured the accuser," Arthur believed he could not "with any propriety continue in their service." Richard Henry, Francis Lightfoot, and Samuel Adams were empowered to plan strategy and execute the best tactics. If congressional debate proved unproductive, Arthur directed that Deane be prosecuted "at common law for a falsehood and scandalous libel." Joseph Reed and Jared Ingersoll were suggested as attorneys who would take up his case. The cause must be pursued "in the most open and direct manner." Arthur would come to America "if Congress have not done me the Justice, and the public are deluded by such a wretch."[8]

7. Arthur Lee to Franklin and John Adams, February 7, 1779, in Franklin Papers, XIII, 1, no. 86; Arthur Lee to Franklin, March 19, 1779, in Arthur Lee Papers, Box 6; Franklin to Arthur Lee, March 26, 1779, Franklin to Jonathan Williams, July 8, 1779, both in Smyth (ed.), *Writings of Franklin*, VII, 272–73, 363.

8. William Lee to Thomas Jefferson, September 28, 1779, in Worthington C. Ford (ed.), *Letters of William Lee*, III, 745–51; Arthur Lee to Governor of Virginia [Thomas Jefferson], September 4, 1779, in Julian Boyd et al. (eds.), *Papers of Thomas Jefferson*, III, 82–83; Arthur Lee to Richard Henry Lee, March 8, 1779, in Hoffman and Molyneaux (eds.), *Lee Family Papers*, V, 778.

Lee selected Hezekiah Ford, his personal secretary, to carry the rebuttal to America. He was as yet unaware that Governor Patrick Henry and the Council of Virginia considered Ford "an enemy to the American cause of independence, and by no means a fit subject to be near the person of an American Commissioner." The suspicion was that the talkative Ford had incited resistance to a militia draft in North Carolina and had even tried his hand at counterfeiting. Thus his attachment to Lee further tarnished Arthur's reputation. When Ford reached Virginia in August, 1779, Richard Henry sent him to Williamsburg to demand a hearing before his accusers, but except for the posting of a £1,000 bond, the historical record reveals nothing of Ford's end. Arthur subsequently enlisted his nephew, Ludwell Lee, as amanuensis.[9]

Lee returned from Nantes to take up residence in the Saint Germain district of Paris. Perhaps Chaillot was too expensive, perhaps it was too close to Passy, or perhaps Arthur was smitten with the charms of a Parisian. Scattered in his papers for 1779 are undated love letters written in a youthful French hand. Three, penned by Mademoiselle Benôit, welcome a visit from the American bachelor. Lee evidently kept these affairs—whether consummated or not—well covered. Though he did preserve these epistles, there is no mention of romantic or sexual relations with women during his career in France. Certainly, Lee's flirtations pale in comparison with Franklin's dalliances. Although the British spies once reported he had taken a mistress, none of Arthur's enemies mention any improprieties in his personal life.[10] Lee may have been enticed by the opposite sex at this time, but he was so deeply committed to his patriotism and his family that he could not contemplate marriage in Europe. There was always the reminder of how disruptive the diplomatic calling was to

9. Arthur Lee to Richard Henry Lee, April 26, 1779, in Hoffman and Molyneaux (eds.), *Lee Family Papers*, VI, 7; Meriwether Smith to Congress, January 26, 1770, in Wharton (ed.), *Correspondence*, III, 32; Butterfield (ed.), *Diary and Autobiography of John Adams*, II, 365n; Richard Henry Lee to Arthur Lee, August 12, 1779, John Page to Arthur Lee, June 7, 1780, both in Hoffman and Molyneaux (eds.), *Lee Family Papers*, VI, 303, 677; Dixon and Nicholson (eds.), *Virginia Gazette*, August 28, October 11, 16, 1779.

10. Mlle. Benoit to Arthur Lee [undated], in Hoffman and Molyneaux (eds.), *Lee Family Papers*, V, 574, VI, 420–421, 503; Marguerite duPont Lee, *Arthur Lee*, 161–66; Paul Wentworth to the Earl of Suffolk, November 10, 1777, in Stevens (ed.), *Facsimiles*, no. 217; Claude Anne Lopez, *Mon Cher Papa: Franklin and the Ladies of Paris* (New Haven, 1966), *passim*.

the family life of brother William. Nor did Arthur Lee want any of the sort of notoriety that Franklin's escapades had received.

The two Lee brothers in Europe spent much of the summer of 1779 in an attempt to cleanse their reputations of Deane's charge that Arthur had leaked news of the Franco-American alliance to the British, seeking reconciliation with them. Deane's source, Samuel Petrie, a London speculator and former acquaintance from Wilkes's banquets, conceded after much badgering, that William, not Arthur, might have been the leak. William Lee thereupon challenged Petrie to a duel. As in an *opéra bouffe*, the antagonists failed to meet, but William returned to Frankfurt with a written vindication from Arthur's friends, certain that Petrie had backed out like a coward.[11] Yet the family honor had not been absolved. Probably even ridicule was heaped on the Lees. Nor can the evidence that William Lee was guilty as charged be brushed aside.

Deane's accusations continued to rankle Arthur Lee, but his animosity toward his former companion had already peaked. Instead, as he relayed views to his American correspondents, he began to worry about what he saw as a growing conspiracy that threatened not only his position, but the fundamental thrust of the Revolution as well. His personal contentions were a microcosm of the international contest. Franklin and Gérard were now his chief targets. The Frenchman he labeled a coconspirator in Deane's "great roguery." Franklin, he condemned for consorting with the "informers," stockjobbers like Bancroft and the Whartons; for treating Arthur "with neglect and ill-humor"; and chiefly for being submissive to the French court. His old fears returned as Arthur extrapolated "that the ultimate object of the faction is to sell us back to the domination from which we have vindicated ourselves." To Samuel Adams, he was more specific on two points. In Franklin's ascendancy, Lee perceived the moral regression of America: "We shall fall into such a vileness soon that nothing will retrieve our character. The meanest of all mean men, the most corrupt of all corrupt men is assimilating everything to his own nature." The remedy was Arthur's proverbial panacea—autonomy. "As to Poli-

11. Certificate of Edmund Jenings, June 1, 1779, Samuel Petrie to Arthur Lee, April 9, 1779, in Hoffman and Molyneaux (eds.), *Lee Family Papers*, VI, 173, 18, 19, 23; William Purdie Treloar, *Wilkes and the City* (London, 1917), 259–89; Worthington C. Ford (ed.), *Letters of William Lee*, I, 216–19, 627–28; Statement of Walter Pollard and William Boush, August 5, 1779, in Hoffman and Molyneaux (eds.), *Lee Family Papers*, VI, 280–285.

tics, I must recur to my former position, that you must depend upon your-selves and not remit any efforts from a confidence in the weakness of the Enemy or the assistance of our Ally." [12]

These refrains are so repetitive in Arthur's correspondence with Sam-uel Adams that they might appear meaningless. For ten years the two had dwelt on little else than the denunciation of Lee's compatriots and a run-ning jeremiad on faltering American self-reliance. The revived Lee-Adams correspondence reinforced these feelings. Adams wrote, "I fore-saw soon after his [Deane's] arrival that your lot would be to suffer per-secution for a while. This is frequently the portion of good men, but they are never substantially injured by it." [13] Arthur's cries of persecution are so frequent as to render him—in the eyes of his contemporaries and of later critics—a paranoid.

Certainly the historical record indicates that Arthur Lee had just cause for believing himself persecuted by numerous enemies. There was no fantasy or illusion about the machinations and mutterings of Deane, Gé-rard, Beaumarchais, Franklin, Bancroft, and others. To the degree that Lee was aware of them, he could not be considered ill. But perhaps he was unable to see that, beyond this very real oppression, much of his anxiety arose from within himself. It is the tone rather than any specific complaint that is revelatory. Arthur in 1769 and in 1779 was writing in the same vein as he had when he was an adolescent in 1759. He was con-tinually harassed, if not persecuted, by his inability to realize his own in-dependence. As long as Franklin overshadowed, outmaneuvered, and spurned him, Lee could never consider himself autonomous. He saw Con-gress—just as his parents had—preparing to disown him. When he felt vulnerable and full of self-doubt, he relied on the same tactics he had used as a student at Edinburgh, a polemicist in London, and a diplomat in France. He denied faults in himself, focused on the faults of his adver-saries, and proclaimed self-righteously that he was suffering personal tor-ment for the benefit of others.

On the last day of May, Arthur drafted a letter resigning his commis-sion to Madrid. He told the president of Congress that he was "willing

12. Arthur Lee to Richard Henry Lee, April 22, May 21, 1779, Arthur Lee to Samuel Adams, March 6, 1779, May 22, 1779, all in Arthur Lee Papers, Box 6.
13. Samuel Adams to Arthur Lee, August 1, 1779, in Cushing (ed.), *Writings of Samuel Adams*, II, 155–57.

to continue to sacrifice, as I have hitherto done, my private interest to the public good," but as long as he stayed at his post, he feared "dissensions" over his position would negate his abilities and contributions. Therefore, "as the public good was the sole motive of my accepting the Commission, the same reason now induces me to desire most earnestly to resign it." Arthur had previously tendered his resignation on March 1, but evidently Richard Henry had not submitted the original letter. Whether Arthur anticipated that it would now be accepted or not cannot be ascertained. Certainly the note was intended to force Congress to confront the issue of his continuance and put an end to the suspense generated by Deane's accusations. Ironically, the letter was not read before Congress until October, 1779, by which time the issue had already been determined.[14]

Uncertainty over his status dogged Lee throughout the spring. Nonetheless, he carried out his mission as best he could despite a lack of instructions from Congress and a lack of encouragement from Franklin. Lee's predicament was exasperating, for prospects had brightened. In April at Aranjuez, Floridablanca consented to a secret pact with Vergennes. When a Spanish ultimatum for mediation was brushed aside by the British, war ensued. The French assured Charles III that they would not treat for a separate peace or stop fighting until Spain won Gibraltar. Although Lee knew nothing of these arrangements, he revived memorials to Madrid when he learned of Spain's war declaration. As before, his entreaties and suggestions received cold replies. The Spaniards wanted no connection with the Continental Congress. Lee was perplexed, for if he did nothing, he could be accused of "negligence," but if he acted and were recalled, his negotiations would be purposeless. So he waited. Franklin hinted that because the prospects and resources for the Madrid commission were dim, it would be "both wise and honest" for Arthur to return to America. The fact that Lee was still dependent upon Franklin for funds raised his old insecurities.[15]

14. Arthur Lee to the President of Congress, May 31, 1779, in Wharton (ed.), *Correspondence*, III, 196; Worthington C. Ford (ed.), *Journals*, XIV, 826, 989, 1008, 1012, XV, 1016, 1161; Oliver P. Chitwood, *Richard Henry Lee*, 114–15.

15. Arthur Lee to Committee of Foreign Affairs, May 12, 1779, Arthur Lee's Memorial to the Court of Spain, June 6, 1779, Lee to the President of Congress, June 21, 1779, Lee to Floridablanca, June 27, 1779, all in Wharton (ed.), *Correspondence*, III, 171–73, 209, 229, 234–35; Arthur Lee to Richard Henry Lee, August 21, 1779, November 7, 1779, Franklin to Arthur Lee, September 30, 1779, in Hoffman and Molyneaux (eds.), *Lee Family Papers*, VI, 321, 443, 381.

Through the summer and into autumn, Lee tarried in Paris, frustrated. The fault lay neither with himself nor the Spaniards. He would not "hazard the public interest and my own honor in undertaking the negotiations uninstructed, unvindicated, and unsupported." He called the failure of Congress to provide for him an "unexampled cruelty." [16] It was the plaintive cry of a frustrated zealot who had labored four years only to find himself in disfavor at home and disused abroad.

Foreign affairs had, in fact, become a central concern of Congress in early 1779. Congress had not only the final disposition of Deane—and perhaps other diplomatic personnel—to be decided, but also the entire foundation and framework of foreign policy to consider. Two different spirits were in contention: one favored reform in the Continental Line, in the means of financing the war effort, and in international affairs, while the other championed the impetus of earlier radicalism. The debates were plagued by parochial and sectional outbursts. The eastern party, of which the Lee-Adams axis was a central faction, had held sway since the opening of the war. But as the element of French influence came to bear, in the person of Gérard, and as British forces moved out of New England into the more southerly theaters of war, eastern domination came under attack by the southern party. This partisan plurality extended into the determination of policies and personnel. As H. James Henderson's recent studies have made abundantly clear, "The history of the Continental Congress had been marked by factional disputes between delegates who spoke (or professed to speak) for the democracy against the aristocracy, between nationalists and parochialists, between agrarian and commercial interests, and between an array of regional coalitions." [17] The party affiliations seemed to Lee but a revival of the Whig-Tory dichotomy of 1774–1776. From the modern perspective the labels radical or purist versus moderate or realist appear more meaningful although less ideologically charged, but all polar perspectives are simplistic.

Gérard, as the representative of France and, to a much lesser extent, of Spain, forced controversy when he asked the Americans to articulate the terms they required for peace. In effect, he asked for the self-prescription

16. Arthur Lee to the Committee of Foreign Affairs, November 6, 1779, in Wharton (ed.), *Correspondence*, III, 400–401.

17. H. James Henderson, "Quantitative Approaches to Party Formation in the United States Congress: A Comment," *William and Mary Quarterly*, 3rd ser., XXX (April, 1973), 315.

of the American mission in the world. The ensuing wranglings were the initial round of a two-century dispute. Some wanted only recognition of American independence, while others insisted that such imperial goals as freedom to navigate the Mississippi River, possession of Nova Scotia or the entirety of Canada, and the guarantee of rights to the Newfoundland fisheries must be achieved. There was question about whether these ambitions should be held as *sine qua non* in the peace ultimatum. Gérard wanted the least aggressive statement he could get. The debates over the fisheries raged from February through August; those over the Mississippi went into the next year. Throughout, Arthur Lee's merits and demerits were simultaneously disputed. In essence the French intention to dominate their American allies found a responsive and compliant following in the more pragmatic delegates of the southern party, giving rise to an apparent anomaly. Generally, southerners—but for "monsters" such as Richard Henry Lee and Henry Laurens—supported Deane, Gérard, and a limited vision of the American republic, while New Englanders and their associates, clinging to stiff and wide-ranging ultimata, rallied to the cause of Arthur Lee and were cast as antigallic, if not worse.[18]

To the Adams-Lee faction, the debates of 1779 unfolded like a morality play. Personal antagonisms were heightened by ideological overtones. Early on, Richard Henry asserted that "All sensible Whigs in this Country, and now the herd of Mankind begin to see clearly into Deane and his party," but he could not be overly optimistic, for if Deane were not exonerated, Arthur's post was still in peril. Samuel Adams and Francis Lightfoot Lee agreed with Richard Henry that liberty and virtue were challenged by dependency and every kind of vice.[19] While it might be too neatly dichotomous to classify the competing parties as radical and moderate, nonetheless the revivalistic impulse of the Lee-Adams faction sharply distinguished itself from the more practical perspective and programs

18. John R. Alden, *The South in the Revolution, 1763–1789* (Baton Rouge, 1957), 300–305; H. James Henderson, "Congressional Factionalism and the Attempt to Recall Benjamin Franklin," *William and Mary Quarterly*, 3rd ser., XXVII (April, 1970), 251. The significance of the fisheries and of Arthur Lee's advocacy are emphasized in Henderson, "Political Factions," 255–60.

19. Richard Henry Lee to Arthur Lee, February 11, 1779, in Ballagh (ed.), *Letters of Richard Henry Lee*, II, 31–32; Richard Henry Lee to Arthur Lee, March 21, 1779, in Burnett (ed.), *Letters*, IV, 110–111; Henderson, *Party Politics*, 192–95.

of their opponents. One insisted on the moral integrity of the republican revolution, the other tolerated Gérard's meddling and Deane's profiteering. Each group had different visions of the social and political orders of the emerging nation as well as its role in the world order. The basic question was whether the Adams-Lee axis, so critical in initiation of the rebellion, would be allowed to play a like role in determining its perpetuation. H. James Henderson notes, "Actually the radical reputation of the easterners was not entirely warranted; at least it must be carefully qualified. There were profoundly conservative dimensions to the 'Christian Sparta' that remained Sam Adams' ultimate revolutionary purpose. . . . The republican purism that had been the mainstay of the eastern faction proved to be as fragile an instrument for sustaining power as it was dynamic in generating the Revolution." [20]

Amidst Silas Deane's pleas and Thomas Paine's polemic, Congress confronted its international mission in January, 1779, by empowering a thirteen-man committee to investigate the conduct of the commissioners. Within three months, the Deane camp had gained control. On March 24, 1779, the stage was set when it was reported, "That suspicions and animosities have arisen among the (late and present) Commissioners (*viz.*, Benjamin Franklin, Silas Deane, Arthur Lee, Ralph Izard, and William Lee) highly prejudiced to the honor and interests of the United States." There was an immediate recommendation that all commissions be vacated and new appointments made.[21] The seven-point indictment brought against Arthur Lee, largely fashioned from earlier testimony offered by Deane and Carmichael, charged that Arthur's contemptuous attitudes toward the French had disgusted the Bourbons and threatened Franco-American harmony, that his captious personality had provoked quarrels with his compatriots, that no success could be reported from his Spanish and Prussian endeavors, and that he had leaked news of the alliance to British friends. The wrong man had been recalled!

It is ironic that the committee's report, which was so unfavorable to Lee, finally affirmed Arthur's recommendations that only one diplomat

20. Kaplan, *Colonies to Nation*, 124–25; Henderson, "Congressional Factionalism," 248–49; H. James Henderson, "The Structure of Politics in the Continental Congress," in Stephen G. Kurtz and James H. Hutson (eds.), *Essays on the American Revolution* (New York, 1973), 183–84.

21. Worthington C. Ford (ed.), *Journals*, XII, 364–67; Henderson, "Congressional Factionalism," 252–56.

be assigned each foreign court, "that no such representatve exercise any other public office while serving," that American accounts in Europe be audited, and that specific salaries be assigned envoys. An added criterion, however, was seemingly targeted at Arthur, for the committee stipulated also that diplomats be United States citizens "and have a fixed and permanent interest therein."[22] Lee's long residence in England was still a sore spot.

Delegates maneuvered in support of or opposition to various diplomats. Several congressmen sought out Gérard for France's opinion. Although under instructions from Vergennes to remain aloof from the Deane-Lee controversy, the French minister was drawn into the fray because, seeing the implications of personnel changes on the formulation of policy, he wanted to influence them. Gérard was also antagonized by the Lee forces, which asserted that Arthur possessed the confidence of the French court. This fabrication vexed Gérard, who in dispatches to Vergennes had labeled Lee "a man very annoying, if not dangerous." Gérard warned Richard Henry Lee not to provoke testimony from the French court. Samuel Adams would not be stilled, however, for he believed that Arthur's value system and priorities, not his temperament, irritated the Francophiles and Gérard. On April 15 Adams reported to Congress that, contrary to previous assertions, Arthur Lee did in fact possess the confidence of Versailles.[23] Gérard had been goaded.

The debate over Arthur Lee's rapport with the French raised the issue of what degree Congress would comply with Bourbon dictates. Laurens, whose rhetoric and previous voting record were both pro-Lee, was not above requesting Gérard's direct testimony. This appeal proved detrimental to Lee's case. On April 21 Laurens offered Congress news of his interview with Gérard. This testimony amounted to damning with faint praise. Overall, it was Gérard's opinion that Arthur Lee's conduct was "disagreeable" to the French, "but in respects" Lee "stood fair."[24] The

22. Worthington C. Ford (ed.), *Journals*, XII, 364–67.

23. Gérard to Vergennes, December 12, 1778, in Meng (ed.), *Despatches and Instructions of Gérard*, 418–23, 557–61; Gérard to Vergennes, March 6, 1779, in Ballagh (ed.), *Letters of Richard Henry Lee*, II, 43n; Samuel Adams to Benjamin Austin, March 9, 1779, in Cushing (ed.), *Writings of Samuel Adams*, IV, 135; Gérard to Samuel Adams, April 21, 1779, in Hoffman and Molyneaux (eds.), *Lee Family Papers*, VI, 44.

24. Statement of Henry Laurens, April 29, 1779, in Burnett (ed.), *Letters*, IV, 166–68.

French were unappreciative of Lee's inflexibility as a negotiator, but despite rumors rampant in France, they did not doubt his fidelity. Thomas Burke, a prominent Francophile, questioned this claim, and the day ended after a "very warm loud and long debate" with Congress determined to consider the recall of each commissioner individually. Between April 22 and June 10, votes gauged the degrees of confidence Congress had in its diplomats.[25] Meanwhile, the controversy spilled into the Philadelphia press.

The opposing parties offered ploys and counterploys. Some staunch supporters of Deane were willing to vote for Franklin's recall if, in turn, a few votes could be swayed to go against Lee's retention. Interestingly enough, the roll call votes were phrased to question whether the emissaries should be recalled or not, although the question was actually that of retention. On April 22, Franklin was continued at Passy by a considerable margin of the state delegations. Consideration then shifted to Arthur Lee, and emotions mounted. Eastern forces rounded up delegates from Pennsylvania and New Jersey. Warm but undecisive deliberations were recorded April 26 and 27. So bitter was debate that a motion was introduced to call in Gérard for his personal testimony. Such overt intervention by the French was rejected, but Richard Henry Lee was nonetheless ill at ease. He wrote Francis Lightfoot, "This day I have heard all the artillery discharged with great vehemence against Dr. Lee, and prodigious aid is derived from the whispers of G[érar]d." James Lovell, proponent of both Franklin and Arthur Lee, reported to the former that "Nothing short of the Ruin of the Reputation" of the latter "will glut the malice of a party" formed by Deane. John Jay, who was presiding over the debate, reported to General Washington, "There is as much Intrigue in this State House as in the Vatican but as little Secrecy as in a boarding school."[26] So despondent was Richard Henry that he openly envied Francis Lightfoot's retreat from the melee of Congress.

The anti-Lees launched a torpedo on April 30 when southerners Wil-

25. Henderson, *Party Politics*, 202–205; Thomas Burke, Account of an Interview with Gérard respecting Arthur Lee [*ca.*, April 21, 1779], John Fell Diary, April 21, 1779, in Burnett (ed.), *Letters*, IV, 168–70, 172–73.

26. Henderson, "Congressional Factionalism," 256, 267; John Fell Diary, April 21, 22, 1779, in Burnett (ed.), *Letters*, IV 172–73; Richard Henry Lee to Francis Lightfoot Lee, April 26, 1779, in Ballagh (ed.), *Letters of Richard Henry Lee*, II, 49–51; James Lovell to Franklin, April 29, 1779, John Jay to General Washington, April 26, 1779, in Burnett (ed.), *Letters*, IV, 182–83, 176–77.

liam Paca of Maryland and William Henry Drayton of South Carolina
tried to scuttle Lee's commission to Madrid by settling once and for all
what the French desired. These delegates, with others like Thomas Burke
of North Carolina and Meriwether Smith of Virginia, formed the core of
the Deane faction. Not only did they advocate and practice the pragmatic
and profit-oriented brand of revolution, but they also possessed additional
motives to oppose Lee. Drayton, for example, who had perhaps vied with
Lee during his schooling in Britain, was now the main adversary of
Laurens for control of his state's delegation. Willingly, Paca and Drayton
conveyed Gérard's best shot to Congress. He repeated for their benefit
what he had written to Vergennes the previous October: "Besides, I confess to you, that I fear Mr. Lee and those about him." In turn, Paca and
Drayton repeated this to Congress and detailed how much Arthur had
proved disgusting to and distrusted by both Bourbon courts.[27] The cres-
cendo of congressional contentiousness mounted. Meanwhile, the memorandum was leaked to the press. Paca and Drayton sought to conclude the
work Deane had begun the previous December: their aim was the total
traducement of Arthur Lee, and Gérard connived in it.

The roll-call vote on Arthur Lee came May 3. William Carmichael,
now a Maryland delegate who favored Deane, made one final argument.
Although the *Journals* of Congress are mute as to the pitch of the deliberations and although Lee's correspondents within Congress were uncommonly reticent or hesitant about the nature of their arguments,
Gérard divulged that "the debates have been incited to the last degree of
animosity and indecency." Later historians rank the entire imbroglio as
the most vituperative in a culture noted for its verbal bloodletting. What
rhetorical contribution Richard Henry Lee made is not known, but the
record shows he excused himself from the vote. His home state was overwhelmingly against the Lees anyway. When the final tally was made, at
the request of Meriwether Smith, who perhaps coveted Arthur's assignment, twenty-two delegates had voted for Lee's recall, while only fourteen believed he should continue as commissioner to Spain, but the Lee

27. Bowers, "Richard Henry Lee," 333–36; Henderson, *Party Politics*, 11–12,
180, 230; William Paca and William Henry Drayton, Memorial to Congress,
April 30, 1779, in Hoffman and Molyneaux (eds.), *Lee Family Papers*, VI, 912;
Gérard to Vergennes, October 20, 1778, in Meng (ed.), *Despatches and Instructions of Gérard*, 358; Stinchcombe, *American Revolution*, 70–71.

faction had not lost. The vote, when recorded properly by states, showed equal divisions of four apiece in the columns of yeas, nays, and divisions. It was most ironic that Arthur Lee, a preacher of nationalism, was obligated to the congressional system of recording votes by states rather than tabulating individual delegates' preferences. Further, because the vote was for recall, Lee was continued at his post. Had it been phrased to consider his continuance, a similar poll would have resulted in his ouster.[28]

The Virginian owed his tenure to the ability of the eastern party to neutralize southern antipathy. Votes between the two sectional parties were equal: the easterners for retaining Lee, the southern states for his recall. Lee survived the recall effort because New Hampshire's single representative cast a pro-Lee vote and because the New Jersey and Pennsylvania delegations were dependent upon the presence of recently returned pro-Lee members. In the pivotal divided states, any one of which could have tipped the vote against Arthur, the momentary attendance of Nicholas Van Dyke of Delaware was the single most crucial vote cast. Such were the often whimsical determinations of Congress.[29]

Reactions indicate that both sides knew that the complex issues had not been settled definitively. Gérard alerted his superior that his team, "Les Patriots," would continue to undermine Arthur Lee, "the least suitable" of emissaries of the American cause. The Lee-Adams faction was no longer simply antigallic, it was now known as the "English faction." Richard Henry Lee recognized that Gérard's antagonism was far more threatening than Deane's. The onslaught had been so vociferous that Richard Henry counseled a tactical retreat. He left Philadelphia to return to the Northern Neck. Although "the uniform, fixed, invariable Whigs" were for Arthur, the Madrid commission seemed untenable. So great was "the violence and wickedness" of the Deaneites that his youngest brother would be wise "to take the first favorable opportunity to resign, or rather ask leave to do so." It was anticipated that Arthur would soon return to America armed with full substantiation of his commission and expendi-

28. William Carmichael, Statement Concerning Silas Deane and Arthur Lee, May 3, 1779, in Burnett (ed.), *Letters*, IV, 189–93; Gérard to Vergennes, May 4, 1779, in Meng (ed.), *Despatches and Instructions of Gérard*, 615–19; Henderson, *Party Politics*, 200–205. Mistaken tallies (such as for Jenifer and Collins) mar Henderson's nonetheless revealing tabulations.

29. Burnett (ed.), *Letters*, III, lii, IV, lii; Richard Henry Lee to Arthur Lee, August 31, 1780, in Hoffman and Molyneaux (eds.), *Lee Family Papers*, VI, 728.

tures. Meanwhile, Richard Henry rallied Laurens, Samuel Adams, and Thomas Jefferson in the cause of "honest Whiggism." The "putrid fabric" of the Deane camp must be annihilated.[30]

The Whigs endured reversals, sacrificed some personnel, but persisted in their campaigns against the Francophiles. In June, Congress deposed Ralph Izard and William Lee from their commissions to Tuscany and Prussia respectively. The cores of the rival factions voted the party line solidly while the unaffiliated delegates swung the tallies against the Lee-Adams faction by a final vote of seven states to four. Izard and Lee retained a measure of honor, however, for they were not required to return to America. That their dismissal was a month later than the vote on Arthur Lee indicates that it was of secondary concern to Congress. At least one delegate found humor in the two-month bickering over the foreign service. A note passed in pro-Lee channels observed, "we had many curious and learned Debates respecting the Meaning and Definition of the Word 'recall' and I at one Time apprehended the Result might have produced the Necessity of Correction in most of our modern Dictionaries."[31]

Congress had yet to render a final decision on Deane's status. On June 10, after nearly a year of pleading, the former commissioner received congressional permission to depart from America if he so desired. Deane's supporters had prevailed. The Lee forces wanted Deane detained until Arthur Lee appeared and could face his accuser. No vote of censure was called in consideration of Deane's appeal over the head of Congress to the public. Lovell's reading of a spirited thirty-two page rejoinder from Arthur Lee to Deane's allegations reportedly moved Deane's side to tears but had no other effect. In August, Congress discharged Deane and paid him for expenses incurred in public service. Within a year he was back in France pursuing profit. The majority of delegates sought to still the

---

30. Gérard to Vergennes, May 4, 1779, in Meng (ed.), *Despatches and Instructions of Gérard*, 614–19; Stinchcombe, *American Revolution*, 38; Richard Henry Lee to Arthur Lee, May 23, 1779, in Burnett (ed.), *Letters*, IV, 227–29; Bowers, "Richard Henry Lee," 335; Richard Henry Lee to Laurens, June 13, 1779, Richard Henry Lee to Samuel Adams, June 20, 1779, Richard Henry Lee to Jefferson, July 8, 1779, all in Ballagh (ed.), *Letters of Richard Henry Lee*, II, 70, 76–77, 82–86.

31. Worthington C. Ford (ed.), *Journals*, XIV, 700–705; Henderson, *Party Politics*, 202–205; Nathaniel Scudder to Richard Henry Lee, June 15, 1779, in Burnett (ed.), *Letters*, IV, 271.

controversy over personnel so that formulation of policy could proceed. Meanwhile, newspapers along the Atlantic seaboard reverberated with charges and countercharges that partisanship in Congress, such as the Lee-Adams junto, was hindering the war effort.[32]

That Congress had cast doubt on his integrity and had not censured Deane added to Arthur Lee's conviction that the revolutionary movement was turning away from him. Certain a revelation of the facts would vindicate his honor, he realized that this must await less critical times. Then he would "prove to my country and to the world" that Congressional "confidence in me was not misplaced." Arthur entreated Jefferson not to permit "our Countrymen" to be lulled into a false sense of security. Although he did not refer specifically to the French alliance, he asserted, "The events of war are always uncertain; but it is most sure, that they who are best prepared for war, make peace upon the most advantageous terms." Here was an echo of his writings in 1774–1775. Another reminder of times past was the note Arthur sent John Dickinson, an ally in 1776, who had voted against him. Arthur, for good reason, felt somewhat betrayed. Finally, Lee sought refuge in the comforting correspondence with Samuel Adams. Lambasting Deane, Carmichael, and Franklin, Arthur concluded with a most sobering thought: "the old man and his Associates, are not to be trifled with; nor is it possible to say, at what Atrocious Acts they will not aim."[33] Although his complaints were pricked by personal pride, they were also encapsuled in patriotism.

Arthur's case before Congress was entrusted to James Lovell, but even though Lovell's attachment to whiggism could not be doubted, his tactics left much to be desired. The departures of Richard Henry Lee and Sam-

---

32. Henderson, *Party Politics*, 201–205; Wharton (ed.), *Correspondence*, III, 216–18; Chitwood, *Richard Henry Lee*, 116–17; Lovell to Samuel Adams, July 16, 1779, in Burnett (ed.), *Letters*, IV, 319–20; "Draft of Arthur Lee's Defense" [undated], in Hoffman and Molyneaux (eds.), *Lee Family Papers*, VI, 508–530; Stinchcombe, *American Revolution*, 66–69; Chitwood, *Richard Henry Lee*, 212, 213; "Rowland," to Editor of *Pennsylvania Packet*, August 10, 17, 24, 31, 1779, all in Ballagh (ed.), *Letters of Richard Henry Lee*, II 108–112, 125–30, 132–38, 138–42.

33. Arthur Lee to Committee of Foreign Affairs, September 19, 1779, in Wharton (ed.), *Correspondence*, III, 329–30; Arthur Lee to Jefferson, September 4, 1779, in Boyd (ed.), *Jefferson Papers*, III, 82–83; Arthur Lee to Dickinson, September 19, 1779, Arthur Lee to Samuel Adams, September 19, 1779, both in Arthur Lee Papers, Box 6.

uel Adams from Congress diminished their faction's ideological fire-power. Lovell did little but read aloud Arthur's letters that, whether addressed to Lee, Adams, or the Committee on Foreign Affairs, arrived in Philadelphia. This was not without effect. Among the Deaneites, one such reading in August spurred "envy, malice and every vindictive passion that disappointed malevolence could inspire. . . . Fiddle head [Meriwether Smith] shook, swivel eye [James Duane?] nestled and turned pale, the Chair [John Jay] changed colour at every sentence, some others forced a sneer, endeavoring to conceal their chagrin and confusion." [34]

Watchful waiting was Lovell's strategy. Rather than force Arthur's cause, he withheld the Virginian's request for recall and his demands that Deane be assailed with civil suits. On September 22 the Congressman alerted Arthur Lee, "I expect in a few hours to be able to show you whether your honor is properly regarded here or not." A decisive moment had arrived. The status of Lee's mission to Madrid was entwined with the question of what demands to include in a peace proposal, which was then in the concluding stages of debate. If Congress chose to include navigation of the Mississippi River and occupation of the Floridas, then a new man might be empowered to treat with Spain. Lovell was hopeful, but cryptic, explaining, "I have papers so arranged as to enlighten new members and make old members sin against conviction, if they so sin." [35] Perhaps the death of William Henry Drayton and Gérard's impending departure for France buoyed Lovell's hopes. It seemed possible that the Whigs would be able to recoup the losses they had suffered in June.

The easterners could not cope with southern strategy in the autumn as they had in the spring. The final struggle over Arthur Lee's commission was swift and fatal to the Lee interests despite Lovell's efforts. The southern party split the Lee-Adams faction when they nominated John Adams for the newly designated post of peace commissioner. In the first round of votes on September 25, Arthur's supporters failed by a wide margin to have his appointment to Madrid renewed. Adams and John Jay then were nominated to treat for peace. A deadlock arose because neither had the

34. Lovell to Franklin, August 6, 1779, in Smyth (ed.), *Writings of Franklin*, VII, 402; William Whipple to Richard Henry Lee, August 23, 1779, in Burnett (ed.), *Letters*, IV, 385–86.

35. Lovell to Arthur Lee, September 17, 22, 1779, in Burnett (ed.), *Letters*, IV, 422–25, 431.

necessary support of seven states. Then the old anti-Lee combination of Meriwether Smith and William Paca moved that a minister plenipotentiary, rather than a commissioner, be assigned Spanish negotiations. This ruse, which passed by a seven-to-three vote, in effect revoked Arthur Lee's mission. The path was then clear for the next set of manuevers.[36]

The key development came September 27. First Congress reaffirmed that the minister to Spain would supersede the commissioner on the rationale that the negotiation of an alliance with Charles III was different from the type of services Lee had performed. Again, this ploy of Paca and Smith prevailed. Lovell, selecting endorsements of Lee from the correspondence of John Adams and Vergennes, offered a defense. Then Laurens nominated Arthur Lee for the Madrid post, Paca nominated John Adams, and James Mercer of Virginia nominated John Jay. The Adams-Lee coalition was broken. Jay squeezed in, while Lee received only the support of New Hampshire. Adams initially found eleven states and then a unanimous Congress in support of his selection as peace commissioner. Lovell was forced to concede "the crowning act of all Deane's base Arts" had transpired, and he asked, "What d——d dirty work is this of politics?" Although the Deaneites and Gérard had been unable to place Jay as chief peace negotiator, they had eliminated Arthur Lee from foreign service. It was not until October 13 that Congress, prompted by Lovell's reading of Arthur's renewed request for recall, remembered to inform him of his fate. Lovell personally desired that the revolutionary come to America immediately "and do himself all that Justice before the World which his Patriotism will permit."[37] He had the unpleasant task of communicating the congressional decision to the fallen commissioner.

The prolonged and violent struggle between Arthur Lee's foes and supporters was over, and analyses of the impact were soon forthcoming. Richard Henry Lee was aghast and wrote to his young brother, "Your enemies have triumphed at last, wicked persevering and under no kind of restraint they have fairly worried out the friends of virtue and their country."

36. Worthington C. Ford (ed.), *Journals*, XV, 1103–1110; Hoffman and Molyneaux (eds.), *Lee Family Papers*, VI, 370–373.

37. Lovell to Richard Henry Lee, September 27, 1779, in Burnett (ed.), *Letters*, IV, 443–45; Henderson, *Party Politics*, 208–210; Worthington C. Ford (ed.), *Journals*, XV, 116; Lovell to Richard Henry Lee, September 27, 1779, in Burnett (ed.), *Letters*, IV, 443–45; Lovell to John Adams, September 27, 1779, in Wharton (ed.), *Correspondence*, III, 337n.

More vociferously, he charged that "Congress have by their treatment of Dr. Lee given a very instructive lesson to future Ministers—that zeal, ability and integrity are qualities which they do not intend their servants shall practice without incurring their utmost displeasure." Other Whigs agreed that a great wrong had been inflicted on a most virtuous American, but they had not the spirit to continue the fight. Lovell wanted to let bygones be bygones. John Dickinson, defending his votes against Lee, conceded that his former associate possessed those attributes listed by Richard Henry plus those of courage and diligence. The Pennsylvanian posited that had not Lovell and others been uncompromising in Congress, Lee might have salvaged another European assignment.[38]

Gérard gloated. Both he and Juan de Miralles, the Spanish observer in America, judged Jay to be pliable to the Bourbon point of view. Further, they anticipated that actual negotiations for peace would be held in Spain so that Adams' powers would be neutralized. One of Gérard's henchmen and simultaneously a business partner of Morris, Carter Braxton of Virginia, fired the final volley at Arthur Lee. In the *Virginia Gazette*, Braxton censured Lee's malicious temperament and anti-French attitude. Of the decision by Congress, Braxton trumpeted, "the united voice of a people have declared him unworthy the confidence of the people."[39] This ridiculing of Lee was not unlike John Camm's in 1766. The defamation of Arthur Lee had been accomplished.

Through the frenzy of the Lee-Deane dispute there were some who evaded the intense politicalization. William Churchill Houston, a new delegate from New Jersey who had not participated in the votes but who had been intrigued by the inflammatory opinions expressed by his colleagues and in the newspapers, took a moderate stance. In subsequent debates he appeared as a member of the ascendant middle-south coalition. He saw Arthur Lee as the epitome of old radicalism: "I take Mr. Arthur

38. Richard Henry Lee to Arthur Lee, October 12, 1779, in Burnett (ed.), *Letters*, IV, 481–82; Henderson, *Party Politics*, 211; Richard Henry Lee to James Searle, October 15, 1779, in Ballagh (ed.), *Letters of Richard Henry Lee*, II 164; Dickinson to Arthur Lee, March 30, 1780, Thomas McKean to Richard Henry Lee, March 25, 1780, both in Burnett (ed.), *Letters*, V, 100, 94–96; Henderson, *Party Politics*, 250.

39. Carter Braxton to Arthur Lee, in Dixon & Nicholson (eds.), *Virginia Gazette*, October 23, 1779.

Lee to be a man of a jealous, suspecting, difficult disposition; trusty, capable and industrious. Indefatigable above others in procuring and transmitting intelligence, accurate and frugal in expenses and money matters, simple, severe, and republican in his manners, so much so, as to be thought by many sour and inimical."[40] The vote to dismiss Lee from the foreign service was interpreted as an effort to calm the turbulence in the diplomatic corps. Lee's talents and verve had been welcomed in 1776. In 1779, they were not only deemed inappropriate, but even castigated.

The moods, alignments, and objectives of the Revolution were altered by the Lee-Deane imbroglio. Gérard's participation in Deane's cause had raised the ire of those Whigs who advocated self-reliance in the war effort and were suspicious of Bourbon aid. In a sense, the alliance of 1778 was still negotiable; the degree of subservience of one ally to the other had not been decided.[41] Gérard, pleading ill health, was preparing to return home. It was a measure of reciprocity for Arthur Lee. The Francophiles had unseated the Lees and Izard, but in turn, the Lee-Adams junto had worried Gérard out of his post. Moreover, the French military contribution had been less than anticipated—as in the bungled Franco-American expedition against Newport, Rhode Island—and this fact enhanced the distrustful position of the Whigs. The Catholic monarchies were to be held at a distance by American republicans.

Formulation of the peace ultimata of 1779—wherein the fisheries had been relegated to a secondary demand and wherein Izard and the two Lees had been sacrificed—marked a turning point in congressional politics. The eastern party, including the Lee-Adams faction, lost control of foreign policy. Historian H. James Henderson has put it aptly, "In the last analysis, the ideological cement of the Old Radical Massachusetts-Virginia axis could hold only with the additional adhesion of sectional self-interest."[42] Jay and Franklin, rather than John Adams, were manning the action posts in Europe. In Philadelphia the Whig retreat left the moderates in command of Congress, resulting in a merging of southern and middle state blocs. As Congress grappled with the problems of sus-

---

40. William Churchill Houston to the Governor of New Jersey, October 5, 1779, in Burnett (ed.), *Letters,* IV, 472.
41. Stinchcombe, *American Revolution,* 72–76.
42. Henderson, *Party Politics,* 212, 250.

taining the war effort from day to day and as practical concerns such as paying the army came to the fore, rabid ideology was pushed aside.

The Whigs' loss of mastery over diplomatic assignments and policy formulation augured a change in American objectives in the War for Independence. By trimming the fisheries, Florida, and the right of Mississippi navigation from their *sine qua nons*, Congress acceded to the desires of her allies. A new list of priorities for the survival of the Revolution was formulated. The primary concern was to end the war and attain recognition of American independence. Although Congress might issue instructions to American negotiators, the course of action would be drawn up by the diplomats in Europe. The peacemakers were to be the policy makers. Ultimately, the trio of Adams, Jay, and Franklin, who had all been participants in the Lee-Deane affair, did put the public welfare and American autonomy ahead of personal profit, partisanship or Bourbon desires.[43]

News of Jay's appointment to Madrid reached Arthur Lee by Christmas, 1779. Instinctively he rushed to confront Vergennes with the Paca-Drayton memorandum and other evidence of Gérard's meddling. The foreign minister no longer needed to show restraint. He acknowledged that the French had no confidence in Arthur, reiterated the stories that Lee was involved with English stockjobbers, and refused to support him in his allegations against Deane or Bancroft. In a characteristic reaction, Arthur suspected the French of subverting him in Europe as they had in America. He even contemplated an appeal to the king "demanding justice against those, who have thus injured me and fomented discord and faction in America." In the following year Lee and Gérard traded angry letters, but the Frenchman would not answer a challenge from the American. Unable to get either justice or revenge, Arthur could only record his "sovereign contempt" for Gérard.[44]

Since Jay proceeded from Philadelphia directly to Madrid, Lee had no need to tarry in Paris to brief his successor. He did, however, offer an appraisal of the Spanish connection. Secrecy and prudence, he counseled,

43. Stinchcombe, *American Revolution*, 76; Richard B. Morris, *The Peacemakers: The Great Powers and American Independence* (New York, 1965), 8–12.

44. Arthur Lee to Count Sarsfield, December 15, 1779, in Hoffman and Molyneaux (eds.), *Lee Family Papers*, VI, 468; Arthur Lee to C. A. Gérard, April 17, 1780, Gérard to Lee, April 28, 1780, Lee to Gérard, May 4, 1780, all in Hoffman and Molyneaux (eds.), *Lee Family Papers*, VI, 637, 645, 648.

should be Jay's forte. Yet, he wrote, "You are to negotiate with a people of honor and a minister of wisdom. They will propose fairly and perform faithfully. You will not be embarrassed by intrigue, at least, none of Spanish origin."[45] On all counts, Madrid offered contrast to Versailles.

Lee planned to depart from France as soon as possible in early 1780. After three years service, he took leave of Louis XVI in January. Like Deane, he was presented a portrait of the monarch set in diamonds atop a gold snuff box. He led Congress to believe that this present redeemed his honor even though he knew it was not so. Nonetheless, a republican to the marrow, he was willing to dispose of the present as the delegates might direct. That Franklin offered no mark of his respects did not surprise Lee, nor would the revelation that the old man was broadcasting to numerous American correspondents biting commentaries about Lee. Franklin judged Lee to have no equal in "malice, subtlety, and indefatigable industry."[46] He did all he could to cement the label of paranoid to Lee's reputation.

While awaiting passage to America, Arthur had time to contemplate his own future and the course of the war. The time he had spent in French ports persuaded him that little benefit would come from Bourbon fleets. He also brooded that the British war effort might be revitalized. It was possible that Americans would be forsaken by the French and left free "to contend for our own Independency." But foremost among concerns was a justification of his activities in the foreign service of the American republic.[47] He was uncertain about the best tactics for vindication. He had also become less prone to outright confrontation. Perhaps he recognized dwindling Whig strength in Congress. However solid were his cases against his accusers, Arthur believed a counterattack not then promising. Congress need not be rent by further reverberations of per-

45. Arthur Lee to John Jay, March 17, 1780, in Thomson, *Spain*, 75.
46. Arthur Lee to Committee for Foreign Correspondence, January 19, 1780, Vergennes to La Luzerne, February 5, 1780, in Hoffman and Molyneaux (eds.), *Lee Family Papers*, VI, 560, 573; Arthur Lee to William Lee, January 22, 1780, in Worthington C. Ford (ed.), *Letters of William Lee*, III, 775–76; Richard Henry Lee, *Life of Arthur Lee*, I, 168–69; Franklin to Richard Bache, June 2, 1779, Franklin to Samuel Cooper, March 16, 1780, Franklin to Joseph Reed, March 19, 1780, Franklin to William Carmichael, March 31, 1780, all in Smyth (ed.), *Writings of Franklin*, VII, 344–45, VIII, 38–39, 51–55.
47. Arthur Lee to Samuel Adams, March 30, 1780, Arthur Lee to Richard Henry Lee, April 3, 1780, both in Arthur Lee Papers, Box 7.

sonal antagonisms. The drive for national independence must not be jeopardized by a spirit of disunity. Perhaps he wrote these things to enable him to brush aside his deep wounds.

Lee's strategy was to retaliate "more by public Acts than private artifice." He may have intended to harass Deane through the courts of law, but he would soon learn that Richard Henry's belated libel suit against Deane had proved fruitless. Possibly he foresaw a reopening of the polemic wars. Arthur's rebuttal of 1779, which had been published by Richard Henry, was judged by the older brother to have "had every good effect that could be wished." Arthur had argued therein that he and William Lee possessed more talents for their missions than rivals such as Deane and Jonathan Williams. Not only had Arthur sworn that Deane's accusations were false, but he went on to detail the self-serving aspects of his antagonists' activities. Arthur's summation presaged the tenor of what his future publications might bring forth if Deane were not punished: "there is an end to all expectation of public justice. The impunity of the past will encourage greater crimes against the public; and all order, virtue, dignity, and decency will be constantly transgressed."[48] He was prepared to ring the clarion in 1780 as he had been a decade earlier.

Franklin could not easily get Lee out of France. It was three months before an American frigate, the *Alliance*, was located in L'Orient and Lee assigned passage. Then another two months elapsed as bickering between officers and crew persisted. Franklin must have recognized that Lee's assignment would be explosive for his antipathy for the ship's commander, John Paul Jones, was both protracted and vociferous.[49] The melodrama that unfolded at the French port and on the Atlantic was not unexpected. The combination of Jones, Lee, Pierre Landais, and others proved highly volatile.

48. Richard Henry Lee to Arthur Lee, April 24, 1780, in Ballagh (ed.), *Letters of Richard Henry Lee*, II, 175–77; *Extracts of a Letter Written to the President of Congress by the Honorable Arthur Lee, Esquire*, in Hoffman and Molyneaux (eds.), *Lee Family Papers*, VII, 204–241. The original letter had been read in Congress July 16, 1779. Worthington C. Ford (ed.), *Journals*, XIV, 843. More vituperative was Worthington C. Ford (ed.), *Reply of William Lee to the Charges of Silas Deane, 1779* (Brooklyn, 1891).

49. Arthur Lee to Franklin and Deane, January 18, 1778, in Arthur Lee Papers, Box 4; John Paul Jones to Arthur Lee, November 21, 1778, in Mrs. Reginald DeKoven, *The Life and Letters of John Paul Jones* (2 vols.; New York, 1913,

On August 17, following Landais' unauthorized sailing from L'Orient and a voyage of seven weeks marked by two uprisings, the *Alliance* made port at Boston. Lee, for the first time in his life, had come to the storm center of American radicalism. While the Navy Board inquired into Landais' conduct, Lee stayed a month to offer testimony, commune with James Warren and others of the Whig perspective, and look over the environs as a possible place to establish a law practice. What struck him most were paper money inflation and the lack of a well-supplied regular army.[50] So burdensome were these handicaps to the American cause that Lee revived an old scheme of 1776. He told a French correspondent that unless the Bourbons appropriated forty thousand livres to buttress the credit of "the government of these states," some sort of "accommodation" would be made with the British. It was an old ploy to extract funds from the French.

The trip from Boston to Philadelphia augmented Lee's impressions. He stopped off to visit such "good and wise Whigs" as John Trumbull of Connecticut and George Clinton of New York, perhaps seeking advice for his case before Congress. A few days' stay at army encampments quickened his concern for the plight of the troops. Although he denied any intention of unsettling Congress or the public, at least one delegate feared that Lee's presence on October 19 heralded "a high quarrel" and "a winter's work." Lee deposited the gift portrait of Louis XVI with Congress and requested a hearing. He asserted that "the manner of my dismission from the service of the United States implies a censure upon my conduct abroad and is unjurious to my character." A committee composed of James Madison, Thomas Bee, and Abraham Clark was selected to review Lee's petition and to determine if he should be granted the "full hearing at their bar" which the lawyer requested.[51]

Congressional inertia resulted in a replay of Deane's treatment. Al-

1930), I, 393. DeKoven, II, 28, in an uncorroborated report, describes a duel between Arthur's nephew and Jonathan Williams at L'Orient at this time.

50. Arthur Lee to Count Sarsfield, August 26, 1780, Arthur Lee to Baron Bretieul, September 19, 1780, both in Hoffman and Molyneaux (eds.), *Lee Family Papers*, VI, 724, 736.

51. Arthur Lee to James Warren, October 30, 1780, in *Warren-Adams Letters*, II, 142–43; Ezekiel Cornell to the Governor of Rhode Island (William Greene), October 24, 1780, in Burnett (ed.), *Letters*, V, 426; Worthington C. Ford (ed.), *Journals*, XVIII, 951–54.

though the committee's report was ready October 30, it was not brought up for debate until December 1. The report permitted Lee to retain the bejeweled portrait of Louis XVI but claimed "there is no particular charge against him before Congress properly supported." No comment on Lee's conduct was offered. Although the delegates denied Arthur's termination was meant as a censure, there is evidence that some so interpreted it. A section which was struck from the *Journals* reveals that the debates of May and September, 1779, over the foreign service "appeared at the time a necessary measure to stop the differences subsisting among . . . Commissioners in Europe greatly detrimental to the Interests of the United States, the particular grounds of which differences it was not then in the power of Congress fully to investigate."[52] This view echoed sentiments expressed earlier by William Churchill Houston: realities were secondary to impressions.

Even though Arthur Lee had denied any desire for confrontation in Philadelphia, he readily marked off friends and foes according to their congressional alignments. Richard Henry offered a list of the pro-Lee forces and observed, "Most of the Eastern Delegates are your friends." But Arthur could not be assuaged. His assessment was pessimistic: "Toryism is triumphant here. They have displaced every Whig." He felt that James Duane of New York, a leader of the antagonists, meant to deny him any favorable mark from Congress. Arthur also accused François Barbé-Marbois, secretary to the French ambassador, who followed Gérard's tactic of indirectly informing Congress of French distaste for the militia diplomat.[53] The substantial forces of the Deaneites were at work to deny Lee gratification.

Arthur intended to unseat Franklin, and Richard Henry and William Lee spurred him on. Evidently Arthur thought the "tory party" and French influence too potent to overcome. Nonetheless, when Congress requested a written appraisal of its state of affairs in Europe, he believed vindication was within grasp. His peroration was pervaded with pa-

52. Worthington C. Ford (ed.), *Journals*, XVIII, 114–15; William T. Hutchinson *et al.* (eds.), *The Papers of Madison*, II, 142–43, 154, 217–18.
53. Richard Henry Lee to Arthur Lee, August 31, 1780, in Ballagh (ed.), *Letters of Richard Henry Lee*, II, 196–200; Arthur Lee to Elbridge Gerry, November 26, 1780, in Arthur Lee Papers, Box 7; Arthur Lee to Count Sarsfield, October 24, 1780, Marbois' estimate of Arthur Lee, October 29, 1780, in Hoffman and Molyneaux (eds.), *Lee Family Papers*, VI, 752, 759.

triotism. Imagining himself the victim of congressional faction, he explained, "I hope to give a lesson to Mankind to show how difficult it is in a free country to fix permanent dishonor upon a faithful servant of the public and that truth and rectitude are superior to abused prerogative and power." Throughout the review he openly conceded his contentious and suspicious nature, but he mitigated the importance of his ill temper and emphasized the jealousy of his critics. No doubt this self-examination was painful. He knew he had become the object of "poisoned insinuations" because he "was considered as a determined opposer of the impositions upon and plunder of the public." In anguish he concluded, "I can call God to witness that I have never laid my head upon my pillow for ten years past, without meditating what I might next day do for the service of my Country and its cause. This is not mentioned as a merit; it was my duty. . . . I did not ask from you reward, but I did not expect ingratitude and persecution."[54] Thus had Congress, under the influence of Deane, Franklin, and Gérard, paid the virtuous revolutionary.

Lee's attack on Franklin was indirect. While he leveled specific charges at Bancroft and other malevolent hangers-on at Passy, Lee wrote of Franklin that he was "much advanced in years, more devoted to pleasure than would become even a young man in his station and neglectful of the public business." The fundamental issue was character. Rather than cite examples of the misconduct of "the most subtle of all my Enemies," Lee said he would give full testimony, "when justice is done to the public by calling Dr. Franklin to a trial for his conduct." Meanwhile, he published a pointed attack on Franklin's commercial dealings and those of his kinsman, Jonathan Williams.[55] Apparently it was a key element in Lee's strategy to utilize his title of esquire and his training as an attorney, components of self-esteem of which he could be assured.

54. Richard Henry Lee to Arthur Lee, August 31, 1780, in Ballagh (ed.), *Letters of Richard Henry Lee*, II, 196–200; Arthur Lee to General [Anthony] Wayne, November 24, 1780, in Arthur Lee Papers, Box 7; Arthur Lee to Count Sarsfield, October 24, 1780, in Hoffman and Molyneaux (eds.), *Lee Family Papers*, VI, 572; Arthur Lee to the President of Congress, December 7, 1780, in Wharton (ed.), *Correspondence*, IV, 182–86.

55. [Arthur Lee], *Observations on Certain Commercial Transactions in France Laid Before Congress by Arthur Lee, Esquire* (Philadelphia, 1780), 6, indicates Lee's inverted perspective of life: "The history of the world in all ages furnishes many examples, that those men who have received the greatest favors of their fellow citizens, have often proved the least deserving of them."

Franklin's removal was one of three reforms Lee proposed for American diplomacy. He also suggested that Congress send a minister to the court of Catherine the Great at Saint Petersburg and that an office, secretary of state for foreign affairs, be established to systemize the American diplomatic effort. His wishes were only partially fulfilled. On December 19 Lee and Alexander Hamilton lost out to Francis Dana when Congress chose a minister to Russia. While a subcommittee looked into computation of Arthur's salary from December 15, 1776, to March 25, 1780, the Congress as a whole refused to consider Franklin's recall. Arthur's aspirations were evaporating.[56]

Arthur's quest to become secretary of state proved as frustrating. It was his belief that his previous experience in the diplomatic corps was eminent qualification for the post, but the opposition considered it a major liability. Creation of the office had been subject to occasional debate since the spring of 1780, but it was not until January, 1781, that it appeared likely. The post was one of a number of bureaucratic reforms envisioned by James Duane and others who had their eyes on more efficient Continental government. The two nominees for the position, Robert R. Livingston of New York and Arthur Lee, were archtypes of two different approaches to the Revolution. They differed in the degree of trust they placed in the legislative process, in how much faith they had in technical skills of leadership over ideology, and in how deep their commitment was to the French allies. Possibly, Lee's candidacy was hampered by news from Boston of the court-martial of the captain and crew of the *Alliance*. There was much comment about Lee's role in fomenting the irregularities aboard ship and about his shipment of private goods at public expense. At this time, though both Livingston and Lee had followings, neither had sufficient backing to win, and no secretary was named for a half year.[57]

Amidst debates on foreign affairs, Congress was shaken when the

56. Arthur Lee to James Bowdoin, December 25, 1780, in Arthur Lee Papers, Box 7; Worthington C. Ford (ed.), *Journals*, XVIII, 1139, 1154–156, XV, 14; David M. Griffiths, "American Commercial Diplomacy," 383; Currey, *Code Number 72*, p. 235.

57. Burnett, *Continental Congress*, 489–92; Worthington C. Ford (ed.), *Journals*, XV, 42–44, 65; Henderson, "Structure of Politics," 184–85; Warren to Arthur Lee, December 18, 1780, April 28, 1781, in Richard Henry Lee, *Life of Arthur Lee*, II, 272, 274–75; Ezekiel Cornell to William Greene (Governor of Rhode Island) January 24, 1781, in Burnett (ed.), *Letters*, V, 549n, 555n.

Pennsylvania line of the Continental army mutinied January 3, 1781, deposed its officers, and marched from Morristown to Princeton, New Jersey. Arthur Lee had foreseen such an event, for he had repeatedly commented on the soldiers' plight since his arrival in America. He had even pressed General George Washington to seek further aid from France and had applauded the congressional decision to send Colonel John Laurens to Versailles to beg. His sensitivity to the welfare of the troops was heightened by the turmoil of allegations from the *Alliance* proceedings and also by his own first-hand observations. The dilemma was how to integrate these realities with his ideology. His perceptions were distorted, for he believed that the delegates who had sought his recall were linked with those "who do not wish to see the Army and Navy prosper, because that must secure our independency, and put an end to their vain hopes of again reducing us under the domination of Great Britain." Although blinded by visions of toryism, Arthur nonetheless was realistic enough to revise the typical Whig fear of standing armies. Now he perceived, "The establishment of a respectable Army is of the utmost importance, and will be the surest means under God, of producting a speedy and honorable peace."[58] Lee's nationalism overcame his inevitable suspicions.

It appeared that Arthur Lee, like Silas Deane, would get no satisfaction from the Continental Congress. A further career in the diplomatic corps or in any form of public service was problematical. Nor could the Board of Treasury decide proper reimbursement for his previous tenure. In the interim Lee decided in January to depart from Philadelphia for Virginia. Delegate Samuel Adams, who had met his compatriot for the first time at Philadelphia, was despondent over Arthur's departure. The fervid fires of the early 1770s had evidently been fanned by conversations between the two zealots, for Adams' estimations of Lee were heavily moralistic. In congressional dissembling and the ill treatment of Lee, Adams saw the demise of American virtue. Much lamented were "the Mistakes and Prejudices of some Men and the Wickedness of others"

58. Arthur Lee to Washington, November 11, 1780, in Arthur Lee Papers, Box 7; Washington to Arthur Lee, November 20, 1780, in Fitzpatrick (ed.), *Writings of Washington*, XX, 374–75; Arthur Lee to Governor Trumbull of Connecticut, December 25, 1780, in Burnett (ed.), *Letters*, V, 490n; Arthur Lee to General [Anthony] Wayne, November 24, 1780, Lee to Samuel Cooper, January 18, 1781, in Arthur Lee Papers, Box 7.

that had caused Arthur's downfall. The deposed diplomat would only gain justice when "the Trustees of the Publick shall have Fortitude enough, to be uninfluenced by great Names and Characters given to Men of base and depraved Minds." His accolades might not be forthcoming "in this Age. But the Historian will in some future time draw forth the Proofs of his Patriotism, and unprejudiced Posterity will acknowledge that Arthur Lee has borne a great Share in defending and establishing the Liberties of America."[59]

Adams' prognosis was overly optimistic. Most subsequent analyses of Arthur Lee's contributions to early American diplomacy have been based on Franklin's perspective. Lee has been stigmatized as a misfit, and he has been relegated to a marginal role in the formulation of policy and the conduct of affairs. A reassessment is in order, for Lee was a most patriotic envoy of the American Revolution. His diplomacy, it must be remembered, covered not only the war years and his various assignments at European capitals, but also the period 1766–1775 in Britain.

In this early era Lee's diplomacy, that is, his representation of the American colonies, was extraordinary. He played three critical roles. In his analysis of parliamentary politics and policies, Lee was ultrasensitive to the rights of Americans. It was Lee who, in a profusion of pamphlets and private communications, perceived grievances and developed a catalog of British misdeeds. Secondly, as penman for numerous petitions, Lee was a crucial channel to convert American protests into constitutional requests or remonstrances for redress and then, when satisfaction was not forthcoming, to justify the right to revolt. Finally, as congressional emissary, Lee fulfilled his assignments. He made contact with the French and established the connection with Beaumarchais that would funnel covert aid to the rebellious colonies. These were greater successes than he would achieve as a militia diplomat. Posterity is obliged to Lee for his early defense and establishment of American liberties.

Lee met more frustration than success from 1776 to 1780 as he served at various European posts. He certainly traveled more than the other commissioners. His reliance on remonstrances yielded, at best, mixed results. He might be credited with aid from Grimaldi and Floridablanca; he cannot be accorded credit for subsidies from France after 1776. The

59. Samuel Adams to Richard Henry Lee, January 15, 1781, in Burnett (ed.), *Letters*, V, 534.

Prussian connection was nominal. During parleys leading to the Franco-American Alliance of 1778 and thereafter, Lee shared with John Adams the desire that America remain autonomous in international affairs. From Europe he constantly preached to his congressional correspondents that dependence upon the Bourbons was an unworthy aim, a tactic that bred corruption. American virtue, self-reliance, and fulfillment were to Lee the appropriate goals of the struggle. Ironically, although Congress chose not to follow his advice, Adams, Franklin, and Jay—in peace negotiation with the British—did.

★ CHAPTER VIII ★

Sordid Pursuits and Servile Attachments

In February, 1781, Arthur Lee returned to Virginia from Europe. In the past when he had returned home, as a schoolboy from Eton or as a newly trained physician from Edinburgh, he had borne hopes along with his credentials. Now, after an absence of twelve years his sanguine expectations were faltering. Once again he had a career choice to face. At Chantilly, the home of his revered brother, Richard Henry, Arthur discussed his own future. Plans to establish a law practice in Boston, Philadelphia, or elsewhere were abandoned. In fact, any sort of private life was cast aside. The Revolution was far from concluded, and Arthur Lee still had a zest for public life. Thus it was decided he should stand for public office. In the late spring he was elected by the freeholders of Prince William County as a delegate to the Virginia Assembly. The Northern Neck constituency was near the Stratford Lee family stronghold of Westmoreland and was also the domain of cousin Henry Lee of Leesylvania. The need to defend his homeland during this critical period of the Revolution coincided with Arthur Lee's own personal needs. He later rationalized that, because he had not settled accounts with Congress and hence had no salary, he could not avoid further public service.[1]

One of Arthur's primary concerns in 1781 was gaining recompense from Congress. A springtime trip to Philadelphia unfortunately only renewed his doldrums. The settlement of his accounts had been forestalled because "Low people, when exalted, love to show they are masters." It seemed that Lee was destined always to be dependent on others for his sustenance. What made matters worse was Arthur's investments

1. Richard Henry Lee to Samuel Adams, February 5, 1781, in Ballagh (ed.), *Letters of Richard Henry Lee*, II, 213; Richard Henry Lee, *Life of Arthur Lee*, I, 109, 164–69; Robert E. and B. Katherine Brown, *Virginia, 1705–1786: Democracy or Aristocracy?* (East Lansing, 1964), 228–30; Arthur Lee to Warren, July 27, 1781, in *Warren-Adams Letters*, II, 169–70.

of hard money in worthless Continental paper currency. He was in need of restitution. By August the Board of Treasury believed it had a firm handle on Lee's affairs. It calculated his expenses at 135,361.3.10 livres, extraordinary expenses of 19,836.14.6 livres, and 66,853.0.10 livres advanced without authorization to the state of Virginia. In sum, it was judged Congress owed Lee and his secretary £2,238.19.9 (approximately $112,000 by 1975 standards). Although it was claimed that accounts were closed, no recommendation was made as to how or when Arthur would be justly compensated.[2] Some problems were perpetual throughout his life.

Whether in Virginia or Philadelphia, Arthur Lee let his opinion of American foreign affairs be known. Perhaps he was campaigning for the post of Secretary of Foreign Affairs. Definitely he saw that Franklin and Vergennes were "plotting against Mr. J. Adams, in the same manner they did against me." The struggle for control of foreign policy was renewed but to little avail. French suasion was paramount. The delegates refused to consider Franklin's recall. Rather Congress voted to combine Franklin and Adams as joint peace negotiators. Arthur moaned, "We shall be betrayed and ruined." Neither such pleadings by Lee nor reminders by John Witherspoon in Congressional debates of the pitfalls of joint commissions stemmed the tide. The delegates seemed determined to permit French dictation of the ways and means of concluding war. Never before had Arthur Lee been so sympathetic to Adams or so venomous toward Franklin as when he wrote, "What I always knew must now be clear to everyone—that it was not Dr. Lee but his principles that were offensive to the French court: since in conjunction with Dr. Franklin they have commenced the very same intrigues against our friend Mr. J. Adams. They know his intentions are too honest and his mind too firm, for their purposes; and therefore they are endeavoring to disgrace him, or shakle [*sic*] him with the wiles of that old corrupt Serpent, who has constantly sold this Country to them."[3] Nowhere in the historical record is there a more

2. Arthur Lee to Richard Henry Lee, May 28, 1781, in Hoffman and Molyneaux (eds.), *Lee Family Papers*, VII, 84–85; Worthington C. Ford (ed.), *Journals*, XX, 522, 574–75, XXI, 832–34.

3. Arthur Lee to John Page [June 4?], 1781, in Miscellaneous Manuscripts, American Philosophical Society, Philadelphia; John Witherspoon, Speech in Congress of the Appointment of Plenipotentiaries, [June 11, 1781?], in Burnett (ed.), *Letters*, VII, 117.

graphic rendition of Lee's self-image and recollection of his years in France. He was a martyr.

Lee was bitter over the French ambassador's successful manipulation of Congress. Gérard's successor, Chevalier Anne C. de la Luzerne, had intervened to halt Lee's August bid for the post of secretary of foreign affairs. In three days of debate after a half year's consideration, Lee lost an early advantage to Robert R. Livingston. The old forces of conspiracy —"the french interest, that of Dr. Franklin and of Mr. Duane or of the Tories"—had frustrated his ambition. The New Jersey and Pennsylvania delegations fell victim to the entreaties of the anti-Lee forces. One Pennsylvanian had been carried on a litter to vote against Lee.[4]

It was evident in a letter that Lee dispatched to his fellow Old Radical Samuel Adams, that his enthusiasm was waning. Arthur rationalized that perhaps he was fortunate in not being chosen, for he would have had to serve in an administration "where the Financier [Robert Morris] and probably the other Ministers would have been in a cabal against me here." Then, as was his habit, Lee leaped from the personal level of conflict to a wider stage. He predicted that all of the executive posts would be manned by New Yorkers doing the French bidding. "If this should succeed. . . . It behooves the friends of Liberty and of America to look about them and bestir themselves. The plot is deep, the times are favorable to it, and we may be fettered before we are aware." Who would not believe the times were still critical? Already Arthur was again being drawn to national politics. He confided his plan to get into Congress whenever ratification of a peace treaty appeared on the horizon.[5] That day came sooner than expected.

Congressional intrigues were cast aside in August, for when Lee returned to Virginia, Cornwallis' army had also entered the state. Here was real crisis. Richard Henry had warned that the consequences of the British invasion "may be very unpleasing to sound and sensible Whiggism." Arthur described the "great ardor" and "wonderful unanimity" of Virginia's defenders and made a plea for aid from neighboring states. "In

---

4. Arthur Lee to Warren, June 15, 1781, *Warren-Adams Letters*, II, 166–68; Merrill Jensen, *The New Nation: A History of the United States During the Confederation, 1781–1789* (New York, 1950) 56; Arthur Lee to Samuel Adams, August 13, 1781, in Arthur Lee Papers, Box 7.

5. Arthur Lee to Samuel Adams, August 13, 1781, in Arthur Lee Papers, Box 7.

the midst of such distress," he wrote, "no man shrinks from the war, or is dispirited." Exactly what role he played in defending native soil is not clear since the record of Arthur's personal correspondence is uncommonly blank for the autumn of 1781, and the records of the Virginia House of Delegates are no more enlightening. It was probably the power of his cousins and brothers in both houses of the state legislature that led to Arthur's selection as a delegate from Virginia to Congress on December 28, 1781. No matter how zealous he might have been in House work on legal, financial, or military matters, it is doubtful he could have secured such a post without substantial support from others as powerful as his relatives.[6]

Other honors, perhaps traceable to Arthur's prominence as an American Whig and man of science, were soon forthcoming. Ironically, both the LL.D. awarded by Harvard in 1781 and the membership in the American Academy of Arts and Sciences bestowed in 1782 linked the Virginian with the French minister, Luzerne. In the latter case, Lee's scholarly bent had been aroused during a summer thunderstorm in Philadelphia. Later he submitted an essay in which he reported his observations of lightning striking the house leased by Luzerne. This membership was added to those in the Royal Society and the American Philosophical Society.[7] Harvard, with perhaps a middle-of-the-road approach, saw fit to honor not only Lee but also John Adams and Luzerne. Although the actual awarding of the degrees was somewhat delayed, Lee was most thankful of this mark of esteem from the Massachusetts school, which he called "Cambridge University." His response was the dictum of a devotee of classical and Whig history: "Liberty and letters sir, are so inseparably connected, that a lover of the one cannot but see with sincere satisfaction the cultivation and prosperity of the other. It is to the light which literature

---

6. Richard Henry Lee to Arthur Lee, June 4, 1781, in Ballagh (ed.), *Letters of Richard Henry Lee*, II, 23; Arthur Lee to Thomas McKean, August 26, 1781, in Arthur Lee Papers, Box 7; *Journal of the House of Delegates of the Commonwealth of Virginia . . . 1781–1785* (Richmond, 1828), December 13, 28, 1781, pp. 38, 62. Lee may have filled the congressional seat unattended by John Blair. Burnett (ed.), *Letters*, VI, lii–liii.

7. Francois Jean Chastellux, *Travels in North America in the Years 1780, 1781, and 1782* (2 vols.; Chapel Hill, 1963), I, 293, 332; Arthur Lee to James Bowdoin, July 29, 1782, in Arthur Lee Papers, Box 7; Bowdoin to Arthur Lee, January 31, 1782, in Hoffman and Molyneaux (eds.) *Lee Family Papers*, VII, 193.

had diffused that we owe the assertion of our liberties, and to the continuance of the same we must owe their establishment and permanency."[8]

Lee's arrival in America and his early service in the Congress of the Confederation coincided with the nadir of the American war effort. Posterity's image of Lee in this period is largely that of a troublemaker and an antinationalist. While it is true that Arthur became one of the most outspoken critics of Robert Morris and those who sought to consolidate the power of the central government, this portrait of Lee is most frequently based on the jaundiced correspondence that passed between James Madison and Edmund Randolph in the 1780s. Randolph, especially, reported every rumor of Lee's politics and continually painted Lee as the *bête noir* of the Virginia delegation. This sort of evidence is testimony to the personal, rather than partisan, nature of Virginia politics. A survey of Lee's early voting record in Congress actually finds him more prone to vote with Madison than with the remnant of eastern radicalism. Perhaps the return to his war-threatened home state had sensitized him to provincial rather than ideological influences. Lee reported to Jefferson, "My colleagues seem to me to be as Faithful to, & watchful over, the interests of our Country as you can possibly wish."[9]

One divisive topic between New England and Virginia that Lee championed was the eternal Lee family interest in empire. Specifically, in April, 1782, the question was the disposition of Vermont. There were at least three issues at work here. One concerned the small state–large state composition of the Confederation. Arthur hoped Vermont could stand independent of New Hampshire and New York, but not be admitted to Congress where it might tip the majority to the "little" states. More populous states like Virginia would then soon be yoked with the "whole burthen of the war." A second factor was Lee's fear that land speculators would corrupt America's prospective empire. He focused on delegate

8. LL.D. diploma from Harvard, December 19, 1781, in Arthur Lee Papers, Box 7; *Publications of the Colonial Society of Massachusetts* (1910–11), XII, 113; Arthur Lee to Rev. Dr. Joseph Willard, April 20, 1782, in Richard Henry Lee, *Life of Arthur Lee*, I, 178–79.

9. James Madison to Edmund Randolph, July 23, 1782, in William T. Hutchinson *et al.* (eds.), *Papers of Madison*, IV, 434–35; Jensen, *New Nation*, 65–66; Henderson, "Political Factions," 314–15; Richard R. Beeman, *The Old Dominion and the New Nation, 1788–1801* (Lexington, 1972), 5; Arthur Lee to Jefferson, March 13, 1782, Arthur Lee Papers, Box 7.

Samuel Wharton of Delaware, an old nemesis from England, as the "agent for the Enemies of our cause and country" on the grounds that he was an "insolvent and a profligate adventurer." Wharton's overt lobbying in Congress irked Lee, for Wharton was using British funds to fête the delegates. Arthur's attempts to have Congress enact a "purifying declaration," whereby each delegate would have to reveal his affiliations with land companies, were defeated.[10] Congressional experience was most discouraging to the zealot, for in Congress self-interest was dominant over patriotism, and virtue was victimized by pelf.

Lee's major consideration was Virginia's claims to western lands. Maryland had withheld approval of the Articles of Confederation until 1781 because of these claims and there were raging debates over the jurisdiction—state or national—of the interior of the American republic. Thomas Paine asserted that the Old Dominion claims to lands on the Ohio River were "not admissible nor manageable." In rejoinder, Arthur wrote a summary of how Virginia's "blood and treasure" had been expended to assert and to affirm sovereignty over the lands. He hoped that his dissertation would legitimate Virginia's claim for a far western boundary. Later in the year Lee thwarted an effort to have Congress recognize Kentucky as a distinct state. This was a case of limited vision. On one hand he could condemn colleagues for their lack of patriotism and support of provincial interests, but on the other hand he could not perceive when his own views were swayed by parochial or personal interest.[11]

By early summer of 1782, when Arthur Lee was reelected to the Continental Congress, the Virginia delegation was beginning to fragment. Madison and Randolph continually exchanged news of the victories and defeats of the Lee forces. Randolph believed that Arthur and Richard

10. Arthur Lee to Samuel Adams, April 21, 1782, in Arthur Lee Papers, Box 7; Arthur Lee to Warren, April 8, 1782, in Burnett (ed.), *Letters*, VI, 326; Arthur Lee to Samuel Adams, April 21, 1782, in Arthur Lee Papers, Box 7; Worthington C. Ford (ed.), *Journals*, XXII, 191–92; Henderson, *Party Politics*, 306.

11. Boyd *et al.* (eds.), *Papers of Thomas Jefferson*, VI, 189; Randolph to Madison, June 1, 1782, in William T. Hutchinson *et al.* (eds.), *Papers of Madison*, IV, 305–308; Arthur Lee's undated draft, "A Concise View of Tittle [*sic*] of Virginia to the Western Lands in replication of a pamphlet called Public Good," in Hoffman and Molyneaux (eds.), *Lee Family Papers*, VII, 180–88; Foner, *Tom Paine*, 189; Henderson, *Party Politics*, 306–310; Madison to Randolph, September 3, 1782, in William T. Hutchinson *et al.* (eds.), *Papers of Madison*, V, 103–105.

Henry were merciless in pursuit of their opponents. Arthur's "factious and vindictive plans" were to be aimed at Robert Morris in upcoming debates. Thus Lee was soon named a member of a committee "to inquire fully" into Morris' domain. Through the next year he periodically filled a seat on the committee; his antagonism toward Morris was constant. His mistrust of all mercantile men and handlers of money, especially those from Philadelphia—"the bosom of *Toryism*"—hardly subsided. His objective was a complete investigation of all congressional contracts, for wherever profit accumulated, corruption arose.[12]

Together with delegate Ralph Izard from South Carolina, Lee moved to revive debate over instructions to the American peace negotiators. They hoped to remove Franklin and to liberate John Adams from subordination to Vergennes, for to Arthur, dependence on the French was a measurement of moral decay. "The yoke is riveted upon us," he wrote, "and the Man who I am sure sold us in the negotiation with France is the sole adjunct with Mr. Adams, in a negotiation on which everything that is dear and honorable to us depend." Lee felt that it was a mistake to abandon patriot claims to the Grand Banks fisheries and to navigation of the Mississippi River. He commented sarcastically, "In short, the most servile display of the most servile principles, is what alone must entitle us to the patronage of our great and generous Protector." Lee could not but be cynical. All that he had worked for was being repudiated. "This is not the sentiment or language, that commenced the revolution, and I pledge myself it is not the sentiment or language that will bring it to a happy issue." The regenerative thrust of American virtue was endangered. The movement spawned by Adams, Lee, and other agitators in 1776 was falling from their grasp. Selfishness was overwhelming self-control. "Sordid pursuits and servile attachments have apparently absolved all the Faculties of our fellow citizens." He could only hope that balances in power—"the jealousy of G. Britain and of the other powers in Europe"—would prevent French abuse of America.[13]

12. Randolph to Madison, June 20, July 6, 1782, in William T. Hutchinson *et al.* (eds.), *Papers of Madison*, IV, 354–62, 386–90, and see also IV, 229, 247, 336; Worthington C. Ford (ed.), *Journals*, XXII, 370–71, 407–408; Arthur Lee to Francis Dana, July 6, 1782, in Burnett (ed.), *Letters*, VI 379; Madison to Randolph, July 16, 1782, in William T. Hutchinson *et al.* (eds.), *Papers of Madison*, IV, 419.
13. Madison to Randolph, July 28, 1782, in William T. Hutchinson *et al.*

Lee and Madison went head to head on July 24 in a dispute over French influence on American foreign policy. Lee wanted the congressional stance toward peace negotiations reconsidered, and Madison, believing Lee's maneuver "was pointed against the ministers as well as the instructions," succeeded in forestalling a vote. The antigallics—for now the term was appropriate—were thwarted but the struggle would continue. Lee denounced the Luzerne-dictated instructions as "derogatory to the honor, dignity, and independence of the United States." He was certain that self-interest would direct Bourbon strategy in concluding the war. He warned Samuel Adams, "France will be for protracting the war, or turning the chief advantages of it to herself and Spain. . . . we have put ourselves shamefully and entirely in her [French] powers to the conditions of Peace."[14] It looked as though the advantage won from the British on the field of battle would now be sacrificed by America's ally at the negotiating table.

Lee differentiated between respectful consultations between American and French negotiators and submission, which he labeled "a negatory independence," and Madison countered his every point.[15] As a moderate, Madison agreed that the instructions to the American negotiators did sacrifice national dignity, but this was unavoidable. His point prevailed. Congress moved to delay a decision and, meanwhile to reconsider such explosive criteria as land claims, navigation of the Mississippi, and the fisheries. By October it was decided to consider these interests "as essential" to American property and posterity but to make no adamant assertions. Meanwhile, the American peace commission was instructed to continue to act in concert with French negotiators. Fortunately, Adams, Jay, and Franklin sidestepped the resolutions and signed a preliminary peace—one largely satisfactory to Lee's imperial aims and his tenet of autonomy—with the British before alerting Vergennes.

(eds.) *Papers of Madison*, IV, 434–36; Arthur Lee to Warren [*ca.* July, 1782], in Burnett (ed.), *Letters*, VI, 389–90.

14. Charles Thomson, Notes of Debates, July 24, 1782, in Burnett (ed.), *Letters*, VI, 390–94; James Madison's notes on debates, August 2, 8, 1782, in William T. Hutchinson *et al.* (eds.), *Papers of Madison*, V, 15–16, 33; Arthur Lee to Samuel Adams, August 6, 1782, in Burnett (ed.), *Letters*, VI 428–30.

15. Charles Thomson, Notes of Debates, August 8, 1782, in Burnett (ed.), *Letters*, VI, 432–33; Burnett, *Continental Congress*, 547–49; Morris, *The Peacemakers*, 440–41.

Arthur's contentiousness led to disputes both in and out of Congress. In the autumn of 1782 he entered into the contest between Radicals and Republicans of Pennsylvania. Two Lee acquaintances, Thomas McKean and Joseph Reed, ranked high in the Radical party, while John Dickinson led the Republicans. As "Virginius," Lee published criticism of Dickinson's trustfulness and excoriated Philadelphians for susceptibility to corruption. When, in turn, Reed's patriotism was questioned by the opposition, a bitter newspaper skirmish ensued. Benjamin Rush and Eleazor Oswald, publisher of the *Independent Gazetteer*, set their sights on Lee. Oswald, matching scurrility with Lee, brought up in the process all of the old allegations of Deane and Beaumarchais. Ultimately Oswald charged Lee with treachery. Madison reported that Arthur was "not in the best of humor," having "been frustrated in several favorite projects" in Congress and "most rudely handled" by the local press. Madison was mystified when Arthur did not accept Oswald's challenge. Perhaps Arthur was losing his spirit. Madison's correspondent, Edmund Randolph, compassionately inquired, "Does the sacred liberty of the press justify such invectives against men in high office?"[16]

The harassment followed Lee home to Virginia where he served in the autumn in the House of Delegates. Rumors of his pro-British sentiments swept through Richmond. A House investigation was undertaken into a letter Lee sent Mann Page, Jr., in which, it was believed, a "matter highly injurious to public interests" had been discussed. Specifically Lee's anti-gallicism was thought documented by his reported query, "Do you not know that a Majority of C. [Congress] are under the influence of the French Minister?" Edmund Pendleton, who had seen "a particular account" of the controversial letter, claimed "the clamor was without foundation," but it nonetheless appeared that Lee would be censured.[17] The

16. Benjamin Rush to Nathanael Greene, September 16, 1782, in Butterfield *et al.* (eds.), *The Letters of Benjamin Rush*, I, 285–87; William T. Hutchinson *et al.* (eds.), *Papers of Madison*, V, 187; Vernon O. Stumpf, "Colonel Eleazor Oswald, Politician and Editor," (Ph.D. dissertation, Duke University, 1968), 78–98; John F. Roche, *Joseph Reed: A Moderate in the American Revolution* (New York, 1957), 194–209; Madison to Randolph, October 8, 1782, Randolph to Madison, November 2, 1782, in William T. Hutchinson *et al.* (eds.), *Papers of Madison*, V, 186–91, 230–231.

17. *Journal of the House of Delegates*, November 20, 1782, p. 27; Randolph to Madison, November 16, 1782, in William T. Hutchinson *et al.* (eds.), *Papers of Madison*, V, 280–287; Edmund Pendleton to Joseph Jones, October 21, 1782,

investigating committee, which included Richard Henry Lee and cousin Richard Lee, concluded that the missive was "a private confidential letter, not intended for the public eye, and does not contain matters injurious to the Commonwealth." Further, the committee saw fit to proclaim "the services rendered by the said Arthur Lee to this community, are such as prevent all suspicions of inimical designs to this state, or America in general." This whitewashing withstood a challenge from the floor, possibly from James Mercer or Henry Tazewell, and a maneuver to reduce Virginia's delegation in Congress was also thwarted.[18] Lee forces had rallied successfully.

Lee's antagonists persisted. On December 18 a motion was made to recall him from Congress, on the rationale that Arthur's conduct "induced in the minds of the people, suspicions respecting his friendship to the French Alliance." Volley after volley was fired at Lee. John Francis Mercer charged, "That it was the public conversation in Philadelphia, that there is a *British party on the continent*, at the head of which are Messrs. Adams, Lee and Laurens." Samuel Griffin alluded to promises of "riches, honors, and dignities" which the British agent Berkenhout had made to the Lees. Vergennes' fears were reintroduced by Meriwether Smith and James Mercer. Thus the House was forced to meet as a committee of the whole on this sensitive topic. Richard Henry Lee was immediately cleared of suspicion, the previous exoneration of Arthur was permitted to stand, and the Lee brothers had weathered this latest onslaught. Edmund Randolph reported it was not so much a case of the Lee defense—indeed extant personal documents hardly mention this episode—as it was a failure of the attack.[19]

Having survived attack at home, Arthur Lee turned to the offensive in

---

Pendleton to Madison, November 8, 1782, both in David J. Mays (ed.), *The Letters and Papers of Edmund Pendleton, 1734–1803* (2 vols.; Charlottesville, 1967), II, 411, 427–28; Reverend James Madison to James Madison, January 16, 1783, in William T. Hutchinson *et al.* (eds.), *Papers of Madison*, VI, 49.

18. William T. Hutchinson *et al.* (eds.), *Papers of Madison*, V, 339n; *Journal of the House of Delegates*, December 11, 1782, p. 62; Randolph to Madison, December 13, 1782, in William T. Hutchinson *et al.* (eds.), *Papers of Madison*, V, 399–406.

19. Randolph to Madison, December 22, 27, 1782, in William T. Hutchinson *et al.* (eds.), *Papers of Madison*, V, 424–27, 453–57; *Journal of the House of Delegates*, December 22, 1782, p. 76.

Congress. If he ranked Benjamin Franklin as the "most meanly envious and selfish" man he knew, then he probably placed Robert Morris in the second place on his public enemies list. When Lee was not lambasting Franklin in congressional debates, he assaulted the domain of Morris. The attacks were similar in that both Franklin and Morris threatened Lee's autonomy; Franklin overshadowed any possibility for Arthur Lee to achieve fame, and Morris continually resisted Lee's claims for financial restitution.

As was his wont, Lee's strictures on Morris were ideologically tinged. His "war against the financier," as Madison termed it, attacked on personal as well as political levels. Lee found the magnitude of powers that Congress had delegated to the Philadelphia empire-builder vexatious, and he despised the personal values of the profiteer. Morris' type of leadership threatened to displace the Lee brand of hegemony, and Arthur thought him "a most dangerous man to the Liberties of the Country." [20]

Arthur usually expressed the Lee-Morris clash as a contest between the virtuous and the vice-ridden. Morris and his henchmen, Lee reported, "have made large fortunes during this war, [and] employ their wealth in a manner not very consistent wtih that unostentatious virtue which ought to animate our Infant republic." In Philadelphia, Lee found, "Extravagance, ostentation and dissipation distinguish what are called the Ladies of the first rank." The alterations in social mores rankled him, for, he wrote, "the generality seem to be intoxicated with a sudden change of manners and unexpected elevation." The Puritan and the aristocrat in Lee denounced the democratic strains of the Revolution. In the clash between commercialization and asceticism social control was lost, and alterations in social hierarchy resulted. Arthur Lee, whose value system pivoted upon denial and whose vision of society emphasized order, was being displaced. More opportunistic men, like Jonathan Williams and Robert Morris, were challenging for position among the elite.[21]

Lee wanted to use Morris' handling of the nation's finances to embarrass him. One way was to push settlements of accounts left over from his

20. Madison to Randolph, July 2, 1782, in William T. Hutchinson, et al. (eds.), Papers of Madison, IV, 386; Arthur Lee to Samuel Adams, August 6, 1782, in Arthur Lee Papers, Box 7.

21. Arthur Lee to Warren, March 12, 1783, in Burnett (ed.), Letters, III, 77–78; Arthur Lee to Warren, December 12, 1782, in Warren-Adams Letters, II, 184–86; Foner, Tom Paine, 159; Henderson, "Structure of Politics," 183–85.

own diplomatic assignments. In 1781 he had accepted a loan certificate "for the balance payable with interest" due him from Congress. As all other American diplomats had been paid in bills of exchange, he demanded in 1782 that his certificate be redeemed. There was little cash available for such a transaction, for Lee was not the only creditor seeking restitution. As Charles Thomson, secretary of Congress, candidly recorded of the forwarding of Lee's case to Morris, "By this step Congress avoided the apparent inconsistency of conduct and partiality in favor of their own members and left it to the superinten't to falsify his own report and incurring the odium of the public creditors by drawing in favor of Mr. Lee, or the resentment of Mr. Lee by a refusal." Morris declined to be impaled by the dilemma and returned the demand to Congress. Finally, on November 18, 1782, Congress permitted Lee's certificate of $9,850.55/90 to be exchanged for £2238.17.9.[22] Also exchanged were many unpleasantries between Lee and Morris, but Lee's assaults in 1782 might have been more irritating to Morris if James Duane of New York had not paired himself with Lee on many of the investigating committees. Lee was allowed to wail, but Duane averted in-depth investigation.

The year 1783 was serious to the Revolution. Although he confessed that the exposure "to perpetual enmities" attendant to his public service had embittered him, Arthur Lee only fleetingly contemplated retirement. He persisted because the crisis was so real to him. Peace seemed elusive; inflation was uncontrollable. In January, Lee debated with Madison the merits of a central fund for the Congress of the United States. Lee advocated no alteration in the state requisition system. A tax payable to Congress would unwisely place "the purse in the same hands with the sword," endangering liberty. Lee suggested that if all state governors were assembled to hear a report on the financial plight of the country, state contributions would be forthcoming. He observed that "the States will never agree to those plans which tended to aggrandize Congress, that they were jealous of the power of Congress, and that he acknowledged himself to be one of those who thought this jealousy not an unreasonable one." He might be classified a parochialist and an anticentralist, but certainly not an antinationalist. The dilemma of Lee and fellow Old Radicals in Congress

22. Worthington C. Ford (ed.), *Journals*, XXII, 727–28; Robert Morris to Arthur Lee, October 9, November 18, 26, 1782, in Arthur Lee Papers, Box 7; William T. Hutchinson *et al.* (eds.), *Papers of Madison*, V, 300.

in 1783 was that they were able to unite in roll call votes only in opposition to a proposed policy and not in favor of one.[23]

Lee preferred to keep Congress rather "a rope of sand than a rod of iron." Unrest in the Continental army stationed outside New York City, he noted, was utilized by delegates advocating permanent taxes and tax collectorships. He equated such a scheme with "tory designs . . . of subverting the Revolution." When Robert Morris resigned on January 24, Lee saw that the true intent of this maneuver was to shock creditors so as "to force the system of funding upon the states."[24] Lee feared that speculators would destroy the nation in their efforts to amass "immense wealth." They would acquire fortunes at the expense of true patriots, who had sold their depreciated loan office certificates at cheap prices. If the congressional debt were funded, profiteers would sell the certificates back to Congress and reap vast rewards. The true patriot would suffer.

Theodorick Bland, delegate from Virginia and Lee's most frequent ally in debate, joined the assault on Morris in early March. The two Virginians disparaged Morris' administration, besmirched his integrity, and termed his threatened resignation an insult to Congress.[25] Lee reportedly declared Morris "unfit" to remain financier, and he seconded Bland's motion that Congress rearrange Morris' department, a move that was rejected overwhelmingly because Congress preferred to devise the most proper steps to be taken in consequence of Morris' letter of resignation.

News of a preliminary peace with Great Britain interrupted the polarized debates over Morris. On March 12 Congress received the provisional treaty signed November 30, 1782. There is no record of Lee's reaction to these momentous tidings, although it appears he rushed a congratulatory message to General Washington. He soon plunged into the debates that swirled around the actions of the peace commission. Lee lauded John Jay

23. Arthur Lee to William Lee, January 26, 1783, in Burnett (ed.), *Letters,* VII, 23; Madison's notes on debates, January 28–29, February 23, 1783, in William T. Hutchinson *et al.* (eds.), *Papers of Madison,* VI, 141–49, 292–95; Worthington C. Ford (ed.), *Journals,* XIV, 96–127; Henderson, *Party Politics,* 310–11, 320–321.

24. Arthur Lee to Samuel Adams, January 29, March 5, 1783, in Arthur Lee Papers, Box 7.

25. Madison's notes on debates, March 4–5, 1783, in William T. Hutchinson *et al.* (eds.), *Papers of Madison,* VI, 304–305; Worthington C. Ford (ed.), *Journals,* XXIV, 165–68.

and John Adams, who had defied instructions to inform Vergennes of the American parleys with the British, but made no mention of Franklin's contributions. Lee asserted that separate negotiations had insured American independence, for "France wanted to sacrifice our interests to her own, or those of Spain." The Virginian correctly anticipated that the French would complain but eventually accept the Anglo-American treaty. The heated debates over this issue quickly cooled when word of a pact between the British and the Bourbons arrived, but it was not until April 15 that sufficient calm was restored to ratify the preliminary peace.[26]

The harassment of Robert Morris resumed. Lee requested that the superintendent give a strict account "of all monies which were in his hands at his coming into office, or have been received since for the public use." Lee wanted each and every expenditure to be itemized as to the date, recipient, and purpose of the payment.[27] Morris' camp was unable to substitute Madison's less severe proposal, but adjournment was called before Lee's measure was brought to a vote. All Arthur had to show for his efforts was a position on the committee resurrected to monitor the department of finance.

The spring of 1783 found Arthur Lee traveling between Virginia and Congress. In April he campaigned for reelection to the Virginia Assembly. Although his antagonist, James Mercer, reported that Lee had abused the electorate, he was returned to office. Similarly he retained membership on that state's congressional delegation. It was during Arthur's attendance at Richmond that Robert R. Livingston resigned as secretary of foreign affairs. Lee had known since January of this pending move but was none too optimistic about his own chances to succeed to an office he continually coveted. He surmised that the opposition would be too formidable. Madison, on the other side, wrote, "A[rthur] L[ee] will be started if the defect of a respectable competitor sh[oul]d be likely to force vote upon him." Ultimately six men, including Arthur Lee, were nominated. Even though the selection of the secretary was an order of the day throughout

26. Arthur Lee to Warren, March 12, 1783, in Burnett (ed.), *Letters*, VII, 77–78; Washington to Arthur Lee, March 20, 1783, in Richard Henry Lee, *Life of Arthur Lee*, II, 172; Madison's notes on debates, March 19, 1783, in William T. Hutchinson *et al.* (eds.), *Papers of Madison*, VI, 355–65; Morris, *The Peacemakers*, 440–443.
27. Worthington C. Ford (ed.), *Journals*, XXIV, 216–22.

1783, it was not until May, 1784, that Congress finally filled the position.[28] Lee withdrew his name in August, 1783. Since the war had ended, foreign policy no longer was a top priority. Lee left no further record of activity aimed at seating himself at the center of American diplomacy. Inexplicably he terminated his decade-long interest and service in the international affairs of the emerging American nation.

Between meetings of the Virginia Assembly and the Congress, Lee had time to pause in the summer of 1783. He used the opportunity to reacquaint himself with Lord Shelburne and to offer appraisal of what the war had wrought. This renewal of correspondence indicated the degree to which Lee identified with the British peer. Perhaps it was Shelburne's reputation as a persecuted public servant that aroused Lee's sympathy. His opening remark noted the rough treatment Parliament and George III had recently given Shelburne. Lee, of course, blamed the king and his cabinet. It was they who were responsible for "the rapacity, cruelty, and profusion" of the war. It was the king who, "though he meant the subjugation of America, would in fact conduct her to independence." Lee painted a whiggish portrait of life in America. He contemplated retirement "under that constitution which I have labored to assist in rearing to liberty, virtue, and public happiness," but he was not totally at ease. He trusted neither the Confederation system nor the corrupt and intriguing officeholders who "are promoted or restrained more by the genius of the people, than by forms of government, or the operations of laws." Yet he was growing fond of his homeland, which possessed more abundant natural charms than any part of Europe. Lee proposed that Shelburne, who shared intense interest in the Ohio Valley, join him in a tour of the interior of America.[29]

Congress, relocated in Princeton, New Jersey, was no longer tempes-

28. Madison to Randolph, April 1, May 13, 1783, in Burnett (ed.), Letters, VIII, 121, 163, lxxvii; James Mercer to John Francis Mercer, May 6, 1783, in John M. Jennings (ed.), "Letters of James Mercer," Virginia Magazine of History and Biography, LIX (January, 1951), 98–99; Journal of the House of Delegates, June 6, 1783, p. 39; Arthur Lee to William Lee, January 26, 1783, Madison to Randolph, June 17, 1783, both in Burnett (ed.), Letters, VIII, 23, 189–91; Burnett, Continental Congress, 583–84; William T. Hutchinson et al. (eds.), Papers of Madison, VII, 127n.

29. Arthur Lee to Lord Shelburne, July 24, 1783, in Richard Henry Lee, Life of Arthur Lee, I, 174–76.

tuous when Lee resumed his post. He was relegated to such lesser tasks as Indian affairs and commissioning a statue of George Washington. As before, his attempts to get at Morris' accounts were checked repeatedly by James Duane. Lee renewed the hue and cry that under Morris' plans for clothing the army, "the public money is lavished away, the Soldiery defrauded and the public plundered." He also renewed his inquisition of the affairs of Silas Deane. Near the conclusion of the war the British published a series of letters from Deane advocating reconciliation, from which evidence Lee correctly surmised that Deane had been bought. Robert Morris, however, successfully repulsed all Lee's efforts to pin any guilt on Deane or to remove any taint from Lee's own reputation.[30] Arthur Lee must have relished the knowledge that he had been right, that his nemesis had in fact betrayed the American cause.

Following ratification of the definitive peace in the autumn of 1783, Congress rapidly dwindled in membership and activity, but Lee loyally remained in attendance. After all, there were problems of some magnitude confronting Congress. Peace with the Indian tribes must be arranged; the national debt must be apportioned to the states; the western territory must be mapped. Once again appointment of a secretary of foreign affairs came up for consideration. One of Arthur's favorite projects was his campaign for Congress to establish permanent residence near Georgetown on the Potomac River. This was no small issue. Arthur hoped to keep the government away from vice-ridden urban areas—especially Philadelphia —and near land holdings of his own family. Perhaps as part of his strategy, Lee was then advocating that the Northern Neck cut away from Virginia and join Maryland. Jefferson was aghast. He advised that Lee "deserves to be well *watched* in our state. He is extremely soured with it and is not cautious in betraying his hostility against it." His aberration was only temporary. Congress soon moved southward to Annapolis and lapsed into a festive mood. Lee recorded, "We have a great deal of dancing, feasting, ogling, and all that." Surprisingly he joined in, even hosting a ball. But as Jefferson merrily reported to Madison, Arthur fell "in the midst of the mud," because his gathering conflicted with another. It was

30. Worthington C. Ford (ed.), *Journals*, September 5, 10, 29, 1783, XXIV, 536–37, 541–44, 628–31; Arthur Lee to Warren, September 17, 1783, in *Warren-Adams Letters*, II, 224–26; Arthur Lee to Morris, September 26, October 9, 1783, Morris to Arthur Lee, October 4, 11, 1783, all in Arthur Lee Papers, Box 7.

also reported that Lee was courting a local belle, Sophia Sprigg, "A *young girl of seventeen* and of *thirty thousand pound*[s] expectation."[31]

Arthur's flirtations were unfulfilled. He found some of the ladies "too pleasing rather to let our hearts stop short of desires which they are not disposed to gratify." His courtship of Miss Sprigg ended in humiliation when his rival in the Virginia delegation, John Francis Mercer, won her hand and dowry in the spring of 1785. Subsequently Mercer moved to Maryland and became governor. Lee continued his romantic sallies, but he was destined to bachelorhood. The objects of his ardor changed as Congress traveled. In New York he reportedly courted Alida Livingston and Esther Cartwright simultaneously. In Pennsylvania he wooed Mary Coxe throughout 1788 and 1789. Arthur tried to appear attractive but to no avail. Whenever his prospects brightened, one observer noted, rumors of the Virginian's infidelity also rose. Arthur later rationalized that readings in the classics had rendered his standards for a wife unrealistic and that "the tempest of my fortune" had hampered his amorous campaigns.[32]

Courtships and travel sent Arthur to commune with his niece, Nancy Shippen. A reigning belle of Philadelphia, Nancy acted as confidant in Arthur's affairs of the heart. From 1782 through 1789 Arthur frequently traded "saucy notes" with her. He enjoyed this opportunity to play surrogate parent, and his attachment strengthened as Nancy's marriage to Henry Beekman Livingston proved unhappy. Trust and love pervaded Arthur's every note, and he particularly adored Nancy's daughter, Peggy. Nancy's estrangement and her mother's despondency evoked her uncle's attentions. He wrote humorous titterings and requests to have Nancy carry

31. William T. Hutchinson *et al.* (eds.), *Papers of Madison*, VII, 389n; Lawrence Delbert Cross, "Whither Columbia? Congressional Residence and the Politics of the New Nation, 1776 to 1787," *William and Mary Quarterly*, 3rd ser., XXXII (October, 1975), 581–600; Arthur Lee to John Hopkins, March 14, 1785, January 1, March 18, 1786, Arthur Lee to Anne Hume Livingston, February 12, 1784, all in Arthur Lee Papers, Box 8, 7; Jefferson to Madison, February 20, 1784, in William T. Hutchinson *et al.* (eds.), *Papers of Madison*, VII, 423–24. Italicized words in cipher.

32. Arthur Lee to Theodorick Bland, February 24, 1784, in Arthur Lee Papers, Box 7; William Grayson to [Richard Henry Lee, 1786?], in Hoffman and Molyneaux (eds.), *Lee Family Papers*, VII, 569–72; Marguerite duPont Lee, *Arthur Lee*, 133–232; Ethel Armes (ed.), *Nancy Shippen: Her Journal Book* (New York, 1968), 214–15, 265–66; Richard Henry Lee, *Life of Arthur Lee*, I, 182.

messages to whomever he was then courting.[33] Perhaps his gallantry was aimed indirectly at herself.

Like affairs of the heart, Lee's financial problems were recurrent through the 1780s. Repeatedly he pestered James Warren and Samuel Adams to look out for his land in Massachusetts. He was indebted to this duo for persuading their legislature to award Lee a grant for the services he had rendered as colonial agent. Arthur evidently considered purchasing farm land in Maine for speculative purposes, for he wrote to Thomas Lee Shippen of a six-thousand acre parcel there. He did purchase nearly 10,000 acres in western Virginia (Kentucky). He perhaps had visions of expanding Virginia's influence westward, but he never ventured to settle on the frontier. Other investments included £1,000 left in European banks to be tended by William Lee. By the time of his death, he had amassed, in addition to these extensive holdings, rights to 8,500 acres more near the Ohio River, lots in Philadelphia, Richmond, Alexandria, Norfolk, and his home plot at Urbanna, Virginia. His annual income was probably never as great as that of brother William, who was numbered among Virginia's truly wealthy, but as his will indicates, he was able to amass a comfortable revenue and to enjoy fine silver, china, and jewelry.[34] He was also considerate enough to apportion his estate to numerous nephews and nieces. While the males were allotted the larger land parcels, the females received household goods and the income-producing urban properties.

Personal and public concerns pushed Lee into the new realm of government—Indian affairs. Before the war Lee had corresponded with Sir William Johnson on the culture of native Americans, and he renewed his

33. Arthur Lee to Anne Hume Livingston, July 28, 1788, March 21, 1789, both in Arthur Lee Papers, Box 18.

34. Arthur Lee to Samuel Adams, October 30, 1777, August, 1781, May 17, 1786, all in Arthur Lee Papers, Boxes 3, 7, 8; Arthur Lee to Warren, July 27, 1781, April 8, 1782, both in *Warren-Adams Letters*, II, 169, 170–171; Arthur Lee to Thomas Lee Shippen, January 2, 1787, in Arthur Lee Papers, Box 8; Willard R. Jillson (ed.), *Old Kentucky Entries and Deeds: A Complete Index to All of the Earliest Land Entries, Military Warrants, Deeds, and Wills of the Commonwealth of Kentucky* (Louisville, 1926), III, 117; Colonel Arthur Campbell to Arthur Lee, December 27, 1782, in Hoffman and Molyneaux (eds.), *Lee Family Papers*, VII, 295; Henderson, *Party Politics*, 371, 381n; Arthur Lee's will, July 27, 1792, in Arthur Lee Papers, Box 20; William Lee to Lotsam [Arthur Lee], May 8, 1782, in

anthropological inquiries in the 1780s. His scholarly inclination was reinforced by the belief that settlement of America's interior would satisfy
many of the republic's dilemmas. The army would be justly rewarded
with land grants. The Confederation Congress, by selling territory, could
pay its debts. Lee family imperialism, more than a century old, might be
consummated. Thus in the spring of 1784 he sought and gained an appointment as one of four commissioners to negotiate a peace with the
Iroquois.[35]

The end of spring, 1784, was a benchmark in Arthur Lee's career. Two
basic concerns in Congress had been settled. John Jay, now esteemed for
his defiant stance against the Bourbons, had been appointed secretary of
foreign affairs, while Thomas Jefferson was named to replace Franklin,
and John Adams assigned to England. Further participation in diplomacy
was no longer an option for Lee, but he no doubt savored the final oust-
ing of Robert Morris as superintendent of finance. Congress had seen fit
to replace Lee's foe with a board of treasury composed of three commissioners. Arthur welcomed the calm that followed the "turbulence and agitation" of the war. He hoped that his compatriots, like himself, would
utilize the time to travel, for such tours would "remove prejudices and
cultivate harmony" among Americans. A sense of nationalism needed to
be developed. After "the happy event of the late glorious revolution," Lee
and other members of Virginia's Constitutional Society pledged to cherish
liberty.[36] Arthur Lee had become an advocate of harmony who intended
to surmount the turmoil that had surrounded the creation of the nation.

Hoffman and Molyneaux (eds.), *Lee Family Papers*, VII, 211; Jackson Turner
Main, "The One Hundred," *William and Mary Quarterly*, 3rd ser., XI (October, 1954), 354–84.

35. Edmund Bailey O'Callaghan (ed.), *The Documentary History of the State
of New York* (4 vols.; Albany, 1849–51), IV, 430–437; Sir William Johnson to
Arthur Lee, March 28, 1772, in James Sullivan (ed.), *The Papers of Sir William
Johnson* (14 vols.; Albany, 1921–45), XII, 950–955; Right Reverend John Ett-
wine to Arthur Lee, n.d., in *Pennsylvania Magazine of History and Biography*,
XXXIX (1915), 219; Arthur Lee to Joseph Reed, April 5, 1784, in Roche, *Joseph
Reed*, 407; Arthur Lee to the Marquis of Lansdowne, March 3, 1786, in Richard Henry Lee, *Life of Arthur Lee*, II, 166–69; Boyd *et al.* (eds.), *Papers of Jef-
ferson*, VII, 9n, 119.

36. Burnett, *Continental Congress*, 601–603; Worthington C. Ford (ed.), *Journals*, XXVI, 355, 372–74; William T. Hutchinson *et al.* (eds.), *Papers of Madison*, VIII, 71–75.

Postwar emphasis for the American republic, as well as for Lee as a mature individual, should be on integration of previous experiences.

Sometime in September, Lee set out for western New York with the commissioners from Congress to treat with the Iroquois. If there was something incongruous about the Virginia gentleman who had frequented Versailles now on his way to back country negotiations, it was not apparent. A fellow traveler simply described Lee as "a gentleman from Virginia of great report, about 35 to 40 years of age; good person; very sensible, polite and apparently agreeable." Lee, Richard Butler, and Oliver Wolcott traveled first to Albany and then westward to Fort Stanwix [Rome] to meet the sachems and warriors of the Six Nations on October 3. There they also encountered the Marquis de Lafayette, who had been enlisted to impress the Indians. James Madison, tending congressional concerns, was able to report that the Frenchman "was the only conspicuous figure. The Commissioners were eclipsed. All of them probably felt it. Le[e] complained to me of the immoderate stress laid upon the influence of the M.[arquis] and evidently promoted his departure." [37] Perhaps Arthur's antigallicism had flared anew; perhaps family pride—for his own father had negotiated at Stanwix during Lee's youth—made him covet a dramatic and leading role.

Negotiations were complicated. Feuds among the various tribes had to be ameliorated; trust for the American Congress had to be cultivated; New Yorkers bent on profiting from liquor sales had to be curbed. This last goal caused much bickering that indicated an uneasy connection between the state and national governments. A sheriff tried to halt a federal officer from enforcing liquor prohibitions, whereupon, Lee, brandishing a sword, leapt into the middle of the ruckus, putting the local official to flight. The Virginian later claimed that the governor of New York had "absolutely done all in his power" to frustrate the commissioners while the settlers kept the Iroquois drunk "so as to prevent our treating with them." [38]

37. Hallock F. Raup, "Journal of Griffith Evans, 1784–1785," *Pennsylvania Magazine of History and Biography*, LXV (April, 1941), 204; Madison to Jefferson, October 17, 1784, in William T. Hutchinson *et al.* (eds.), *Papers of Madison*, VIII, 118–21; Neville B. Craig (ed.), *The Olden Time* (2 vols.; Pittsburgh, 1848), II, 406–408.
38. Arthur Lee to Jacob Reed, October 29, 1784, Arthur Lee Papers, Box 7; Craig (ed.), *Olden Time*, II, 411.

The parleys proved tedious although Arthur sought to press the issues with "a most spirited grand speech." The commissioners' secretary recorded that Lee's oration "alarmed us very much but had a very good effect and deserves great credit." Arthur's dramaturgical inclinations were rewarded. Evidently he tried a variation of militia diplomacy on the Indian leaders, Cornplanter, Red Jacket, and Aaron Hill. Those tribes which had recently aided the British, Lee asserted, were to be considered a "subdued people" and forced to seek American mercy at the negotiation table. Later he reflected, "I did not conceive, till I delivered the last speech to them and the articles of the treaty, that they could be brought to such submission. But they are Animals that must be subdued and kept in awe or they will be mischievous, and fear alone will affect [*sic*] this submission." Ultimately the chiefs conceded the boundaries outlined in the peace of 1783 between the British and the Americans. Lee was certain his team had won an advantageous pact that would secure "valuable Country" for the American republic. The Six Nations gave up claims to holdings south of the Great Lakes and east of the Mississippi River.[39] Lee's imperial visions moved closer to realization.

Since the other tribes in the northwest demanded separate negotiations, the commissioners traveled to Pennsylvania. Accompanied by a guard of artillery, Lee, Butler, and George Rogers Clark reached Fort Pitt in December. Lee, once more faithfully tending a diary, was careful to record all he saw of frontier and Indian culture as well as the lay of the land. He wrote down his observations on childbirth among the Indians and occasionally became moderately poetic. Frequently he inserted a line from Milton or Pope. Crossing the Appalachians in a blizzard, the world traveler wrote, "The ocean in a storm with its billows and their white tops rising behind and above each other, resemble the various ridges of snowcapt hills which compose this immense chain." Less lyrical entries noted recurrent sickness among his companions, endless cold, and a chaotic brawl by drunken officers that Lee and Butler had to quell at Fort Pitt.[40]

39. Arthur Lee to [?], November 19, 1784, in Arthur Lee Papers, Box 7; Craig (ed.), *Olden Time*, II, 413–15; Raup, "Journal," 211, 215; Treaty of Fort Stanwix, October 22, 1784, in William R. Palmer (ed.), *Calendar of Virginia State Papers* (11 vols.; Richmond, 1875–93), III, 618–19.

40. Arthur Lee, "Indian Journal" [1784], in Richard Henry Lee, *Life of Arthur Lee*, II, 377–99; John W. Harpster (ed.), *Pen Pictures of Early Western Pennsylvania* (Pittsburgh, 1938), 151–59.

These were wondrous experiences for so cultivated a gentleman as Arthur Lee.

Christmas Eve, 1784, found Arthur Lee, scion of Virginia gentry and product of Britain's best schools, sick in a frontier hut at Fort Pitt. He had already bled himself copiously and fasted but to no avail. Now he was confined to his room. Perhaps his recent birthday had jostled his mind. In his diary he "could not avoid meditating" on his future prospects. He could foresee three options. To return to native Virginia "without a wife," he wrote, "is hardly practicable." He considered himself to be too old and too idealistic about love to find a proper match in the Old Dominion, and he seems to have equated residence in his home state with marriage. To venture to Kentucky "and try my fortune in a young country and a rising region" appeared too challenging to the forty-four-year-old lawyer. Presciently he asked himself, "For whom should I sacrifice present enjoyment, to secure a future fortune?" In western Virginia he foresaw joining another movement for "separation and independence."[41]

Recollections of 1774 came to mind. Arthur felt certain that a bachelor with an annual income of £600 could be fully satisfied as a man about town in London. He yearned to "be restored to the situation that I enjoyed before the revolution . . . that is as happy a man without domestic cares, domestic anxiety, and domestic love, could be." In all his life he had found no place so satisfying as London. It appealed to his need to be in politics, and it satisfied his desire to be a cultured man. Had he continued as a lawyer there, he believed he could have risen "to place and profit," but "the great contest . . . the revolution" had changed all that. A return now to the land of George III would repudiate all of Lee's labors for the past fifteen years, for he had "hazarded everything to establish republican liberty." Pragmatism ultimately triumphed, as Lee sighed, "What then remains for me but to take the world as I find it—to remain in the midst of this odd chapter of accidents." He sustained himself with pessimistic poetry.[42]

Lee's indisposition soon vanished. Representatives of the western tribes appeared, and at Fort McIntosh, on January 21, 1785, all but the Shawnee agreed to the commissioners' proposals. In return for some gifts,

41. Arthur Lee, "Indian Journal" [December 24, 1784], in Richard Henry Lee, *Life of Arthur Lee*, II, 389–93.
42. *Ibid.*

the Indians ceded all territory northwest of the Ohio River except for a few scattered districts and watering places. When he returned to Congress in February, Lee received congratulations for gaining an estimated 30 million acres. The Lee family was at work to open the west and to sustain the Confederation government.[43]

On the crest of this achievement Arthur Lee suddenly found himself unemployed. Under the Articles of Confederation he was not allowed to serve more than three consecutive years in Congress. One noteworthy success was that after four years he finally settled accounts from his European service. Richard Henry Lee's selection as president of Congress was helpful. In April Arthur was commissioned to treat with the Indians at Kaskaskia, and he also became a member of the Board of Treasury. The appointments caused uneasiness in some quarters. James Monroe, delegate from Virginia, lamented that Congress "can get none better than Mr. A. L." Lee just would not retire from public service! When Jefferson heard about the appointments, he voiced fears that the zealot would fragment the board by rummaging old accounts of the treasury in order to rekindle his "eternal war with Morris." On the other hand if the contentious Virginian were dispatched to Kaskaskia, Jefferson predicted "a revolt of that settlement from the United States." Jaundiced views of the Lees were not restricted to the personal notes of Jefferson, Monroe, Madison, and Randolph. There was now enough anti-Lee sentiment in the Virginia Assembly to unseat Arthur as representative from Prince William County because he had accepted a "lucrative office" from Congress.[44] In consequence he became identified as a national, not a state or local, official. At various times in his career he had usually been labeled an easterner (1780–1782), a parochialist (1782–1784), or an independent (1784).

43. James Alton James, "Some Phases of the History of the Northwest, 1783–1786," *Proceedings of the Mississippi Valley Historical Association*, VII (1913–14), 169–72; Elbridge Gerry to Jefferson, February 25, 1785, in Boyd *et al.* (eds.), *Papers of Thomas Jefferson*, VII, 651–52.

44. Richard Henry Lee to Dr. William Shippen, February 7, 1785, James Monroe to Madison, December 18, 1784, Monroe to Jefferson, April 12, 1785, all in Burnett (ed.), *Letters*, VIII, 23n, VII, 633, VIII, 92; Jefferson to Monroe, June 17, 1785, in Boyd *et al.* (eds.), *Papers of Jefferson*, VIII, 229–30; Henderson, *Party Politics*, 356–57; Burnett (ed.), *Letters*, VII, 623n, 633; *Journal of the House Delegates*, October 31–November 1, 1785, p. 15–17.

Lee served on the Board of Treasury from 1785 until 1789, when he retired in favor of the administration of President George Washington. Firsthand experience as a member of the national government caused him to reassess the Confederation. As time went by, he changed from a defender of states' rights to an advocate of reform of the Articles. His patience and perseverance were severely tested by the jumble of accounts the Board examined. In March, 1786, he declared, "the states have proved shamefully defective" in providing revenue for the national government. He testified that the Confederation was "not good—but it is better than a dishonest bankruptcy." His eternal fears of ruining American virtue "by the rapacity of speculation" were joined to an increasing discontent with the structure of government. To Richard Henry he blurted, "We have independence, without the means of attaining it; and are a nation without one source of national defense . . . we don't seem to feel these things are necessary to national existence. The Confederation is crumbling to pieces." Arthur played the familiar role of doomsayer more frequently as he aged. By the end of 1787 the Board could only lament the "dreadful" and "Embarrased situation of Finances." Lee was dispatched to his home state to make special pleas for requisitions. Privately he had already advised Virginia to buy up public securities in anticipation that prices would improve if the Articles were strengthened by the Constitution. He spoke passionately but to deaf ears.[45]

The time was ripe for a change. From New York City in 1787 Arthur was broadcasting the dirge of the Confederation: "We are just as we were, scrambling —hoping—at sixes and sevens—without a revenue— without a Congress and without a President." Turmoil in Massachusetts exacerbated Lee's pessimism and moralism. He exclaimed, "It is most manifest that we do not have the public virtue and private temperance which are necessary to the establishment at least of free Republics." At

45. Arthur Lee to Marquis of Lansdowne, March 3, 1786, in Richard Henry Lee, *Life of Arthur Lee*, II, 166–69; Arthur Lee to Thomas Lee Shippen, March 1, July 18, 1786, Arthur Lee to Samuel Adams, February 14, 1786, Arthur Lee to Richard Henry Lee, September 19, 1786, all in Arthur Lee Papers, Box 8; Arthur Lee to Governor of Virginia, May 20, 1787, January 30, 1788, Samuel Osgood and Walter Livingston to Governor Randolph, December 26, 1787, all in Palmer (ed.), *Calendar of Virginia State Papers*, IV, 288–89, 398–99, 372–73; Joseph Jones to Madison, June 7, 1787, in William T. Hutchinson *et al.* (eds.), *Papers of Madison*, X, 36–38.

first he did not believe the states would answer the call to convene "a National Convention" to amend the Confederation, but then he prayed for it. As the drama of the Constitutional Convention unfolded during the summer, Lee was an intense observer from his federal post in New York. His early reaction was that "The Convention is composed of the first men among us for wisdom, character, and property." He told Shelburne that improvement in American government would evolve out of such periodic conventions. Delegates could do no wrong if they modeled their document on the British Constitution. Later, when he transmitted a copy of the draft of the Constitution to Shelburne, Lee noted his criticism of the plan —"a little too manifest aristocratical"—but predicted its adoption.[46]

Lee was voluble in his reactions to the change in American government. Throughout 1787 he developed extensive correspondence with a nephew, Thomas Lee Shippen, brother of Nancy Shippen, whom Arthur had previously befriended. Nancy and Thomas were the surviving children of Arthur's sister Alice and her husband, Dr. William Shippen. The Shippen family was much afflicted, and perhaps therefore, became an object of Lee's attentions. It appears Arthur set about to tutor Thomas as though he were his own son. Arthur analyzed contemporary politics, unlimbered artillery against his enemies, and confessed his own failures to his adopted pupil. While it existed, it was one of the most meaningful relationships Arthur ever developed, but it ended tragically. Arthur and William Shippen became embittered over debts, Nancy was cast into melancholy after her divorce, Thomas died of tuberculosis, and Alice Lee Shippen became a recluse.[47]

Arthur Lee's epistles to Thomas Lee Shippen in 1787 are lectures on nation-building. Lee recognized his land as "an infant nation" that required British "nursing." The governments of the states and the country were "yet experimental, unknit, and unestablished." An Anglo-American rapprochement would be beneficial. As he aged, his faith in regenerating a virtuous people dwindled while his trust in the British structures of gov-

46. Arthur Lee to Richard Henry Lee, January 13, 1787, Arthur Lee to Thomas Lee Shippen, January 2, 30, 1787, Arthur Lee to William Lee, March 12, 1787, Arthur Lee to Lord Shelburne, June 1, October 1, 1787, all in Arthur Lee Papers, Box 8, 17.

47. Betsy Chopping Corner, *William Shippen, Jr.: Pioneer in American Medical Education* (Philadelphia, 1951), 96, 117; Marguerite duPont Lee, *Arthur Lee*, 229.

ernment intensified. His early diatribes against speculators now gave way to generalized jeremiads. The pillars of republicanism, such as sacrifice, integrity, and virtue, would perish under the onslaught of "the most baneful of all luxuries, the luxury of the common people, who are more extravagant than any people in the world of the same rank." He offered a most depressing diagnosis of his society: "the corruption of manners, the insecurity of property and the destruction of national faith, character and confidence." Such degeneracies particularly infested the state assemblies and were traceable to "considerable external commerce." The only remedy Lee could prescribe for the Constitutional Convention was to entrust national government to "one Sovereignty consisting of an imperial head, a Senate for life, and an elective house of commons." These thoughts were not unlike those of Alexander Hamilton and not far afield from those of John Adams. Democracy must be curbed, "order . . . [and] a proper balance" restored to American government.[48]

In trying to apply Whig ideology in his analysis of events in 1787, Lee ended with some convoluted thinking. To Shelburne, Arthur could label the proposed Constitution too aristocratic, but to Shippen he could point out that a natural elite should govern. "The Science of Government," he pontificated, "is no trifling matter. It requires education, and experience —it requires the habits of the great world and great men—it requires the leisure which independent fortune gives, and the elevation of mind which birth and rank impart." This was a prescription for rule by an oligarchy— by Lees, for example! From his angle of vision Lee believed too powerful a senate had been created by the Constitution. He confided, "Now tho I wish to see the Aristocracy have its due weight yet, I can never agree that they shall trample upon the People, and I am persuaded that a due balance is the best guard to the Aristocracy itself." Like his brother Richard Henry, Arthur Lee was an opponent of the proposed Constitution, largely on the grounds that the document lacked "a declaration of rights" to protect personal freedoms. He possessed little faith in the people but even less in state governments. A nationalist but not a centralist, a libertarian, and an elitist, he followed Richard Henry Lee and George Mason in the unsuccessful campaign to provide a bill of rights and to reconvene a sec-

48. Arthur Lee to Thomas Lee Shippen, May 2, 29, June 4, 6, 1787, all in Arthur Lee Papers, Box 8; Arthur Lee to Marquis de Rosignan, July 6, 1778 in Richard Henry Lee, *Life of Arthur Lee*, II, 159.

ond constitutional convention. Yet Arthur's antifederalism was not rabid; he left to Richard Henry the duties of corresponding with Samuel Adams and publishing arguments against ratification. Although he had not mellowed, Arthur certainly was less voluble. His political trinity was to curb democracy and "establish a proper balance" in the national government, to safeguard personal freedoms from possible central interference, and to gradually evolve a "reformation" of the Confederation. There was no concern for state prerogatives or sovereignty in Lee's critiques of the Constitution.[49] Personal liberties need not be dependent on either state or national government. Yet even though he opposed the Constitution, Lee did not seek assignment to the ratifying convention in Richmond, nor did he write voluminously against it. Perhaps age had tempered him or perhaps he was a constitutionalist at heart.

Ratification of the Constitution deprived Arthur Lee of his job on the Board of Treasury. Once again the opportunity for retirement presented itself, but once again he felt compelled to participate in public affairs. While brother Richard Henry, through a revived friendship with Patrick Henry, won selection as a federal senator from Virginia, Arthur offered himself to the voters between the Potomac and York rivers as a candidate for Congress. A handbill announcing Arthur's candidacy evinced a brand of populism. He declared his principles were to submit to majority opinion and endorsement of the Constitution. His stated goal was "the Prosperity of the People, under the new Government." If elected, he would strive "to promote, as far as may be in my Power, the particular interests of this District." Despite these commitments, despite a pledge to seek amendments to the Constitution so "as to remove the Apprehension and secure the Confidence of the People," despite Arthur's twelve years experience "in the high and confidential office of Government," he failed. He then gave up pursuit of elective office. His world view, ethnocultural perspective, and family record were not compatible with local preferences

49. Arthur Lee to Thomas Lee Shippen, July 30, August 1, 1787, Arthur Lee to John Rutledge, October 28, 1787, all in Arthur Lee Papers, Box 8; Arthur Lee to John Adams, October 3, 1787, in Charles Francis Adams (ed.), *Works of John Adams*, IX, 554–55; George Mason to Arthur Lee, May 21, 1787, in Hoffman and Molyneaux (eds.), *Lee Family Papers*, VII, 628–30; Boyd *et al.* (eds.), *Papers of Jefferson*, XII, 321, 281, 423; Arthur Lee to Thomas Lee Shippen, May 2, 29, June 4, 6, 1787, Arthur Lee to John Rutledge, October 29, 1787, all in Arthur Lee Papers, Box 8.

in the Middle Tidewater.[50] John Page, a Federalist, was elected instead by voters of the Seventh Congressional District.

Lee's hopes of furthering his career in public service were not totally quashed. Not reticent about his own qualifications, Lee seems to have approached George Washington asking to be named an associate justice on the Supreme Court or secretary of treasury. When these national aspirations went unfulfilled, Richard Henry Lee lobbied on Arthur's behalf in Virginia, praising his brother's devotion to liberty, his sacrifices for the public, his well-bred training in law, and his record in American politics. Patrick Henry, however, could find no place for him. The experience of job hunting was embittering for Arthur. Other intriguers for places were successful. He complained to his nephew, "I am now cast off with as much disgrace as they can fix upon me, and must spend the remainder of my life in circumstances hardly above indigence." Again he questioned his self-worth; again he fancied himself the victim of the plots of Robert Morris; again the menacing fear of dependency reemerged. His investments in land had not yielded high returns. How and where would he live now that he was relegated to a private life?[51]

Retirement from public service forced Lee to act independently in choosing the next step in his career. He would not move in with Richard Henry or Francis Lightfoot on their plantations. His training in the law as well as almost continuous residence in cities on two continents made Alexandria, Virginia, more attractive to him. There he occasionally practiced law. The state of Virginia was sufficiently impressed by his professional credentials to appoint him a member of the committee to revise state statutes. Perhaps Arthur had visions of speculating in the surround-

50. Arthur Lee, 1788 Handbill, Arthur Lee to Richard Henry Lee, February 19, 1788, in Hoffman and Molyneaux (eds.), *Lee Family Papers*, VII, 663, 685; Jackson Turner Main, *Political Parties Before the Constitution* (New York, 1973), 244–67, 386–90; Norman K. Risjord and Gordon DenBoer, "The Evolution of Political Parties in Virginia, 1782–1800," *Journal of American History*, LX (March, 1974), 964.

51. Washington to Madison [August, 1789], in Fitzpatrick (ed.), *Writings of Washington*, XXX, 393–94, 413; Richard Henry Lee to Patrick Henry, September 27, 1789, in Ballagh (ed.), *Letters of Richard Henry Lee*, II, 504–507; Arthur Lee to Anne Hume Livingston, March 21, 1789, Arthur Lee to Francis Lightfoot Lee, August 29, 1789, both in Arthur Lee Papers, Box 8; Arthur Lee to Thomas Lee Shippen, n.d. [1789?], in *Magazine of the Society of the Lees of Virginia*, I, (December, 1922), 28–29.

ing lands in hopes that the federal city would move near the falls of the Potomac. Meanwhile he continued to keep an eye on the affairs of his country and the world. He was an early commentator on the evolution of partisanship in federal politics, a booster of the developing national economy, a devotee of Washington's leadership, and an opponent of the stand on natural rights taken by Thomas Paine in the French Revolution. Lee grew more reactionary. Where before he had written that society was improving as citizens became enlightened, in 1790 he recorded, "To me it appears very doubtful whether the increase of knowledge in this age, has increased our happiness—either political or moral." Further reflection brought him to observe, "I am most sure that the People of America are much less happy than before the revolution, and I believe it will soon be the same with the People of France." [52] He was ever the misfit.

The search for happiness took Arthur Lee to the Chesapeake Bay. In 1791 he moved to Urbanna in Middlesex County, Virginia. There he purchased two plots of land, one of 300 acres and one of $8\frac{1}{2}$ acres. The latter estate he named Lansdowne in honor of Lord Shelburne. His concerns revolved around maintenance of a productive life rather than passive retirement. He continued to look after Nancy and Thomas Lee Shippen. With the latter he had toured Virginia in 1790 and continued to share his thoughts on life. Theirs was more than a simple mentor-pupil relationship, for Arthur found his nephew to be a compassionate confessor. The older man wished to impress on the younger's mind his view of the world: "I am apt to think with Hamlet that it is a congregation of pestilent vapors—an unweeded garden, and that things rank and gross in nature do possess it merely. There is certainly far more prudery than virtue in the world. Everyone pretends to love and admire virtue, and very few practice it." Lee hoped his ward would follow his cardinal tenet: "the good of the public must be above all things most dear to me—that is the very essence of true republicanism." [53]

52. Governor Beverly Randolph to Arthur Lee, February 20, 1791, in Hoffman and Molyneaux (eds.), *Lee Family Papers*, VII, 820; Arthur Lee to Randolph, February 25, 1791, Arthur Lee to Richard Henry Lee, May 9, 1789, Arthur Lee to Thomas Lee Shippen, April 25, 1790, Arthur Lee to Thomas Shippen, n.d. [April, 1789?], Arthur Lee to Lord Shelburne, September 24, 1789, September 14, 1790, May 5, 1782, all in Arthur Lee Papers, Box 8, 17.

53. Arthur Lee to Lord Shelburne, May 10, 1792, in Arthur Lee Papers, Box 17; C. C. Chowning, "Some Colonial Houses of Middlesex County," *William and*

Arthur's fondness for nieces and nephews coincided with his somewhat paternal wish to transmit to posterity his interpretation of the events
of his era. Writing a history of the American Revolution would be compensation for disengagement from public life, and as early as June of
1777, he had this project in mind. He had secured copies of his own correspondence and had reminded Washington to preserve his papers in
order to disprove "the forgeries which will be offered to the world." During the war Lee and Franklin had discussed the events in which they participated. Both men saw that the American rebellion was founded on "the
opinion and voice of the majority of the people. . . . It was not a tumul-
tuous resolution, but a deliberate system." This interpretation might have
been more appropriate for Franklin than for Lee, or it might show Lee's
later editing. Ultimately Lee chose to begin a memoir rather than a history, for he was still trying to purge his reputation of taint. He observed
that memoirs, having "less dignity" but not "less utility" than history,
enabled historians "to trace their true though secret motives." [54] He failed
to complete the project.

Lansdowne provided Lee the role of gentleman farmer. With characteristic energy he turned toward this potentially productive life. By 1792
he had amassed 1,147 acres in Middlesex County. Arthur intended to
apply science to farming, as he had observed when a student in Scotland.
He hoped to make the soil more fruitful and to order the yield of his
lands. As a bachelor husbandman he found a degree of happiness, for he
reported to Shippen, "I have been occupied totally with my farm, planning fields, ditches and enclosures. . . . I take to my Farm as naturally as

---

Mary Quarterly, 2nd ser., XXII (April, 1942), 157–58; Middlesex County Records, Deedbook, April 1791–1799, August 29, 1791; Robert Beverly of Blandfield
to Arthur Lee of Fairfax County, in Arthur Lee Papers, Box 17; Marguerite duPont
Lee, *Arthur Lee*, 247; Arthur Lee to Thomas Lee Shippen, March 26, 1792, in Arthur Lee Papers, Box 8. Ironically Arthur's final will failed to provide a token to
his love to either Nancy or Thomas Shippen. Richard Henry Lee to Thomas Lee
Shippen, April 15, 1793, in Ballagh (ed.), *Letters of Richard Henry Lee*, II, 555–
59.

54. Arthur Lee to George Washington, June 15, 1777, in Richard Henry Lee,
Life of Arthur Lee, II, 86–88; William Gordon to Arthur Lee, July 26, 1782, in
Hoffman and Molyneaux (eds.), *Lee Family Papers*, VII, 249; Arthur Lee's Jour-
nal, October 25, 1777, in Richard Henry Lee, *Life of Arthur Lee*, II 344–46; Ar-
thur Lee's "Memoir of the American Revolution," in Richard Henry Lee, *Life of
Arthur Lee*, I, 243–46.

your little Boy does to his Bottle, and am not less fond of it." He especially liked the ornamental fruit trees he raised and the rosebushes. On a
raw December day in 1792 he helped plant a new orchard. Within days
he was bedridden with a fever and then became violently ill. On December 12, less than a fortnight before his fifty-second birthday, Arthur Lee
died. He was buried at Lansdowne rather than at distant Stratford as his
will directed.[55]

Arthur Lee's eulogies in Virginia emphasized his virtue. One newspaper contended that "greater sacrifices of a personal nature were made
by none in America for the promotion of her liberty and happiness."
Nephew Ludwell Lee composed verses in his uncle's memory:

> Closed are those eyes that beamed celestial fire,
> Shut is that mouth that virtue did inspire;
> Cold is that heart, which beat for public good,
> Fled is that mind, which most things understood.

Such portraits reflected the self-image Arthur had striven to achieve, but
this appraisal was contradicted by many of Lee's contemporaries. None
other than George Washington, as he formed his presidential administration in 1789, was forced to a contrary assessment. Of a possible appointment of Arthur to the Supreme Court, Washington confided, "The opinion entertained of him by those with whom I am most conversant is
unpropitious and yet few men have received more marks of public favor
and confidence than he has. These contradictions are embarassing."[56] In
Washington's eyes, Arthur Lee was a revolutionary manqué.

Indeed, in the last stage of his life, as the Revolution denied him any
further role and repudiated his values, Arthur Lee was cast into despair.
His faith in the American republic and his fidelity at the personal level
were challenged. He had a ready rationalization, with which he protected
his self-image and which he offered nephew Thomas Lee Shippen, "Every-

55. Arthur Lee to Thomas Lee Shippen, March 26, 1792, in Arthur Lee Papers,
Box 8; Richard Henry Lee, *Life of Arthur Lee*, I, 180; Cazenove G. Lee, Jr., *Lee
Chronicle*, 82–84.

56. *Virginia Gazette and General Advertiser* (Richmond), December 19, 1792,
quoted in Marguerite duPont Lee, *Arthur Lee*, 267–68; Ludwell Lee, "Lines on
the Death of Mr. Arthur Lee," in *Magazine of the Society of the Lees of Virginia*,
I (April, 1923), 51; Washington to Madison [August, 1789], in Fitzpatrick (ed.),
Writings of Washington, XIX, 393–94.

one pretends to love and admire virtue, and very few practice it. Nay worse, they do not seem in truth to like those who practice it." [57]

Lee's contributions to the American Revolution should not be underestimated. Although certain of his goals were unfulfilled and his personal tactics proved defective, he played a major role during a formative period of American diplomacy. In the decade before the Declaration of Independence, as a representative not only of a Virginia dynasty, but also of the American resistance movement, Lee performed critical tasks with remarkable industry. Through an outpouring of private correspondence and public pamphleteering, he broadcast a distinctive analysis of events in the British empire. From Massachusetts to South Carolina, and throughout radical circles in Britain, his writings spread the corrosive fears and evangelical millennialism that comprised the core of Anglo-American whiggism. Critically situated at the center of opposition politics in England, close to both Wilkes and Shelburne, Lee provided his countrymen with an all-inclusive rendering of the machinations behind policies emanating from the crown, the ministry, or Parliament. These tracings of interest groups, disclosures of personal motives, connections of divers events, and condemnations of incompetent administrators were broadcast by Lee to his network of friends and family in America, who in turn rebroadcast them throughout the American colonies. Arthur Lee was a key transmitter of the Real Whig component of the ideology of the American Revolution. There was no more productive or more skillful polemicist.

Lee's most critical talent was his articulation of the alternatives available to the American resistance movement. Initially he had attempted, through the institution of the Society of the Bill of Rights, to keep American grievances yoked with those expressed by the Opposition in English political circles. Further, through a myriad of remonstrances, Arthur tried to use constitutional mechanisms to seek redress. By 1774 he perceived, in the failure to arouse the British people, the total corruption of the nation. He therefore turned to the task of legitimizing the cause of American independence. Arthur's accomplishments between 1774 and 1776 were twofold. First, his experiences in factuality, his perceptions of reality, and his visions of actuality—compounded of classical and Real Whig sources—caused him to narrow the alternatives to one: the imperative to rebel. In-

---

57. Armes (ed.), *Nancy Shippen*, 266; Arthur Lee to Thomas Lee Shippen, March 26, 1792, in Arthur Lee Papers, Box 8.

creasingly, he emphasized the dichotomy between freedom and slavery. Increasingly, he saw life within the empire leading to a forcible depriva- tion of the fruits of one's labors. Hence Lee was able to portray the dissi- dent colonists as revolutionaries. They aimed at restitution of rights of the people. Later he would reflect, "we must remember that the revolu- tion was not directed by the leaders of faction, but by the opinion and voice of the majority of the people." Second, he endowed the movement with a sense of destiny: "the greatest revolution the world ever saw." Repeatedly he exhorted Old Radical correspondents to persist in the quest for "the noble fabric we have labored so much to rear to liberty, honor, and Independence."[58] Lee's contributions to the ideology of the Ameri- can Revolution were manifold. His goals, values, and world view were widely shared amongst the early leaders of the movement.

As Arthur's role changed in 1775–1776 from colonial agent to na- tional diplomat, his enthusiasm for the American cause was challenged. Samuel Adams urged him: "You are now called to act in a still more enlarged sphere. Go on, my friend, to exhort yourself in the cause of lib- erty and virtue. You have already the applause of virtuous men, and may be assured of the smiles of heaven."[59] Arthur Lee brought to diplomatic assignments not only his customary energy, but also a repertoire of tactics —subsequently labelled militia diplomacy—which he had developed for more than a decade. Further, his formulation of goals and strategies would interact with congressional instructions, the diverse aims of his fellow commissioners, and the desires of European policy makers. His missions over the map of western Europe often miscarried or came up short of his personal goals, for the aggressive stance of militia diplomacy, intensified by his personal quirks, was not productive. The Prussians proved un- yielding, and the Spaniards grudgingly made nominal concessions. French intervention, Arthur ultimately concluded, jeopardized American autono- my. Character traits and temperament, especially his mistrust and initia- tive, made Lee ill suited for these assignments. He appeared abrasive to

58. Arthur Lee's Journal, October 25, 1777, in Richard Henry Lee, *Life of Ar- thur Lee*, II, 344–45; Arthur Lee to Samuel Adams, February 14, 1786, in Arthur Lee Papers, Box 8.

59. Samuel Adams to Arthur Lee, January 2, 1777, in Cushing (ed.), *Writings of Samuel Adams*, III, 339–40.

most fellow American agents and contentious to potentates of the *ancien régime*. Neither set of men agreed with Lee's grand objective—that America be free from all European connections. In 1775–1776 Lee had seen a future for himself, his family, and his country in independence that could never be realized in continued union with Britain. It is readily apparent in Lee family papers that this "band of brothers" deemed themselves highly competent as provincial politicians and that family and personal ambitions, often coded as "virtue" or "independence," were thwarted by imperial interference. This same vision was a common thread from 1776 to 1783. Arthur Lee wished that Congress would not subject its policies tò the whims of Bourbon policy makers or the temptations of European creditors. Congressional debate, precipitated by Lee's feud with Silas Deane, rejected the Virginian's aims, and led to his recall. Ironically his replacements, John Jay and John Adams, achieved Lee's goals in negotiating the peace treaty of 1782–1783.

Lee proved a caustic critic of the Confederation and the Constitution. He could not tolerate the expansive individualism and pluralistic politics unleashed in the actual creation of the American republic. In 1792 he wailed "that I think the modern contenders for liberty, are actually for dissolving all government; and substituting, whatever they may profess— licentiousness for liberty." The rising democratical tide could be measured in "the sacrifice of the public honor & interests to the selfish objects of individuals" in state assemblies as well as "the most baneful of all luxuries, the luxury of the common people."[60] His prognosis could apply equally to the American and the French revolutions in Lee's eyes.

To his contemporaries Arthur Lee appeared ubiquitous and feisty. His enthusiasm for "liberty and virtue" had dictated his public career, which he later charted as "a continued scene of agitation and commotion." Most of the maelstroms that swirled around him can be traced not to his ideology or political stances, but to his personality. His childhood and formal education developed his exaggerated traits and his attitudes toward his fellow man. Such peculiarities as Lee's hyperbolic mistrust and autonomy, proved congruent to the ideology widely shared with other American radicals through 1776. Thereafter, as he clung rigidly to the hope of

60. Arthur Lee to Earl of Shelburne, May 5, 1792, Arthur Lee to Thomas Lee Shippen, May 2, 29, June 4, 6, 1787, all in Arthur Lee Papers, Box 17, 8.

regenerating the social values of an illusive past, Lee became more of a misfit. His opponents and rivals, the more pragmatic and modern men like Benjamin Franklin and Robert Morris, were able to direct the Revolution toward more materialistic and less communal goals than those envisioned by Lee.[61]

61. Arthur Lee, "Indian Journal," in Richard Henry Lee, *Life of Arthur Lee*, II, 389–90; William G. McLoughlin, "The Role of Religion in the Revolution: Liberty of Conscience and Cultural Cohesion in the New Nation," in Stephen G. Kurtz and James H. Hutson (eds.), *Essays on the American Revolution* (New York, 1973), 188, 202.

Bibliography

Primary Sources

Manuscript Collections

Manuscripts Department, University of Virginia Library, Charlottesville
  Arthur Lee Papers (Accession No. 8709).
  Lee Family Papers.
American Philosophical Society, Philadelphia, Pa.
  Duane Collection.
  Sol Feinstone Collection.
  Benjamin Franklin Papers.
  Miscellaneous Manuscripts.
National Archives, Washington, D.C.
  "Marine Committee Letterbook, 1776–1780," Miscellaneous Papers of the
    Continental Congress, 1774–1789, in Record Group 11, Microcopy 332,
    Roll 6.
  Navy Board of the Eastern Department (Captain John Barry presiding).
    "Courtmartial of Captain Peter Landais, November 20, 1780–January 7,
    1781, and Lieutenant James Degge, January 11–25, 1781." Papers of the
    Continental Congress, 1774–1789, in Record Group 360, Microcopy
    247, Roll 200.

Printed Documents

Abbott, Claude C. *A Catalogue of Papers Relating to Boswell, Johnson, and
  Sir William Forbes Found at Fettercairn House.* Oxford: Clarendon Press,
  1936.
Abernethy, Thomas P., ed. *A Summary View of the Rights of British Ameri-
  ca.* New York: Scholars Facsimiles and Reprints, 1943.
Adair, Douglas and John A. Schutz, eds. *Peter Oliver's Origin and Progress*

of the American Rebellion: A Tory View. San Marino: Huntington Library, 196⁻.

Adams, Charles F., ed. *Familiar Letters of John Adams to His Wife Abigail Adams, During the Revolution.* Boston: Houghton-Mifflin, 1875.

Adams, Charles Francis, ed. *The Works of John Adams, Second President of the United States with a Life of the Author.* 10 vols. Boston: Little, Brown, 185⁻.

Adams, Richard, to Thomas Adams, March 24, 1772, in *Virginia Magazine of History and Biography,* VI (October, 1898), 389–91.

The Annual Register; or, A View of the History, Politics, and Literature for the Year 1765 . . . 1783. Vols. VIII–XXVI. 3rd edition; London: J. Dodsley, 1802–1820.

Austen-Leigh, Richard A., ed. *The Eton College Register 1753–1790.* Eton: Ballantyne, 1921

Ballagh, James C., ed. *The Letters of Richard Henry Lee.* 2 vols. New York: Macmillan, 1911–14.

Bland, Colonel Richard, to Thomas Adams, August 1, 1771, in *Virginia Magazine of History and Biography,* VI (October, 1898), 133–34.

The Bowdoin and Temple Papers. In the Massachusetts Historical Society. *Collections.* 6th Series. IX; Boston, 1897.

Boyd, Julian *et al.,* eds. *The Papers of Thomas Jefferson.* 19 vols. Princeton: Princeton University Press, 1950–.

Burnett, Edmund C., ed. *Letters of Members of the Continental Congress.* 8 vols. Washington, D.C.: Carnegie Institute of Washington, 1921–1936.

Butterfield, Lyman, *et al.,* eds. *Letters of Benjamin Rush.* 2 vols. Princeton: Princeton University Press, 1951.

Butterfield, Lyman H., ed. *The Diary and Autobiography of John Adams.* 4 vols. Cambridge: Harvard University Press, 1961.

Campbell, Charles, ed. *The Bland Papers.* 2 vols. Petersburg, Va.: Edmund and Julian Ruffin, 1840.

Cappon, Lester J., ed. *The Adams-Jefferson Letters.* 3 vols. Chapel Hill: University of North Carolina Press, 1959.

Chastellux, Francois Jean. *Travels in North America in the Years 1780, 1781, and 1782.* 2 vols. Chapel Hill: University of North Carolina Press, 1963.

Colbourn, H. Trevor. "A Pennsylvania Farmer at the Court of King George: John Dickinson's London Letters, 1754–1756," *Pennsylvania Magazine of History and Biography,* LXXXVI (July, October, 1962), 241–86, 417–53.

Corner, George W., ed. *The Autobiography of Benjamin Rush: His Travels Through Life Together with his Commonplace Book for 1789–1793.* Princeton: Princeton University Press, 1948.

Crane, Verner W., ed. *Franklin's Letters to the Press, 1758–1775.* Chapel Hill: University of North Carolina Press, 1950.

Cushing, Harry Alonzo, ed. *The Writings of Samuel Adams.* 4 vols. New York: G.P. Putnam's Sons, 1904–1908.

The Deane Papers: Correspondence Between Silas Deane, His Brothers and Their Business and Political Associates. Hartford, 1870, 1930. Vols. II and XXII of the Connecticut Historical Society, *Collections.*

Deas, Anne Izard, ed. *Correspondence of Mr. Ralph Izard, of South Carolina, from the Year 1774 to 1804, with a Short Memoir.* New York: Charles S. Francis, 1844.

Dexter, Franklin B., ed. *The Literary Diary of Ezra Stiles.* 3 vols. New York: Charles Scribner's Sons, 1901.

Durand, John, ed. *New Materials for the History of the American Revolution.* New York: H. Holt, 1889.

Ettwein, Right Reverend John, to Arthur Lee, n.d., in *Pennsylvania Magazine of History and Biography,* XXXIX (1915), 219.

The Farmer's and Monitor's Letters to the Inhabitants of the British Colonies. Williamsburg: William Rind, 1769.

Fitzpatrick, John C., ed. *The Writings of George Washington.* 39 vols. Washington, D.C.: U.S. Government Printing Office, 1931–44.

————, ed. *The Diaries of George Washington.* 4 vols. New York: Houghton-Mifflin, 1925.

Force, Peter, ed. *American Archives, Fourth Series: Containing a Documentary History of the English Colonies in North America, from the King's Message to Parliament of March 7, 1774, to the Declaration of Independence by the United States.* 6 vols. Washington, D.C.: U.S. Government Printing Office, 1837–46.

Ford, Paul L., ed. *Political Writings, 1764–1774.* Philadelphia: Historical Society of Pennsylvania, 1895. Vol. I of Ford, ed. *The Writings of John Dickinson.*

————, ed. *The Writings of Thomas Jefferson.* 10 vols. New York: G.P. Putnam's Sons, 1892–99.

Ford, Worthington C., ed. *Letters of William Lee.* 3 vols. New York: B. Franklin Reprint, 1968.

————, ed. *Journals of the Continental Congress, 1774–1789.* 34 vols. Washington, D.C.: U.S. Government Printing Office, 1904–37.

————, ed. *Reply of William Lee to the Charges of Silas Deane, 1779.* Brooklyn: Historical Publishing Club, 1891.

Fortesque, Sir John, ed. *The Correspondence of King George the Third from 1760 to December 1783.* 6 vols. London: Macmillan and Co., 1927–28.

Genet, George, ed. "Beaumarchais' Opinion of Silas Deane and Arthur Lee: A Secret Memoir for the Ministers of the King," *Magazine of American History*, III (1879), 631–35.

Gordon, Thomas, trans. *The Works of Sallust, Translated into English with Political Discourses upon that Author, to Which Is Added a Translation of Cicero's Four Orations against Cataline.* London: T. Woodward and J. Peele, 1744.

Greene, Jack P., ed. *The Nature of Colony Constitutions: Two Pamphlets on the Wilkes Fund Controversy in South Carolina By Sir Egerton Leigh and Arthur Lee.* Columbia: University of South Carolina Press, 1970.

Harpster, John W., ed. *Pen Pictures of Early Western Pennsylvania.* Pittsburgh: University of Pittsburgh Press, 1938.

Hoffman, Paul R. and John L. Molyneaux, eds. *The Lee Family Papers.* 8 reels microfilm. Charlottesville: University of Virginia Library, 1966.

Hutchinson, Peter O., ed. *The Diary and Letters of His Excellency Thomas Hutchinson, Esq.* 2 vols. London: Sampson, Low, Marston, Searle, and Rivington, 1883–86.

Hutchinson, William T., *et al.*, eds. *The Papers of James Madison.* 12 vols. Chicago: University of Chicago Press, 1962–.

Isham, Charles, ed. *The Deane Papers.* New York, 1887–91. Vols. XIX–XXIII of the New York Historical Society, *Collections.*

"Jared Ingersoll Papers," *Papers of the New Haven Colony Historical Society.* IX. New Haven, 1918.

Jennings, John M., ed. "Letters of James Mercer," *Virginia Magazine of History and Biography*, LIX (January, 1951), 89–103.

Journal of the House of Delegates of the Commonwealth of Virginia ... 1781–1785. Richmond: Thomas W. White, 1828.

Labaree, Leonard W., *et al.*, eds. *The Papers of Benjamin Franklin.* 21 vols. New Haven: Yale University Press, 1959–.

Landais, Pierre de. *Memorial, to Justify Peter Landais' Conduct During the Late War.* Boston: Peter Edes, 1784.

———. *The Second Part of the Memorial, to Justify Peter Landais' Conduct During the Late War.* New York: Samuel Loudon, 1785.

[Lee, Arthur]. *An Appeal to the Justice and Interests of the People of Great Britain in the Present Disputes with America, By An Old Member of Parliament.* London: J. Almon, 1774.

[———]. *An Essay in Vindication of the Continental Colonies of America, From A Censure of Mr. Adam Smith, in his Theory of Moral Sentiments.* London: T. Becket and P. A. DeHondt, 1764.

———. *Extracts of a Letter Written to the President of Congress by the Honourable Arthur Lee, Esquire.* Philadelphia: Francis Bailey, 1780.

————. *Inauguralis De Cortica Peruviano*. Edinburgh: Donaldson and J. Reed, 1764.

[————]. *Observations on Certain Commercial Transactions in France Laid Before Congress by Arthur Lee, Esquire*. Philadelphia: Francis Bailey, 1780.

[————]. *The Political Detection; or, The Treachery and Tyranny of Administration, both at Home and Abroad; Displayed in a Series of Letters, Signed Junius Americanus*. London: J. & W. Oliver, 1770.

[————]. *A Second Appeal to the Justice and Interests of the People on the measures Respecting America by the Author of the First*. London: J. Almon, 1775.

[————]. *A Speech, Intended to Have Been Delivered in the House of Commons, in Support of the Petition from the General Congress at Philadelphia, by the Author of An Appeal to the Justice and Interest of Great Britain*. London: J. Almon, 1775.

————. to Thomas Lee Shippen, n.d. [1789?], in *Magazine of the Society of the Lees of Virginia*, I (December, 1922), 28–29.

[————]. *A True State of the Proceedings in the Parliament of Great Britain, and in the Province of Massachusetts Bay, Relative to the Giving and Granting the Money of the People of that Province, and of all America, in the House of Commons, in Which They Are Not Represented*. London: William Strahan, 1774.

Lee, Ludwell. "Lines on the Death of Mr. Arthur Lee," *Magazine of the Society of the Lees of Virginia*, I (April, 1923), 51.

Macgeagh, Sir Henry F., ed. *Register of Admissions to the Honorable Society of the Middle Temple, from the Fifteenth Century to the Year 1944*. London: Butterworth, 1949.

Mathews, Albert, ed. "Letters of Dennys DeBerdt, 1757–1770," *Publications of the Colonial Society of Massachusetts*, XIII (March, 1911), 316–29.

Mays, David J., ed. *The Letters and Papers of Edmund Pendleton, 1734–1803*. 2 vols. Charlottesville: University Press of Virginia, 1967.

Meng, John J., ed. *Dispatches and Instructions of Conrad Alexandre Gérard, 1778–1780*. Baltimore: The Johns Hopkins Press, 1939.

Miller, David Hunter, ed. *Treaties and Other International Acts of the United States of America*. 8 vols. Washington, D.C.: U.S. Government Printing Office, 1931–48.

Morton, Brian N., ed. *Beaumarchais Correspondence*. 2 vols. Paris: A.G. Nizet, 1969–.

Mulkearn, Lois, ed. *George Mercer Papers Relating to the Ohio Company of Virginia*. Pittsburgh: University of Pittsburgh Press, 1954.

O'Callaghan, Edmund Bailey, ed. *The Documentary History of the State of New York*. 4 vols. Albany: Weed, Parsons, 1849–51.

Palmer, William R., ed. *Calendar of Virginia State Papers.* 11 vols. Richmond: R. F. Walker, Supt. of Public Printing, 1875–93.

Raup, Hallock F. "Journal of Griffith Evans, 1784–1785," *Pennsylvania Magazine of History and Biography,* LXV (April, 1941), 202–233.

Royal Society of London. *Philosophical Transactions,* LVI. (1766), 47–51.

Smyth, Albert H., ed. *The Writings of Benjamin Franklin Collected and Edited with a Life and Introduction.* 10 vols. New York: Macmillan, 1905–1907.

Sparks, Jared, ed. *Correspondence of the American Revolution; Being Letters of Emminent Men to George Washington . . .* 4 vols. Boston: Little, Brown, 1853.

Steuart, A. Francis, ed. *The Last Journals of Horace Walpole During the Reign of George III from 1771–1783.* 25 vols. New York: John Lane, 1889–1910.

Stevens, Benjamin F., ed. *Facsimiles of Manuscripts in European Archives Relating to America, 1773–1783.* 25 vols. London: Malby & Sons, 1889–

Sullivan, James, ed. *The Papers of Sir William Johnson.* 14 vols. Albany: University of the State of New York, 1921–45.

[Swem, Earl G.?]. *A Provisional List of Alumni, Grammar School Students, Members of the Board of Visitors of the College of William and Mary in 98. Virginia from 1693 to 1888.* Richmond: n.p., 1941.

Van Doren, Carl, ed. *The Letters of Benjamin Franklin and Jane Mecom.* Princeton: Princeton University Press, 1950.

Wade, John, ed. *Junius.* 2 vols. London: H. G. Bohn, 1850–55.

Warren-Adams Letters: Chiefly a Correspondence Among John Adams, Samuel Adams, and James Warren. Cambridge: 1917, 1925. Vols. LXXII–LXXIII of the Massachusetts Historical Society, *Collections.*

Wharton, Francis, ed. *The Revolutionary Diplomatic Correspondence of the United States.* 6 vols. Washington, D.C.: U.S. Government Printing Office, 1882–89.

Wickersham, Cornelius W. and Gilbert H. Montague, eds. *The Olive Branch Petition.* New York: New York Public Library, 1954.

Secondary Sources

Books

Abernethy, Thomas P. *Western Lands and the American Revolution.* New York: D. Appleton–Century, 1937.

Adams, Thomas R. *American Independence: The Growth of An Idea.* Providence: Brown University Press, 1965.

Albanese, Catherine L. *Sons of the Fathers: The Civil Religion of the American Revolution.* Philadelphia: Temple University Press, 1976.

Alden, John R. *A History of the American Revolution.* New York: Alfred A. Knopf, 1969.

―――. *The South in the Revolution, 1763–1789.* Baton Rouge: Louisiana State University Press, 1957.

―――. *The American Revolution, 1775–1783.* New York: Harper & Row, 1954.

Allen, Gardner W. *A Naval History of the American Revolution.* 2 vols. New York: Russell & Russell, 1972.

Allport, Gordon W., ed. *Letters From Jenny.* New York: Harcourt, Brace, & World, 1965.

Alvord, Clarence W. *The Mississippi Valley in British Politics.* 2 vols. Cleveland: Arthur H. Clark, 1917.

Alvord, Clarence W. and Clarence E. Carter, eds. *The Critical Period, 1763–1765.* Springfield, 1915. Vol. X of the *Collections of the Illinois State Historical Library.*

Armes, Ethel, ed. *Nancy Shippen: Her Journal Book.* New York: Benjamin Bloom, 1968.

―――. *Stratford Hall: The Great House of the Lees.* Richmond: Garrett & Massie, 1936.

Augur, Helen. *The Secret War of Independence.* New York: Duell, Sloan, and Pearce, 1955.

Bailyn, Bernard. *Education in the Forming of American Society: Needs and Opportunities for Study.* New York: W. W. Norton, 1972.

―――. *The Ideological Origins of the American Revolution.* Cambridge: Harvard University Press, 1967.

―――. *The Ordeal of Thomas Hutchinson.* Cambridge: Harvard University Press, 1974.

―――. *The Origins of American Politics.* New York: Vintage Books, 1968.

Bailyn, Bernard, *et. al.*, eds. *The Great Republic.* Lexington: D.C. Heath, 1977.

Bancroft, George. *History of the United States of America from the Discovery of the Continent.* 6 vols. New York: D. Appleton, 1883–1885.

Barber, James D. *The Presidential Character: Predicting Performance in the White House.* Englewood Cliffs: Prentice-Hall, 1972.

Bargar, B. D. *Lord Dartmouth and the American Revolution.* Columbia: University of South Carolina Press, 1965.

Beeman, Richard R. *The Old Dominion and the New Nation, 1788–1801.* Lexington: University Press of Kentucky, 1972.

Bell, Whitfield J., Jr. *John Morgan: Continental Doctor.* Philadelphia: University of Pennsylvania Press, 1965.

Bemis, Samuel Flagg. *The Diplomacy of the American Revolution.* Bloomington: Indiana University Press, 1957.

Bendiner, Elmer. *The Virgin Diplomats.* New York: Alfred A. Knopf, 1976.

Black, Eugene C. *The Association: British Extra Parliamentary Political Organization, 1769–1793.* Cambridge: Harvard University Press, 1963.

Blanton, Wyndham B. *Medicine in Virginia in the Eighteenth Century.* Richmond: Garrett & Massie, 1931.

Boatner, Mark A., III, ed. *Encyclopedia of the American Revolution.* New York: D. McKay, 1966.

Boulding, Kenneth E. *The Image: Knowledge in Life and Society.* Ann Arbor: University of Michigan Press, 1961.

Boulton, James T. *The Language of Politics in the Age of Wilkes and Burke.* London: Routledge & Kegan Paul, 1963.

Bridenbaugh, Carl. *Seat of Empire: The Political Role of Eighteenth Century Williamsburg.* Williamsburg: Colonial Williamsburg, 1950.

Brown, Robert E. and B. Katherine Brown. *Virginia, 1705–1786: Democracy or Aristocracy?* East Lansing: Michigan State University Press, 1964.

Brown, Weldon A. *Empire or Independence: A Study in the Failure of Reconciliation, 1774–1783.* Baton Rouge: Louisiana State University Press, 1944.

Burnett, Edmund C. *The Continental Congress.* New York: W. W. Norton, 1964.

Chitwood, Oliver P. *Richard Henry Lee: Statesman of the Revolution.* Morgantown: West Virginia University Library, 1967.

Clark, Dora M. *British Opinion and the American Revolution.* New Haven: Yale University Press, 1930.

Clarke, M. L. *Greek Studies in England, 1700–1830.* Cambridge, England: Cambridge University Press, 1945.

Colbourn, H. Trevor. *The Lamp of Experience: Whig History and the Intellectual Origins of the American Revolution.* Chapel Hill: University of North Carolina Press, 1965.

Corner, Betsy Chopping. *William Shippen, Jr.: Pioneer in American Medical Education.* Philadelphia: American Philosophical Society, 1951.

Corwin, Edward S. *French Policy and the American Alliance of 1778.* Hamden: Archon Books, 1962.

Craig, Neville B., ed. *The Olden Time.* 2 vols. Pittsburgh: Wright and Charlton, 1848.

Crane, Verner W. *Benjamin Franklin and a Rising People.* Boston: Little, Brown, 1954.

Cremin, Lawrence A. *American Education: The Colonial Experience, 1607– 1783.* New York: Harper and Row, 1970.

Cunliffe, Marcus. *George Washington: Man and Monument.* New York: Mentor Books, 1958.

Currey, Cecil. *Code Number 72 / Ben Franklin: Patriot or Spy?* Englewood Cliffs: Prentice-Hall, 1972.

———. *Road to Revolution: Benjamin Franklin in England, 1765–1775.* Garden City: Anchor Books, 1968.

DeKoven, Mrs. Reginald. *The Life and Letters of John Paul Jones.* 2 vols. New York: C. Scribner's Sons, 1913, 1930.

Doniol, Henri. *Histoire de la participation de la France à l'établissement des Etats-Unis d'Amerique: Correspondence diplomatique et documents.* 5 vols. Paris: Imprimie nationale, 1886–92.

Donoughue, Bernard. *British Politics and the American Revolution: The Path to War, 1773–1775.* London: Macmillan, 1964.

Dull, Jonathan R. *The French Navy and American Independence: A Study of Arms and Diplomacy, 1774–1787.* Princeton: Princeton University Press, 1975.

Earl, D. C. *The Political Thought of Sallust.* Amsterdam: Adolf M. Hakkert, 1966.

Einstein, Lewis. *Divided Loyalties: Americans in England During the War of Independence.* Boston: Houghton, Mifflin, 1933.

Ellëgard, Alvar. *Who Was Junius?* Stockholm: Almquist and Wiksell, 1962.

Erikson, Erik H. *Dimensions of a New Identity.* New York: W. W. Norton, 1974.

———. *Childhood and Society.* New York: W. W. Norton, 1963.

———. *Life History and the Historical Moment.* New York: W. W. Norton, 1975.

———. *Young Man Luther: A Study in Psychoanalysis and History.* New York: W. W. Norton, 1962.

Ferguson, E. James. *The Power of the Purse: A History of American Public Finance, 1776–1780.* Chapel Hill: University of North Carolina Press, 1961.

Lord Fitzmaurice. *Life of William Earl of Shelburne Afterwards First Marquess of Landsdowne with Extracts from His Papers and Correspondence.* 2 vols. London: Macmillan, 1912.

Foner, Eric. *Tom Paine and Revolutionary America.* New York: Oxford University Press, 1976.

Freeman, Douglas S. *George Washington: A Biography.* 7 vols. New York: Charles Scribner's Sons, 1949–57.

Frothingham, Richard. *The Life and Times of Joseph Warren.* Boston: Little, Brown, 1865.

Gilbert, Felix. *To the Farewell Address: Ideas of Early American Foreign Policy.* Princeton: Princeton University Press, 1970.

Gipson, Lawrence Henry. *The Coming of the Revolution, 1763–1775.* New York: Harper and Row, 1954.

Gottschalk, Louis. *LaFayette Between the American and French Revolution (1783–1789).* Chicago: University of Chicago Press, 1950.

Granger, Bruce I. *Political Satire in the American Revolution.* Ithaca: Cornell University Press, 1960.

Grant, Sir Alexander. *The Story of the University of Edinburgh During Its First Three Hundred Years.* London: Longmans, Green, 1884.

Greven, Philip. *The Protestant Temperament: Patterns of Child-Rearing, Religious Experience, and the Self in Early America.* New York: Alfred A. Knopf, 1977.

Gummere, Richard M. *The Colonial Mind and the Classical Tradition: Essays in Comparative Culture.* Cambridge: Harvard University Press, 1963.

Hamilton, Edith. *Mythology.* Boston: Little, Brown, 1946.

Harlow, Ralph Volney. *Samuel Adams: Promoter of the American Revolution: A Study in Psychology and Politics.* New York: Henry Holt, 1923.

Hawke, David Freeman. *Paine.* New York: Harper and Row, 1974.

Henderson, Herbert James. *Party Politics in the Continental Congress.* New York: McGraw Hill, 1974.

Hendrick, Burton J. *The Lees of Virginia: Biography of a Family.* Boston: Little, Brown, 1935.

Henretta, James A. *The Evolution of American Society, 1700–1815: An Interdisciplinary Analysis.* Lexington: D. C. Heath, 1973.

Herr, Richard. *The Eighteenth Century Revolution in Spain.* Princeton: Princeton University Press, 1958.

A History of the College of William and Mary, from Its Foundation, 1660 to 1874. Richmond: J. W. Randolph, 1874.

Hollis, Christopher. *Eton: A History.* London: Hollis and Carter, 1960.

Horn, D. B. *A Short History of the University of Edinburgh, 1556–1889.* Edinburgh: University of Edinburgh Press, 1967.

Jacobson, David L. *John Dickinson and the Revolution in Pennsylvania, 1764–1776.* Berkeley: University of California Press, 1965.

James, Alfred P. *The Ohio Company: Its Inner History.* Pittsburgh: University of Pittsburgh Press, 1959.

James, Coy Hilton. *Silas Deane: Patriot or Traitor?* East Lansing: Michigan State University Press, 1975.

Jensen, Merrill. *The New Nation: A History of the United States During the Confederation, 1781–1789.* New York: Alfred A. Knopf, 1950.

Jesse, James Heneage. *Memoirs of Celebrated Etonians.* London: Richard Bentley and Sons, 1875.

Jillson, Willard R., ed. *Old Kentucky Entries and Deeds: A Complete Index to All of the Earliest Land Entries, Military Warrants, Deeds, and Wills of the Commonwealth of Kentucky.* Louisville: Standard Printing, 1926.

Jones, E. Alfred. *American Members of the Inns of Court.* London: St. Catherine Press, 1924.

Jordan, Winthrop D. *White over Black: American Attitudes Toward the Negro, 1550–1812.* Chapel Hill: University of North Carolina Press, 1968.

Kammen, Michael G. *A Rope of Sand: The Colonial Agents, British Politics, and the American Revolution.* Ithaca: Cornell University Press, 1968.

Kaplan, Lawrence S. *Colonies into Nation: American Diplomacy, 1763–1801.* New York: Macmillan, 1972.

Knollenberg, Bernhard. *Origin of the American Revolution, 1759–1766.* New York: Free Press, 1965.

Laistner, M. L. W. *The Great Historians.* Berkeley: University of California Press, 1947.

Lee, Cazenove G., Jr. *Lee Chronicle: Studies of the Early Generation of the Lees of Virginia.* Edited by Dorothy Mills Parker. New York: New York University Press, 1957.

Lee, Edmund Jennings. *Lee of Virginia, 1642–1892: Biographical and Genealogical Sketches of the Descendents of Richard Lee.* Philadelphia: n.p., 1895.

Lee, Marguerite duPont. *Arthur Lee, M.D., LL.D., F.R.S.* Richmond: n.p., 1936.

Lee, Richard Henry. *Life of Arthur Lee, LL.D., Joint Commissioner to the Court of France, and Sole Commissioner to the Courts of Spain and Prussia, During the Revolutionary War.* 2 vols. Boston: Wells and Lilly, 1829.

―――. *Memoir of the Life of Richard Henry Lee and His Correspondence.* 2 vols. Philadelphia: H. C. Carey and I. Lea, 1825.

Lomenie, Louis de. *Beaumarchais and His Time.* 4 vols. London: Addey, 1856.

Lonn, Ella. *The Colonial Agents of the Southern Colonies.* Chapel Hill: University of North Carolina Press, 1945.

Lopez, Claude-Anne. *Mon Cher Papa: Franklin and the Ladies of Paris.* New Haven: Yale University Press, 1966.

Lopez, Claude-Anne and Eugenia W. Herbert. *The Private Franklin: The*

Man and His Family. New York: W. W. Norton, 1975.

Lorenz, Lincoln. *John Paul Jones: Fighter for Freedom and Glory*. Annapolis: U. S. Naval Institute, 1943.

Maccoby, Simon. *English Radicalism, 1762–1785: The Origins*. London: George Allen and Unwin, 1955.

Magazine of the Society of the Lees of Virginia, I (December, 1922–April, 1923).

Maier, Pauline. *From Resistance to Revolution: Colonial Radicals, and the Development of American Opposition to Britain, 1765–1776*. New York: Vintage Press, 1974.

Main, Jackson Turner. *Political Parties Before the Constitution*. New York: W. W. Norton, 1973.

Marshall, Dorothy. *Dr. Johnson's London*. New York: John Wiley and Sons, 1968.

Meng, John J. *Comte de Vergennes: European Phases of His American Diplomacy*. Washington: Catholic University of America, 1932.

Merli, Frank J. and Theodore A. Wilson, eds. *Makers of American Diplomacy*. 2 vols. New York: Charles Scribner's Sons, 1974.

Miller, John C. *Sam Adams: Pioneer in Propaganda*. Boston: Little, Brown, 1936.

Morales, Francisco Padron. *Spanish Help in American Independence*. Madrid: Publicaciones Espanolas, 1952.

Morgan, Edmund S. *Virginians at Home: Family Life in the Eighteenth Century*. Williamsburg: Colonial Williamsburg, 1952.

Morison, Samuel E. *John Paul Jones: A Sailor's Biography*. Boston: Little, Brown, 1959.

Morris, Richard B. *The Peacemakers: The Great Powers and American Independence*. New York: Harper and Row, 1965.

Morton, Richard L. *Westward Expansion and Prelude to the Revolution, 1710–1763*. Chapel Hill: University of North Carolina Press, 1960. Vol. II of Morton. *Colonial Virginia*.

Nicholson, Nigel and Ian Graham. *Great Houses*. London: Weidenfeld and Nicholson, 1968.

Osborne, J. A. *Williamsburg in Colonial Times*. Richmond: Dietz Press, 1935.

Palmer, Robert R. *The Challenge*. Princeton: Princeton University Press, 1959. Vol. I of Palmer. *The Age of Democratic Revolution: A Political History of Europe and America, 1760–1800*.

Pares, Richard. *George the Third and the Politicians*. Oxford: Clarendon, 1953.

Paullin, Charles Oscar. *The Navy of the American Revolution: Its Administration, Its Policy, and Its Achievements.* Chicago: Burrows Brothers, 1906.

Perkins, James B. *France in the American Revolution.* New York: B. Franklin, 1970.

Pocock, J. G. A. *The Machiavellian Moment: Florentine Political Thought and the Atlantic Republican Tradition.* Princeton: Princeton University Press, 1975.

Pottle, Frederick A. *James Boswell: The Earlier Years, 1740–1769.* New York: McGraw Hill, 1966.

Reed, William B. *The Life of Esther DeBerdt, Afterwards Esther Reed of Pennsylvania.* Philadelphia: C. Sherman, 1853.

Ritcheson, Charles. *British Politics and the American Revolution.* Norman: University of Oklahoma Press, 1954.

Roche, John F. *Joseph Reed: A Moderate in the American Revolution.* New York: Columbia University Press, 1957.

Rudé, George. *Wilkes and Liberty: A Society Study of 1763 to 1774.* Oxford: Clarendon Press, 1962.

Rutman, Darrett B. *The Morning of America, 1603–1789.* Boston: Houghton-Mifflin, 1971.

Sachse, William L. *The Colonial American in Britain.* Madison: University of Wisconsin Press, 1956.

Sanders, Jennings B. *Evolution of Executive Departments of the Continental Congress, 1774–1789.* Gloucester: Peter Smith, 1971.

Schoenbrun, David. *Triumph in Paris: The Exploits of Benjamin Franklin.* New York: Harper and Row, 1976.

Schlesinger, Arthur M. *Prelude to Independence: The Newspaper War on Britain, 1764–1776.* New York: Alfred A. Knopf, 1958.

Shaw, Peter. *The Character of John Adams.* Chapel Hill: University of North Carolina Press, 1976.

Shyrock, Richard. *Medicine and Society in America, 1660–1860.* New York: New York University Press, 1960.

Smelser, Marshall. *The Winning of Independence.* New York: New Viewpoints, 1973.

Sosin, Jack M. *Agents and Merchants: British Colonial Policy and the Origins of the American Revolution, 1763–1775.* Lincoln: University of Nebraska Press, 1965.

———. *Whitehall and the Wilderness: The Middle West in British Colonial Policy, 1760–1775.* Lincoln: University of Nebraska Press, 1961.

Stephens, Alexander. *Memoirs of John Horne Tooke Interspersed with Original Documents.* 2 vols. London: J. Johnson, 1813.

Stinchcombe, William C. *The American Revolution and the French Alliance.* Syracuse: Syracuse University Press, 1969.

Stourzh, Gerald. *Benjamin Franklin and American Foreign Policy.* Chicago: University of Chicago Press, 1954.

Sumner, William G. *The Financier and the Finances of the American Revolution.* New York: A. M. Kelley, 1968.

Sutherland, Lucy S. *The City of London and Opposition to Government, 1768–1774.* London: University of London—The Athlone Press, 1959.

———. *The East India Company in Eighteenth Century Politics.* Oxford: Clarendon Press, 1952.

Thomson, Buchanan Parker. *Spain: Forgotten Ally of the American Revolution.* North Quincy, Mass.: Christopher Publishing, 1976.

Time—Special 1776 Issue: Educational Edition. Boston: Little, Brown, 1975.

Treloar, William Purdie. *Wilkes and the City.* London: John Murray, 1917.

Trench, Charles Chevenix. *Portrait of a Patriot: A Biography of John Wilkes.* Edinburgh: W. Blackwood, 1962.

Tyler, Moses C. *The Literary History of the American Revolution.* 2 vols. New York: Barnes and Noble, 1941.

Van Doren, Carl. *Benjamin Franklin.* New York: Viking Press, 1938.

———. *Secret History of the American Revolution.* New York: Viking Press, 1941.

Wallace, David D. *The Life of Henry Laurens.* New York: G. P. Putnam's, 1915.

Watson, J. Steven. *The Reign of George III, 1760–1815.* Oxford: Clarendon Press, 1960.

Wegelin, Oscar. *Early American Poetry.* New York: Peter Smith, 1930.

Wills, Gary. *Inventing America: Jefferson's Declaration of Independence.* Garden City: Doubleday, 1978.

Wood, George C. *Congressional Control of Foreign Relations During the American Revolution, 1774–1789.* Allentown: R. H. Haas, 1919.

Wood, Gordon S. *The Creation of the American Republic, 1776–1787.* Chapel Hill: University of North Carolina Press, 1969.

Wright, Esmond. *Fabric of Freedom, 1763–1800.* Rev. ed. New York: Hill and Wang, 1978.

Wright, Louis B. *The First Gentlemen of Virginia: Intellectual Qualities of the Early Colonial Ruling Class.* San Marino: Huntington Library, 1940.

———. *The Atlantic Frontier: Colonial American Civilization, 1607–1763.* Ithaca: Cornell University Press, 1965.

Yarborough, Minnie Clare. *John Horne Tooke.* New York: Columbia University Press, 1926.

Yela Utrilla, J. F. *Espana ante la independencia de los Estados Unidos.* 2
vols. Lerida, Spain: Garficos Academia Mariana, 1925.
Youngson, A. J. *The Making of Classical Edinburgh, 1750–1840.* Edinburgh:
Edinburgh University Press, 1966.

Articles

Abernethy, Thomas P. "Commercial Activities of Silas Deane in France,"
American Historical Review, XXXIX (April, 1938), 477–85.
————. "The Origins of the Franklin-Lee Imbroglio," *North Carolina His-
torical Review,* XV (January, 1938), 1–12.
Alden, John E. "John Mein: Scourge of the Patriots," *Publications of the
Colonial Society of Massachusetts,* XXXIV (February, 1942), 571–99.
Appleby, Joyce. "The Social Origins of American Revolutionary Ideology,"
Journal of American History, LXIV (March, 1978), 935–58.
Bailyn, Bernard. "The Central Themes of the American Revolution: An In-
terpretation," in Stephen G. Kurtz and James H. Hutson, eds. *Essays on
the American Revolution.* New York: W. W. Norton, 1973, pp. 3–31.
————. "Political Experience and Enlightenment Ideas in Eighteenth Cen-
tury America," *American Historical Review,* LXVII (January, 1962),
339–51.
Barber, James D. "Adult Identity and Presidential Style: The Rhetorical
Emphasis," *Daedalus,* XCVII (Summer, 1968), 938–68.
Bell, Whitfield J., Jr. "Some American Students of 'That Shining Oracle of
Physic,' Dr. William Cullen of Edinburgh, 1755–1766," *Proceedings of the
American Philosophical Society,* XCIV (June, 1950), 275–81.
Bemis, Samuel F. "British Secret Service and the French-American Alliance,"
American Historical Review, XXIX (April, 1924), 474–95.
Black, Eugene C., review of John Norris, *Shelburne and Reform* in *William
and Mary Quarterly,* 3rd ser., XXI (October, 1964), 611.
Blassingame, John W. "American Nationalism and Other Loyalties in the
Southern Colonies, 1763–1775," *Journal of Southern History,* XXXIV
(February, 1968), 50–75.
Bonwick, C. C. "English Dissenters and the American Revolution," in H. C.
Allen and Roger Thompson, eds. *Contrast and Connection: Bicentennial
Essays in Anglo-American History.* London: G. Bell and Sons, 1976, pp.
88–112.
Boyd, Julian. "Silas Deane: Death by a Kindly Teacher of Treason?" *Wil-
liam and Mary Quarterly,* 3rd ser., XVI (April–October, 1959), 165–87,
319–42, 515–50.

Bridenbaugh, Carl. "Violence and Virtue, 1766; or, The Importance of the Trivial," *Massachusetts Historical Society Proceedings*, LXXVI (1964), 3–29.

Brown, Vera Lee. "Studies in the History of Spain in the Second Half of the Eighteenth Century," *Smith College Studies in History*. XV (October, 1929–January, 1930), 1–92.

Burnett, Edmund C. "Ciphers of the Revolutionary Period," *American Historical Review*, XXII (January, 1917), 329–34.

Burrows, Edwin G. and Michael Wallace. "The American Revolution: The Ideology and Psychology of National Liberation,"*Perspectives in American History*, VI (1972), 167–308.

Bushman, Richard L. "On the Use of Psychology: Conflict and Conciliation in Benjamin Franklin," *History and Theory*, V (1968), 225–40.

———. "Corruption and Power in Provincial America," in *The Development of a Revolutionary Mentality*. Washington, D.C.: Library of Congress, 1972, pp. 63–91.

Canby, Courtlandt. "The Commonplace Book of Doctor George Gilmer," *Virginia Magazine of History and Biography*, LVI (October, 1948), 379–407.

Chowning, C. C. "Some Colonial Houses of Middlesex County," *William and Mary Quarterly*, 2nd ser., XXII (April, 1942), 144–60.

Christie, Ian R. "The Wilkites and the General Election of 1774," *Guildhall Miscellany*, XI (October, 1962), 155–64.

Commager, Henry Steele. "America and the Enlightenment," in *The Development of a Revolutionary Mentality*. Washington D.C.: Library of Congress, 1972, pp. 7–29.

Cross, Laurence Delbert. "Whither Columbia? Congressional Residence and the Politics of the New Nation, 1776–1787," *William and Mary Quarterly*, 3rd ser., XXXII (October, 1975), 581–600.

Currey, Cecil B. "Ben Franklin in France: A Maker of American Diplomacy," in Frank J. Merli and Theodore A. Wilson, eds. *Makers of American Diplomacy*. 2 vols. New York: Charles Scribner's Sons, 1974, pp. 1–25.

deMause, Lloyd. "The Formation of the American Personality Through Psychospeciation," *Journal of Psychohistory*. IV (Summer, 1976), 1–30.

Demos, John. "Developmental Perspectives of the History of Childhood." In Theodore K. Rabb and Robert I. Rotberg, eds., *The Family in History: Interdisciplinary Essays*. New York: Harper & Row, 1971, pp. 127–39.

Donnelly, Lucy Martin. "The Celebrated Mrs. Macaulay," *William and Mary Quarterly*, 3rd ser., VI (April, 1949), 173–207.

Duff, Stella F. "The Case Against the King: The *Virginia Gazettes* Indict George III," *William and Mary Quarterly*, 3rd ser., VI (July, 1949), 383–90.

Elsey, George W., ed. "John Wilkes and William Palfrey," *Publications of the Colonial Society of Massachusetts*, XXXIV (February, 1941), 411–28.

Erikson, Erik H. "Psychological Reality and Historical Actuality," in Erikson, *Insight and Responsibility*. New York: W. W. Norton, 1964, pp. 159–216.

Ferguson, E. James. "Business, Government, and Congressional Investigation in the Revolution," *William and Mary Quarterly*, 3rd ser., XVI (April, 1959), 293–318.

Geertz, Clifford. "Ideology as a Cultural System," in David E. Apter, ed. *Ideology and Discontent*, New York: Free Press, 1964, pp. 47–76.

George, Alexander L. "Assessing Presidential Character," *World Politics*, XXVI (1974), 234–82.

Giddens, Paul H. "Arthur Lee, First United States Envoy to Spain," *Virginia Magazine of History and Biography*, XL (January, 1932), 3–13.

Greene, Jack P. "Changing Interpretations of Early American Politics," in Ray A. Billington, ed., *The Reinterpretation of Early American History*. San Marino: Huntington Library, 1966, pp. 151–84.

———. "Search for Identity: An Interpretation of the Meaning of Selected Patterns of Social Response in Eighteenth Century America," *Journal of Social History*, III (Spring, 1970), 189–200.

———. "Society, Ideology and Politics: An Analysis of the Political Culture of Mid-Eighteenth Century Virginia," in Richard M. Jellison, ed., *Society, Freedom and Conscience*. New York: W. W. Norton, 1976, pp. 14–76.

———. "An Uneasy Connection: An Analysis of the Preconditions of the American Revolution," in Stephen G. Kurtz and James H. Hutson, eds., *Essays on the American Revolution*. New York: W. W. Norton, 1973, pp. 32–80.

Griffiths, David M. "American Commercial Diplomacy in Russia, 1780 to 1783," *William and Mary Quarterly*, 3rd ser., XXVII (July, 1970), 379–410.

Harris, Richard D. "French Finances and the American War, 1777–1778," *Journal of Modern History*, XLVIII (June, 1976), 233–58.

Haworth, Paul L. "Frederick the Great and the American Revolution," *American Historical Review*, IX (April, 1904), 460–78.

Henderson, H. James. "Congressional Factionalism and the Attempt to Recall Benjamin Franklin," *William and Mary Quarterly*, 3rd ser., XXVII (April, 1970), 246–67.

————. "Quantitative Approaches to Party Formation in the United States Congress: A Comment," *William and Mary Quarterly*, 3rd ser., XXX (April, 1973), 307–323.

————. "The Structure of Politics in the Continental Congress," in Stephen G. Kurtz and James H. Hutson, eds., *Essays on the American Revolution.* New York: W. W. Norton, 1973, pp. 157–96.

Howe, Mark A. DeWolfe. "The English Journal of Josiah Quincy, Junior, 1774–1775," *Massachusetts Historical Society Proceedings*, L (June, 1917), 445–53.

Hutson, James H. "Early American Diplomacy: A Reappraisal," in Lawrence S. Kaplan, ed. *The American Revolution and "A Candid World,"* Kent: Kent State University Press, 1977, pp. 40–68.

————. "Intellectual Foundations of Early American Diplomacy," *Diplomatic History*, I (Winter, 1977), 1–19.

Isaac, Rhys. "Dramatizing the Ideology of Revolution: Popular Mobilization in Virginia, 1774 to 1776," *William and Mary Quarterly*, 3rd ser., XXXIII (July, 1976), 357–85.

————. "Religion and Authority: Problems of the Anglican Establishment in Virginia in the Era of the Great Awakening and the Parsons' Cause," *William and Mary Quarterly*, 3rd ser., XXX (January, 1973), 3–36.

James, James Alton. "Some Phases of the History of the Northwest, 1783–1786," *Proceedings of the Mississippi Valley Historical Association*, VII (1913–14), 168–96.

Jordan, Winthrop D. "Familiar Politics: Thomas Paine and the Killing of the King," *Journal of American History*, LX (September, 1973), 294–308.

Kammen, Michael G. "The Colonial Agents, English Politics, and the American Revolution," *William and Mary Quarterly*, 3rd ser., XXII (April, 1965), 244–63.

Kaplan, Lawrence S. "Toward Isolationism: The Rise and Fall of the Franco-American Alliance, 1775–1801," in Kaplan, ed. *The American Revolution and "A Candid World,"* Kent: Kent State University Press, 1977, pp. 134–60.

Ketcham, Ralph L. "France and American Politics, 1763–1793," *Political Science Quarterly*, LXXVIII (June, 1963), 198–223.

Kite, Elizabeth S. "French 'Secret Aid' Precursor to the French American Alliance, 1776–1777," *French-American Review*, IV (April, 1948), 143–52.

MacMaster, Richard K. "Arthur Lee's 'Address on Slavery': An Aspect of Virginia's Struggle to End the Slave Trade, 1765–1774," *Virginia Maga-*

zine *of History and Biography*, LXXX (April, 1972), 141–57.

Maier, Pauline. "Coming to Terms with Samuel Adams," *American Historical Review*, LXXXI (February, 1976), 12–36.

———. "John Wilkes and American Disillusionment with Britain," *William and Mary Quarterly*, 3rd ser., XX (July, 1963), 373–95.

Main, Jackson Turner. "The One Hundred," *William and Mary Quarterly*, 3rd ser., XI (October, 1954), 354–84.

Martin, Gaston, "Commercial Relations Between Nantes and the American Colonies," *Journal of Economic and Business History*, IV (August, 1932), 812–29.

Matthews, John C. "Two Men on a Tax: Richard Henry Lee, Archibald Ritchie, and the Stamp Act," in Darrett B. Rutman, ed., *The Old Dominion: Essays for Thomas Perkins Abernethy*. Charlottesville: University Press of Virginia, 1964, pp. 96–108.

Mazlish, Bruce. "Leadership in the American Revolution: The Psychological Dimension," *Leadership in the American Revolution*. Washington, D.C.: Library of Congress, 1974, pp. 113–33.

McLoughlin, William G. "The Role of Religion in the Revolution: Liberty of Conscience and Cultural Cohesion in the New Nation." In Stephen G. Kurtz and James H. Hutson, eds., *Essays on the American Revolution*. New York: W. W. Norton, 1973, pp. 197–255.

Meng, John J. "A Footnote to Secret Aid in the American Revolution," *American Historical Review*, XLIII (July, 1938), 791–95.

Middlekauff, Robert. "The Ritualization of the American Revolution," in Robert Middlekauff and Lawrence W. Levine, eds., *The National Temper*. New York: Harcourt, Brace, Jovanovich, 1972, pp. 100–110.

Montague, Ludwell Lee. "Richard Lee, The Emigrant, 1613–1664," *Virginia Magazine of History and Biography*, LXII (January, 1954), 3–49.

Morgan, Edmund S. "The Puritan Ethic and the American Revolution," *William and Mary Quarterly*, 3rd ser., XXIV (January, 1967), 3–18.

Morris, Richard B. "The Revolution's Caine Mutiny," *American Heritage*, XI (April, 1960), 10–13, 88–91.

Murphy, Orville T. "Charles Gravier de Vergennes: Profile of an Old Regime Diplomat," *Political Science Quarterly*, LXXXIII (September, 1968), 400–418.

Musto, David F. "The Youth of John Quincy Adams," *Proceedings of the American Philosophical Society*, CXIII (1969), 269–82.

"Notes and Queries," *Virginia Magazine of History and Biography*, XVI (October, 1908), 206.

Onuf, Peter. "Toward Federalism: Virginia, Congress, and the Western
Lands," *William and Mary Quarterly,* 3rd ser., XXXIV (July, 1977),
353–76.

Paullin, Charles O. "Admiral Pierre Landais," *Catholic Historical Review,*
XVII (October, 1931), 296–307.

Peckham, Howard. "Dr. Berkenhout's Journal, 1778," *Pennsylvania Magazine
of History and Biography,* LXV (January, 1941), 79–92.

Pocock, J. G. A. "Virtue and Commerce in the Eighteenth Century," *Journal
of Interdisciplinary History,* III (Summer, 1972), 119–34.

Potts, Louis W. "Arthur Lee: A Life History in the American Revolution,"
Journal of Psychohistory, IV (Spring, 1977), 513–28.

Riggs, A. R. "Arthur Lee, A Radical Virginian in London, 1768–1776," *Virginia Magazine of History and Biography,* LXXVIII (July, 1970),
268–80.

Risjord, Norman K. and Gordon DenBoer. "The Evolution of Political Parties in Virginia, 1782–1800," *Journal of American History,* LX (March,
1974), 961–84.

Rudé, George. "Wilkes and Liberty," *History Today,* VII (September, 1957),
571–79.

Sainsbury, John. "The Pro-Americans of London, 1769 to 1782," *William and
Mary Quarterly,* 3rd ser., XXXV (July, 1978), 423–54.

Savelle, Max. "Colonial Origins of American Diplomatic Principles," *Pacific
Historical Review,* III (September, 1934), 334–50.

Schatzman, Morton. "Paranoia or Persecution: The Case of Schreber," *History
of Childhood Quarterly,* I (Summer, 1973), 62–88.

Schlesinger, Arthur M. "A Note on Songs as Patriot Propaganda, 1765–1776,"
William and Mary Quarterly, 3rd ser., XI (January, 1954), 78–88.

"Sketch of John Camm," *William and Mary Quarterly,* 1st ser., XIX
(1910–11), 28–30.

Smart, George K. "Private Libraries in Colonial Virginia," *American Literature,* X (March, 1938), 24–52.

Smith, Glenn Curtis. "An Era of Non-Importation Association, 1768–1773,"
William and Mary Quarterly, 2nd ser., XX (January, 1940), 85–89.

Sparks, Jared. "Early Diplomatic History of the United States," in James B.
Scott, ed., *The United States and France, 1778–1783: Some Opinions of
International Gratitude.* New York: Oxford University Press, 1926, pp.
3–71.

———. Review of R. H. Lee, *Life of Arthur Lee* in *North American Review,*
XXX (April, 1830), 454–511.

Stearns, Raymond P. "Colonial Fellows of the Royal Society of London, 1661–

1788," *William and Mary Quarterly*, 2nd ser., XX (January, 1940), 85–89.

Stillé, Charles J. "Beaumarchais and the 'Lost Million': A Chapter on the Secret History of the American Revolution," *Pennsylvania Magazine of History and Biography*, XI (1887), 1–36.

Stinchcombe, William. "A Note on Silas Deane's Death," *William and Mary Quarterly*, 3rd ser., XXXII (October, 1975), 619–24.

Stout, Harry S. "Religion, Communications, and the Ideological Origins of the American Revolution," *William and Mary Quarterly*, 3rd ser., XXXIV (October, 1977), 519–41.

Sutherland, Lucy S. "The City of London in Eighteenth Century Politics," in Richard Pares and A. J. P. Taylor, eds., *Essays Presented to Sir Lewis Namier*. London: Macmillan, 1956, pp. 49–74.

Tyler, Lyon G. "The Medical Men of Virginia," *William and Mary Quarterly*, 1st ser., XIX (January, 1911), 155–56.

Van Alstyne, Richard W. "Thomas Walpole's Letters to the Duke of Grafton on American Affairs, 1776–1778," *Huntington Library Quarterly*, XXX (November, 1960), 12–20.

Van Tyne, Charles H. "French Aid Before the Alliance of 1778," *American Historical Review*, XXXI (October, 1925), 20–40.

———. "Influences Which Determined the French Government to Make the Treaty with America," *American Historical Review*, XXI (April, 1916), 528–42.

Walzer, John F. "A Period of Ambivalence: Eighteenth Century American Childhood," in Lloyd deMause, ed., *The History of Childhood*. New York: Harper & Row, 1974, pp. 351–82.

Waters, John J. "James Otis, Jr.: An Ambivalent Revolutionary," *History of Childhood Quarterly*, I (Summer, 1973), 143–50.

Weir, Robert K. "Who Shall Rule at Home: The American Revolution as a Crisis of Legitimacy for the Colonial Elite," *Journal of Interdisciplinary History*, VI (Spring, 1976), 679–700.

Whitridge, Arnold. "Beaumarchais and the American Revolution," *History Today*, XVII (1967), 98–105.

Wood, Gordon S. "Rhetoric and Reality in the American Revolution," *William and Mary Quarterly*, 3rd ser., XXIII (January, 1966), 3–32.

Wood, Gordon S. "The Democratization of Mind in the American Revolution," in *Leadership in the American Revolution*. Washington, D.C.: Library of Congress, 1974, pp. 63–90.

Yarbrough, Minnie C. "John Horne Tooke: Champion of the American Colonies," *South Atlantic Quarterly*, XXXV (October, 1936), 374–92.

Unpublished Manuscripts

Bowers, Paul C. "Richard Henry Lee and the Continental Congress, 1774–1779," Ph.D. dissertation, Duke University, 1965.

Henderson, Herbert James, Jr. "Political Factions in the Continental Congress, 1774–1783," Ph.D. dissertation, Columbia University, 1962.

Matthews, John C. "Richard Henry Lee and the American Revolution," Ph.D. dissertation, University of Virginia, 1939.

Moore, Stanley Joel. "The Character of Arthur Lee," M.A. thesis, University of South Florida, 1977.

Oh, Wonyung Hyun. "Opinions of Continental American Leaders on International Relations, 1763–1775," PhD. dissertation, University of Washington, 1963.

Potts, Louis W. "Arthur Lee: American Revolutionary," Ph.D. dissertation, Duke University, 1970.

Riggs, Alvin R. "Arthur Lee and the Radical Whigs, 1768–1776," Ph.D. dissertation, Yale University, 1967.

Stumpf, Vernon O. "Colonel Eleazor Oswald, Politician and Editor," Ph.D. dissertation, Duke University, 1968.

Newspapers

Virginia Gazette, John Dixon and Thomas Nicholson, eds., 1779–1790.
Virginia Gazette, John Pinckney, ed., 1774–1776.
Virginia Gazette, Alexander Purdie and John Dixon, eds., 1766–1775.
Virginia Gazette, William Rind, ed., 1766–1773.

Index